Skagen

Frederikshavn

**NORTHWESTERN
ZEALAND**
Pages 116–151

**SOUTHERN
ZEALAND AND
THE ISLANDS**
Pages 152–171

COPENHAGEN
Pages 46–111

Grenå

Ebeltoft

Frederiksværk

Helsingør

Odden
Færgehavn

Hillerød

Hørsholm

Birkerød

Frederikssund

Kalundborg

Holbæk

Copenhagen
(København)

Roskilde

Tåstrup

**NORTHWESTERN
ZEALAND**

Sorø

Køge

BORNHOLM
Pages 216–227

Slagelse

Ringsted

Korsør

**SOUTHERN
ZEALAND AND
THE ISLANDS**

Odense

Nyborg

FUNEN

Næstved

Svendborg

Rudkøbing

Vordingborg

Stege

Nakskov

Nykøbing F.

Bagenkop

BORNHOLM

Denmark

Bornholm

Rødbyhavn

Gedser

0 km   400

0 miles   20

Puttgarden

EYEWITNESS TRAVEL
DENMARK

EYEWITNESS TRAVEL

DENMARK

MONIKA WITKOWSKA
JOANNA HALD

DK

LONDON, NEW YORK,
MELBOURNE, MUNICH AND DELHI
www.dk.com

Produced by Wydawnictwo Wiedza i Życie, Warsaw

SENIOR GRAPHIC DESIGNER Paweł Pasternak
EDITORS Maria Betlejewska, Joanna Egert-Romanowska
AUTHORS Joanna Hald, Marek Pernal, Jakub Sito,
Barbara Sudnik-Wójcikowska, Monika Witkowska

CARTOGRAPHERS Magdalena Polak, Olaf Rodowald,
Jarosław Talacha
PHOTOGRAPHERS Dorota and Mariusz Jarymowiczowie
ILLUSTRATORS Michał Burkiewicz, Paweł Marcza
GRAPHIC DESIGN Paweł Pasternak
DTP Elżbieta Dudzińska

For Dorling Kindersley
TRANSLATOR Magda Hannay
EDITOR Matthew Tanner
SENIOR DTP DESIGNER Jason Little
PRODUCTION CONTROLLER Rita Sinha

Printed and bound in China by L. Rex Printing Co. Ltd

First American Edition, 2005
13 14 15 16 10 9 8 7 6 5 4 3 2 1

Published in the United States by DK Publishing,
375 Hudson Street, New York, New York 10014

Reprinted with revisions 2008, 2010, 2013

Copyright 2005, 2013 © Dorling Kindersley Limited, London

Published in the UK by Dorling Kindersley Limited.

A catalog record for this book is available from the Library of Congress.

ISSN 1542-1554
ISBN: 978-0-75669-507-1

FLOORS ARE REFERRED TO THROUGHOUT IN ACCORDANCE WITH EUROPEAN
USAGE; IE THE "FIRST FLOOR" IS THE FLOOR ABOVE GROUND LEVEL.

Front cover main image: Svaneke Church, Bornholm, Denmark

MIX
Paper from
responsible sources
FSC™ C018179
www.fsc.org

CONTENTS

HOW TO USE
THIS GUIDE **6**

Church organ, Copenhagen

INTRODUCING
DENMARK

DISCOVERING
DENMARK **10**

PUTTING DENMARK
ON THE MAP **12**

A PORTRAIT
OF DENMARK **14**

DENMARK THROUGH
THE YEAR **28**

THE HISTORY OF
DENMARK **32**

Amalienborg and Marmorkirken,
Copenhagen, seen from the water

◁ Colourful 18th-century houses and yachts on Nyhavn, Copenhagen

COPENHAGEN AREA BY AREA

COPENHAGEN AT A GLANCE **48**

NORTH COPENHAGEN **50**

CENTRAL COPENHAGEN **64**

SOUTH COPENHAGEN **80**

FURTHER AFIELD **90**

SHOPPING IN COPENHAGEN **98**

ENTERTAINMENT IN COPENHAGEN **102**

The Lille Tårn (Little Tower), Frederiksø

SOUTHERN ZEALAND AND THE ISLANDS **152**

FUNEN **172**

SOUTHERN AND CENTRAL JUTLAND **182**

NORTHERN JUTLAND **200**

BORNHOLM **216**

GREENLAND AND THE FAROE ISLANDS **228**

TRAVELLERS' NEEDS

WHERE TO STAY **240**

WHERE TO EAT **262**

SHOPPING IN DENMARK **286**

ENTERTAINMENT IN DENMARK **288**

OUTDOOR ACTIVITIES **290**

SURVIVAL GUIDE

PRACTICAL INFORMATION **296**

TRAVEL INFORMATION **304**

INDEX **314**

Trumpeters' monument standing near Copenhagen's Rådhus

STREET FINDER **106**

DENMARK REGION BY REGION

DENMARK AT A GLANCE **114**

NORTHWESTERN ZEALAND **116**

Christiansborg, Copenhagen

HOW TO USE THIS GUIDE

This guide will help you get the most out of a visit to Denmark. The first section, *Introducing Denmark*, provides information about the country's geographic location, its history and culture. The sections devoted to the capital and other large cities, as well as to individual regions, describe the major sights and visitor attractions. Information on accommodation and restaurants can be found in the *Travellers' Needs* section. The *Survival Guide* provides practical tips on everything a visitor may need to know, from money and language to getting around and seeking medical care.

COPENHAGEN

This section has been divided into three parts, each devoted to a separate part of the city. Sights outside the capital's centre are described in the *Further Afield* section. All sights are numbered and plotted on the area map. Detailed information for each sight is given in numerical order.

Sights at a Glance lists the sights in an area by category: churches, museums and art galleries; streets and squares; parks and gardens.

Pages referring to Copenhagen are marked in red.

A locator map shows where visitors are in relation to other areas of the city.

1 Area Map
For easy reference the sights are numbered and plotted on the area map, as well as on the main map of Copenhagen (see pp108–11).

A suggested route for sightseeing is indicated by a dotted red line.

2 Street-by-Street Map
Provides a bird's-eye view of the town centre described in the section.

Star Sights indicate parts of buildings, historic sights, exhibits and monuments that no visitor should miss.

3 Detailed Information
All the major sights of Copenhagen are described individually. Practical information includes addresses, telephone numbers, the most convenient buses and trains, and opening hours.

1 Introduction
This section deals with the landscape, history and character of each region, revealing how it has changed over time, and describing its current attractions.

DENMARK REGION BY REGION

In this guide Denmark is divided into seven regions, each of which has a separate section devoted to it. The most interesting cities, towns, villages and sights worth visiting are marked on each regional map.

2 Regional Map
The regional map shows the main road network and the overall topography of the region. All sights are numbered, and there is also information on public transport and getting around.

Boxes highlight interesting aspects or people associated with a sight.

Each region of Denmark can be found by using the colour code. The colours are explained on the inside front cover.

3 Detailed Information
Towns, villages and major tourist attractions are listed in numerical order, corresponding with the area map. Each entry contains information on important sights.

The Visitors' Checklist provides practical information to help plan your visit.

4 Major Sights
At least two pages are devoted to each major sight. Historic buildings are dissected to reveal their interiors. Major towns and town centres have street maps with the principal sights marked on them.

INTRODUCING DENMARK

DISCOVERING DENMARK 10–11
PUTTING DENMARK ON THE MAP 12–13
A PORTRAIT OF DENMARK 14–27
DENMARK THROUGH THE YEAR 28–31
THE HISTORY OF DENMARK 32–45

DISCOVERING DENMARK

An island kingdom, linked to Germany by a land border and to Sweden by a magnificent bridge, Denmark has a substantial coastline: a mix of sandy beaches, fjords and pretty fishing villages. Inland lie colourful towns, forests, castles, lakes and Viking

Visitors at Legoland®

remains. Jutland is the country's mainland and Zealand its largest island. Funen is known as "the Garden of Denmark" and Bornholm "Scandinavia in miniature". The vibrant capital, Copenhagen, shares the relaxed friendliness that pervades the entire country.

The colourful illuminations of Tivoli by night

COPENHAGEN

- **Architectural surprises both old and new**
- **Fabulous shops and bars**
- **The magic of Tivoli**

City of castles and canals, palaces, parks and gorgeous gardens, Denmark's capital offers many architectural surprises. Amid a skyline of copper roofs, domes and redbrick towers, the strange spires of **Børsen** (see p85) and **Vor Frelsers Kirke** (see p88) intrigue, while the modern "**Black Diamond**" (see p88), the stunning **Operaen** (see p89) and **Tycho Brahe Planetarium** (see p92) dare to be different.

For art lovers, the **Statens Museum for Kunst** (see pp62–3) and **Ny Carlsberg Glyptotek** (see pp78–9) are a must, while style queens will be spoilt by the shops, restaurants and nightlife that the city is renowned for.

Joyous **Tivoli** (see pp76–7) delights visitors of all ages and any trip should include a visit to the **Little Mermaid**

(see p54) – "small and close to the sea" – said to be the perfect symbol of Denmark.

NORTHWESTERN ZEALAND

- **Hamlet's castle, Kronborg**
- **On the Viking trail**
- **Karen Blixen's home**

This region is packed with historic sights, including the great castles of **Kronborg Slot** (Elsinore in Shakespeare's Hamlet, see pp126–7), **Frederiksborg Slot** (see pp132–3) and **Fredensborg Slot** (see p129). Follow in the wake of the Vikings at **Trelleborg** (see p147) and **Roskilde** (see pp140–41), where the cathedral (see pp142–3) is a World Heritage Site. Culture vultures enjoy writer **Karen Blixen**'s evocative home (see p121) and modern art at the striking **Louisiana Museum** (see pp122–3).

Outdoors, choose between sandy beaches, beautiful lakes (see pp130–31), forests, or the world's oldest fun park at **Bakken** (see p120).

SOUTHERN ZEALAND AND THE ISLANDS

- **Pristine beaches**
- **The spectacular white cliffs of Møn Klint**
- **Family-friendly resorts**

This relaxed, family-friendly region has miles of coastline, pristine beaches, lakes and a scattering of islands. Worth a visit are the cliffs at **Møns Klint** (see p168) and **Stevns Klint** (see p170), the moated **Vallø Slot** (see p171) and medieval **Køge** (see p171).

Children love the giant roller coaster at **BonBon-Land** (see p157), **Knuthenborg Safari Park** (see pp160–61), and the family activity resorts such as **Lalandia** (see p162) and **Marielyst** (see p167).

Chalk cliffs of Møns Klint, rising up out of the Baltic

FUNEN

- **Odense, birthplace of Hans Christian Andersen**
- **Preserved towns and sights**
- **Sealife encounters**

The writer Hans Christian Andersen was born in **Odense** (see pp178–9), but there is a fairytale old-world

Regal Egeskov Slot, surrounded by water

feel to the whole island: market towns have cobbled streets and half-timbered houses; manor houses, palaces and castles dot the rolling landscape. Romantic **Egeskov Slot** *(see p177)* is particularly well preserved.

For getting close to the local sea life there is Fjord&Bælt in **Kerteminde** *(see p176)*.

SOUTHERN AND CENTRAL JUTLAND

- **Family fun at LEGOLAND®**
- **Peaks and lakes of Silkeborg**
- **Lively Aarhus**

Denmark's peninsula is packed with attractions, including the very popular **LEGOLAND®** *(see pp192–3)*. Historic towns and excellent museums compete for your attention while walkers and cyclists flock to the **Silkeborg Lake District** *(see p187)*. **Rømø** *(see p196)* has one of the widest beaches in Europe.

Also worth a visit are runic stones in **Jelling** *(see p191)*, medieval **Ribe** *(see p195)* and, when night falls, the friendly bars of **Aarhus** *(see pp188–9)*, Denmark's second city.

NORTHERN JUTLAND

- **Peaceful Limfjorden**
- **Remote and artistic Skagen**
- **Aalborg's medieval quarter**

The peaceful **Limfjorden** *(see pp210–11)* cuts its watery way across this region of forest and farmland, famed for its picturesque towns, windswept dunes and diverse birdlife.

Artists have found much inspiration from the extraordinary light here, many

settling in the fishing village of **Skagen** *(see p205)*.

Historic sights include manor houses, a "living history" open-air museum, **Hjerl Hedes Frilandsmuseum** *(see p207)* and the bustling medieval quarter of **Aalborg** *(see pp208–9)*. Try the potent *akvavit* (Danish schnapps), produced in the town.

Picturesque Gudhjem, seaside centre for arts and crafts

BORNHOLM

- **Mild climate**
- **Fortified round churches**
- **Art and crafts**

This tranquil "sunshine island", where vineyards and Mediterranean flowers thrive, boasts steep cliffs, rift valleys, moors, bogs and memorable beaches. Bornholm is also known for its white **round churches** *(see p221)* and the atmospheric ruins of **Hammershus Slot** *(see p220)*.

Artists and craftsmakers flock here, and there are workshops and galleries all over the island – the pretty, well-preserved towns of **Svaneke** *(see p223)* and **Gudhjem** *(see p226)* are good places to start looking.

GREENLAND AND THE FAROE ISLANDS

- **Life outdoors from whale-watching to dog-sledding**
- **Unspoilt island life on the Faroe Islands**

Greenland, a huge ice-covered island lying within the Arctic Circle, offers adventure: from whale-spotting trips out of **Nuuk** *(see p232)*, dog-sledding across frozen fjords from **Uummannaq** *(see p233)*, to cruising among icebergs in Disko Bay and summer hikes in the "**Valley of Flowers**" *(see p233)*, near Tasiilaq – even hunting and fishing with the Inuit. In this unforgettable landscape, visitors encounter brightly coloured towns and ice in all its forms and pristine beauty.

Close-knit communities snuggle by fjords on the **Faroe Islands** *(see pp234–7)* where craggy mountains meet the sea and millions of seabirds nest on soaring cliffs. The air is clean and clear, the ever-changing light plays on a steep landscape, and the views are magnificent.

Coast of Mykines, one of the Faroe Islands

Putting Denmark on the Map

Denmark is situated between the North Sea to the
west and the Baltic Sea to the southeast. Most of
Denmark consists of Jutland, a peninsula that covers
29,766 sq km (11,493 sq miles). The rest of the
country consists of some 400 islands, of which the
largest are Bornholm, Funen and Zealand. Far to
the north, Greenland and the Faroe Islands are
self-governing overseas regions of Denmark.

KEY

✈ Airport

⛴ Ferry port

▬ Motorway

▬ Major road

— Other road

–·– National border

FAROE ISLANDS *(see p234)*

Streymoy
Borðoy
Eysturoy
Vágar
• Tórshavn
Sandoy
Suðuroy

0 km   15
0 miles   15

GREENLAND *(see p230)*

• Qaanaaq
(Thule)

• Oeqertarsuaq
(Godhavn)

Tasilaq
(Ammassalik)
Nuuk
(Godthåb)

Qaqortoq
(Julianehåb)

0 km   400
0 miles   400

Skagerrak

Oslo
Larvik
Moss

Kristiansand

Hirtshals
E 39
55
Hjørring
E 39
Brønderslev
11 55
Egersund
Bergen
Tórshavn
Hanstholm
11 29
11
26
Thisted
Limfjorden
Aalborg
26
11
Nykøbing
Mors
29
13
Hobro
E 45
507
Nissum
Bredning
Lemvig
Skive
Klejtrup Sø
Randers
16
Struer
16
Viborg
Gudenå
26
E 45
28
Holstebro
Storå
Skive Å
13
Nissum
Fjord
16
18
Herning
Silkeborg
15
Aa
15
15
15
Julsø
Ringkøbing
Skanderborg
Ringkøbing
Fjord
Mossø
E 45
Omme Å
30
Horsens
28
18
30
11
28
Varde
30
✈
Vejle
28
Esbjerg
E 20
Fredericia
Fanø
Kolding
Middelfart
25
A45
317
Ribe
Fladså
11
24
47
Haderslev
313
Fanø Bugt
Helnæs
323
Rømø
25
Faaborg
11
Abenrå
Als
8
E 45
Tønder
8
Sønderborg
5
Flensburg
A7 E 45

GERMANY

Schleswig

EUROPE

Gothenburg

CANADA

GREENLAND

RUSSIA

ICELAND

FAROE
ISLANDS

FINLAND

SWEDEN

ESTONIA

NORWAY

LATVIA

LITHUANIA

BELARUS

Copenhagen

UKRAINE

POLAND

MOLDOVIA

IRELAND

GREAT
BRITAIN

GERMANY

CZECH REP.

SLOVAK REP.

HOLLAND

BELGIUM

0 km   100

0 miles   100

Læsø

havn

Anholt

Kattegat

Grenå

15

Ebeltoft

Bugt

Odden
Færgehavn

Oslo

Angelholm

E6 E20

24

24

21

Helsingør

Helsingborg

21

23

Frederiksværk

Arresø

6

E6 E20

E22

amsø

Sejerø

16

Hillerød

19

Hørsholm

Landskrona

Frederikssund

6

Birkerød

Øresund

Sejerø Bugt

04

E47 E55

COPENHAGEN
(KØBENHAVN)

Lund

Røsnæs

23

Holbæk

6

Tåstrup

E22

Kalundborg

21

Roskilde

E20 E47 E55

E20

Malmö

Tissø

57

Amager

Køge Bugt

E6 E22

E65

22

E20

14

Slagelse

Sorø

Ringsted

Køge

9

Trelleborg

Nyborg

Korsør

22

54

Baltic
Sea

Agersø

Næstved

22

Fakse Bugt

Rønne

Rostock
Travemünde

Knudshoved
Odde

Svendborg

Småландsfarvandet

59

Møn

Langeland

Vordingborg

Stege

ing

305

9

Nakskov

E47

Falster

Søndersø

Nykøbing F.

pp

Lolland

E47

E55

BORNHOLM (see p216)

159

158

Rønne

38

Kiel
Bay

Rødbyhavn

Gedser

E55

0 km   50

0 miles   50

0 km   10

0 miles   10

Puttgarden

Rostock

A PORTRAIT OF DENMARK

*D*enmark is most famous for its association with the Vikings and the writer Hans Christian Andersen. It has, of course, far more to offer visitors, including miles of sandy coastline, beautiful countryside and historic buildings. Copenhagen, the country's capital, has a rich cultural life and world-class museums.

Denmark, the southernmost and most continental of the Scandinavian countries, occupies over 480 islands, of which about 100 are inhabited. It acts as a bridge between mainland Europe and Scandinavia and is linked with the European continent by a narrow stretch of land, in the southern part of the Jutland peninsula, at the border with Germany.

Although not part of the Scandinavian peninsula, the Danes are linked with their northern neighbours by ties of common history and culture. There are also linguistic similarities and Danes can easily converse with people from Sweden or Norway.

Porcelain doll in traditional costume

The country has strong links with two autonomous regions: the Faroe Islands and Greenland, both of which are represented in the Danish parliament. Denmark exercises control over their banking, foreign policy and defence.

Denmark is a low-lying country with wide stretches of cornfields, moors and forests, and several national parks. In addition, it has vast sand dunes, fjords and long stretches of beach. The country's immaculate towns and villages, with colourful houses adorned with flowers, include many examples of half-timbered design.

Picturesque houses along the bank of Nyhavn, Copenhagen

◁ The "Black Diamond" extension to Det Kongelige Bibliotek (The Royal Library), Copenhagen

Changing of the guards at Amalienborg Slot, Copenhagen

Majestic castles, palaces and historic churches pepper the Danish landscape. There are also many Viking ruins, as well as older remains including ancient dolmens dating from the Stone Age.

Denmark is acknowledged to be a peaceful and liberal country, with a well-organized transport system and a comprehensive system of social welfare. It has enviably low levels of crime and corruption. In rural areas it is not unusual to see stalls by the roadside on which local farmers have left their produce on sale unattended.

Statue of the Little Mermaid – a symbol of Copenhagen

Charming half-timbered house in Rønne, on the island of Bornholm

TRADITIONS AND POLITICS

The national flag – the Danneborg – is the world's oldest and the Danes demonstrate their patriotism by unfurling it during state and family celebrations. According to legend, the flag takes its origin from a banner, bearing a white cross on a red background, which was dropped from heaven to rally the Danish knights during a battle fought in present-day Estonia in the early 13th century.

The Danes are proud of their heritage, and historic villages – dating from the 1800s right back to Viking times and the Stone Age – are popular excursion destinations. Most Danes regard the fact that their monarchy is the oldest in the world with pride. The present queen, Margrethe II, has been on the throne since 1972 and is the first female monarch in Denmark since the 14th century. In addition to performing all ceremonial functions, this popular queen is credited with transforming the monarchy into a modern institution.

In political matters, the monarchy's influence is limited by the Danish constitution. The direction of national policy is determined in the Folketinget, the chamber in Christiansborg Slot, Copenhagen, where the country's 179 members of parliament sit. About a dozen parties are represented in parliament. Elections take place every four years and over 90 per cent of those eligible to vote turn out at election time. Most important national issues are decided by popular vote, however. Decisions made in referenda have included the Danes' approval of a constitutional amendment allowing a woman to inherit the throne in 1953 and, in 2000, the rejection of the euro.

View of Gammel Estrup, Jutland, surrounded on all sides by water

SOCIETY AND EVERYDAY LIFE

Denmark is largely inhabited by ethnic Danes who are ancestors of the Teutonic tribes that once populated all of Scandinavia.

Harald I (Bluetooth), Denmark's second king, was baptised as a Catholic in 960 and Denmark remained a Catholic country until well into the 16th century, when the ideas of the German Protestant reformer Martin Luther won widespread support. Lutheranism became the official religion of Denmark with the accession of Christian III in 1534. Today, about 90 per cent of the population are Protestant, and although the churches remain fairly empty, many Danes subscribe to a tax that supports the Church and observe traditions such as christenings and confirmations.

Although Denmark is largely an ethnically homogenous country, relaxed immigration policies introduced in the 1960s helped to establish small communities of foreign nationals from outside Europe. Copenhagen is home to significant numbers of Turks and Palestinians as well as new arrivals from Iraq and Afghanistan.

When it comes to bringing up children, many parents continue with their careers after taking parental leave. The progressive welfare system enables most women to return to work, at least part time.

Harbour and sailing boat jetty, Maribo (Lolland)

Denmark's famous liberalism is perhaps best illustrated by "Christiania", a hippy commune that sprang up in 1971. Allowed to remain as a social experiment, it is inhabited by about 900 people seeking an alternative lifestyle.

The Danes are similarly relaxed when it comes to issues such as marriage. The country's divorce rate is one of the highest in Europe and nearly 20 per cent of couples co-habit without ever getting married. Abortion has been available "on demand" since the 1960s.

Father and son feeding pigeons in one of Copenhagen's open squares

ECONOMY AND ECOLOGY

The Danish economy is fairly robust and the country has the EU's highest per-capita Gross National Product and a high standard of living.

Denmark was for centuries a land of farmers and fishermen. Today less than 5 per cent of the country's population are employed in agriculture. Fishing, however, is still an important sector of the economy. The country is a major exporter of fish and is also known for its dairy and pork products. Other exports include beer, furniture and home electronics.

The Danes attach great importance to environmental issues. The country has an extensive network of alternative energy sources and the state-subsidized power-generating windmills are a common feature of the landscape. These supply over 20 per cent of the country's electricity. Major investments are also made in the use of solar power and the island of Ærø, south of Funen, has one of the world's largest solar power stations. All new building projects are scrutinized to minimize the impact on the environment. Danes take great care of their coastline, many resorts have been awarded the blue flag, denoting clean beaches. Recycling domestic waste is normal practice in Denmark, as is the use of environmentally friendly packaging (a large amount of the country's paper production comes from recycled sources).

Seaside scenery in Allinge, Bornholm

CULTURE, ART AND DESIGN

Denmark's cultural events range from major music festivals to local parades and concerts. Even smallish towns consider it a point of honour to organize festivals and concerts, putting on anything from classical music to pop and rock.

Oven-smoked fish, a popular delicacy

One of the largest events is the July rock festival in Roskilde, which attracts over 70,000 visitors. Copenhagen's July jazz festival, held every year since 1979, is one of the top events of its kind in Europe and has attracted top performers including Dizzy Gillespie, Miles Davis and Oscar Peterson.

Denmark has a wide variety of wonderful museums, including the Ny Carlsberg Glyptotek *(see pp78–9)* and the Nationalmuseet *(see pp84–5)*, both in Copenhagen, as well as the Arken and Louisiana

Sculpture from Holmegård

museums, which are within easy reach of the capital. The Nationalmuseet devotes much of its space to exhibits relating to Danish culture and history, but it also has world-class collections of Greek, Roman and Egyptian artifacts. Among the Glyptotek's collection are examples of 19th-century European painting, representatives of Denmark's "Golden Age" *(see pp42–3)* and works by major international artists such as Edgar Degas and Paul Gauguin.

Many smaller museums and galleries are spread throughout the country. Some of these are devoted to the life and work of famous Danish individuals such as the composer Carl Nielsen and sculptor Bertel Thorvaldsen. Then there are more unusual museums, such as Roskilde's Viking Ship Museum *(see p141)*.

Among the country's best-known architects and designers are Ole Kirk Christiansen, inventor of LEGO®; Jørn Utzon, creator of the Sydney Opera House; and Arne Jacobsen, a pioneer of Danish modernism famous for his furniture and minimalist tableware. Prominent examples of Danish applied art include jewellery by Georg Jensen and sleek audio and visual equipment by Bang & Olufsen.

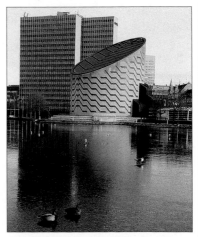

The unmistakable silhouette of the modern Tycho Brahe Planetarium, Copenhagen

Danish Landscape and Flora

More than three quarters of Denmark is less than 100 m (330 ft) above sea level. Most of its landforms are of glacial origin, which adds variety to the lowland scenery. Forests, whose wholesale destruction was halted in the 19th century, occupy only a small percentage of the landscape and include commercial forests planted with spruce and fir, and natural forests dominated by beech and oak. Pastures and meadows are also distinctive features of the landscape and most of these are given over to crop cultivation and the rearing of livestock. A large portion of Denmark's highly diversified coastline consists of dunes, marshland and tidal flats.

DANISH FAUNA

Many mammals, including elks and bears, have disappeared in Denmark. What forests remain provide a habitat for deer, marten, wild boar and hare. Excellent nesting grounds are a haven for many birds including geese, storks, swans and sandpipers. The largest wild animal to be found in Denmark is the red deer, while polar bears can still be found in Greenland.

ZEALAND
The island covers an area of 7,000 sq km (2,702 sq miles), and has a diverse landscape. In its northern section, on the outskirts of Copenhagen, there are fragments of natural forests – all that remains of a vast former wilderness. Elsewhere, the island has lakes, beaches and pasture land.

BORNHOLM
This island, largely composed of volcanic rock, has a mild climate. Its rugged granite cliffs, with stone rubble at their base, rise to over 80 m (262 ft) in height. At its northeastern end the well-preserved deciduous forests grow to the edge of the cliffs. The southern coast has long stretches of white sand beaches.

Seaside Centaury (Centaurium littorale) *is a species associated with salt flats, but can also sometimes be found growing on seaside sands.*

Bird's Eye Primrose (Primula farinosa) *is a rare peat bog species, which in Denmark is found only in isolated clusters.*

Common Wintergreen (Pyrola minor) *has a distinctive rosette of slightly leathery leaves; it grows in forests and deciduous woodlands, on acid soil.*

White Helleborine (Cephalanthera damasonium) *is an orchid with creamy-white flowers, and is often found in forests.*

Helleborine (Epipactis) *is found in several different varieties in Denmark. This orchid can be recognized by its labium, which is divided into two parts.*

Wild Strawberry (Fragaria vesca) *grows on woodland glades and banks. Its small red berries are sweet and fragrant.*

Five species of seal *can be found on the coast of Greenland. The largest of these is the hooded seal, the male of which can weigh up to 400 kg (884 lbs). The Inuit still rely on seals for clothing and food.*

The greylag goose *is one of Denmark's largest wild geese. Pairs mate for life; some 10,000 pairs are thought to be breeding in Denmark.*

The mute swan *is Denmark's national bird and can be found in many parks and ponds throughout the country.*

White storks, *which winter in Africa, can be seen in summer in Denmark's marshes, meadows and pastures.*

FUNEN

The island that separates Jutland from Zealand is famous for its scenery and is known as the "garden of Denmark" because it produces much of the country's fruit and vegetables. The terrain in the north of the island eventually levels out into marshland, while in the south it is more hilly.

JUTLAND

Lakes, which occupy about one per cent of Denmark's total area, are clustered mainly in central Jutland. Yding Skovhøj and Møllehøj, Denmark's highest peaks, can also be found here – rising a little over 170 m (560 ft) above sea level. Himmelbjerget is 147 m (482 ft) above sea level and is a famous viewpoint.

Mountain Arnica (Arnica montana), *contrary to its name, is also found growing on lowlands, meadows, pastures and by roads. It is a valuable medicinal plant.*

Field Fleawort (Senecio integrifolius) *is a rare species, found in meadows, grasslands, pastures and woodlands.*

Sea Rocket (Cakile maritima) *is a delicate plant associated solely with Funen's sandy coast.*

Field Gentian (Gentiana campestris) *is in danger of extinction and is legally protected in Denmark and many other European countries.*

Sea Holly (Eryngium maritimum) *is a typical plant of the seaside dunes and comes in white and grey varieties.*

Cinquefoil (Potentilla) *belongs to the rose family. There are several varieties growing in Denmark with yellow flowers.*

Danish Architecture

Denmark's architecture includes many of the styles found elsewhere in Europe. The country's vernacular architecture includes 17th-century fortress churches and half-timbered houses. The influence of Baroque and Dutch Renaissance dominated the style of palaces built in the 17th and 18th centuries. Denmark's native character re-established itself with Neo-Classicism at the end of the 19th century and this trend has continued with contemporary landmark designs.

Dutch Renaissance Frederiksborg Slot, built mainly in the 17th century

ROMANESQUE ARCHITECTURE

The first Danish churches were built of wood, but they were quickly replaced by Norman structures that were usually constructed of granite. The 10th to 12th centuries marked the arrival of brick and stone Romanesque architecture, exemplified by the churches in Viborg and Ribe. Village churches, such as the one in Hover, Jutland, were usually built as single-aisle structures, with an apse or presbytery. The historic round churches found on Bornholm represent a very distinctive style. These medieval fortress-like buildings were built in the 12th century and were used not only for religious purposes but as places of refuge. Three-storeys high, the top two storeys were used for storage rooms and also provided shelter for the local population in times of danger.

Portal finial in the form of a pediment, with ornamental carvings

The portal tympanum has been decorated with a granite relief depicting the Deposition from the Cross, reminiscent of the reliefs found in the churches of northern Spain.

Ribe Domkirke *is a prime example of a Romanesque cathedral. Built on the site of a wooden structure, this stone building was begun in 1150. One of its most notable features is the "Cat's Head" door on the south side.*

Sankt Bendts Kirke, *Ringsted, was built during the reign of Valdemar I (1152–82) as a tomb for his father, Canute III. Later, more royals were buried here including Valdemar I. Its rich architecture encompasses an imposing edifice with a front tower, a presbytery enclosed with an apse and a mighty transept.*

Round churches were used as shelters during enemy raids.

Nylars' round church on Bornholm, built around 1150

GOTHIC ARCHITECTURE

One of the earliest Gothic buildings in Denmark is Roskilde's Domkirke (Cathedral), founded by Bishop Absalon in 1170. The most prominent example of the mature Gothic is the cathedral church in Odense. The introduction of red brick is an important element of the Danish Gothic style. Other typical features of Gothic architecture are its severe forms, ornate decorations and a façade that features stepped peaks. Many Gothic buildings have whitewashed or polychromatic interiors.

Sankt Knuds Domkirke *in Odense is a magnificent example of pure Gothic church brickwork. Most of the cathedral is 13th-century but the finely detailed gilded altar dates from the early 16th century and is the work of Claus Berg, a master craftsman from Lübeck.*

RENAISSANCE ARCHITECTURE

Danish Renaissance architecture grew out of the church's practice of importing architects for major projects in the late 16th century. Dutch architects and craftsmen were employed by Frederik II, and later by Christian IV in the 17th century, to build grand palaces such as Frederiksborg Slot in Hillerød and Kronberg Slot in Helsingør.

Triton figure from the Neptune fountain at Frederiksborg, by Adrian de Vries (c.1615)

Gables with richly-carved ornaments

Kronborg Slot, a stately castle built in 1585 by Frederik II, and later rebuilt by Christian IV

Jens Bangs Stenhus, Aalborg, *is, along with the Børsen (Stock Exchange), Copenhagen, and the quaint streets and crooked houses of Christianshavn, a fine example of town architecture from this period.*

BAROQUE ARCHITECTURE

From the mid-17th to mid-18th centuries Baroque in Denmark left its mark mainly on residential architecture. The best examples are Copenhagen's palaces – Charlottenborg and Christiansborg – along with the grand residence in Ledreborg. The main force behind Baroque in Denmark was the architect Nicolai Eigtved. His greatest achievement was the Frederikstad district in Copenhagen, which was built in a French style and intended as a royal quarter.

Audience Room in Frederiksborg Slot with moulded decorations

Fredensborg Slot *is a sumptuous early-18th-century castle and was built by Frederik IV to a design by Johann Cornelius Krieger in an Italian Baroque style.*

Altar from Vor Frelsers Kirke (Our Saviour's Church), Copenhagen

20TH-CENTURY ARCHITECTURE

In the early part of the 20th century Danish architecture began to reflect a desire for better design in housing and everyday objects, resulting in Modernism and, subsequently, Functionalism. A major result of this trend was the creation of the Design Council at the Association of Architects, in 1907. Characteristics of modern Danish architectural practice are an honest use of materials, clean lines and an abundance of natural light.

Water emphasises the visual link with a ship

The "Black Diamond", *an extension of Det Kongelige Bibliotek (The Royal Library), Copenhagen, represents a Neo-Modernist trend that has gained favour in Denmark.*

Arken's Museet for Moderne Kunst *(Museum of Modern Art) was designed by the then 25-year-old architect Søren Robert Lund, in metal and white concrete, and is a splendid example of Danish Deconstructivism.*

Danish Design

LEGO® bricks, chairs by Arne Jacobsen, audio-visual equipment by Bang & Olufsen, jewellery by Georg Jensen: all are recognized throughout the world as examples of a Danish aesthetic. Design has a high profile in Denmark and constitutes an important source of revenue for the country, as well as being a major element of the national identity, supported by many institutions. Two good places to learn more about the traditions and history of Danish design are the DesignMuseum Danmark and the Danish Design Centre, both of which are in Copenhagen.

Danish glass *is admired throughout the world. The Holmegård factory was founded in the first half of the 19th century and initially employed workers brought over from Norway.*

Large windows blur the boundary between a room's interior and the outside.

Bang & Olufsen *high-fidelity products have been manufactured since 1925. The beauty of these products resides in the discreet use of the latest technology, which is coupled with audiophile performance.*

Furniture designer Kaare Klint *was fascinated by the possibility of combining ergonomics with traditional furniture design. His designs draw on many sources including pieces from 18th-century England.*

The Bodum company *was founded at the end of World War II by Peter Bodum. His smart and simple kitchen appliances, designed in the 1950s, are produced to this day and still enjoy great popularity.*

LEGO® *is the name of the toy company founded in 1932 by Ole Kirk Christiansen. Christiansen started by producing wooden toys and, in 1958, introduced the now familiar plastic building bricks. The well-known brand name is a contraction of the Danish phrase* leg godt *("play well").*

The Cylinda-Line *(1967) series of tableware is one of Arne Jacobsen's best-known creations. It is made of steel which, along with wood and plastic, was one of his preferred materials.*

The "Pins" stool *(2002), by Hans Sandgren Jacobsen, is an example of modern design that still maintains Danish precision and aesthetics.*

Light, open space

Functional, simple furniture

This Lamp by Poul Henningsen, *from a series of lamps produced for Louis Poulsen & Co, is the result of a persistent endeavour by the designer to create lamps that give maximum natural light, while eliminating all shadows. He achieved the desired result by employing sets of shaped shades to produce a soft, dispersed light.*

Innovative use of material

Danish porcelain, *particularly the* Flora Danica *dinner service (1789), is famous throughout the world. This service is decorated with floral motifs drawn by the botanist Teodor Homskjal, a pupil of Linnaeus.*

DESIGN FOR LIVING

Following World War II, Danish architects began to take an interest in the architectural styles of a number of other countries, drawing on many influences to produce open-plan house designs. This trend is, perhaps, best exemplified by houses that architects have built for themselves, such as the home of Jørn Utzon in Hellebæk, erected in 1952.

ARNE JACOBSEN

Born in 1902, Arne Jacobsen is the unquestionable "star" of Danish design. In his youth, Jacobsen was fascinated by the work of the Swiss-born architect Le Corbusier, especially his focus on functionality. As a designer Jacobsen created many well-known pieces including the Ant (1951). This plywood chair could be stacked and was the forerunner of chairs found in schools and cafés all over the world today. The majority of Jacobsen's chair designs, including the Egg and the Swan, are still being produced. He died in 1971.

Danish Art

Both painting and sculpture have an important place in the history of Danish art. Sculpture flourished particularly during the Late Gothic and Mannerist periods, but above all, thanks to the genius of sculptor Bertel Thorvaldsen, during the so-called "Golden Age" in the early 19th century, which saw a flowering of Danish expression. Painting also flourished during this period and the formal portraiture of earlier painters such as Jens Juel began to be replaced with lively depictions of everyday life by artists such as Christoffer Wilhelm Eckersberg and his student Christen Købke.

View from the Loft of the Grain Store at the Bakery in the Citadel (1831), Christen Købke

Wounded Philoctetes (1774–75), Nicolai Abildgaard (Statens Museum for Kunst)

Danish painting came with the founding of the Royal Academy of Fine Arts in 1754. Its alumni included many prominent painters from the period such as Jens Juel and Nicolai Abildgaard, who studied in Rome, from 1772 to 1776.

belief that truth is beauty. He brought back the precision of Neo-Classicism and made it a dominant trait in Danish painting. Portraiture during the "Golden Age" was also of a very high standard. Among the other outstanding artists of the period are Christian Albrecht Jensen and Christen Købke.

OLD MASTERS

There are many well-preserved medieval works of art in Denmark, including Romanesque paintings and, in the churches of Zealand, the cycles of frescoes dating mainly from the 12th century.

The subsequent centuries were dominated by formal portraiture. Among the most outstanding, and the largest in size, are the oil paintings on display in Rosenborg Slot in Copenhagen, produced after 1615 by Dutch artists including Reinchold Timm and Rembrandt. The artists working for Christian IV, in Kronborg, included the Dutch painter Gerrit van Honthorst, who painted for the court of Denmark between 1635 and 1641. During the reign of Frederik IV the influences of French painting became more pronounced. During the Rococo period a French influence was also present and can be seen in the works of Scandinavians such as Johan Salomon Wahl and Carl Gustaf Pilo. The turning point in the development of

THE "GOLDEN AGE"

The period between 1800 and 1850 saw a great surge in creativity. One of the prime movers of the "Golden Age" *(see pp42–3)* was Christoffer Wilhelm Eckersberg, who drew much of his inspiration from the native Danish landscape, as well as from scenes of everyday life. He had studied in Paris where he was taught by Jacques Louis David to see nature for what it was. Eckersberg returned to Denmark, fired with the

MODERN ART

After 1880 Realism and Naturalism ruled supreme in Danish painting. Their most famous exponents was the Skagen School, which placed an emphasis on natural light and its effects. Among the leading members of this school were Peder S. Krøyer and Anna and Michael Ancher. Around 1900, Danish painting came to be dominated by Symbolism. The situation changed just before World War I, when new trends, such as the

Dead Drunk Danes (1960), Asger Jorn

experiments with form by the Expressionists and Cubists, began to challenge existing traditions in art. The ranks of Danish Cubists included Jais Nielsen and Vilhelm Lundstrom. One of the most important phenomena of the 1950s was CoBrA (Copenhagen–Brussels–Amsterdam), a movement that tried to give free expression to the unconscious. One of the movement's founders was the Danish artist Asger Jorn, whose vivid abstract paintings have received international acclaim.

High altar of Roskilde Domkirke, 16th century

SACRED ART

Before turning to Protestantism Danish churches were richly decorated. In the 16th century, after the Reformation, many frescoes were painted over, as they were considered to be examples of Catholic flamboyance. Surviving to this day are a few gilded altars dating from the Romanesque period (12th–13th centuries); two of them are still found in their original locations, in Sahl and Stadil churches. Some outstanding altarpieces were created in the Late Gothic period (late 15th and early 16th centuries) by woodcarvers from Lübeck, notably Claus Berg. Berg's work, which includes the main altar in the cathedral in Odense, is particularly striking. Filled with

emotional charge and high in drama, his carving maintains a realism of detail that is typical of work found in southern Germany.

The Renaissance high altar in Roskilde Domkirke was made in Antwerp in 1560. It was originally intended for Gdansk, until it was requisitioned by Danish customs authorities.

The 17th century saw a culmination of the Reformation. At that time large sums of money were spent on building churches and chapels, notably Holmens Kirke in Copenhagen, for which Frederik III ordered a sumptuously decorated altarpiece sculpted from raw oak wood.

SEPULCHRAL SCULPTURE

With the passing of the medieval era, funereal or sepulchral sculpture began to enjoy success in Denmark. Characteristic of this period are the works of the sculptor and architect Cornelius Floris of Antwerp, who designed the tomb of Christian III (d.1559) in Roskilde Domkirke (Cathedral), west of Copenhagen. It is made of multi-coloured marble and extraordinarily richly ornamented, with an open plan colonnade that contains two statues of the monarch. This is one of Europe's largest royal tombs from this period.

Renaissance tombs and epitaphs of the aristocracy, found in great numbers throughout Denmark, were more modest, and usually limited to a single slab of stone bearing the image of the deceased in a prostrate position, with an inscription. A new type of tombstone appeared in the 17th century. Its main creator

Tomb of Christian III in Roskilde Domkirke, by Cornelius Floris

was Thomas Quellinus of Antwerp. His marble tombs realistically depicted the deceased, and were accompanied by personified images of his virtues.

MODERN SCULPTURE

Prior to the 19th century sculpture was treated in Denmark solely as a means of portraying the monarchy. This art form began to be taken more seriously with the establishment of the Royal Academy, however, and among its early exponents were Johanes Wiedeweilt (d.1802) and Nicolai Dajon (d.1823). Sculpture was only elevated to a high form of art, however, by Bertel Thorvaldsen (d.1844), who created an austere variety of Classicism based on his in-depth studies of classical antiquity while in Rome. After working in southern Europe for many years, Thorvaldsen returned home to a hero's welcome in 1838. He bequeathed many of his finest works to the city of Copenhagen on condition that a museum was established in which to house them (Thorvaldsens Museum, *see p85*).

Self-portrait, by Bertel Thorvaldsen

DENMARK THROUGH THE YEAR

Denmark is roughly on the same latitude as Moscow and southern Alaska but has a fairly mild climate. The coldest months are January and February, and most events and festivals are scheduled for spring and summer. The Danes like to enjoy themselves, and during the summer holiday season the whole country comes alive, with almost every town having its own festival. Denmark is not a large country yet it hosts many world-class events, including one of the oldest rock-music festivals, in Roskilde, which is attended by many major international acts. The world-famous Copenhagen jazz festival also attracts top performers. As elsewhere in Europe, religious festivals such as Christmas are widely observed and provide an opportunity for people to spend time with their families.

A clown dressed for Copenhagen's carnival

Royal family at the official celebrations of the Queen's 64th birthday (2004)

SPRING

Spring arrives slowly in Denmark, but its advent is welcomed with great celebration around the country. The biggest of the festivals is Copenhagen's Whitsun Carnival, when the streets fill with Danes dressed in colourful costumes to mark the end of the long winter.

MARCH

Aalborg Opera Festival
(1st half of Mar), Aalborg. In early March opera lovers congregate to hear some of the world's best performers.

APRIL

Birthday of Queen Margrethe II *(16 Apr)*, Copenhagen. The Danish queen is very popular, and on this day large crowds of loyal Danes congregate outside Amalienborg Slot to sing "Happy Birthday", which is accompanied by the ceremonial changing of the Livgarden (royal guards).
Store Bededag *(4th Friday after Easter)*. Common Prayer Day or Great Prayer Day is a movable Easter feast. Following the introduction of Protestantism to Denmark in the 16th century, the church calendar was revised and several feasts were combined into one – the Store Bededag. On this day many Danes eat wheat buns – *varme hveder*.
CPH:PIX *(2nd half of Apr)*, Copenhagen. This is the biggest international film festival in Denmark. Film entries include Scandinavian producers, as well as many world-famous directors.

MAY

Arbejdernes Kampdag *(1 May)*. Rallies are held to mark International Workers' Day.
Pinsedag. Whitsunday.
Viking Market *(1st weekend in May)*, Ribe. Held at the Viking Museum, this annual event recreates a Viking marketplace complete with displays of Viking crafts.
Aalborg Carnival *(Whitsun weekend)*, Aalborg. A week of celebrations leading up to Whitsun, including a fireworks display and Northern Europe's biggest parade.
Ølfestival *(mid-May)*, Copenhagen. This lively beer festival includes stalls, music and, of course, lots of beer to sample.
Copenhagen Marathon *(late May)*, Copenhagen. This race attracts amateur and elite runners from many European countries.
Whitsun Carnival *(Whitsun weekend)*, Copenhagen. This three-day event includes a parade, dancing and special activities for children.

Viking Market, Ribe

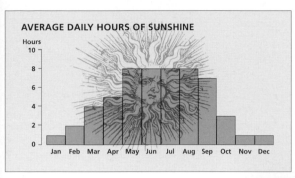

AVERAGE DAILY HOURS OF SUNSHINE

Hours

Jan Feb Mar Apr May Jun Jul Aug Sep Oct Nov Dec

Hours of Sunshine
Most sunny days occur in late spring and early summer but visitors can also expect some fine weather through until September. November, December and January are generally the cloudiest months.

SUMMER

Summer festivities begin with Sankt Hans Aften (23 June) when bonfires are lit on many beaches. Numerous attractions are scheduled for the summer holidays – from local one-day events to major festivals.

Roskilde Festival – one of
Denmark's most popular events

JUNE

International Sand Sculpture Festival *(from early Jun)*, various towns. Competition to build the best sand sculptures.
International Kite Festival *(mid-Jun)*, Fanø.
River Boat Jazz Festival *(end Jun)*, Silkeborg. Jazz bands perform all around Silkeborg, some on boats.
Sankt Hans Eve *(23 Jun)*. Midsummer Night is celebrated around camp fires.

JULY

Ringridning *(Jul)*, several towns in Sønderjylland. At this colourful festival, horse riders use a lance or spear to target a series of metal rings suspended in mid-air.

Roskilde Festival *(begin Jul)*, Roskilde. This rock festival has been attracting some of the biggest names in music since 1971. Past performers include Bob Dylan, Bob Marley and David Bowie.
Copenhagen Jazz Festival *(early Jul)*, Copenhagen. For two weeks jazz, blues and fusion blast out of almost every public space in the city.
Aarhus International Jazz Festival *(mid-Jul)*, Aarhus. A second opportunity in this month to hear some top-class jazz.
Hans Christian Andersen Plays *(end Jul–early Aug)*, Odense. Each year, one of Andersen's tales is performed outside in Den Fynske Landsby (Funen Village).

AUGUST

Cultural Harvest. Festivals celebrated in castles and stately homes, including exhibitions and theatre.

Jazz Festival, Copenhagen

Hamlet Summer *(early to mid-Aug)*, Helsingør. Performances of Shakespeare's *Hamlet* and other works are staged in Kronborg Slot.
International Film Festival *(mid-Aug)*, Odense.
Schubertiade *(mid-Aug–early Sep)*, Roskilde. Top musicians perform a selection of the works of Franz Schubert.
Copenhagen Cooking *(end of Aug)*, Copenhagen. Ten days of cooking events, from tastings and street kitchens to special menus.
European Medieval Festival *(end of Aug)*, Horsens. For two days the town is transformed into a 15th-century city.

Re-creating the Middle Ages at Horsens's European Medieval Festival

AVERAGE MONTHLY RAINFALL

mm												Inches
80												3
60												
40												2
20												1
0	Jan	Feb	Mar	Apr	May	Jun	Jul	Aug	Sep	Oct	Nov	Dec	0

Rainfall
July is one of the warmest, but also one of the wettest, months. The best time to visit is in late spring, when it is warm and there is very little rain.

AUTUMN

Early autumn provides the final opportunity to stage outdoor performances of jazz and theatre. The beginning of October marks a transition between the carefree holiday season and the beginning of the new school year with months of hard work and study ahead. Theatres stage their first-night performances, and cold autumn evenings bring music-lovers into the clubs.

Father Christmas Parade during Christmas celebrations in Tønder

Israels Plads flower market, Copenhagen, in early autumn

SEPTEMBER

Golden Days *(2 weeks in Sep)*, Copenhagen. This bi-annual event celebrates Copenhagen's rich cultural heritage and city life through a series of lectures, concerts, debates and themed walks.
Around Limfjorden Race *(early or mid-Sep)*, Løgstør, Thisted, Struer, Nykøbing Mors, Fur and Skive. The biggest annual sailing event in Scandinavia is an exciting five-day race in traditional boats around the Limfjord Bay.

Tourde Gudenå *(mid-Sep)*, Skanderborg. Kayak and canoe contest attracting many participants and spectators.

OCTOBER

Night of Culture *(2nd Fri in Oct)*, Copenhagen. A night when it is possible to visit many exhibitions, museums, castles, theatres and churches, including some buildings that are usually closed to visitors.
Tivoli Halloween *(3rd week Oct)*, Copenhagen. Witches, lanterns and pumpkins.
Mix Copenhagen *(2nd half of Oct)*, Copenhagen. International gay, lesbian, bi and transgender film festival.

NOVEMBER

Tivoli Christmas *(Nov–Dec)*, Copenhagen. Events for the young and young at heart in Tivoli as Christmas draws closer. Among the attractions are a Christmas market, ice-skating on a frozen artificial lake and the chance of spotting a Christmas pixie.

Copenhagen Irish Festival *(1st half of Nov)*, Copenhagen. Four days of celebrations and plenty of Irish music.
Feast of St Morten *(10 Nov)*. St Morten's Evening is often marked by roasting a goose.
CPH:DOX *(early to mid-Nov)*, Copenhagen. This is the largest documentary-film festival in northern Europe.
Tønder – The Christmas Town *(mid-Nov)*, Tønder. A colourful parade featuring a multitude of Father Christmases, accompanied by marching bands, passes along the main street of the town.

Street vendor roasting almonds on a Copenhagen pavement

AVERAGE MONTHLY TEMPERATURE

Temperature
This chart shows the average maximum and minimum temperatures for each month. Summer temperatures reach about 20° C (68° F), although temperatures can top 25° C (77° F). Winters can be cold with the temperature often dropping below zero, though severe frosts are rare.

WINTER

Winter is the quietest time of the year. Little happens and the weather is not conducive to outdoor entertainment. The Christmas period abounds in concerts, however- er. These are often staged in churches and feature choral ensembles singing psalms and carols. Denmark's streets are beautifully decorated and illuminated at this time and Christmas fairs are held throughout the country, with plenty to eat and drink, and the occasional parade.

DECEMBER

Jul *(24–26 Dec)*. The Danes celebrate Christmas in family circles. As in most of Europe, children play a central role. Danes tend to celebrate on Christmas Eve, decorating the tree the night before Christmas and often hanging it with real candles. The traditional Christmas dinner is also eaten on the 24th and usually consists of roast duck with red cabbage and potatoes. Rice pudding is eaten for dessert; whoever finds the hidden almond gets a prize.

JANUARY

Nytårsdag *(1 Jan)*. New Year's Day witnesses a boisterous welcome to the New Year in Denmark. Many towns stage firework displays, while classical concerts are performed in most major cities.

FEBRUARY

Copenhagen International Fashion Fair *(early Feb)*, Copenhagen. Top Scandinavian and European fashion designers present their latest collections.
Wondercool *(early Feb)*, Copenhagen. A fusion event,

Symphony orchestra performing for Aalborg's New Year concert

mixing music, art, food, design and architecture.
Fastelavn *(last Sun before Lent)*. Shrovetide is a time for fun and games. The Danish tradition of "knocking a cat out of the barrel" is still practised by children in fancy-dress. Originally the barrel, hanging from a string, contained a real cat, which was held to be a symbol of evil. Today, the barrel contains sweets, toys and fruit, which eventually fall to the ground.

PUBLIC HOLIDAYS

New Year *Nytår* (1 Jan)
Maundy Thursday
Good Friday
Easter Day *Påske*
International Workers' Day *Arbejdernes Kampdag* (1 May)
Common Prayer Day *Store Bededag* (Apr/May)
Ascension Day *Kristihimmelfartsdag*
Whitsunday,
Whitmonday *Pinse*
Constitution Day *Grundslovsdag* (5 Jun)
Christmas Day (25 Dec)
Boxing Day (26 Dec)

New Year fireworks in Tivoli, Copenhagen

THE HISTORY OF DENMARK

enmark's history has long been associated with the sea. Viking raids on England and elsewhere between the 9th and 11th centuries marked the beginnings of Danish influence and by the late Middle Ages Denmark had a tight grip on trade in the Baltic. The country later lost its position as a world power, but continues to play an important role in the international arena.

The earliest evidence of human existence to be found in Denmark dates from about 12,000 BC. Between 3900 and 1700 BC the first agricultural settlements began to emerge. Denmark's Bronze Age dates from around 1800 BC and jewellery and cult objects have been unearthed from this period. By about 500 BC iron had largely replaced bronze.

Bronze-Age cult object displayed at the Nationalmuseet

UNIFICATION

During the late Iron Age (5th and 6th centuries AD) a Nordic tribe known as Danes began to take control of the Jutland peninsula, forming a social order based around tribal structures.

As a result of the threat from the south presented by the Frankish empire under Charlemagne, these clans began to co-operate as a defensive measure. The Danish strategic position was strengthened in about AD 737 by the building of the Danevirke, a rampart that cut across the Jutland peninsula. This wall, and the forces of Godfred, king of Jutland, forced Charlemagne to recognize the local Eider River as the Franco-Danish border in AD 811.

After Godfred's death, rivalry between different clans again brought chaos. The first ruler to restore unity was Gorm the Old, the son of a Norwegian chieftain who had conquered the Jutland peninsula in the late 9th century. Gorm's son, Harald I (Bluetooth) took the throne in AD 950 and extended his power base across the rest of Denmark. Harald I's conquest enabled the widespread adoption of Christianity, which not only unified the country but also appeased Denmark's Frankish neighbours.

Increased security gave new impetus to a series of Viking (*see pp34–5*) raids on the British Isles and Ireland. These raids made it possible for Danish kings to win control of England and, for a period, an Anglo-Danish kingdom was formed under Canute I (The Great), who ruled as monarch of Denmark, England and Norway until his death in 1035.

TIMELINE

12,000 BC	4000 BC	AD 500	750	1000	1100

12,000 BC Earliest evidence of man in Denmark

Cover of a stone urn from the Bronze Age

9th century Danish Viking raids on British Isles and France

811 Army of Charlemagne stopped by Danevirke wall

1018–1035 Reign of Canute I. Unification of Denmark, England and Norway

3900–1700 BC Earliest agricultural settlements

737 Building of the Danevirke rampart

Clay pot, 1700–500 BC

1013 Sweyn I conquers England

5th–6th century Danes occupy the Jutland peninsula

c.985 Harald I (Bluetooth) unites Jutland, the islands and southern Sweden

◁ **Danish flag descending from heaven during Valdemar II's campaign in present-day Estonia in 1219**

The Vikings

The term Viking is generally used to refer to the Scandinavian peoples who journeyed overseas in wooden ships, between AD 800 and 1100, to raid and trade throughout the North and Irish seas and along the rivers of eastern and western Europe. Early Viking raiders targeted monasteries for their wealth and the ferocity of these lightning raids spread terror throughout Christian Europe, giving rise to the image of Vikings as plunderers and rapists. In fact these pagan people were expert sailors and ventured as far as North America where they traded in such items as tusks and pelts.

Ornament
This silver ornament, found in Lindholm Høje in 1952, represents a typical piece of Viking jewellery.

Strong ropes holding the mast

Silver Coin
The Vikings established trade routes to the East and the West. From the 9th century, silver coins, such as this one from the market place of Hedeby, were used as currency.

Sails were made from sheep's wool or flax and were often worth more than the rest of the boat.

Viking Chieftain
In the 19th century a view of Vikings began to take hold, which saw them as barbarians. This portrait by Carl Haag is typical of the common image. Actually they were skilled craftsmen, traders, and hunters.

The bow and stern of a Viking ship had the same shape, enabling it to make a rapid change in direction.

Figurehead
The stems of ships were decorated with figureheads, in the form of a snake or a dragonhead. The loss of a figurehead was believed to be a bad omen.

Keel produced from a trunk of hard oak

VIKING SHIP

Viking warships were usually about 28 m (92 ft) in length. The longest one ever found measured nearly 70 m (230 ft). Along with a 60-strong crew of oarsmen, they could carry as many as 400 people.

KEY

— Viking expeditions

Woman Statuette
The independent and self-reliant Viking women ran their homes and farms for many months when their men went out to sea.

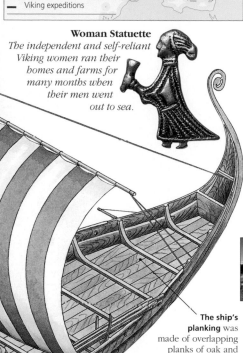

The ship's planking was made of overlapping planks of oak and joined together with nails. Any gaps between the planks were sealed with tarred wool or fur.

Viking sailing ships had a very shallow draught and could sail in waters less than 1 m (3.3 ft) deep.

Viking Raids
Early raids were carried out only during spring and summer. From about 845, Vikings began wintering at the mouths of foreign rivers, making raids possible throughout the year.

VIKING ARCHITECTURE

Few Viking buildings, which were built of earth, wood and stone, have survived. The best preserved are the round fortresses erected during the reign of Harald I (Bluetooth), in the late 10th century, at strategic points around Fyrkat (eastern Jutland), Aggersborg (northern Jutland), Trelleborg (Zealand) and Nonnebakken (Funen). These fortified settlements were surrounded by circular embankments 120 m (394 ft) in diameter, 12 m (39.4 ft) wide and rising to a height of 4 m (13 ft).

The Frykat fortress included 16 huge buildings containing domestic quarters, and was probably inhabited by between 800 and 1,000 people. Close to where the fortress stood, there is now a replica Viking farmstead including houses and outbuildings.

This replica longhouse, *near Fyrkat, was built using authentic tools and materials, with knowledge gained from archaeological research.*

Viking house doors, *such as this one in Frederikssund, was heavily built as a defence against intruders as well as the forces of nature.*

Valdemar I removing a pagan statute on the coast of Rugia

number of laws which for the time were quite progressive. These changes included the end of imprisonment without just cause (1282) and the establishment of the first supreme court in 1360.

THE MIDDLE AGES

King Canute's son Hardicanute died in 1042 and the Anglo-Danish kingdom disintegrated as the successors of Denmark's eighth monarch, Sweyn II (1047–74), began fighting each other for the throne. As royal supremacy weakened, the power of wealthy landowners and church leaders grew and this early medieval period of Denmark's history is scarred by internal strife and corruption.

This period of unrest came to an end with the succession of Valdemar I (The Great) in 1157. He reunited the country and enacted Denmark's first written laws (the Jutland Code). With help of the powerful Bishop Absalon, he made a series of successful raids against the Wends in eastern Germany. By the time of Valdemar II's succession, Denmark had won control of Meklenburg, Holstein, Lübeck and Estonia, making it one of the greatest powers in northern Europe.

Denmark's pre-eminence ended in 1227 when the country was defeated by its German vassals at the Battle of Bornhøved. As a result, Denmark was forced to give up much of its recently acquired territory and, following the death of Valdemar II in 1241, the Danish monarchy lost much of its power. As a result, successive monarchs were forced into enacting a

THE KALMAR UNION

One of the greatest achievements of King Valdemar IV (1340–75) was to arrange the marriage of his daughter Margrete to Norway's King Haakon. Margrete succeeded in forming the Kalmar Union, an alliance uniting Denmark, Norway and Sweden under a common sovereign. The main aim of the union was to counter the dominance of the Hanseatic League, which under the influence of Germany dominated trade in the region.

Queen Margrete, regent of Denmark and the initiator of the Kalmar Union

TIMELINE

Bronze amulet

1167 Founding of Copenhagen

1227 Denmark defeated at the Battle of Bornhøved

1397 Creation of the Kalmar Union

1361 Conquest of Gotland

1100	1175	1250	1325

1157 Reunification of Denmark by Valdemar I (The Great)

1241 Death of Valdemar II

1282 Erik V signs an agreement to create an annual assembly (*hof*) of feudal lords

1286 Assassination of Erik V

c.1350 Arrival of the bubonic plague in Denmark

Gustav Vasa persuading Lübeck authorities to join in the attack on Christian II

addition to these battles, the major European conflict, the Thirty Years War, took place (1616–48). Denmark was involved from 1625 to 1629 and suffered a disastrous defeat, while Sweden, joining in 1630, gained power and wealth through the conflict. Renewed warring between the two countries ended in 1658 with Denmark losing all of its territories on the Swedish mainland. Two more wars occurred, 1675–79 and 1709–20.

While each country remained free to follow their own policies, they were obliged to fight any wars together and elect a common monarch. In 1397, Margrete's grand-nephew Erik of Pomerania was crowned king of Denmark, Norway and Sweden.

Initially, a long line of military successes, the introduction of customs duties in the Øresund (Sound) and a growing demand for Danish produce strengthened the country's position. Soon, however, Denmark's domination in the Baltic was challenged by the growing power of Sweden, which sought a greater influence in its own internal affairs. In 1520 the Danish king, Christian II, ruthlessly suppressed an insurrection by what is known as the Stockholm Bloodbath. Three years later, however, Sweden elected its own king, Gustav Vasa, effectively putting an end to the union.

Wooden altar by Abel Schrøder, 1661, in Holmens Kirke, Copenhagen

TOWARDS ABSOLUTE MONARCHY

The strength of the monarchy had been increased by the introduction of Lutheranism in 1536, which placed the wealth of the Catholic church in the hands of the Crown. The king, however, was still elected by the nobility. Although political power was divided between the Crown and Council, the nobles often had the last say, especially in financial matters. After the defeats of 1658, state coffers were empty and King Fredrik III needed to assert himself and take control. This led to the instatement of absolute monarchy (see pp38–9).

WARS WITH SWEDEN

Denmark's and Sweden's aims to gain control of Øresund lead to a long series of wars between the two countries during the 16th and 17th centuries. In

Christian IV, King of Denmark, welcomed in Berlin by the Brandenburg Elector, 1595

Christian II, King of Denmark (1513–23)

1520 Stockholm Bloodbath

1660 Establishment of hereditary monarchy; rise of an absolute monarchy

1658 Treaty of Roskilde. Denmark loses its territories on the Swedish mainland

1665 Denmark begins to establish colonies in the Virgin Islands

1475	1550	1625	1700

1479 Founding of Copenhagen University

1536 Introduction of Lutheranism in Denmark

1523 Termination of the Kalmar Union

Two-crown coin dating from 1618

The Era of Absolute Monarchy

Frederik III introduced hereditary monarchy in 1660 in an effort to curtail the power of the nobles of the Council *(see p37)*. In 1665, he took the matter further and passed the Royal Act, which declared the sovereign to be beyond the law and inferior only to God. Five years later Christian V became the first monarch to be crowned under the new system. The people seemed to prefer an almighty king to the old nobility, and kings continued to rule as absolute monarchs until 1848.

Frederik III
Crowned King of Denmark and Norway in 1648, Frederik III ruled until his death in Copenhagen castle in 1670. To this day, his grave can be found in Roskilde cathedral.

Academy of Knights
Denmark's elite schools were established by Frederik III. These academies became popular in the 17th century.

Holmens Kirke, built in 1619 to serve the Royal Navy

Holmens Canal

The Holmens Drawbridge enabled ships to enter the canal.

Frederiksborg Chapel
The Slotskirken (Palace Chapel) is where Danish kings were crowned from 1670 to 1840.

Copenhagen (c.1700)
Following the introduction of absolute monarchy the Danish capital's defences were strengthened.

THE INTRODUCTION OF ABSOLUTISM IN DENMARK

The decision by Frederik III to introduce absolute monarchy in Denmark in 1665 was met with general approval. The ceremonial meeting between the king and the parliament has been immortalized in minute detail in many paintings including examples found in Rosenborg and Frederiksborg.

Corfitz Ulfeldt

Corfitz Ulfeldt, son-in-law of Christian IV, was a typical example of the powerful nobility. After a disagreement with Frederik III, he switched sides and negotiated the Roskilde Treaty on Sweden's behalf in 1658.

Colourful burgher homes were built in the form of narrow-fronted terraced houses.

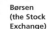

Børsen (the Stock Exchange)

Numerous inhabitants of the capital attended the celebrations marking the introduction of absolute monarchy.

Boats moored along the canal

The king's troops

Frederik VII

In 1848 Frederik VII renounced absolute power and, with a new constitution, turned Denmark into a democratic country, with guaranteed freedom of speech.

ARCHITECTURE

The period of absolute monarchy brought with it many magnificent buildings. The most opulent examples of the residential architecture of this period include Charlottenborg in Kongens Nytorv, Copenhagen, which was completed in 1683 as a palace for the royal family *(see p69)*. Other outstanding buildings from this period are Ledreborg, a stately home designed by the architect Lauritz de Thurah *(see p139)*, Copenhagen's Børsen (Stock Exchange) and Amalienborg Slot *(see pp56–7)*, which was designed by Nicolai Eigtved, the architect also responsible for Copenhagen's Frederiksstad district.

Vor Frelsers Kirke *was built in 1696 by Lambert van Haven in Dutch Renaissance style. The spire was added by Lauritz de Thurah in 1752 (see p88).*

Christian VII's Palace *at Amalienborg has typically opulent Rococo interiors, designed by Nicolai Eigtved and the sculptor Le Clerk.*

Painting by C.A. Lorentzen of the British attack on the Danish fleet, 1801

THE AGE OF REFORM

A peace treaty with Sweden signed in 1720 marked the beginning of the longest war-free period in Denmark's history. The absence of external threats encouraged economic growth and this in turn brought about a period of social change, which became more urgent as the French Revolution gathered pace. Under Frederik VI (1808–39) feudal obligations such as compulsory labour were abolished and large tracts of land were broken up and redistributed to peasants. At the same time landowners were given a role in government and compulsory education was introduced for all children under the age of 14.

THE NAPOLEONIC WARS

The outbreak of the Napoleonic Wars in 1796 eventually brought this period of peace and reform to a halt. Denmark, which derived major benefits from trade, tried to remain neutral in the face of the conflict in Europe but, in 1801, Britain accused Denmark of breaking the British trade embargo and attacked and destroyed the Danish fleet in Øresund. In 1807 the British, fearing the strengthening of a Franco-Danish alliance, struck again and bombarded Copenhagen for four days, inflicting heavy damage. By the end of the attack much of the city was ablaze and the naval yard was destroyed. The British then sailed away with what remained of the Danish fleet, which included 170 gunboats. In the aftermath of this assault, Denmark joined the continental alliance against Britain and Britain in turn blockaded Danish waters.

The war ended with the signing of the Kiel Peace Treaty in 1814 under the terms of which Denmark lost some 322,000 sq km (124,292 sq miles) of territory, including Norway. The new boundaries left Denmark

Peasants give thanks to Christian VII for abolishing serfdom, painting by C.W. Eckersberg

TIMELINE

1720 End of war with Sweden

1721 Denmark regains Schleswig

1750 Increase in foreign trade; end of economic crisis

1807 Bombardment of Copenhagen by Wellington's army

| 1720 | 1740 | 1760 | 1780 | 1 |

Armchair from the Chinese Room in Amalienborg Slot, Copenhagen

First Danish banknote, dating from 1713 during the reign of Frederik IV

1788 Abolishment of serfdom

1801 British attack Danish fleet

Painting by C.W. Eckersberg depicting bombardment of Copenhagen in 1807

with a mere 58,000 sq km (22,388 sq miles), which included the Duchy of Schleswig, with its Danish-German population, and the Holstein and Lauenburg dukedoms.

The Napoleonic Wars had a catastrophic effect on Denmark. The British blockade led to famine and starvation while territorial losses and wartime destruction resulted in a bankrupt state treasury. Culturally, however, this was the beginning of Denmark's Golden Age *(see pp42–3)*.

Denmark's national emblem, 1774–1820

SCHLESWIG CONFLICT

Events in Europe, including the 1830 July Revolution in France, contributed to the weakening of absolute monarchy. With increasing force, demands were made for the creation of a representative government. Eventually, in 1848, pressure from liberal circles resulted in the enactment of a new constitution, putting an end to absolute monarchy.

The new constitution included the incorporation of the duchies of Schleswig and Holstein as permanent regions of Denmark. With the support of Prussia, the armies of Schleswig and Holstein rose up against the Danish authority. War ensued and ended in 1851 with the defeat of the duchies, but failed to solve the conflict. Trouble erupted again with even greater force, in 1863, when the Danish parliament agreed a new joint constitution for the Kingdom of Denmark and the Duchy of Schleswig. A year later, on the pretext of defending the German populations within the duchies, Prussia and Austria declared war on Denmark. Within months Denmark was defeated and the contested duchies were lost to Prussia and Austria.

The shock of defeat led Denmark to declare its neutrality and concentrate its efforts on rebuilding the economy. Danish agriculture entered a period of rapid growth, assisted by a high demand for grain in Britain, and the railway system was extended to cover much of the country. By the end of the 19th century Denmark had a well-developed economic base that included mature shipbuilding and brewing industries.

Return of Danish soldiers to Copenhagen in 1864, painting by Otto Bache

---

1813 State Treasury declared bankrupt

1814 Kiel Peace Treaty; loss of Norway

1848–51 Civil war over the duchies of Schleswig and Holstein

Christian VIII, King of Denmark (1839–48)

1873 Banning of child labour

1820	1840	1860	1880

1835 First edition of Hans Christian Andersen's *Fairy Tales*

1843 First philosophical works by Søren Kierkegaard published

1848 End of absolute monarchy

1864 War with Prussia and Austria

1884 First Social Democrats elected to parliament

Denmark's Golden Age

The period of political and economic turmoil
that occurred during the Napoleonic wars,
and the years immediately following them,
witnessed an unprecedented flourishing of
culture. The leading figures of Denmark's
"Golden Age", which lasted throughout the first
half of the 19th century, achieved recognition
far beyond the borders of Denmark. Among the
most prominent are the sculptor Bertel
Thorvaldsen, the painter Christoffer Wilhelm
Eckersberg and the romantic poet Adam
Oehlenschläger. More famous than these,
however, are the writer Hans Christian Andersen
and the philosopher Søren Kierkegaard.

Bella and Hanna Nathansson
*This portrait was painted by
the "father of Danish painting"
Christoffer Wilhelm Eckersberg.*

Interior of a House
*The drawing room of a
Copenhagen merchant, portrayed
in this painting by Wilhelm
Marstrand, represents a typical
interior of a middle-class home
during the 1830s.*

Gottlieb Bindesbøll

Martinus Rørbye

Constantin
Hansen

Bertel Thorvaldsen
*This sculpture (1817) of a shepherd
boy is one of many Neo-Classical
statues by Bertel Thorvaldsen.*

Parade
*Festivals, parades and fairs coloured the
lives of Copenhagen's citizens.*

H.C. Andersen Telling his Stories *An illustration from one of the earliest editions of Hans Christian Andersen's tales, which are some of the most famous works of children's literature.*

Wilhelm Morstrand, Albert Küchler and Dietlev Blunck on a balcony

Jørgen Sonne

H.C. Andersen *Born in humble circumstances in 1805, the popular writer later socialized with the bourgeoisie and at court.*

Andersen's Inkpot *As well as writing nearly 200 fairy tales, Andersen also wrote novels, librettos and other works.*

Søren Kierkegaard *One of the forerunners of Existentialism, Kierkegaard (1813–55) described human life in terms of ethics, aesthetics and religion.*

ARTISTS OF THE GOLDEN AGE

This painting, entitled *A Group of Danish Artists Visiting Rome* was painted in 1837 by Constantin Hansen. Like many painters of this period, Hansen learnt his craft abroad and returned to Denmark with a fresh perspective.

THE GOLDEN AGE IN COPENHAGEN

Following the ravages that befell Copenhagen at the turn of the 18th and 19th centuries, including the 1807 British bombardment *(see p40)*, the city was rebuilt in a new form. Classicism became the dominant architectural style. Christian Frederik Hansen and other Danish architects often drew their inspiration from antiquity. Office buildings, as well as the new bourgeois residences, were adorned with columns, porticoes and tympanums. The most interesting buildings include Thorvaldsens Museum, the Domhuset (Court House) in Nytorv, and the Harsdorff Hus in Kongens Nytorv.

Thorvaldsens Museum *was built in 1848 and approved personally by the sculptor who had bequeathed his work to the city. This building is decorated with friezes by Jørgen Sonne (see p85).*

Vor Frue Kirke *was designed by Christian Frederik Hansen, who got his inspiration from Classical buildings. It had an imposing façade, but no tower until Frederik VI declared that a tower was essential (see p72).*

Stockholm, Copenhagen and Oslo portrayed in a satirical magazine, in 1906

WORLD WAR I

Before World War I Denmark had maintained good relations with both Britain and Germany and with the outbreak of war the Danish government declared its neutrality. This brought considerable benefits to the country's economy, although a third of Denmark's merchant fleet was sunk during the conflict. Also, the war drew attention to the commercial and strategic importance of Denmark's colonies in the West Indies, and the USA bought the Virgin Islands from Denmark in 1917.

Germany's defeat in 1918 revived the old Schleswig-Holstein problem. Under the Treaty of Versailles, the area was divided into two zones and, after a referendum in 1920, the northern part of the former duchy was returned to Denmark. The southern zone remained with Germany.

WORLD WAR II

In September 1939, during Hitler's invasion of Poland, Denmark again confirmed its neutral status. This failed to stop the Third Reich from invading Denmark on 9 April 1940, and after a brief period of resistance by the royal guards at Amalienborg Slot Germany began a "peaceful occupation". Hoping to minimize casualties, the government in Copenhagen decided on a policy of limited co-operation. Opposition among ordinary Danes to this occupation was widespread, however, and in 1943 an increasingly strong resistance movement brought an end to the policy of collaboration. Following a wave of strikes and anti-German demonstrations, the government resigned and was replaced by a German administration.

The Nazis disarmed the Danish army and fleet and began to round up Danish Jews. Fortunately, most were spirited away at night in fishing boats by the Danish Resistance to neutral Sweden.

The final 18 months of the war saw the Danish Freedom Council, an underground movement that organized the Resistance, become

US State Secretary hands the Danish minister a cheque in payment for the Virgin Islands

TIMELINE

1914–18 World War I. Denmark remains neutral

Frederik VIII with his wife, Louise

1940 Denmark occupied by the Third Reich

1944 Iceland becomes a republic

1900 — 1915 — 1930 — 1945

1901 Adoption of democratic parliamentary government

1933 Implementation of first social reform programmes

1949 Denmark becomes a co-founder of NATO

1960 Denmark joins EFTA

1917 Sale of the Virgin Islands to the United States

1920 Schleswig-Holstein referendum

Christian X (1912–47)

Germans on the streets of Copenhagen during World War II

the throne. These new rules were applied in 1972 when Queen Margrethe II ascended the throne following the death of her father, Frederik IX.

Denmark did not participate in the talks which in 1957 resulted in the formation of the European Union, but in 1973, after a referendum, it became the first Scandinavian country to join the EU. Denmark's EU membership has remained a controversial subject with many Danes, however, and 87 per cent of the country voted against the adoption of the euro.

increasingly active. The Danish Resistance, which by 1945 had some 50,000 operatives ready to assist the Allies, did all it could to hamper the German war effort, including blowing up railway lines and sabotaging German-run factories. With the German surrender in 1945, a new government composed of Resistance leaders and pre-war politicians was formed in Denmark.

Margrethe II, Queen of Denmark

Throughout the 1960s and 1970s a series of reforms, including a generous system of social welfare and a virtual lack of censorship, bolstered the country's reputation as a liberal country. In the 1970s and 1980s Denmark entered a conservative phase with calls for curbs on immigration and tax cuts. However, it is still acknowledged as a tolerant society, with a high standard of living, a strong sense of social conscience and many positive policies towards protecting the environment. In 2009, Anders Fogh Rasmussen, the country's former prime minister, was appointed secretary general of NATO.

POSTWAR DENMARK

Thanks to the activities of the Resistance, Denmark was recognized as a member of the Allied Forces and joined the United Nations in 1945. In 1949 it joined the ranks of NATO. This move marked a departure from a policy of neutrality, which the country had followed since 1864. Denmark's participation in the Marshall Plan enabled the country to thoroughly modernize its industry and agriculture and laid the foundations for postwar prosperity. A new constitution, enacted in 1953, introduced a single-chamber parliament and changed the rules governing female succession to

Anders Fogh Rasmussen, secretary general of NATO

1972 Queen Margrethe II ascends the throne of Denmark

2002 Copenhagen Summit; negotiations end on the enlargement of the EU

2000 Denmark rejects adoption of the euro

2005 Bicentenary of H.C. Andersen

2009 Anders Fogh Rasmussen appointed secretary general of NATO

1975 | 1990 | 2005 | 2020

1973 Denmark joins the European Union

1992 Rejection of the Maastricht Treaty, by public referendum

2004 Wedding of the Crown Prince

Marriage of Prince Frederik and Mary Donaldson

COPENHAGEN AREA BY AREA

COPENHAGEN AT A GLANCE 48–49

NORTH COPENHAGEN 50–63

CENTRAL COPENHAGEN 64–79

SOUTH COPENHAGEN 80–89

FURTHER AFIELD 90–97

SHOPPING IN COPENHAGEN
98–101

ENTERTAINMENT IN COPENHAGEN
102–105

STREET FINDER 106–111

Copenhagen at a Glance

Copenhagen's main attractions include its three royal palaces (Rosenborg, Amalienborg and Christiansborg), as well as numerous museums, churches and monuments, including the much-loved Little Mermaid. There is no shortage of parks. The most famous of these is Tivoli in the heart of the city. The city centre is compact and can easily be explored on foot. Enjoyable alternatives to walking are touring the city on a bicycle or riding one of the waterbuses that run along some of the most interesting canals.

0 metres 200
0 yards 200

Marmorkirken
The Marble Church, with its vast dome, is also known as Frederikskirken, after Frederik V who had it built. Visitors may climb the dome with a guide (see p58).

ØSTRE ANLÆG

BOTANISK HAVE

ROSENBORG HAVE

KONGENS HAVE

Nørreport M

CENTRAL COPENHAGEN

Gefion Springvandet
The biggest fountain in Copenhagen is inspired by a popular Scandinavian myth about the creation of Zealand (see p55).

◁ Royal guards sporting red uniforms and busbies and carrying drums

KASTELLET

NORTH COPENHAGEN

SOUTH COPENHAGEN

PUSHER STREET

M Christianshavn

Livgarden
The royal guards are one of the symbols of Copenhagen. They can be seen in front of Amalienborg Slot, the official residence of Queen Margrethe II (see p57).

Statens Museum for Kunst
The National gallery has a great treasure of European art dating from the 13th to 19th centuries (see pp62–3).

Rådhuspladsen
The city's main square is a good starting point to explore Strøget; it is also the seat of the city hall (see p75).

KEY

🕆	Church
⊠	Post office
M	Metro

NORTH COPENHAGEN

The north of the city is particularly attractive and includes the famous statue of the Little Mermaid *(Den Lille Havfrue)* and two royal palaces: Amalienborg Slot and Rosenborg Slot. The area also contains several interesting museums of a highly diverse nature – ranging from the Statens Museum for Kunst (Danish National Gallery), through to the Geologisk Museum (Geological Museum) and the Frihedsmuseet (Danish Resistance

Emblem from a frieze decorating Marmorkirken

Museum). Standing close to one another are sacred buildings belonging to three different religions: the Protestant Marmorkirken, the Roman Catholic Sankt Ansgars Kirke and the Russian orthodox Alexander Newsky Kirke. North Copenhagen has masses of greenery. The gardens and waterfalls of Botanisk Have (Botanical Gardens) are well worth exploring, as is the King's Garden (Kongens Have), which surrounds Rosenborg Slot.

SIGHTS AT A GLANCE

Churches
Marmorkirken **8**
Sankt Albans Kirke **3**

Historic Buildings and Monuments
Amalienborg Slot pp56–7 **7**
Gefion Springvandet **4**
Kastellet **2**
The Little Mermaid **1**
Rosenborg Slot pp60–61 **12**

Museums and Galleries
Davids Samling **9**
DesignMuseum Danmark **6**
Frihedsmuseet **5**
Geologisk Museum **14**
Hirschsprungske Samling **15**
Livgardens Historiske Samling **11**
Statens Museum for Kunst pp62–3 **16**

Places of Interest
Botanisk Have **13**
Kongens Have **10**

GETTING AROUND
This part of Copenhagen can be reached by taking the S-tog to Østerport or Nørreport or the metro to Kongens Nytorv and walking from there. Amalienborg is served by buses 1A and 15; Rosenborg by 6A and 173E.

KEY

Street-by-Street Map
See pp52–3

🕀 Church

0 m   200
0 yards   200

◁ **Marble Hall with 17th-century stuccowork, Rosenborg Slot**

Street-by-Street: Around Amalienborg Slot

The main reason to come to this part of Copenhagen is to visit Amalienborg Slot, the official residence of Queen Margrethe II, which is guarded by soldiers in traditional uniforms. The best time to visit is at noon, when the daily ceremony for the changing of the guard takes place. Frederik V made Amalienborg Slot the focal point of a new, smart district, which he built to mark the 300th anniversary of the Oldenburg dynasty, celebrated in 1748. In honour of the king the district was named Frederiksstaden.

Medicinsk-Historisk Museum, a medical museum, is housed in the former Danish Academy of Surgery and has on display some gruesome human remains as well as an old operating theatre.

Alexander Newsky Kirke is a Russian Orthodox church and was completed in 1883. It was a gift from Tsar Alexander III to mark his marriage to a Danish princess.

FREDERICIAGADE

BREDGADE

FREDERIKSGADE

★ **Marmorkirken**
Also known as Frederiks-kirken, this church is just west of Amalienborg. Its huge dome rests on 12 pillars and is one of the biggest of its kind in Europe, measuring 31 m (102 ft) across ❽

KEY

– – – Suggested route

STAR SIGHTS

★ Amalienborg Slot

★ DesignMuseum Danmark

★ Marmorkirken

★ **Amalienborg Slot**
Consisting of four almost identical buildings, the palace has been the main residence of the Danish royal family since 1794 ❼

★ **DesignMuseum Danmark**
Looking at the exhibits in this museum of art and design, it is hard to imagine that in the 18th century this building served as the city hospital **6**

LOCATOR MAP
See Street Finder Map 2

NORTH COPENHAGEN

CENTRAL COPENHAGEN

Sankt Ansgars Kirke
is on the site of a Roman Catholic chapel and was once used by Copenhagen's foreign population. The present building was completed in 1842 and consecrated 23 years later.

Afstøbningssamling,
or Royal Cast Collection, has over 2,000 sculpture casts, including a copy of the *Venus de Milo* and copies of statues from the Acropolis.

Amaliehaven
is a modern park, donated to the city by the A.P. Møller shipping company in 1983. The gardens are next to Nyhavn and are a popular place for a walk.

0 m   20

0 yards   20

The Little Mermaid ❶

Langelinie. **Map** 2 F3. 🚌 *1A, 15, 19, 26.*

The tiny figure of the Little Mermaid *(Den Lille Havfrue)*, sitting on a rock and gazing wistfully at the passing ships, is Denmark's best-known monument. The sculpture, commissioned by Carl Jacobsen, head of the Carlsberg brewery, was inspired by the ballet version of *The Little Mermaid*, which in turn was based on Hans Christian Andersen's tale about a mermaid who falls in love with a prince.

The sculptor, Edvard Eriksen (1876–1959), wanted to use as his model Ellen Price, a prima ballerina who had played the part of the mermaid. However, when the dancer learned where the statue was to be located she refused to continue posing and allowed only her face to be used. As a result, the body was modelled on that of the sculptor's wife.

The final bronze cast was placed at the end of the harbour promenade in 1913. Since then, the sculpture has fallen victim to vandals and pranksters on a number of occasions. In 1961 she had her hair painted red. In 1964 her head was cut off; some time later she lost both arms and in 1998 she lost her head once again. Now, moved a little further towards the sea, she enjoys more peace.

One of the buildings inside the Kastellet

Kastellet ❷

Map 2 E3. **Tel** 33 47 95 11 (for tours of the grounds). Ⓢ *Østerport.* 🚌 *1A, 15, 19, 26.* ⬚ fortress grounds only. 🅿

A fortress was first built on this site in 1626 but a Swedish attack in 1658 revealed its numerous weak points and on the orders of Frederik III the defences were rebuilt. The works were completed in 1663. The final structure, known as the Kastellet (Citadel), consisted of a fort in the shape of a five-pointed star surrounded by high embankments and a deep moat. In the 19th century the fortress was partially demolished and rebuilt once more. During World War II it was taken over by the occupying German forces who used it as their headquarters. It is now used by the Danish military, although the grounds and ramparts are open to visitors.

In the 19th century Kastellet served as a prison. The prisoner's cells were built against the church so that the convicts, unseen by the public, could participate in the mass by peering through small viewing holes cut into the walls.

Sankt Albans Kirke ❸

Churchillparken. **Map** 2 E3. **Tel** *33 11 85 18.* 🚌 *1A, 15, 19.* ⬚ summer: 10am–4pm Mon–Fri.

This church was built in 1887 to serve the city's Anglican community and is named after Saint Alban, a 4th-century Roman soldier who converted to Christianity and suffered a martyr's death.

Churchillparken, just south of Kastellet

THE STORY OF THE LITTLE MERMAID

The heroine of Andersen's tale is a young mermaid who lives beneath the waves with her five sisters. The little mermaid rescues a prince from a sinking ship and falls in love with him. Desperate to be with the prince, she is seduced by a wicked sea witch into giving up her beautiful voice in return for legs so that she can go ashore. The price is high, and the witch warns the mermaid that should the prince marry another she will die. For a long time the prince adores his new, mute lover but in the end he is forced into marrying a princess from another kingdom. Before the wedding is to take place on board a ship, the mermaid's sisters swim to it and offer her a magic knife. All she need do is stab the prince and she will be free to return to the water. The mermaid cannot bring herself to murder the prince and, as dawn breaks, she dies.

Andersen surrounded by fairytale characters

The Little Mermaid, Copenhagen's most famous landmark

For hotels and restaurants in this region see pp244–7 and pp268–74

Situated not far from the Gefion fountain, along Langelinie promenade in Churchillparken, the elegant Gothic church was a gift from Edward, Prince of Wales, who at the time was vying for the hand of Princess Alexandra, the daughter of Christian IX. They married in 1863, and the prince ascended to the throne as Edward VII in 1901. The church's interior has attractive stained-glass windows and a miniature copy of Bertel Thorvaldsen's sculpture – *St John the Baptist Praying in the Desert*. Religious services are still held here in English and the congregation often includes visitors to the city.

Gefion Springvandet **❹**

Map 2 F4. 🚌 *1A, 15, 19.*

Built in 1908, the Gefion fountain is an impressive work by Anders Bundgaard and one of Copenhagen's largest monuments. Its main feature is a statue of the goddess Gefion – a mythical Scandinavian figure. According to legend, the king of Sweden promised to give the goddess as much land as she could plough in one night. Gefion, who took him at his word, turned her four sons into oxen and harnessed them to a plough. By the time the cock crowed she had managed to plough a sizeable chunk of Sweden. She then picked it up and threw it into the sea, and so formed the island of Zealand. The hole left behind became Lake Vänern (whose shape closely resembles that of Zealand).

Danish armoured car in front of the Frihedsmuseet

Frihedsmuseet **❺**

Churchillparken. **Map** 2 E4. ***Tel*** *33 47 39 21.* Ⓢ *Østerport.* 🚌 *1A, 15, 19.* 🕙 *May–Sep: 10am–4pm Tue–Sun; Oct–Apr: 10am–3pm Tue–Sun.* **www**.frihedsmuseet.dk

The armoured car standing in front of the Danish Resistance Museum was built by members of the Danish underground movement and is one of the star attractions of this fascinating museum, which tells the story of Denmark's role during World War II.

Many of the secrets of sabotage are revealed and exhibits include a makeshift printing press, home-made weapons and police reports. Another section is devoted to the evacuation of Denmark's Jewish population, who were spirited away to Sweden by the Resistance.

Photographs of resistance workers killed in action are especially moving, as are letters to family and friends written by those sentenced to be executed by firing squad.

The thorny issue of Denmark's collusion with Germany during World War II is also covered, and uniforms from the Danish Freikorps – volunteers who signed up to fight with the German army – are on display. It is estimated that almost 4,000 Danes died fighting for Germany.

DesignMuseum Danmark **❻**

Bredgade 68. **Map** 2 E4. ***Tel*** *33 18 56 56.* Ⓢ *Østerport.* Ⓜ *Kongens Nytorv.* 🚌 *1A, 15.* 🕙 *11am–5pm Tue–Sun (to 9pm Wed).* 📷 **www**.designmuseum.dk

Designed by the Danish architect Nicolai Eigtved and erected in the mid-18th century, the buildings that now house the Museum of Art and Design were originally the city hospital; it was here that the philosopher Søren Kierkegaard died in 1855. The hospital was closed in 1919 and today contains one of the largest collections of royal porcelain in Denmark including pieces from the famous *Flora Danica* service *(see p93)*, as well as furniture, Japanese ceramics, silverware and textiles. Exhibits on display range from medieval items to examples of contemporary design.

Nearby, on the same side of the street, is **Sankt Ansgars Kirke**, a Roman Catholic church that has a small exhibition devoted to the history of Danish Catholicism.

The goddess Gefion and her oxen, from the Gefion Springvandet

Amalienborg Slot ⑦

The Amalienborg Palace complex consists of four buildings around an octagonal square. They were meant as residences for four wealthy families, but when Christiansborg Slot burned down in 1794, Christian VII bought one of the four palaces and turned it into a residence for the royal family. Designed by Nicolai Eigtved, Christian VII's Palace is renowned for its Great Hall, which has splendid Rococo woodcarvings and stucco decoration. Since 1885, the palace has been used mostly for royal guests and ceremonial purposes.

Balustrade Statues
All the palace statues were renovated in the late 1970s by sculptor Eric Erlandsen with the help of experts from the Statens Museum for Kunst (Danish National Gallery).

Gallery
The palace gallery has a beautiful ceiling and is the work of Fossatti. The French architect Nicolas-Henri Jardin designed the furniture.

Velvet Chamber
The tiled stove in this room comes from a factory in Lübeck. The silk velvet wall hangings were presents from Ludwig XV to an important high court official named Count Moltke.

★ Entrance Hall
The entrance hall has been renovated to appear as it would have done when the palace was first built. Its decorations have been recreated according to period designs. The statue of Andromeda is a cast of the original marble sculpture.

★ Knights' Chamber

This elegant room is an example of the artistry of Nicolai Eigtved and is the most beautiful Rococo chamber in Denmark.

VISITORS' CHECKLIST

Amalienborg Slot, Christian VII's Palace, Amalienborg Slotsplads. **Tel** *33 92 64 51.* Ⓜ *Kongens Nytorv.* Ⓢ *Nørreport.* 🚌 *1A, 15, 19, 26, 29, 650S.* ◻ *Jul–Sep: Sat & Sun.* 📷 🎟 compulsory: 11:30am (Danish); 1pm & 2:30pm (English). **www**.ses.dk/amalienborg

The royal guards, sporting bearskin hats, stand watch, day and night, in front of the palace.

Clock

This grandfather clock is one of many objects on display in the palace that were once used by the Danish royal family.

Changing of the Guard

Every day at noon, the Livgarden (royal guards) walk from Amalienborg Palace to Rosenborg Castle for the Changing of the Guard.

ROYAL RESIDENCE

KEY

☐ Christian IX's Palace

☐ Christian VII's Palace

☐ Christian VIII's Palace

☐ Frederik VIII's Palace

The name Amalienborg actually refers to an earlier palace, built in 1669 by Frederik III for his young bride Sophie Amalie. The present complex consists of four palaces grouped around a square, collectively known as Amalienborg Slot, which is in the heart of Frederiksstaden. The equestrian statue of Frederick V in the middle of the complex is the work of French sculptor Jacques Saly who spent 30 years working on it. The statue reputedly cost as much as the entire complex.

STAR FEATURES

★ Entrance Hall

★ Knights' Chamber

Marmorkirken ⑧

Frederiksgade 4. **Map** 2 D4.
Tel 33 15 01 44. ▦ 1A, 15, 19, 26.
Church ◯ 10am–5pm Mon–Thu
& Sat, noon–5pm Fri & Sun.
Dome ◯ 1pm, 3pm Sat & Sun.
▨ www.marmorkirken.dk

The vast dome of the
Baroque Frederikskirken,
also known as Marmorkirken
or the Marble Church, leads
many visitors to suspect that
its architect, Nikolai Eigtved,
based his design on St
Peter's Basilica in Rome.
The church was named after
Frederik V who wanted to
celebrate the fact that his
family had ruled Denmark
for 300 years by building a
new district in Copenhagen –
Frederiks-
staden – with
the church as
its focal point.
When work began,
in 1749, it was
assumed that the
church would
be constructed
of marble imported from
Norway (hence its alternative
name). However, it quickly
became apparent that the
cost of such a venture
would exceed the financial
resources of the treasury
and in 1770 work was
abandoned.

A century later the building
was completed using local
Danish marble. The most
obvious feature of the church
is its dome – one of the
largest in Europe. Visitors
can climb the 260 steps to
enjoy wonderful city views
from the top of the bell
tower. Inside the church

are frescoes by Danish artists.
On the outside, the building
has statues of Danish saints.

Davids Samling ⑨

Kronprinsessegade 30–32. **Map** 2 D5.
Tel 33 73 49 49. Ⓢ Ⓜ Nørreport.
▦ 1A, 15, 19, 26, 42, 43, 350S.
◯ 1–5pm Tue & Fri, 10am–9pm
Wed, 10am–5pm Thu, 11am–5pm
Sat & Sun. www.davidmus.dk

The museum's founder,
Christian Ludvig David (1878–
1960), was a lawyer who
donated his collection to the
state in 1945. The main museum building is 19th century
and, like others on this street,
has a characteristic L-shaped
floor plan. David's family had
lived there since
1810, although
he did not per-
sonally take possession
of it until 1917. In 1968
the state donated
the adjacent
house, helping to
accommodate the
museum's growing collection.

**17th-century bronze vessel
from India, Davids Samling**

The museum is best known
for its extensive collection of
Islamic art, which includes
items from Spain, Persia,
India and elsewhere. Among
the many treasures, some of
which date as far back as the
6th century, are ceramics,
silks, jewellery and ancient
daggers inlaid with jewels.
The museum also houses a
small collection of European
art, as well as examples of
18th-century English, French
and German furniture. There
is also a collection of Danish
silver dating from the 17th
and 18th centuries.

Kongens Have ⑩

Map 1 C5. ◯ 7am–dusk daily.

The King's Garden was
established by Christian IV
in 1606 and is Copenhagen's
oldest park, retaining most of
its original layout. In the 17th
century the gardens supplied
the royal court with fresh
fruit, vegetables and roses to
adorn the royal apartments.

Today, the shady gardens,
criss-crossed by paths and
with numerous benches, are
one of the favourite places
for Copenhagen's citizens
to walk and relax. Here,
visitors can also find one of
the capital's most famous
monuments. Unveiled in
1877, it is a statue of Hans
Christian Andersen enchanting a group of children with
some of his fairy tales.

**Leafy Kongens Have surrounding
Rosenborg Slot**

Livgardens Historiske Samling ⑪

Gothersgade 100. **Map** 1 B5.
Tel 45 99 40 00. Ⓢ Ⓜ Nørreport.
▦ 5A, 6A, 14, 42, 43, 150S,
173E, 184, 185, 350S.
◯ 11am–3pm Sat & Sun.
www.forsvaret.dk/lg

The Livgarden or royal
guards, dressed in
colourful uniforms and
sporting furry busbies, are
one of the symbols of
Copenhagen. Many people
come to watch them during
the daily ceremony for the
changing of the guard in front
of Amalienborg Slot, but even
their daily marches between
Rosenborg and Amalienborg
palaces are a popular sight.

Circular grand nave of Marmorkirken, decorated with wall paintings

Vast palm house, built in 1874, in Copenhagen's Botanisk Have

The museum is housed in a cluster of 200-year-old barracks and contains background information on the guards' history. Examples of their uniforms are on display along with weapons, paintings, documents, and musical instruments played by the guardsmen.

Rosenborg Slot ⑫

See pp60–61.

Botanisk Have ⑬

Gothersgade 128. **Map** 1 B4.
Tel 35 32 22 22. 🚌 5A, 6A, 14, 40, 42, 43, 150S, 173E, 184, 185, 350S.
Ⓢ Ⓜ Nørreport. ⬜ May–Sep: 8:30am–6pm daily; Oct–Apr: 8:30am–4pm Tue–Sun.
www.botanik.snm.ku.dk

The 20,000 species of plants gathered in the Botanical Gardens include native Danish plants, as well as some highly exotic ones collected from around the world. The garden was established in 1872, on the grounds of old town fortifications. Bulwarks have been turned into rockeries, and the moat that once surrounded the fortified walls is now a lake filled with water and marsh plants.

The gardens themselves have much to offer. There is a small forest, waterfalls and greenhouses, one of which contains over 1,000 varieties of cactus. Elsewhere, it is

possible to see coffee and pineapples growing. A special attraction is the roof-top walk in the steamy palmhouse.

Geologisk Museum ⑭

Øster Voldgade 5–7. **Map** 1 B4.
Tel 35 32 23 45. Ⓢ Ⓜ Nørreport.
🚌 6A, 26, 42, 43, 184, 185.
⬜ 10am–1pm Tue–Fri, 1–4pm Sat & Sun. 🖥 **www**.geologi.snm.ku.dk

Standing close to the eastern end of Botanisk Have, the Geological Museum opened in 1893 and occupies an Italian Renaissance-style building. Its carved stone decorations include rosettes, columns and arches.

The earliest museum exhibits are the meteorites on display in the courtyard. The biggest of these was found in Greenland in 1963 and, at 20 tonnes (17.86 tons), is the sixth largest in the world. On the ground and first floors are glass cabinets filled with minerals and fossils including the imprint of a jellyfish made over 150 million years ago. Elsewhere, there is an exhibition devoted to volcanoes, displays relating to the history of man and collections of dinosaur bones.

A separate section is devoted to oil and gas exploration and the geology of Denmark. Colourful stones and rock crystals are on sale in the museum shop.

Hirschsprungske Samling ⑮

Stockholmsgade 20. **Map** 1 C3.
Tel 35 42 03 36. Ⓢ Østerport.
🚌 6A, 14, 26, 40, 42, 43, 150S, 184, 185. ⬜ 11am–5pm Wed–Mon.
🖥 **www**.hirschsprung.dk

This gallery, one of Copenhagen's best, owes its existence to the art patronage of Heinrich Hirschsprung (1836–1908), a Danish tobacco baron who supported many Danish artists. The Hirschsprung collection has been on public display since 1911 and is housed in a Neo-Classical building on the outskirts of Østre Anlæg park.

The collection includes works by prominent Danish artists from the 19th and 20th centuries such as Eckersberg, Købke, Bendz, Hansen, Anna and Michael Ancher, Johannes Larsen and Peder S. Krøyer. Among the works on display is a portrait of Hirschsprung himself, smoking a cigar, which was painted by Krøyer.

One of the exhibition rooms displaying the Hirschsprungske Samling

Rosenborg Slot ⑫

This royal palace is one of Copenhagen's most visited attractions and contains thousands of royal objects including paintings, trinkets, furniture and a small armoury. Most impressive of all is the underground treasury containing the crown jewels and other royal regalia. The exquisite Dutch-Renaissance brick palace was erected in 1606, on the orders of Christian IV, to serve as a summer residence. It was used by successive monarchs until the early 18th century when Frederik IV built a more spacious palace at Fredensborg. In the early 19th century Rosenborg was opened to the public as a museum.

Marble Hall
The hall's Baroque décor was commissioned by Frederik III. The Italian decorator Francesco Bruno gave the ceilings new stuccowork and clad the walls with imitation marble.

The spire-topped towers were converted from bays

★ Long Hall
17th-century tapestries decorate the walls of the hall, which also contains a collection of 18th-century silver furniture including three silver lions that once guarded the king's throne.

Tower Stairway
Equestrian paintings, portraits, and a series of 17th-century floral water colours by Maria Merian are hung on the walls.

Christian IV's Winter Room
The most important of King Christian IV's private chambers has a fine collection of Dutch paintings and a speaking tube connected to the wine cellar below.

STAR FEATURES

★ Long Hall

★ Treasury

★ Treasury
The underground treasury rooms house the royal jewels, including the Crown of Christian IV which weighs 2.89 kg (6.4 lbs).

VISITORS' CHECKLIST

Øster Voldgade 4A.
Map 1 C4. **Tel** *33 15 32 86.*
Ⓢ Ⓜ *Nørreport.* 🚌 *6A, 26, 150S, 173E, 184, 185.*
🗓 *Jan–May & Sep–Oct: 11am–4pm; Jun–Aug: 10am–5pm; Nov–Dec: 11am–4pm Tue–Sun.*
🗓 *1 Jan, 21–26 & 31 Dec.* 🏷
www.rosenborgslot.dk

The Main Tower was originally shorter and was raised in the 1620s.

Glass Cabinet
This second-floor room, designed in 1714 and commissioned by King Frederik IV, contains his elaborately displayed collection of Venetian glass. It is the only known cabinet of its kind.

The third floor was completed in 1624 and was designed to provide space for the magnificent, long banqueting hall.

Chinese Drawing Room
This room was used by Sophie Hedevig, sister of Frederik IV. Some of its most distinctive items are the Chinese-style chairs, a guitar encrusted with ivory and tortoiseshell and bearing the princess's monogram, a 17th-century Japanese porcelain jug and an ebony table.

Royal Chamber of Frederik IV
The table standing at the centre of the room was given to Frederik IV in 1709 by the Grand Duke of Tuscany. The magnificent rock crystal chandelier was probably made in Vienna.

Statens Museum for Kunst ⑯

The Danish National Gallery houses a fascinating collection of European art. Among the Danish painters represented here are artists from the "Golden Age", such as Christoffer Wilhelm Eckersberg and Constantin Hansen, and members of the Skagen School, including Anna and Michael Ancher. There are also works by Old Masters like Bruegel, Rubens and Rembrandt, as well as masterpieces by 20th-century giants such as Picasso, and contemporary installation art. Children have their own gallery and an inspiring workshop.

The Last Supper (1909)
Emil Nolde, a well-known representative of German Expressionism, has often pursued religious themes in his art.

1st floor

A Mountain Climber (1912)
This Expressionist painting explores the relationship between humans and nature. It is one of a number of works by the Danish artist J.F. Willumsen.

Ground floor

★ Portrait of Madame Matisse (1905)
This portrait by Henri Matisse combines some of the most typical elements of Fauvism including simple lines and sharply contrasting colours.

Main entrance

Bookshop

2nd floor

VISITORS' CHECKLIST

Sølvgade 48–50. **Map** 1 C4.
Tel 33 74 84 94. ⑤ *Østerport.*
Ⓜ *Nørreport.* 6A, 26, 43,
150S, 173F, 184, 185, 350S.
◯ 10am–5pm Tue–Sun (to 8pm
Wed). (for special exhibitions
only). **www**.smk.dk

★ Christ as the Suffering Redeemer (1495–1500)
The Italian artist Andrea Mantegna's depiction of the garments of Christ is reminiscent of many of Donatello's sculptures.

The Strife of Lent with Shrove-Tide (1550–69)
This detail from a 16th-century Renaissance painting by Pieter Bruegel is typical of his earthy moralizing.

The New Wing, a striking Modernist structure by Anna Maria Indrio, opened in 1998 and is linked to the old building by a glass-roofed atrium.

KEY

- European art, 1300–1800
- The X-Room
- Children's workshop
- Sculpture Street
- Danish and international art after 1900
- Temporary exhibitions
- Danish and Nordic art, 1750–1900

GALLERY GUIDE

Contemporary art exhibitions are held in the X-Room, while Sculpture Street is the venue for contemporary Danish and international sculpture. The permanent collection is on the first floor and in the New Wing. The museum also has a number of spaces reserved for temporary exhibitions on particular artists or eras.

Danish National Art Library

STAR PAINTINGS

- ★ Christ as the Suffering Redeemer
- ★ Portrait of Madame Matisse

CENTRAL COPENHAGEN

The Strøget, a chain of five pedestrianized streets, links the city's two main squares, Kongens Nytorv and Rådhuspladsen. Shops and restaurants line the promenade, which bustles with activity well into the night. Lined with café terraces and restored 18th-century houses, Nyhavn is a quayside street that is particularly lively in the summer months. Central Copenhagen's many museums include the Ny Carlsberg Glyptotek, housing one of the world's best collections of painting and sculpture, and the Guinness World Records Museum. On a fine day it is well worth visiting the famous Tivoli amusement park and gardens. The Latin Quarter, located around the old university, has some pleasant traffic-free streets, such as Fiolstræde, which is lined with second-hand bookshops. A climb up the spiral walkway of the 17th-century Rundetårn (Round Tower) is rewarded by magnificent views over the city.

Façade detail, Latin Quarter

SIGHTS AT A GLANCE

Churches
Helligåndskirken ❾
Sankt Petri Kirke ⓯
Vor Frue Kirke ⓰

Museums and Galleries
Guinness World Records
   Museum ❺
Kunstforeningen
   GL Strand ⓬
Nikolaj, Copenhagen
   Contemporary Art Centre ❼
*Ny Carlsberg Glyptotek
pp78–9* ㉒
Post & Tele Museum ❻
Ripley's Believe
   It Or Not! ⓲

Streets and Squares
Gråbrødretorv ⓭

Højbro Plads ❽
Kongens Nytorv ❸
Nyhavn ❶
Nytorv ⓱
Rådhuspladsen ⓴

Historic Buildings
Charlottenborg Slot ❷
Det Kongelige Teater ❹
Rådhus pp74–5 ⓳
Rundetårn ⓫
Universitet ⓮

Gardens
Tivoli pp76–7 ㉑

Theatres
Skuespilhuset ❿

GETTING AROUND
Kongens Nytorv is served by metro and buses 1A, 15, 19, 26, 350S. The main transport terminal is Rådhuspladsen, served by buses 2A, 5A, 6A, 10, 12, 14, 26, 29, 33, 67, 68, 69, 173E, 250S.

KEY

Street-by-Street Map
See pp66–7

ℹ Tourist information

✚ Church

✡ Synagogue

⊠ Post office

Ⓜ Metro

0 m   400
0 yards   400

◁ **The picturesque Moorish façade of the Nimb Building in Tivoli**

Street-by-Street: Around Kongens Nytorv

During the late 17th century, Kongens Nytorv (King's New Square) was laid out to link the medieval parts of the city with its newer districts. Today, it is Copenhagen's biggest square and makes an excellent starting point for exploring the city. To the southeast it joins the picturesque Nyhavn district where the historic ship *Anna Moller*, part of the National-museet's collection, can be admired from a canal-side café. It also marks the beginning of Strøget, which has plenty of restaurants and bars as well as specialist shops and boutiques to tempt visitors.

Hotel d'Angleterre is one of the oldest and most exclusive hotels in Scandinavia *(see p68)* and has entertained many celebrities visiting Denmark.

Guinness World Records Museum
The museum collection includes numerous curios, including a figure of the world's tallest man (2.72m/8 ft 11 inches) ⬤

0 m   30
0 yards   30

Nikolaj
This 13th-century former church has had a number of other purposes since the early 1800s. It was used for "hap-penings" in the 1960s and now houses the Copenhagen Contemporary Art Center ⬤

KEY

--- – – – Suggested route

Magasin du Nord is more than 100 years old and is one of the biggest and most exclusive department stores in Scandinavia.

★ Kongens Nytorv
Built in 1680 by Christian V, whose huge equestrian statue is at its centre, Kongens Nytorv is one of Copenhagen's most elegant squares and contains some of the city's finest buildings ❸

An anchor from a 19th-century sailing vessel has been transformed into a monument to the victims of World War II.

LOCATOR MAP
See Street Finder Map 4

Charlottenborg Slot
This is the oldest building in Kongens Nytorv, and is used by Det Kongelige Kunstakademi (The Royal Academy of Fine Arts) ❹

★ Nyhavn
The northern side of the canal is lined with colourful houses, many of which were once brothels frequented by sailors after months at sea ❶

Pleasure boat rides along the 17th-century canal are one of the main visitor attractions. It has became a tradition that each year old sailing ships arriving in Copenhagen moor alongside Nyhavn.

★ Det Kongelige Teater
This 19th-century building houses a prominent theatre, staging both drama and ballet ❺

STAR SIGHTS

★ Det Kongelige Teater

★ Kongens Nytorv

★ Nyhavn

Nyhavn, lined with bars, restaurants and cafés

Nyhavn **❶**

Map 4 E1.

Lined on both sides with colourful houses, this 300-m (328-yard) long canal, known as the New Harbour, was dug by soldiers between 1671 and 1673 and was intended to enable ships loaded with merchandise to sail into the centre of Copenhagen. Today, stylish yachts and old wooden boats are moored at many of the quays.

When Hans Christian Andersen lived here, the area north of the canal was a notorious red-light district with a seedy reputation thanks to the cheap bars, rough-and-ready hotels, tattoo parlours and numerous brothels. Since then Nyhavn has smartened up a great deal (though a few tattoo

parlours still remain) and is now one of the city's best-known districts. The boozy joints packed with sailors are long gone and have been replaced with bars, cafés and restaurants targeting a more prosperous clientele. The place is especially popular on warm summer evenings, and many of the restaurants and bars can get extremely busy – particularly on the north side of the harbour. The huge anchor found at the Kongens Nytorv end of the canal once belonged to *Fyen*, a 19th-century frigate, and has been used to commemorate Danish sailors who lost their lives during World War II.

Charlottenborg Slot **❷**

Nyhavn 2. **Map** 4 D1. **Tel** 33 36 90 50. Ⓜ *Kongens Nytorv.* ▦ *1A, 15, 19, 26, 350S.* ◯ *11am–5pm Tue–Sun (to 8pm Wed).* 🅰 **www.**kunsthalcharlottenborg.dk

This Baroque palace was built between 1672 and 1683 for Queen Charlotte Amalie (wife of Christian V), and was named after her. In the mid-18th century King Frederik V handed over the palace to the newly created Royal Academy of Fine Arts, and it is now filled with faculty and students. A section of the palace, known as Charlottenborg Kunsthal, is used as a venue for temporary art exhibitions.

One of Charlottenborg's portals

Kongens Nytorv **❸**

Map 4 D1.

King's New Square was created more than 300 years ago. This is one of Copenhagen's central points and the site of Det Kongelige Teater (The Royal Theatre) and Charlottenborg Slot. As well as marking the end of Nyhavn, it is also a good starting point for exploring Strøget, Copenhagen's famous walkway, which is lined with shops and restaurants.

At the centre of this oval square is an equestrian statue of Christian V, on whose orders the square was built. The original sculpture was made in 1688 by a French artist. Unfortunately, with time, the heavy lead monument, which depicts Christian V as a sombre Roman general, began to sink, distorting the proportions of the figure. In 1946 the monument was recast in bronze.

Each June graduates gather in the square to dance around the statue as part of a traditional matriculation ceremony.

HOTEL D'ANGLETERRE'S ROMANTIC ORIGINS

In the mid-18th century Jean Marchal, a young hairdresser and make-up artist travelling with a troupe of actors, arrived in Copenhagen. Jean decided to settle in town and took the job of valet to Count Conrad Danneskiold Laurvig. At a reception, to which he accompanied the count, he met Maria Coppy, daughter of the court chef. They married in 1755 and, exploiting the culinary talents of Maria, opened a restaurant with a handful of bedrooms for passing travellers. Unfortunately neither lived long enough to fully enjoy the fruits of their enterprise. Their small hotel has survived and thrived, having undergone a great many changes including the addition of around 100 or so rooms. It now receives some of the world's most distinguished figures.

Hotel d'Angleterre

Equestrian statue of Christian V in Kongens Nytorv

Kongens Nytorv was once filled with elm trees, planted in the 19th century. Sadly, these fell prey to disease in 1998 and the square has since been replanted.

Det Kongelige Teater ❹

August Bournonvilles Passage, Kongens Nytorv. **Map** 4 D1. *Tel 33 69 69 33.* **www**.kgl-teater.dk

Anyone visiting the area around Kongens Nytorv is usually struck by the sight of the Royal Theatre, a vast Neo-Renaissance building that has been the main venue in Denmark since it was founded in 1748. The present building, which occupies the original site, dates from 1872. For many years, this theatre set itself apart by putting on ballet, opera and theatre in the same space. The complex includes two theatres – Gamle (old) Scene and Nye (new) Scene, the latter popularly known as Stærekassen and built in 1931. Since the opening of Operaen, the striking opera house across the harbour from Amalienborg Slot in 2005 *(see p89)*, Det Kongelige Teater only hosts ballet, while drama is staged at the Skuespilhuset *(see p71)*.

The statues at the front of the theatre celebrate two distinguished Danes who made contributions to the development of theatre and the arts. One is the playwright Ludvig Holberg, often hailed as the father of Danish theatre, the other is the poet Adam Oehlenschlager.

Guinness World Records Museum ❺

Østergade 16. **Map** 4 D1. *Tel 33 32 31 31.* Ⓜ *Kongens Nytorv.* 🚌 *1A, 15, 19, 26, 350A.* 🕐 *Jan–mid-Jun: 10am–6pm daily (to 8pm Fri & Sat); mid-Jun–Aug: 10am–10pm daily; Sep–Dec: 10am–6pm daily (to 8pm Fri & Sat).* ● *1 Jan, 24–25 Dec, 31 Dec.* 📷 **www**.guinness.dk

Visitors to the Guinness World Records Museum are welcomed at the entrance by a replica of the world's tallest man. Inside is a collection of the biggest, smallest, fastest, heaviest, longest and shortest, as well as a number of rooms in which visitors can try to beat a world record or experience how it feels to drive a car at 500 km/h (311 mph). A film showing how people from all over the world have trained for their record-breaking attempts can also be seen.

Post & Tele Museum ❻

Købmagergade 37. **Map** 3 C1. *Tel 33 41 09 00.* Ⓢ *Nørreport.* Ⓜ *Kongens Nytorv.* 🚌 *1A, 15, 19, 26, 350S.* 🕐 *10am–4pm daily.* ● *1 Jan, 24, 25 & 31 Dec.* ♿ ▢ 🏠 **www**.ptt-museum.dk

This museum dedicated to postal and telecommunication services grew from a core collection gathered by Jens Wilken Mørch, who started his career in the Danish Post in 1856 and eventually became head postmaster. The museum opened to the public in 1913; the exhibits relating to telecommunications were incorporated in 1931, when the museum absorbed the collection of an engineer named Hans Haller.

The permanent collection consists of three sections that give an overview of the many developments in the world of postal and telecommunication services. The highlight of The King's Post Office (1624–1848) is a full-size replica of a spherical mail coach; there are also uniforms and portraits of eminent figures within the mail service. The Age of Invention (1849–1920) focuses on maritime postal history and the early years of telegraphy and telephony. The final section looks at postal and telecommunication services after the 1920s, all the way through to the Internet age. There are also temporary exhibitions and a children's playground located inside a giant three-dimensional stamp.

Entrance to the Guinness World Records Museum

Café situated in the former Sankt Nikolaj Kirke

Nikolaj, Copenhagen Contemporary Art Centre 🔢

Nikolaj Plads 10. **Map** 3 C1.
Tel *33 18 17 80.* Ⓢ *Nørreport.*
Ⓜ *Kongens Nytorv.* 🚌 *1A, 2A, 15, 19, 26, 350S.* 🕐 *noon–5pm Tue–Sun (to 9pm Thu).* 🎫 *(free on Wed).*
www.kunsthallennikolaj.dk

This unique exhibition space, housed in a renovated 16th-century church, focuses on Danish and international modern art.

The first art exhibitions were held here in 1957 but the art centre really came to prominence in the 1960s when it was used by Fluxus, an important international group of avant-garde artists, that staged a number of innovative "Fluxus-performances" here. Some unique works remain from this period including a "juke box" by Fluxus organiser

Knud Petersen, which has since been developed to contain more than 22 hours of experimental music, sound poetry, and the latest in audio art. The "Crying Space" by Eric Andersen is filled with tear-inducing objects and suggestions on the wall. Eleven hollow stones are there to collect visitors' tears.

As well as these permanent exhibits, Nikolaj puts on a number of temporary shows including an annual art exhibition for children.

Højbro Plads 🔢

Map 3 C1.

This cobbled square is one of the most enchanting places in Copenhagen. Although at first glance it looks like a single large unit, it is in fact divided into Højbro Plads and Amagertorv.

Højbro Plads contains a vast monument to Bishop Absalon, who from his horse points out towards Christiansborg Slot on the other side of the canal. In Amagertorv, the former city market, is a 19th-century fountain with three birds about to take flight. It is named Storkespringvandet (The Stork Fountain) though the birds are actually herons.

The northern section of Amagertorv has an interesting twin-gabled house, built in

1616, in the style of the Dutch Renaissance. It is one of the city's oldest buildings and houses the Royal Copenhagen Porcelain Shop. Adjacent to it is the showroom of Georg Jensen, which specializes in upmarket silverware. A small museum is devoted to the work of Jensen and contains some of his early pieces.

Portal of Helligåndskirken – one of Copenhagen's oldest churches

Helligåndskirken 🔢

Niels Hemmingsensgade 5.
Map 3 C1. **Tel** *33 15 41 44.*
🕐 *noon–4pm Mon–Fri; also 7pm–1am Fri.* **www.**helligaandskirken.dk

Dating originally from the early 15th century when it was an Augustinian monastery, the "Church of the Holy Spirit" was built on an even an earlier religious site, founded in 1238. The church, which is one of the oldest in Copenhagen, acquired its towers in the late 16th century and its sandstone portal, originally intended for the Børsen (Stock Exchange), early in the 17th century. The building was ravaged by one of the city's great fires in 1728, and has been largely rebuilt, although some original 14th-century walls in the right-hand wing can still be seen. Now surrounded by a park, the church still holds religious services. It is also used for art shows and exhibitions, which provide an occasion to admire its magnificent vaults.

In the churchyard is a memorial to Danish victims of the Nazi concentration camps.

STRØGET

The word "Strøget" ("pedestrian street") cannot be found on any of the plates bearing street names; nevertheless, all those who know the city are familiar with it. Copenhagen's main walkway runs east to west. It is made up of five inter-connected streets: Østergade, Amagertorv, Vimmelskaftet, Nygade and Frederiksberggade. Pedestrianized in 1962, it has since become one of the town's favourite strolling grounds. Shops range from exclusive boutiques to souvenir and toy stores, along with numerous cafés and restaurants. There are also some pretty churches and squares and a handful of museums. Every day (when the Queen is in residence), at about 11:45am, the Livgarden or royal guards march along Østergade, heading for Amalienborg Slot for the changing of the guards.

Tourist train running along Strøget

Skuespilhuset ⑩

Sankt Annæ Plads 36. **Map** 2 D5.
Tel 33 69 69 33. 🚻 🅿️
www.kglteater.dk

Throughout the 1900s, a number of venues across the city were used to house the Royal Danish Theatre's Drama Department – with varying degrees of success. Although the need for a suitable playhouse was recognized as early as the 1880s, it was not until 2001 that the government unveiled plans to build a dedicated theatre.

Skuespilhuset, the Royal Danish Playhouse, was inaugurated in 2007. The strikingly modern building offers a range of performance spaces, including two main auditoria – the Main Stage and the Portscenen, seating 650 and 200 respectively – and the Studio Stage, which has seats for 100 people. There are also several open-air spaces, such as the waterfront foyer and the footbridge terrace, which are used for children's activities and other events. In addition to its seasonal repertoire of plays, the theatre hosts ballets, public lectures, concerts and Q&As with playwrights, directors and actors. Note that all drama performed here is in Danish.

Designed by Danish architects Boje Lundgaard and Lene Tranberg, the theatre incorporates a variety of materials: the dark cladding on the external walls was created with ceramic tiles; the outside of the stage tower is covered with copper; and the footbridge linking the foyer to the harbourfront promenade is made out of oak.

Rundetårn's cobbled spiral ramp winding to its top

Rundetårn ⑪

Købmagergade 52A. **Map** 3 C1.
Tel 33 73 03 73. 🕐 21 May–20 Sep: 10am–8pm daily; 21 Sep–20 May: 10am–5pm daily. 🎫
www.rundetaarn.dk

The round tower, 35 m (115 ft) tall and 15 m (49 ft) in diameter, provides an excellent vantage point from which to view Copenhagen. Access to the top is via a cobbled spiral ramp, 209 m (686 ft) long, which winds seven and a half times around to the top. Over the years the Rundetårn has been damaged by several fires and part of the observatory was rebuilt in the 18th century.

Rundetårn was erected on the orders of Christian IV, and was originally intended as an observatory for the nearby university. It is still used by the university, making it the oldest working observatory of its kind in Europe.

In 1642, during the tower's opening ceremony, Christian IV is said to have ridden his horse up the spiralling pathway to the very top. Later on, in 1716, the Tsar of Russia, Peter the Great, allegedly repeated this stunt during a visit to Copenhagen and was followed by his wife Tsarina Catherine II, who, as legend would have it, climbed to the top in a coach drawn by six horses.

The modern-day equivalent of such antics is an annual bicycle race; the winner is the person who cycles to the top and back again in the fastest time, without dismounting or falling off.

Kunstforeningen GL Strand ⑫

Gammel Strand 48. **Map** 3 C1.
Tel 33 36 02 60. 🚇 Kongens Nytorv. 🚌 1A, 2A, 6A, 15, 26, 29. 🕐 11am–5pm Tue–Sun (to 8pm Wed & Thu). 🎫 🅿️
www.glstrand.dk

Copenhagen's Gallery of Modern and Contemporary Art was founded in 1825 by the artist and professor C.W. Eckersberg as a way to bridge the gap between the elitist art establishment and the viewing public, thereby making art more accessible. Its mission today is also to focus on and support young, emerging artists. The gallery has occupied its current premises, a building on Gammel Strand designed by the 18th-century architect Philip de Lange, since 1952. GL Strand doesn't have a permanent collection, relying instead on temporary shows spotlighting individual artists. During the course of its history, the gallery has played host to many fascinating exhibitions by the likes of Edvard Munch (1908), Asger Jorn (1953) and the American film director and visual artist David Lynch (2010).

Skuespilhuset, on the Copenhagen waterfront

Outdoor restaurant tables in Gråbrødretorv

Gråbrødretorv ⑬

Map 3 C1. 🚌 6A.

This charming, cobblestone square is filled with music from buskers in summer when the restaurant tables spill out into the street. It is an excellent place in which to stop for a lunch. The square dates back to 1238, and its name refers to the so-called Grey Brothers, Franciscan monks who built the city's first monastery here. A great fire in 1728 destroyed the surrounding buildings; the present buildings date mainly from the early 18th century.

Universitet ⑭

Vor Frue Plads. **Map** 3 B1. Ⓢ Ⓜ
Nørreport. 🚌 5A, 6A, 14, 42, 43,
150S, 173E, 184, 185, 350S.
www.ku.dk/english

The cobbled Vor Frue Plads and its surrounding university buildings are the heart of the so-called Latin Quarter (Latin was once spoken here). Despite the fact that the university was founded by Christian I in 1479, the buildings that now stand in Vor Frue Plads date from the 19th century. They house only a handful of faculties including law; the remaining departments and staff have moved to the main campus, on the island of Amager, east of Copenhagen.

The vast, Neo-Classical university building stands opposite Vor Frue Kirke. It has an impressive entrance hall decorated with frescoes depicting scenes from Greek mythology, which are the work of Constantin Hansen. Adjacent to the university building is the 19th-century university library. On the library's main staircase is a glass cabinet containing fragments from a cannon ball that was fired during the British bombardment in 1807. The ball struck the library and ironically hit a book entitled *The Defender of Peace*. A number of second-hand bookshops are located along Fiolstræde, which runs up to the Universitet.

Sankt Petri Kirke ⑮

Larslejstræde 11. **Map** 3 B1.
Tel 33 13 38 33. Ⓢ Ⓜ Nørreport.
🚌 5A, 6A, 14, 42, 43, 173E, 150S,
350S. ☐ Apr–Sep: 11am–3pm daily.
🎫 💷 burial chapel only.
www.sankt-petri.dk

Saint Peter's church has been the main church for Copenhagen's German community since 1586. It dates from 1450 but suffered serious damage in the course of a series of fires and the British bombardment of 1807. However, many of the bricks used in the building work are from the original structure. Particularly noteworthy is the "burial" chapel containing

Statue of Christ from the high altar in Vor Frue Kirke

numerous tombs and epitaphs, mainly from the 19th century. There are also some interesting tablets commemorating the dead which can be seen on the church's outside wall.

Vor Frue Kirke ⑯

Nørregade 8. **Map** 3 B1.
Tel 33 37 65 40. Ⓢ Ⓜ Nørreport.
🚌 5A, 6A, 14, 42, 43, 150S, 173E,
184, 185, 350S. ☐ 8am–5pm daily.
www.koebenhavnsdomkirke.dk

Copenhagen's cathedral, Vor Frue Kirke (Church of Our Lady), has a somewhat sombre look and is the third consecutive church to be built on this site. The first, a small 12th-century Gothic church, was consumed by fire in 1728, while the next one was destroyed by British bombs in 1807 (the tower presented an excellent target for the artillery). The present structure dates from 1820 and was designed by Christian Frederik Hansen. Its interior is a veritable art gallery, full of sculptures by the prominent Danish sculptor Bertel Thorvaldsen *(see p85)*. Standing on both sides are marble statues of the 12 apostles; the central section of the altar has a kneeling angel and a vast figure of Christ – one of the artist's most famous masterpieces. Thorvaldsen

The imposing Neo-Classical façade of the Universitet

Interior of Vor Frue Kirke, with statues by Bertel Thordvaldsen

is also the creator of the relief depicting St John the Baptist, seen at the entrance to the cathedral. During Sunday mass it is sometimes possible to see Queen Margrethe II among the congregation. In the past she used to occupy a special royal box. But attitudes have changed and today, not wishing to distance herself from her subjects, the Danish monarch is to be found sitting in the pews.

Nytorv ⑰

Map 3 B1.

Although Nytorv looks like one big square, it is in fact made up of two separate areas – Gammeltorv (Old Square) and Nytorv (New Square) which are separated by the Nygade section of the Strøget walkway. To the northwest of Strøget, Gammeltorv was a busy market place in the 14th century and therefore has the longest trading tradition in Copenhgen. Today, it is dominated by a small fruit and vegetable market along with stalls selling jewellery and all kinds of handicrafts.

Standing at the centre of the square is Caritas Springvandet (The Charity Fountain), which dates from 1609. This Renaissance treasure is the work of Statius Otto, and depicts a pregnant woman carrying one child in her arms and leading another by the hand – a symbol of charity and mercy. Water flows from the woman's breasts and also from the urinating boy at her

feet (the holes were blocked with lead for reasons of decency in the 19th century). The fountain was commissioned by Christian IV to draw the public's attention to his charitable virtues. At one time it supplied the city's inhabitants with water brought along wooden pipes from a lake 5 km (3 miles) north of Copenhagen.

Nytorv was established in 1606 and for a long time was used by the authorities as a place of execution. The squares were joined together and given their present form soon after the city hall was destroyed by fire in 1795. The outline of the city hall can still be seen in Nytorv's pavement.

The striking Neo-Classical Domhuset, or Court House, with its six large columns, on the south side of Nytorv was completed in 1815 to a design by Christian Frederik Hansen, the Danish architect who worked on rebuilding the town after a fire in 1795. The materials used in the rebuilding work included those taken from the ruined Christiansborg Slot, and the resulting building is redolent of an ancient temple. The building was first used as the city hall, becoming the fifth seat of the town's authorities. In the early 20th century the city hall was moved to the Rådhus. The inscription seen on the front of the Domhuset refers to more recent

function as a court house and quotes the opening words of the Jutland Code of 1241: "With law the land shall be built".

Ripley's Believe It Or Not! ⑱

Rådhuspladsen 57. **Map** 3 B2.
Tel 33 32 31 31. ▭ 2A, 5A, 6A, 10, 12, 14, 26, 29, 33, 67, 68, 69, 173E, 250S. ◯ Sep–mid-Jun: 10am–6pm Sun–Thu, 10am–8pm Fri–Sat; mid-Jun–Aug: 10am–10pm daily. ● 1 Jan, 24, 25 & 31 Dec. ▨ www.ripleys.dk

This museum is part of an American chain that is based on an idea of Robert L. Ripley, a radio presenter, comic book writer and adventurer, who dreamt up a freakshow in the early 20th century to stun and amaze his American audience.

The museum may well prove popular with children. Many strange exhibits are on display, some of which were collected by Ripley himself. Here, visitors can marvel at a man who eats bicycles or a doll covered in 7,000 buttons, wince at a collection of medieval torture instruments and shrunken voodoo heads, and be astounded by various freaks of nature including a fish covered in fur and a two-headed cow.

Nytorv, a colourful and bustling square

Rådhus 🄉

The red-brick Rådhus (City Hall), which opened in 1905, was designed by the Danish architect Martin Nyrop (1849–1921), who was inspired by Italian buildings but also employed some elements of Danish medieval architecture. Its large main hall, sometimes used for exhibitions and official events, is decorated with statues of Nyrop as well as three other prominent Danes – Bertel Thorvaldsen, H.C. Andersen and Niels Bohr.

Though it is an official building, the Rådhus is open to visitors. It is well worth climbing the 298 stairs to the top of the 105-m (344-ft) tower to reach the city's highest viewpoint.

Copenhagen's Emblem
This has changed little since the 13th century. It consists of three castle towers, symbolically drawn waves of the Øresund and images of the sun and moon.

Ceilings
The Rådhus rooms and chambers are full of details and architectural flourishes such as intricate brickwork, mosaics and decorated ceilings.

National flag of Denmark

★ Main Hall
This vast, rectangular hall on the first floor is flanked by cloisters and topped with a glazed roof. It has Italianate wall decorations and a number of sculptures.

Absalon's Statue
Standing above the main entrance is a gilded statue of Bishop Absalon, the 12th-century founder of Copenhagen.

Main entrance

★ World Clock
Jens Olsen spent 27 years building this clock. Its extraordinary mechanism was set in motion in 1955. One of its many functions is to provide a calendar for the next 570,000 years.

Clock Tower
The peals from the tower's bells are heard throughout the streets of Copenhagen and are also transmitted by radio across the whole of Denmark.

VISITORS' CHECKLIST

Rådhuspladsen. **Map** 3 B2.
Tel 33 66 25 82. ⑤ *Central Station.* 🚌 *2A, 5A, 6A, 10, 12, 14, 26, 29, 33, 67, 68, 69, 250S.*
◯ 7:45am–5pm Mon–Fri.
🎦 *(in English) 3pm Mon–Fri, 10am Sat.* 🆓 **Tower** ◯ *11am & 2pm Mon–Fri, noon Sat.* 🆓
World Clock ◯ *8:30am–4:30pm Mon–Fri, 10am–1pm Sat.* 🆓 **www**.kk.dk

Staircase
The stately rooms on the top floors are reached by graceful stairs with marble balustrades.

STAR SIGHTS

★ Main Hall

★ World Clock

Rådhuspladsen ⑳

Map 3 A2 & B2. ⑤ *Central Station.* 🚌 *2A, 5A, 6A, 10, 12, 14, 26, 29, 33, 67, 68, 69, 173E, 250S.*

This open space is the second biggest square in the Danish capital (after Kongens Nytorv). City Hall Square was established in the second half of the 19th century, following the dismantling of the western gate that stood on this site, and the levelling of the defensive embankments. Soon afterwards it was decided to build the present city hall, providing further impetus to the development of the surrounding area. The square has been pedestrianized since 1994 and is popular with shoppers and sightseers. It is also a gathering point on New Year's Eve.

A number of monuments in Rådhuspladsen are worthy of note. Standing immediately by the entrance to the city hall is the Dragon's Leap Fountain, erected in 1923. A little to one side, by Rådhus's tower, is a tall column, unveiled in 1914, featuring two bronze figures of Vikings blowing bronze horns. Close by, in Hans Christian Andersens Boulevard, is a sitting figure of Andersen, facing Tivoli gardens. Another curiosity is an unusual barometer hanging on a building that is covered with advertisements, located at the corner of Vesterbrogade and H.C. Andersens Boulevard. It includes a figure of a girl, who in fine weather rides a bicycle. When it rains she opens her umbrella. A nearby thermometer gives a reading of the daily temperature.

The Rådhus with its red brick elevations

Tivoli ㉑

When Tivoli first opened in 1843 it had only two attractions: a carousel with horses and a roller coaster. Today Tivoli is an altogether grander affair. Part amusement park, part cultural venue, part wonderland, it is one of the most famous places in Denmark and much loved by the Danes themselves, who regard it as one of their national treasures. Situated in the heart of the city, this large garden is planted with almost one thousand trees and blooms with 400,000 flowers during the summer. At night, when it is lit by myriad coloured bulbs, it is a truly breathtaking sight.

The Ferry Inn
Located next to the jetty, this is one of 30 restaurants in Tivoli. It also houses a micro-brewery.

Frigate
The huge St George's Frigate III, *a pirate-themed family restaurant, is moored on Tivoli's picturesque lake – the remains of a former moat.*

Pantomime Theatre
Pantomime in Denmark dates back to the early 19th century. The Chinese-style pavilion hosts regular performances and is the oldest building in Tivoli gardens.

Main Entrance
The main gate, in Vesterbrogade, was built in 1896.

STAR SIGHTS

★ Pagoda

★ Nimb Building

For hotels and restaurants in this region see pp244–7 and pp268–74

★ Pagoda

The tower, built in the style of a Chinese pagoda, houses a restaurant that has been here since its construction in 1900; it specializes in pan-Asian cuisine.

VISITORS' CHECKLIST

Vesterbrogade 3. **Map** 3 A2. *Tel* 33 15 10 01. Ⓢ Central. 🚌 1A, 2A, 5A, 6A, 10, 11A, 15, 26, 30, 40, 47, 65E, 250S. ☐ 11am–10pm daily (to midnight Fri & Sat). Summer season: mid-Apr–mid-Sep; Halloween season: last 2 wks in Oct; Christmas season: mid-Nov–end Dec. 🚼 www.tivoli.dk

Concert Hall

Tivoli's pastel-coloured concert hall was built in 1956 and updated in 2005. Concerts range from rock to symphonies, and in the basement is Europe's longest seawater aquarium.

Amusements

Rides and other amusements, including vintage cars for smaller children, are scattered throughout the park.

TIVOLI BOYS GUARD

A group of boys dressed in smart uniforms and marching to the beat of drums is a frequent sight when strolling along the park's avenues on weekends. According to promoters of the gardens, "the Queen has her own guards and the Tivoli has its own". Made up of about 100 boys, aged between 8 and 16, the Tivoli Boys Guard is smartly dressed in red jackets and busbies and covers some 300 km (186 miles) a year. The marching band was founded in 1844 and is one of Tivoli's four orchestras, the other three being the Symphony Orchestra, the Tivoli Big Band and the Tivoli Promenade Orchestra.

Boys Guard marching through Tivoli

★ Nimb Building

This palatial Moorish-style building houses three restaurants and two bars, as well as an upmarket boutique hotel.

Ny Carlsberg Glyptotek ㉒

This world-class art museum boasts over 10,000 treasures including Ancient Egyptian art, Greek and Roman sculptures and a huge collection of Etruscan artifacts. It also exhibits a wealth of Danish paintings and sculptures from the era known as the Golden Age *(see pp42–3)* and exquisite works by French Impressionist masters such as Degas and Renoir. It has grown from the fine collection of sculptures *(glyptotek)* donated by Carl Jacobsen, founder of the New Carlsberg Brewery, and the museum now consists of three architecturally different buildings, the first one built in 1897 and the latest added in 1996.

★ Ancient Egyptian Art
The outstanding collection of Egyptian art ranges from delicate vases to monumental statues, such as this granite figure of Ramses II from the 2nd millennium BC.

Danish Sculpture
Sculptures representing the great artistic flourishing of Denmark's Golden Age include works such as Jens Adolph Jerichau's Penelope *(1840s), as well as many pieces by H.W. Bissen.*

★ The Kiss
This famous pair of lovers is one of 35 works by Auguste Rodin, which constitutes the largest collection of the artist's works anywhere outside France.

STAR EXHIBITS

★ Ancient Egyptian Art

★ Head of Satyr

★ The Kiss

Alabaster Relief
This 9th-century BC relief depicting the Assyrian King Assurnasirpal II is part of the multifaceted collection representing the Middle East.

Win
gar

VISITORS' CHECKLIST

Dantes Plads 7. **Map** 3 B3. **Tel** 33
41 81 41 ☐ 11am–5pm Tue–
Sun. ● 1 Jan, 5 Jun, 24 & 25
Dec. ⚅ (free Sun and to under-
18s). ☷ 2A, 11A, 33, 69, 173E,
250S. **www**.glyptoteket.dk

Landscape from Saint-Rémy

*Along with this picture painted by Vincent
van Gogh during his stay in a psychiatric
hospital in 1889, the museum has numerous
works by many of the Impressionists and
Post-Impressionists, including Gauguin,
Toulouse-Lautrec, Monet and Degas.*

2nd floor

The Little Dancer

*The statue of a 14-year-old
dancer dates from 1880
and is one of the most
famous sculptures
to be produced by
Edgar Degas.*

★ Head of Satyr

*This beautiful painted terracotta Head
of Satyr is part of the Etruscan collection,
which includes vases, bronze sculptures
and stone sarcophagi dating from the
8th to the 2nd century BC.*

1st floor

GALLERY GUIDE

*The horseshoe-shaped Dahlerup Building
(1897) contains mainly Danish and
French sculpture. Ancient artefacts from
the Mediterranean and Egypt are
found via the Winter Garden in the
Kampmann Building (1906). The
Larsen Building (1996), rising
within one of the courtyards of
the Kampmann Building,
houses French painting.*

KEY

☐	Ancient Mediterranean
☐	French painting and sculpture
☐	Danish painting and sculpture
☐	Egyptian, Greek and Roman sculpture
☐	Temporary exhibitions
☐	Non-exhibition space

Ground
floor

WINTER GARDEN

This green oasis of palm trees, planted
under a glass dome, was included in
the original design as a way of
attracting visitors who might not
normally be interested in art. It has
always provided a pleasant place in
which to stroll
during a visit.
Many visitors are
drawn to the *Water
Mother* sculpture
by Kai Nielsen.
Unveiled in 1920,
it depicts a naked
woman reclining
in a small pool,
surrounded by a
group of babies.
The Winter Garden
is also used as a
concert venue.

SOUTH COPENHAGEN

Criss-crossed by canals and waterways, this part of Copenhagen contains two areas that both complement and contrast each other. The islet of Slotsholmen is dominated by Christianborg Slot, standing on the site of a fort built by Bishop Absalon in the 12th century, when there was nothing here but a tiny fishing village. The area flourished and in 1443 København, or "merchant's port", was made the Danish capital. Many historical sights are situated here.

Across the water is Christianshavn where the "free state of Christiania", an alternative community, has been in existence since the 1970s. Both Christianshavn and nearby Holmen have undergone a period of redevelopment, and the area has become one of Copenhagen's more fashionable districts. The city's striking opera house has taken centre stage with its location on Dokøen, an islet that was once used as a naval base.

Waterbus tours provide an enjoyable way of getting to know the area. Alternatively, a bicycle can be useful for exploring the many nooks and crannies of Christianshavn.

Dragon's tails on Børsen's spire

SIGHTS AT A GLANCE

Churches
Vor Frelsers Kirke ❾

Museums
Nationalmuseet pp84–5 ❶
Thorvaldsens Museum ❷
Tøjhusmuscet ❻

Historic Buildings
Børsen ❺
Christiansborg Slot pp86–7 ❹
Det Kongelige Bibliotek ❼
Folketinget ❸

Places of Interest
Christiania ⓫
Christianshavn ❽
Operaen ⓬

KEY

▉	Street-by-Street Map See pp82–3
✚	Church
Ⓜ	Metro
⊠	Post office

GETTING AROUND

Christiansborg and Børsen can be reached by metro (getting off at Kongens Nytorv), and also by buses 1A, 2A, 15, 26 and 29. Christianshavn also has metro links with the rest of the city. Buses 2A, 19, 47, 66 and 350S stop close to Christiania. Waterbuses depart from Nyhavn.

0 m		300
0 yards		300

◁ **Three-storey organ, with a bust of Christian V, in the 17th-century Vor Frelsers Kirke**

Street-by-Street: Around Christiansborg Slot

Christiansborg Slot, with its adjoining palace buildings including the palace church, former royal coach house and royal stables, as well as Tøjhusmuseet, Det Kongelige Bibliotek and Børsen, are all situated on the islet of Slotsholmen. The palace derives its name from a castle that was built on this site in 1167 by Bishop Absalon. Opposite the palace, on the other side to the canal, is the Nationalmuseet, which has many exhibits relating to the history of Copenhagen and the rest of Denmark.

Thordvaldsens Museum
The collection confirms the genius of the Danish sculptor, whose tomb can be found in the museum courtyard **2**

★ Nationalmuseet
This museum was founded in 1807, though its origins date back to 1650 when Frederik II established his own private collection **1**

VINDEBROGADE

FR. HOLMS KANAL

NY VESTERGADE

TØJHUSGADE

NY KONGENSGADE

FR. HOLMS KANAL

BRYGHUSGADE

CHRISTIA BRYGG

0 m   50
0 yards   50

Tøjhusmuseet
Visitors interested in militaria will enjoy the huge array of arms and armour in this museum **6**

STAR SIGHTS

★ Christiansborg Slot

★ Nationalmuseet

★ Christiansborg Slot

Although this has not been the home of the royal family for more than 200 years, the palace rooms are still used for grand occasions, such as state banquets attended by Queen Margrethe II ❹

LOCATOR MAP
See Street Finder Maps 3 & 4

KEY

‒ ‒ ‒ Suggested route

Folketinget

The Danish parliament building is open to visitors during the summer, when its members are on vacation ❸

Børsen

The former Stock Exchange, with its spire sculpted in the form of entwined dragon tails, represents an outstanding example of 17th-century public architecture ❺

Det Kongelige Bibliotek

The library's "Black Diamond" extension, utilizing black glass and granite imported from Zimbabwe, is one of the capital's most innovative buildings ❼

Nationalmuseet ❶

Exhibits in this prestigious museum include many items relating to Denmark's history as well as artifacts from all over the world. It is worth allocating several hours for a visit. Among the vast array on display are Inuit costumes and tools, rune stones, priceless Egyptian jewellery and medieval church interiors. There is a good children's section, where kids will enjoy trying on armour or "camping out" in a Bedouin tent. All exhibits are labelled in English.

Antiquities
Greek pottery, Etruscan jewellery and Egyptian mummies are on display in the Egyptian and Classical section.

★ **Inuit Culture**
Included in the ethnographic section are rooms devoted to the Inuit containing many costumes, including a suit made of bird feathers, as well as traditional kayaks and harpoons.

3rd floor

Ethnography
Items from around the world include exhibits from Africa, India and Japan. One room is devoted to world music.

1st floor

KEY

- Pre-history (1300 BC–AD 1050)
- Middle Ages & Renaissance (1050–1660)
- Tales of Denmark (1660–2000)
- Ethnography
- History of the Museum
- Royal Collection of Coins
- Ethnographic Treasures
- Near East & Antiquities

Children's Museum

Helmet
This Bronze Age helmet, in the museum's pre-history department, dates from the 9th century BC and was found at Viksø on Zealand.

Main entrance

VISITORS' CHECKLIST

Ny Vestergade 10. **Map** 3 B2.
Tel 33 13 44 11. 🚌 1A, 2A,
6A, 12, 15, 26, 29, 33, 650S.
🕙 10am–5pm Tue–Sun.
www.natmus.dk

GALLERY GUIDE

The collection is spread over four floors with pre-history on the ground floor. The medieval department shares the first floor with Ethnography, which continues on the second floor with a exhibits relating to the Inuit. A section designed to appeal to children aged between four and 12 is on the ground floor.

2nd floor

★ **Guldhorn**
The pre-history section contains, among other exhibits, fragments of golden horns forged around 400 BC.

Ground floor

STAR EXHIBITS

★ Guldhorn

★ Inuit Culture

Thorvaldsens Museum ❷

Bertel Thorvaldsens Plads 2.
Map 3 C2. **Tel** 33 32 15 32.
Ⓢ Central. Ⓜ Nørreport, Kongens Nytorv. 🚌 1A, 2A, 15, 26, 29.
🕙 10am–5pm Tue–Sun. 🖼
www.thorvaldsensmuseum.dk

Located behind the palace church (Christiansborg Slotskirke), Thorvaldsens Museum was the first art museum in Denmark and opened in 1848. The Danish sculptor Bertel Thorvaldsen (1770–1844) lived and worked in Rome for more than 40 years, but towards the end of his life he bequeathed all his works and his collection of paintings to his native Copenhagen The collection is placed in Christianborg's old Coach House. The building is worth a visit in its own right, with a frieze on the outside by Jørgen Sonne and mosaic floors within.

Despite the fact that he worked on some of his pieces for 25 years, Thorvaldsen's output is staggering and includes sculptures based on classical mythology, busts of well-known contemporaries such as the English poet, Lord Byron, monumental studies of Christ and a number of self-portraits. The museum also displays Thorvaldsen's drawings and sketches and includes items from his private collection of paintings and Egyptian and Roman artifacts.

Vaulted ceiling and decorative floor in Thorvaldsens Museum

Folketinget ❸

Christiansborg. **Map** 3 C2.
🎫 Jun–Sep: daily.

The Folketinget is the Danish parliamentary chamber. Seating for the 179 members is arranged in a semi-circle with "left wing" MPs positioned on the left and "right wing" MPs on the right. The civil servants' offices occupy the largest section of the palace. Separate offices are used by Queen Margrethe II, whose duties include chairing weekly meetings of the State Council and presiding over the annual state opening of parliament in early October.

Christiansborg Slot ❹

See pp86–7.

Børsen ❺

Slotsholmsgade. **Map** 4 D2.
⚫ to visitors.

Copenhagen's former Stock Exchange was built between 1590 and 1640 on the orders of Christian IV, to a design by Lorentz and Hans van Steenwinckel. Today, the building houses the city's Chamber of Commerce and is not open to the public, but its stunning Renaissance façade, copper roofs, numerous gables and

Dragon tails forming Børsen's tower

unusual spire have made it one of Copenhagen's best-known sights. Its sleek 54-m (177-ft) spire, carved to resemble the entwined tails of four dragons, is a city landmark. Topping the spire are three crowns representing Denmark, Sweden and Norway. Trade in goods continued at Børsen until 1857, when it was purchased by a private association of wholesalers who pledged to maintain the historic building.

Christiansborg Slot ❹

This palace stands on the site of four former buildings. A 12th-century fortress built by Bishop Absalon was torn down in 1369 and replaced by the Copenhagen Castle. Christian VI replaced this building with the first Christiansborg Palace, one of the grandest palaces in Europe. This burned down in 1794, forcing the royal family to move to Amalienborg. A second Christiansborg Palace, completed in 1828, was also damaged by fire in 1884. Work on the present palace was completed in 1928.

★ **Throne Room**
As in every royal palace, the Throne Room is one of the grandest rooms in Christiansborg. However, Queen Margrethe II is famous for her "common touch" and has apparently never sat on this magnificent royal seat.

Velvet Room
Completed in 1924, this room is noteworthy for its grand marble portals, reliefs and luxurious velvet wall linings.

Decorative Vase
This 18th-century vase can be found in the Frederick VI Room, one of the many state rooms in the palace. It was a gift to Queen Juliane Marie of Brunswick, second wife of monarch Frederik V.

The Dining Hall
is decorated with portraits of Danish kings and contains two crystal chandeliers.

STAR FEATURES

★ Castle Ruins
―――――――――――――
★ Great Hall
―――――――――――――
★ Throne Room

★ **Great Hall**
The 17 tapestries on display here were commissioned in 1990 for Queen Margrethe II's 50th birthday and completed in 2000. Made by Bjørn Nørgaard, they depict key events in Danish history.

Tower Room

Copenhagen's tallest tower is 106 m (348 ft) high and topped with a 5-m (16-ft) crown. The tower's interior has a series of tapestries created by Joakim Skovgaard depicting scenes from Danish folk tales.

★ Castle Ruins

Under the palace are the ruins of the previous castles, including parts of Bishop Absalon's castle and the Copenhagen Castle.

Library

A small portion of the vast royal collection is housed here. The remaining volumes are kept at Amalienborg Slot (see pp56–7).

Alexander Room

Bertel Thorvaldsen's frieze depicting Alexander the Great entering Babylon is displayed in this room.

Tøjhusmuseet ❻

Tøjhusgade 3. **Map** 3 C2.
Tel 33 11 60 37. 🚌 *1A, 2A, 15, 26,
29.* ⬜ *noon–4pm Tue–Sun.* 🎫 *(free
on Wed).* **www**.thm.dk

The Royal Danish Arsenal
was built between 1598 and
1604 and was one of the
earliest of Christian IV's
building projects. When
completed, the 163-m (535-ft)
long complex was one of the
largest buildings in Europe
and was capable of equipping
an entire army. In 1611 the
building was extended to
include a harbour pool, which
was situated next door in what
are today the Library Gardens.
The building now serves as a
museum. Its collection
covers the history
of artillery from the
invention of
gunpowder up
to the present
day (exhibits
include artillery
guns as well as
firearms). Suits
of armour and
military uniforms are also
on display.

**Cannon from the
Tøjhusmuseet collection**

Det Kongelige Bibliotek ❼

Christians Brygge, entrance from
Søren Kierkegaards Plads. **Map** 4 D2.
Tel 33 47 47 47. 🚌 *66.* 🚢 *901,
902.* ⬜ *10am–9pm Mon–Sat.* 🎫
www.kb.dk

The Royal Library is an
excellent example of how
to merge two very different
architectural forms. The

**Gate leading to the old section of
Det Kongelige Bibliotek**

original library building is 19th
century. The Neo-Classical
building's courtyard has been
transformed into a garden
and contains a statue of the
Danish philosopher and
theologian Søren Kierkegaard.
Next to the old building is the
ultra-modern library, linked
by a special passage to
its historic
predecessor.
Nicknamed
the "Black Diamond"
because of its
angular black glass-
and-granite exteri-
or, the extension
houses library and
exhibition areas,
the National Photography
Museum, a concert hall and
a restaurant and café. It is
worth stepping inside, if only
to see the vast ceiling mural
by Per Kirkeby.

Christianshavn ❽

Map 4 D & 4 E.

This district, which is
sometimes referred to as
"Little Amsterdam" because
of its many canals, can be
explored on foot, by bicycle

or by hopping aboard a
waterbus. Built in the first
half of the 17th century by
Christian IV, Christianshavn
was originally intended both
as a fortified city and a naval
base. The area was the site of
the first boatyards established
in Copenhagen, as well as the
warehouses belonging to
major shipping lines. It is
also where most sailors and
boatyard workers lived. Up
until the 1980s, Christianshavn was known only as
the site of the "free state
of Christiania" and was
considered to be unattractive,
poor and neglected. Since the
1990s, however, Christianshavn, together with nearby
Holmen, has blossomed thanks
to a sustained programme
of urban redevelopment.
Run-down warehouses have
been transformed into trendy
restaurants, cafés, company
offices and smart apartments,
which are favoured by artists
and young professionals.

Vor Frelsers Kirke ❾

Sankt Annæ Gade 29. **Map** 4 E2.
Tel 32 54 68 83. Ⓜ *Christianshavn.*
🚌 *2A, 19, 47, 66, 350S.* ⬜ *11am–
3:30pm daily.* **Tower** ⬜ *10am–4pm
Mon–Sat, 10:30am–3:30pm Sun &
hols (late Jun–mid-Sep: open until
7pm daily).* 🚫 *in heavy rain or strong
winds.* 🎫 **www**.vorfrelserskirke.dk

Our Saviour's Church is most
famous for its extraordinary
spire, completed in 1752,
and accessible via a spiral
staircase that runs around the
exterior. Be warned – it takes

Yachting marina and houses built out over the water, in Christianshavn

For hotels and restaurants in this region see pp244–7 and pp268–74

considerable stamina to climb all 400 steps, not to mention a good head for heights. The spire is Copenhagen's second-highest panoramic viewpoint and once you have caught your breath at the top you will be rewarded with a fabulous view of the city from 90 m (295 ft) up.

The spire's creator was the architect Lauritz de Thurah, who struck upon the idea of a spiral staircase while visiting the church of Sant'Ivo alla Sapienza in Rome. Legend has it that Thurah was so obsessed with his work that when it was alleged that his encircling staircase wound up the wrong way he committed suicide by leaping from the top of the tower. The truth is more prosaic, however, as the architect died in his own bed, poor and destitute, seven years after completing the tower. The tale was nevertheless made into a movie by the Danish director Nils Vest in 1997.

The church itself is also worth visiting. It was built in 1696, to a design by Lambert von Haven. Inside, a Baroque altar by the Swede Nicodemus Tessin is adorned with cherubs. The huge three-storey organ dates from 1698. It has more than 4,000 pipes and is supported by two giant elephants.

Spiral stairs of Vor Frelsers Kirke's tower

Orlogsmuseet ⑩

Overgaden oven Vandet 58.
Map 4 E2. *Tel* 33 11 60 37.
Ⓜ *Christianshavn.* ⊞ *2A, 19, 47, 66, 350S.* ◯ *noon–4pm Tue–Sun.*
▦ www.orlogsmuseet.dk

The Royal Danish Naval Museum's building dates from 1780 and was once a sailors' hospital. Among its exhibits are navigation instruments, ships' lights, figureheads that were once

Entrance to Christiania – a successful example of alternative living

fixed to the bows of windjammers, and uniforms. A collection of over 300 model ships includes one that dates back to 1687.

Christiania ⑪

Map 4 D3 & E3. Ⓜ *Christianhavn.* ⊞ *2A, 19, 47, 66, 350S.* **www**.christiania.org

The "free state of Christiania" has been in existence since 13 November 1971, when a group of squatters took over some deserted military barracks to the east of Christianshavn and established a commune. The local authorities initially tried to force the squatters to leave, but as the community's numbers swelled, the government decided to treat Christiania as a "social experiment". Today the community has about 900 residents.

The community has its own schools, infrastructure and system of government, which are financed in part by the proceeds of its cafés and restaurants and the sale of locally made handicrafts.

Christiania was initially linked with hippy drug culture, and cannabis was openly sold and smoked here until the trade was outlawed in 2004.

Operaen ⑫

Ekvipagemestervej 10. **Map** 2 F5.
Tel 33 69 69 69. ⊞ *66.* ⊠ *901, 902.* ◯ *foyer: 3 hours before a performance.* ▣ *Jul–late Aug: 2pm and 4pm daily (in English).*
www.kglteater.dk

The stunning Copenhagen Opera House opened in January 2005 on the island of Holmen in Copenhagen Harbour. For over a century the Danish Royal Opera shared a space with the Danish ballet and theatre companies at Det Kongelige Teater. The auditorium was designed by the prominent Danish architect Henning Larsen, whose works include the Ny Carlsberg Glyptotek extension and the Danish Design Centre. The modern building is clad in German limestone and covers 41,000 sq m (441,300 sq ft). It includes a 1,500-seat auditorium as well as a second, smaller stage.

Striking façade of Copenhagen's opera house

FURTHER AFIELD

There is plenty to see outside the city centre. Some attractions, such as the Tycho Brahe Planetarium, are within walking distance. Others, like the Carlsberg Brewery, Zoological Garden or Assistens Kirkegård, can be reached by bus. Sights even further afield are served by a network of modern suburban trains.

A visit to one or more of these places provides an alternative to the bustle of inner-city Copenhagen.

Tuborg brewery sign

Charlottenlund, in an affluent coastal suburb close to Danmarks Akvarium, has a patch of surrounding woodland that is perfect for gentle walks, as is the park area around Frederiksberg Slot. And, thanks to the bridge and tunnel that spans the Øresund (Sound), the sandy beach and many attractions of Malmö in Sweden are only half an hour away. The bridge is a marvel of modern engineering and can be admired from the harbour of the charming fishing village of Dragør.

SIGHTS AT A GLANCE

Historic Buildings
Frederiksberg Slot and Have ❹

Places of Interest
Amager and Ørestad ⓬
Carlsberg Brewery ❷
Cisternerne ❺
Danmarks Akvarium ❿
Dragør ⓭
Experimentarium ❽
Tycho Brahe Planetarium ❶
Øresund Bridge ⓫

Parks and Gardens
Charlottenlund ❾
Zoologisk Have ❸

Museums
Arken Museum For Modern Kunst ⓮

Churches
Grundtvigs Kirke ❼

Cemeteries
Assistens Kirkegård ❻

KEY

▮	City centre
▮	Greater Copenhagen
🚉	Railway station
✈	Airport
━	Motorway
━	Major road
═	Other road

OUTSIDE COPENHAGEN'S CITY CENTRE

Tycho Brahe Planetarium in the shape of a bevelled cylinder

Tycho Brahe Planetarium ❶

Gl. Kongevej 10. **Tel** 33 12 12 24.
Ⓢ Vesterport. 🚌 14, 15, 29.
🕐 9:30am–8:30pm daily (from
11:30am Mon, from 10:30am Fri).
📧 www.tycho.dk

Copenhagen's planetarium
is the largest of its kind in
western Europe and is named
after Tycho Brahe (1546–
1601), the renowned Danish
astronomer. Brahe is credited
with the discovery of a new
star in the constellation of
Cassiopeia, in 1572, and with
making important advances in
our knowledge of planetary
motion. These advances
are especially impressive as
they were made before the
invention of the telescope.

The planetarium opened in
1989 in a cylindrical building
designed by Knud Munk. Built
from sand-coloured brick, it
appears at its most attractive
when viewed from across the
small lake, which is one of a
series that continues right up
to Østerbro and that was created in the late 18th century
by damming the local river.
The planetarium is located on
the Old Royal Route (Gammel
Kongevej), which was once
travelled by royal processions
heading for Frederiksberg Slot.

The planetarium houses a
small astronomical collection,
including antique telescopes.
The biggest draw, however,
is the huge IMAX® cinema;
films are screened daily,
including one on the wonders
of space travel.

Carlsberg Brewery ❷

**Carlsberg Visitors Centre &
Jacobsen Brewhouse** Gamle
Carlsberg Vej 11. **Tel** 33 27 12 82.
Ⓢ Enghave, Valby. 🚌 18, 26.
🕐 10am–5pm Tue–Sun. 📧
www.visitcarlsberg.dk

Carlsberg Brewery was
founded in 1847 by Jacob
Christian, whose father
had worked at the king's
brewery in Copenhagen.
Jacob Christian chose this site
on Valby Hill because of the
quality of the water nearby,
and named his company
Carlsberg (Carl's Hill) after his
son. By the late 19th century
the business had an international reputation. In 1882 Carl
founded his own brewery,
Ny (New) Carlsberg, while
his father's brewery continued
as Gamle (Old) Carlsberg.
The two merged in 1906.

East entrance gate to the
Carlsberg Brewery

In 2005, the Jacobsen Brewhouse opened in part of the
old brewery, with the aim of
developing speciality beers.
This brand is now the only
one still produced at this site.

The rest of the brewery is
an exhibition centre where
visitors can learn about the
manufacturing process and
history of beer during a
90-minute self-guided tour
that ends with a beer tasting
in a bar overlooking the
shining copper kettles used in
the brewing process.

In addition to the Visitors
Centre, there is a cluster of
small art galleries, the exhibition space Fotografisk Center
and Europe's largest centre for
modern dance, Dansehallerne.

The brewery site also
features many interesting
examples of industrial architecture, including the intrigu-
ing Elephant Gate (1901),
which consists of four 5-m
(16-ft) high granite elephants
shipped from Bornholm.

Giraffes in the city zoo, near
Frederiksberg Have

Zoologisk Have ❸

Roskildevej 32. **Tel** 72 20 02 00.
Ⓢ Valby. Ⓜ Frederiksberg.
🚌 4A, 6A, 18, 26. 🕐 Jan–Mar,
Nov & Dec: 10am–4pm daily (Mar:
to 5pm Sat & Sun); Apr, May & Sep:
10am–5pm daily (to 6pm Sat & Sun);
Jun & mid-Aug–late Aug: 10am–6pm
daily; Jul–mid-Aug: 10am–9pm
daily; Oct: 10am–5pm daily. 📧
www.zoo.dk

Copenhagen's zoological
garden was established
close to Frederiksberg Slot
in 1859, making it one of
Europe's oldest zoos. In the
1940s it was expanded to

Frederiksberg Slot, headquarters of the Danish Military Academy

include part of Søndermarken, with the two areas connected by a tunnel under Roskildevej. Although not large by international standards, the zoo has a good record of breeding in captivity. A wide selection of animals are kept here, including giraffes, polar bears, hippos, elephants and lions. The Norman Foster-designed Elephant House is especially noteworthy for its large glass domes and groundbreaking architecture. An enclosure for seals, elks and polar bears, The Arctic Ring, opened in 2012.

A tropical section houses butterflies and birds, as well as some crocodiles. Smaller children will enjoy the petting zoo, which offers close-up contact with domestic animals, pony rides and the chance to let off steam in a large play area laid out like a child-size rabbit warren. The 42-m (138-ft) high wooden observation tower, built in 1905, affords views as far as the coast of Sweden.

Frederiksberg Slot and Have ❹

Roskildevej 28. *Tel 36 13 26 00*. Ⓜ *Frederiksberg*. ▦ *4A, 6A, 18, 26, 832*. **Palace** ◐ *to visitors*. **Garden** ◯ *7am–sunset daily*.

Built between 1700 and 1735 this palace was the summer residence of Frederik IV who used it to entertain visitors including, in 1716, the Tsar of Russia, Peter the Great. The king is said to have enjoyed sailing along the park canals, while Copenhagen's inhabitants lined the banks and cheered.

The palace was designed in the Italian style by the architect Ernst Brandenburger following the king's visit to

Italy. During the reign of Christian IV the building was enlarged with two additional wings, giving it its present horseshoe shape.

Since 1869 Frederiksberg Slot has been used by the Danish Military Academy. Having its origins in the Cadets' Corp established by Frederik IV in 1713, the school's emblem still bears the king's monogram. The school is not open to the public, though visitors are free to explore the grounds. The palace gardens, known as Frederiksberg Have, were laid out in a French style in the early 18th century. Later on they were transformed into a romantic rambling English park, criss-crossed with a network of canals and tree-lined paths, and dotted with statues and park benches.

Frederiksberg Slot stands on top of a hill and, for the people of Copenhagen, marks a notional boundary of the city. In the 18th century, when it was built, the palace stood outside the city limits.

Cisternerne ❺

Søndermarken. *Tel 33 21 93 10*. Ⓢ *Enghave, Valby*. ▦ *4A, 6A, 18, 26, 171E*. ◯ *2–6pm Thu & Fri (Feb & Nov: to 5pm); 11am 5pm Sat, Sun & pub hols*. ◼ *Jan & Dec*. 🈳 **www**.cisternerne.dk

Praised by *Forbes* magazine as one of the most unique museums in Europe, the Museum of Modern Glass Art is atmospherically housed in the cisterns that formed Copenhagen's water supply system back in the 19th century. The cisterns are located under the park of Søndermarken; at ground level, the presence of the museum is given away only by two modern portals, designed by the sculptor Max Seidenfaden and resembling two glass pyramids. Among the artists exhibited here are Robert Jacobsen, Jette Vogt, Leif Sylvester and Adi Holzer.

Colourful glass artwork on display at Cisternerne

FLORA DANICA

This dinner service, decorated with floral designs copied from the *Flora Danica* encyclopedia of plants, was ordered in 1790 by Christian VII. The set was intended as a present for Catherine II of Russia. However, during the 12 years when the first *Flora Danica* was in production the Tsarina died, and the king decided to keep the set for himself. It was used for the first time in 1803 during a reception to celebrate the king's 37th birthday. Over 1,500 of the original 1,802 pieces have survived and are now in the possession of Queen Margrethe II. Copies of individual items are made to order and the methods of production hardly differ from those employed over 200 years ago. The pieces are hand-painted by artists who train for over 10 years to master the exquisite flower paintings. This kind of quality is expensive – a plate costs upwards of 5,000 Dkr.

An example of *Flora Danica* tableware

Assistens Kirkegård, both a park and a cemetery

Assistens Kirkegård ❻

Kapelvej 2. *Tel 35 37 19 17.*
Ⓢ Ⓜ *Nørreport.* 🚌 *5A, 350S.*
⏰ *Jan–Mar & Oct–Dec: 7am–7pm daily; Apr–Sep: 7am–10pm daily.*
www.assistens.dk

In 1760 Copenhagen's graveyards were too small to accommodate victims of a plague that was assailing the city at this time. The plague first struck in 1711 and claimed 23,000 lives in all, reducing the city's population by a third. Assistens Kirkegård was established to supplement the existing provisions for burials.

Initially the cemetery was used only for burying the poor but, from the late 18th century, burial plots at Assistens came into fashion. The list of famous people who are buried here include Søren Kierkegaard, Niels Bohr and Hans Christian Andersen, as well as the artists Christoffer Wilhelm Eckersberg and Christian Købke.

The cemetery is also a pleasant park, and popular with many locals. Visitors are as likely to see buskers, joggers, cyclists and sunbathers as people tending the graves.

Grundtvigs Kirke ❼

På Bjerget 14B. *Tel 35 81 54 42.*
Ⓢ *Emdrup.* 🚌 *6A, 42, 43, 66, 69.*
⏰ *9am–4pm Mon–Sat (to 6pm Thu), noon–4pm Sun (to 1pm in winter).*
www.grundtvigskirke.dk

This unusual yellow brick church, remarkable not only for its size but also its highly original shape, was designed in 1913 by P.V. Jensen Klint. Standing almost 49 m (161 ft) high, it ranks as one of Denmark's largest churches and is designed in a Danish Modernist style. It was built between 1921 and 1940 on Bisperbjerg, the highest hill in Copenhagen, and paid for through public donations to honour the memory of Nicolai Frederik Severin Grundtvig (1783–1872) – a prominent clergyman, theologian and philosopher. In addition to his social work, this versatile man found time to write books and treatises, and composed some 1,500 hymns, many of which are sung to this day in Danish churches. For more than 10 years Grundtvig was a member of the Danish Parliament, and in 1861 he became

Front elevation of Grundtvigs Kirke, inspired by small village churches

an honorary bishop of the Danish Church.

The charismatic clergyman became famous in his country as the founder of the Danish Folkehøjskole (People's High School), a system that enabled those from the lower ranks of society to gain access to education. The shape of the church building symbolizes this sphere of his activities, being reminiscent of a typical Danish village church. On the other hand, the top of the tower is designed to resemble a church organ and alludes to the many religious hymns written by Grundtvig.

Hands-on fun for kids at Experimentarium

Experimentarium ❽

Tuborg Havnevej 7. *Tel 39 27 33 33.* Ⓢ *Hellerup or Svanemøllen.*
🚌 *1A, 14, 21.* ⏰ *9:30am–5pm Mon–Fri (to 9pm Tue), 11am–5pm Sat, Sun & hols.* ⏰ *1 Jan, 23–25 Dec, 31 Dec.* 📷 💳 🏪 🏬
www.experimentarium.dk

The main idea behind this innovative science centre, in the Hellerup district of Copenhagen, is to bring science to life through hands-on exploration. Almost all the exhibits are of the interactive kind; there are about 300 experiments that can be independently performed by anyone.

The display area is enormous and, not surprisingly, the place is hugely popular with children who run about trying out all the exhibits. Adults, too, will find much of interest, whether it be testing the latest in virtual technology, programming

Some of the many aquatic creatures to be found at Danmarks Akvarium

Danmarks Akvarium ⑩

Den Blå Planet, Kajakvej 15, Kastrup. *Tel* 39 62 32 83. 🚆 14. ◻ Nov–Jan: 10am–4pm daily; Feb–May, Sep & Oct: 10am–5pm daily; Jun–Aug: 10am–6pm daily. ● 1 Jan, 24, 25 & 31 Dec. 🖼 www.akvarium.dk

Copenhagen's aquarium opened in spring 2013 in Den Blå Planet (The Blue Planet), a modern building in Kastrup harbour, on the island of Amager. Although not as large as Nordsøen Oceanarium in Hirtshals (see p204), it offers the chance to admire a wide variety of marine life; it also plays a major role in conservation, research and education.

It contains more than 90 glass tanks, the largest holding 85,000 litres (18,700 gallons) of water. The tanks are populated by over 300 species of fish from all over the world including sharks and sharp-teethed piranha. Among the other aquatic wildlife are a giant octopus, crocodiles and an electric eel (capable of producing up to 2,000 volts), as well as turtles, sponges, lobsters and many hundreds of brightly coloured tropical fish.

Feeding times (displayed on the aquarium website and at the entrance) are especially animated. In the basement, children can come close to small marine life in the touch pools.

robots or experiencing an earthquake of 5.5 degrees on the Richter scale.

At every point, children are confronted with exhibits and puzzles to fire their curiosity, and tested with such imponderable questions as "Are there green rabbits?" and "Can you lift yourself?". Kids can try their hand at guiding a cargo vessel into harbour, test their emotions, check their hearing from the lowest to the highest frequencies, and learn how ice-dancers' hands affect the speed of their pirouettes. Environmental issues are high on the agenda, and topics include how winds develop, what kind of climate can be expected in 100 years' time by simulating various concentrations of carbon dioxide emissions into the atmosphere, and methods of water conservation.

The Kids' Pavillion is a section where younger visitors between 3 and 6 years old can experiment with magnetism, build a house using a crane, hear what their voice sounds like backwards and decide whether the sounds of bird song or rain should fill a colourful section known as the "Poppy Wood".

There are also shows during which fun chemistry and physics experiments are carried out, and demonstrations where audience participation is encouraged. All the exhibits are labelled in Danish and English, and there are numerous lectures and special exhibitions staged throughout the year.

Charlottenlund ⑨

🚆 14. Ⓢ Charlottenlund St. **Palace** ● to visitors. **Gardens** ◻

A royal residence has stood on this site since 1690, but the present palace was built between 1731 and 1733 on the orders of Princess Charlotte Amalie. The princess, who remained single all her life, liked the place so much that it was soon named after her. She used it as her summer residence until her death in 1782.

The building was remodelled in the 19th century, when its Baroque character gave way to a Renaissance style. A number of other Danish royals have enjoyed staying here including Frederik VIII and his wife, Princess Louise, who remained here until her death in 1926. The couple are commemorated by an obelisk at the rear of the building.

The palace is now used by the Danish Institute for Fisheries, but it is still possible to stroll in its surrounding gardens. The appearance of the park, with its pruned conifers and pleasant avenues, dates from the 1990s, though marked pathways and ponds remain from the 17th century. The vegetable garden dates from 1826 and once grew herbs and produce for the palace kitchen. There are a number of ancient trees in the grounds, notably two larches that stand at the rear of the palace and are considered to be the oldest of their kind in Denmark.

Charlottenlund Slot, surrounded by parkland

Øresund Bridge ⓫

Tel *70 23 90 60. Toll charge:*
165–620 Dkr, depending on vehicle
size; no bicycles allowed; toll and
passport control points are located
on the Swedish side. 🗺️
www.oresundsbron.com

In 2000, when Queen
Margrethe II and King Carl
XVI of Sweden jointly
opened the Øresund Bridge,
it was the first time that the
Scandinavian peninsula had
been connected to mainland
Europe since the Ice Age.
Now, thanks to the bridge,
the delights of Malmö, the
largest city in southern
Sweden, are only 35 minutes
away from Copenhagen.

The bridge is the second
longest fixed-link bridge in
the world. The entire crossing
is 16 km (10 miles) long and
consists of (from the Danish
side): a 430-m (1,411-ft) long
artificial peninsula, a tunnel
measuring more than 3.5 km
(2.2 miles) and running
10 m (33 ft) below the
water, a 4-km (2-mile) long
artificial island and a 7,845-m
(25,738-ft) long cable-stayed
bridge. From either side of
the sound, the sight of the
structure, with its huge
204-m (670-ft) high pylons,
is truly impressive.

The bridge is a marvel of
modern engineering. It has
a two-level structure; the
top is for motor traffic, the
bottom for rail. At its highest
point the bridge is suspended
57 m (187 ft) above the
water. At the tunnel entrance,
on both sides, are light filters

Wind turbines rising from the seabed east of Amager

designed to allow drivers to
adjust to the dimmer conditions. About one thousand
sensors are installed along
the route as part of a fire
alarm system.

The bridge has proved to
be popular and over 20,000
rail passengers and 10,000
cars make the crossing every
day. It also forms part of
an annual marathon run,
the first of which took place
in June 2000, before the
official opening.

Amager and Ørestad ⓬

3 km (2 miles) southeast of
Copenhagen city centre.

For a great number of visitors
arriving by plane, the island
of Amager, southeast of
Copenhagen's city centre,
is the starting point of their
exploration of Denmark, since
it is the site of Copenhagen's
international airport.

Since the opening of the
Øresund Bridge in 2000,
Amager has gone from being
a relatively undeveloped

area to one characterized by
groundbreaking architecture
and housing developments.
The urban conglomeration of
Amager, with its residential
blocks, shops and restaurants,
blends into the almost
futuristic Ørestad. Landmark
buildings here include the
23-floor skyscraper Bella
Sky Comwell Hotel, whose
two towers lean away from
each other with insulating,
alternating glass panels, and
the DR Koncerthuset *(see
p102)*. This world-class
performance venue and
studio space was designed
in the shape of a giant blue
cube by acclaimed French
architect Jean Nouvel. Its
glass façade, opaque by
day, acts like blue-screen
technology at night, project-
ing images of the activity
within. Most of the University
of Copenhagen *(see p72)* is
now based on Amager, and
Scandinavia's largest shopping centre, Fields *(see p101)*,
can be found right next to
Ørestad metro station. Convenient metro connections
to Copenhagen have further
helped rejuvenate the district.

Øresund Bridge linking Denmark and Sweden

Those looking for outdoor attractions can still find them here, however: Naturcenter Vestamager is an oasis for families, with play areas, pony rides and a lake, while the recreated Amager Strandpark, which replaced the former 1930s bathing huts, is a landscaped area of man-made beaches, including a lagoon and an island.

Dragør ®

12 km (7 miles) southeast of Copenhagen. **Museum** Havnepladsen 2. **Tel** 32 53 93 07. ☐ Jun–Sep: noon–4pm Wed, Thu, Sat & Sun. 🖼 www.museumamager.dk

This picturesque town to the southeast of Amager used to be the place to catch a ferry for Limhamn, on the Swedish side of the Øresund (Sound), which ran from 1934 until 1999. The opening of a bridge brought about the closing of this route, and Dragør has since become a destination for those wishing to escape the hustle of central Copenhagen.

As far back as the Middle Ages, Dragør was a major centre for the Baltic herring trade. Later on, its inhabitants profited by piloting the boats that sailed across the Øresund. Many houses in Dragør still have distinctive observation towers, known as "Kikkenborg". The biggest of these (now a museum) stands by Lodshuset, a building that houses the local pilot service headquarters, which was established in 1684. Surprisingly, for a long time Dragør had no proper harbour and the boats were simply dragged ashore. The word "dragør" means a sandy or pebbly strip of land up which the boats were hauled. It was not until 1520 that Dutch settlers, inhabiting nearby Store Magleby, built a proper harbour. Once built, it developed fast and by the 19th century it was the third-largest

Cutters moored in Dragør's harbour

port in Denmark (after Copenhagen and Helsingør), receiving large sailing ships. Today these maritime traditions are kept alive by a pleasant marina overlooking nearby Sweden and the stunning bridge.

The town is a pleasant place for a stroll with cobbled streets and pretty 18th-century yellow walled houses decorated with flowers. The local museum, housed in the old town hall building and a 17th-century harbour warehouse, has a collection of items devoted to Dragør's rich maritime past.

An exhibit from Dragør's museum

A combined ticket allows admission to four museums in the area: the Dragør Museum, the Amagermuseet in Store Magleby, the Lodshuset building and the Mølsted Museum, which is dedicated to the Danish seascape painter Christian Mølsted.

Arken Museum For Moderne Kunst ®

20 km (12 miles) south of Copenhagen city centre. Ishøj, Skovvej 100. **Tel** 43 54 02 22. Ⓢ to Ishøj and from there 🚌 128. ☐ 10am–5pm Tue–Sun (to 9pm Wed). 🖼 www.arken.dk

Located a stone's throw from the beach, Arken Museum For Moderne Kunst (Arken Museum of Modern Art) is housed in a building intended to resemble a marooned ship.

The museum's permanent collection is comprised of contemporary Danish, Nordic and international art, with an emphasis on installations, sculpture and graphic art. Many of the works on display are by Danish artists such as Asger Jorn and Per Kirkeby. One of the most fascinating installations in the gallery is Olafur Eliasson's *Your Negotiable Panorama*, where a pump mechanism and a light shining into a pool of water give the viewer the sensation of bathing in an endless void. There are also nine huge, abstract paintings by German artist Anselm Reye, whose neon colours reference Pop Art, Minimalism and Expressionism, and nine works by Damien Hirst, which are exhibited separately in the Damien Hirst Room. In addition, the museum presents at least two major temporary exhibitions a year, ranging from international retrospectives to large group shows.

Opened in 1996, the building has proved to be as controversial as much of the work inside. Designed by Søren Robert Lund when he was 25 years old and still a student, it follows few conventional rules. Extensions built in different materials have softened the original raw finish and provide a more welcoming exterior.

Bold outline of Arken Museum For Moderne Kunst

SHOPPING IN COPENHAGEN

Copenhagen has long been the commercial centre not only of Denmark, but also of an entire region that includes Zealand and, on the Swedish side, Skåne (Skania). Shopping here is a pleasurable experience, with many of the most interesting stores concentrated in just a few areas, often in buildings as interesting as their merchandise. Strøget and the adjacent pedestrian streets offer everything from designer labels and casual

Sign for a toyshop

fashion, to porcelain, crystal and antiques. Copenhagen is synonymous with the best in interior style and the decorative arts, while young Danish talent has turned the city into a fashion capital, too. An array of hip boutiques and quirky shops have helped to revitalise some previously run-down areas of the city and they deserve to be explored. Along the way, dozens of picturesque squares and cafés offer welcome respite for tired feet.

Magasin du Nord, one of Copenhagen's best-known department stores

WHAT TO BUY

Denmark is the home of applied design, and those looking for homewares are spoilt for choice by the vast array of ingenious, smart, unusual and extravagant items on offer. The Danes like to dress smartly too, without spending a fortune, so it is worth checking out the sales for good quality clothes and footwear at bargain prices. The best times are in July and January.

While all of the high-profile international designer labels are available, one of the pleasures of shopping in Copenhagen is discovering unusual and unique items unavailable back home.

WHERE TO SHOP

Most of the major international brands can be found along the city's two longest pedestrian streets, Strøget *(see p70)* and Købmagergade.

Shops range from cheerful and inexpensive to designer and upmarket department stores (towards Kongens Nytorv). If you take detours into the side streets there is plenty of more alternative shopping on offer. On parallel Læderstræde and Kompagnistræde you will discover a variety of small independent shops; the latter is especially good for antiques. Those on tighter budgets should head west of Strøget, to Larsbjørnsstræde and Studiestræde for street fashion, secondhand shops and music stores.

On the outskirts of the old town, the Nansensgade area mixes traditional and trendy boutiques with attractive bars and cafés. There is everything here from sushi restaurants and chocolate shops to vintage clothes and accessories.

To the west of the central station, the former red light district of Vesterbro has undergone a complete

transformation and is now one of Copenhagen's most vibrant areas. At its centre, Halmtorvet is a trendy café-filled square. Head to Istedgade for art and speciality shops.

Those in search of a quirky bargain should try the multi-cultural Nørrebro district, north of the city. Elmegade and Fælledvej are lined with secondhand stores, new Danish design and recycled goods. For secondhand jewellery try Ravnsborggade.

OPENING HOURS

It is not worth trying to shop in Denmark for anything other than foodstuffs before 10am. Early in the week most shops close at around 5:30pm, although many stores remain open on Fridays until 6 or 7pm. On Saturdays some shops close at 2pm, but the majority now stay open until 4 or 5pm. Department stores tend to have the longest opening hours. While smaller shops in Denmark stay closed on Sundays, larger stores and shopping centres now open on the first and last Sundays of the month.

HOW TO PAY

The country's currency is the Danish krone (Dkr). Some shops also accept the Swedish krone and the euro, although the rate of exchange applied in such cases may not be advantageous. A few of the smaller shops may expect payment in cash, however the vast majority of outlets accept credit cards. The prices quoted always include VAT and excise tax. Non-EU residents are entitled to a VAT refund (see p286).

DEPARTMENT STORES AND SHOPPING CENTRES

Magasin du Nord was Scandinavia's first department store and is still a huge favourite. As well as clothes, cosmetics and luxury household goods it sells books, jewellery, delicious chocolate and foodstuffs. Also popular is the light and airy **Illum** on Strøget, which has several elegant floors selling high-quality goods under a glass dome, and the added advantage of a rooftop café.

Copenhagen has several shopping centres, with shops, cafés, restaurants, and cinemas under one roof. Vesterbro's **Fisketorvet**, situated on the site of an old fish market facing the Sound, is arguably one of the best. It is also worth taking a trip out to **Fields**, the biggest shopping centre in Scandinavia with a total of 150 shops under one roof. Although a little way out of the city, it is conveniently situated at the Ørestad metro station.

DESIGN AND INTERIOR DECORATION

Denmark is justly famous for combining attractive design with functionality and quality materials. Most of its best-known brands have their own shops in the city centre. The **Bang & Olufsen** showroom

has listening rooms where customers can appreciate the quality of its audio products. For a good selection of interior design under one roof, head for **Illums Bolighus**, which keeps an eye on tradition while displaying the latest trends in furnishing and lighting.

Winner of numerous awards for innovative design, **Normann Copenhagen** has converted an old cinema in Østerbro into a stunning showroom. As well as its own collection of kitchen accessories, here you can find a variety of contemporary lifestyle products and high-profile fashion brands from around the world – all in a truly unforgettable setting.

The **Louis Poulsen** showroom offers various designer lighting solutions set against a minimalist background, and young furniture designers display their talent for creating classics with a contemporary twist at **Hay Cph**, which has two branches in the city centre. Another sleek furniture store is **Paustian** in the dock area. Designed by architect Jørn Utzon, of Sydney Opera House fame, there is also a stylish restaurant.

Back in town, the design centre **Casa Shop** is well worth a look, as is the **Danish Design Centre (DDC)**, which hosts changing exhibitions showcasing Danish innovation. **Designer Zoo**, in Vesterbro, is a working design store for eight Danish designers who create furniture, jewellery, knitwear and artistic glass. **Bolia** is a nationwide interior design store that celebrates Scandinavian traditions.

Minimalist interior of leading fashion store Munthe plus Simonsen

CLOTHES AND ACCESSORIES

From high fashion to second-hand chic, Copenhagen has it all. Top international designers congregate at the Kongens Nytorv end of Strøget, while less expensive labels stretch down the street towards the town hall. Købmagergade is good for mid-price clothes whilst Kronprinsensgade, which runs off it, is known as "Copenhagen's Catwalk" for the cutting-edge clothes shops located here. **Bruuns Bazaar** is a favourite, selling men's and women's modern designs.

The narrow streets of the Grønnegade quarter are lined with half-timbered buildings housing Danish streetwear and classic labels. **Munthe plus Simonsen**, renowned for classy yet casual ladieswear, is found here. Nearby, on Pilestræde, **Designers Remix** have opened a large flagship store of their sexy, edgy womenswear. **Day Birger et Mikkelsen**, has also gathered all of their seven lines under one roof here: women's, men's and children's wear, lingerie, jewellery, accessories and home. **Holly Golightly** sells elegant Danish womenswear and accessories.

Secondhand chic lies in the "Pisserenden" area adjacent to Strøget, on streets like Læderstræde and Studiestræde; **Carmen & Fantasio** is one of the best. For vintage frocks and clever accessories, head to Nansensgade or try **Glam Vintage** in Silkegade 7. The collection of high-end 1960–70s glad rags is particularly pleasing.

Interior of a shop selling Bodum kitchenware, a popular Danish product

JEWELLERY

Danish jewellery has a reputation for fine design and attention to detail. The city's most famous jewellery shop is silversmith **Georg Jensen**, but Julie Sandlau (stocked at **Magasin du Nord**), who creates pretty gold designs, is the name on many a celebrity's lips. Similarly trendy (and expensive) are the gold and silver creations of Marlene Juhl Jørgensen at **Figaros Bryllup**. For jewellery fit for Denmark's Queen, visit **Peter Hertz**. Amber washed up on Denmark's west coast makes its way into jewellery at **The Amber Specialist** and branches of **House of Amber**, which also has an amber museum.

ROYAL SHOPPING

While historic royals have left their mark on Copenhagen's architecture, fans of today's very popular royal family like to follow in their footsteps to the shops. The Queen, a talented artist, book illustrator, and designer of ecclesiastical textiles and stage costumes, can often be seen shopping in the city centre while several family members frequent Copenhagen's two big department stores, **Illum** and **Magasin du Nord**.

Grand stores carrying the coveted words "Purveyors to her Majesty, the Queen of Denmark" cluster together on the Amagertorv section of Strøget – the great silversmith **Georg Jensen**, **Royal Copenhagen**, which also boasts a charming tea room, and **Illums Bolighus**, a shrine to modern design.

Crown Princess Mary is a fashion and style icon in Denmark. Among her favourite clothes designers are Julie Fagerholt at **Heart Made**, known for her subtle detailing, the sexy and sophisticated look of **By Malene Birger**, and the innovative yet classic lines of Baum und Pferdgarten, stocked at **Urban Factory**.

Should you wish to take home wine bottled on Prince Henrik's estate in France, visit **Kjaer & Sommerfeldt**.

MARKETS

Hours can be spent bargain hunting in Copenhagen's outdoor flea markets that pop up around the city between April or May and mid-October. The flea market on **Thorvaldsens Plads**, in front of the museum, sells antiques, Danish design, posters, paintings and ceramics. It is particularly popular with its canalside setting and outdoor cafés.

Torvehallerne København, the purpose-built covered food market on Israel Plads, offers more than 60 stands, from fruit and vegetables to meat and fish, and from handmade chocolate and cupcakes to gourmet ready meals.

Flea market in one of Copenhagen's picturesque squares

ART AND ANTIQUES

Bredgade, in the financial district, and Ravnsborggade in Nørrebro are packed with antiques shops, bric-a-brac sellers and collectibles, especially modern Danish classics and funky retro designs. Come here for pieces by the great names in 20th-century Danish design, such as Arne Jacobsen, famed for his Egg, Ant and Swan chairs, Hans J Wegner, Kaare Klint and lighting by Poul Henningsen. Out of town but worth the trek, **Dansk Møbelkunst**, in Østerbro, and **Green Square**, out on Amager, are essential browsing territory for collectors of modern Danish classics.

Great furniture and style from the 1950s, 60s and 70s can also be found at **Klassik**,

while **Lysberg** is popular for the timeless quality of its designs. Bredgade is also the home of the traditional art galleries and auction houses. Sotheby's have a house here as do the long-established Danish auction houses, such as **Bruun Rasmussen**. These offer a good potential source of finds in art, antiques, furniture and jewellery.

In vibrant Vesterbro, the side streets off Istedgade and the meat-packing district of Kødbyen are the places to look for galleries displaying work by up-and-coming artists. The small streets in the Islands Brygge area are a hotbed of galleries specialising in experimental art. Off Strøget, Kompagnistræde is a quiet haven for collectors. Among the cluster of antiques shops there are specialists in porcelain and china, vintage watches and books, prints and comics. For the finest porcelain, silver and crystal, visit **Royal Copenhagen**.

SPECIALIST SHOPS

The array of individual and innovative little shops make strolling Copenhagen's streets a pleasure. They are also a great way to find gifts and souvenirs to take home from the city. Buy specialist teas in one of Europe's oldest tea-shops, **A.C. Perch's Thehandel**, which dates from 1834. Having retained its original interior, the shop and tearoom are a highlight on fashionable Kronprinsensgade. **Sømods Bolcher** is an old-fashioned sweet shop where you can watch traditional treats being made in time-honoured fashion. For the finest foods, take a look at the delicious pastries at **Trianon Bakery** and the specialist breads at **Meyers Bakery**, or explore Vaernedamsvej in Vesterbro, a great street for gourmets, with specialist cheese, wine, fish and chocolate shops, as well as cafés and grocers.

Buy a posy, or just soak up the colour and scent of **Bering Flowers**, who not only do the flowers for the Royal Theatre but royal weddings and other glitzy occasions too.

DIRECTORY

DEPARTMENT STORES AND SHOPPING CENTRES

Fields
Arne Jacobsens Allé 12.
Tel 70 20 85 05.
www.fields.dk

Fisketorvet
Kalvebod Brygge 59.
Map 3 A5.
Tel 33 36 64 00.
www.fisketorvet.dk

Illum
Østergade 52. **Map** 3 C1.
Tel 33 14 40 02.

Magasin du Nord
Kongens Nytorv 13.
Map 4 D1.
Tel 33 11 44 33.
www.magasin.dk

DESIGN AND INTERIOR DECORATION

Bang & Olufsen
Kongens Nytorv 26.
Map 2 D5.
Tel 33 11 14 15.

Bolia
Chr. IX gade 7. **Map** 1 C5.
Tel 70 10 00 55.

Casa Shop
Store Regnegade 2.
Map 1 C3.
Tel 33 32 70 41.

Danish Design Centre
H.C. Andersens Blvd 27.
Map 3 B2.
Tel 33 69 33 69.
www.ddc.dk

Designer Zoo
Vesterbrogade 137.
Tel 33 24 94 93.
www.dzoo.dk

Hay Cph
Pilestræde 29–31.
Map 3 C1.
Tel 42 82 08 20.

Hay House
Østergade 61,
2nd/3rd Floors.
Map 3 C1.
www.hay.dk

Illums Bolighus
Amagertorv 10.
Map 3 C1.
Tel 33 14 19 41.

Louis Poulsen
Gammel Strand 28.
Map 3 C1.
Tel 70 33 14 14.

Normann Copenhagen
Østerbrogade 70.
Map 1 B1.
Tel 35 27 05 40.

Paustian
Kalkbrænderiløbskaj 2.
Tel 39 16 65 65.
www.paustian.dk

CLOTHES AND ACCESSORIES

Bruuns Bazaar
Kronprinsensgade 8–9.
Map 3 C1.
Tel 33 32 19 99.

Carmen & Fantasio
Larsbjørnsstræde 11.
Map 3 B1.
Tel 33 14 30 36.

Day Birger et Mikkelsen
Pilestræde 16. **Map** 3 C1.
Tel 33 45 88 80.

Designers Remix
Pilestræde 8D.
Map 3 C1.
Tel 33 14 33 00.

Glam Vintage
Silkegade 7. **Map** 3 C1.
Tel 35 38 50 41.

Holly Golightly
Møntergade 5.
Map 1 C5.
Tel 33 14 19 20.

Munthe plus Simonsen
Grønnegade 10.
Map 2 D5.
Tel 33 32 00 12.

JEWELLERY

The Amber Specialist
Frederiksberggade 28.
Map 3 B2.
Tel 33 11 88 03.

Figaros Bryllup
Store Regnegade 2.
Map 1 C3.
Tel 33 93 09 92.

Georg Jensen
Amagertorv 4.
Map 3 C1.
Tel 33 11 40 80.

House of Amber
Kongens Nytorv 2.
Map 4 D1.
Tel 33 11 67 00.

Magasin du Nord
(See Department Stores)

Peter Hertz
Købmagergade 34.
Map 3 C1.
Tel 33 12 22 16.

ROYAL SHOPPING

By Malene Birger
Antonigade 10. **Map** 3
C1. *Tel 35 43 22 33.*

Georg Jensen
(See Jewellery)

Illum
(See Department Stores)

Illums Bolighus
(See Design and Interior Decoration)

Heart Made
Pilestræde 45.
Map 3 C1.
Tel 33 38 08 80.

Kjaer & Sommerfeldt
Gammel Mønt 4.
Map 1 C5.
Tel 70 15 65 00.

Magasin du Nord
(See Department Stores)

Royal Copenhagen
Amagertorv 6.
Map 3 C1.
Tel 33 13 71 81.

Urban Factory
Ny Østergade 12.
Map 1 C5.
Tel 33 91 70 75.

MARKETS

Thorvaldsens Plads Antique Market
Bertil Thorvaldsens Plads 2
(in front of Thorvaldsens
Museum). **Map** 3 C2.
⬜ May–Oct: Fri & Sat.

Torvehallerne København
Frederiksborggade 21.
Map 1 B5.
Tel 70 10 60 70.
www.torvehallerne
kbh.dk

ART AND ANTIQUES

Bruun Rasmussen
Bredgade 32. **Map** 2 E5.
Tel 88 18 11 11.

Dansk Møbelkunst
Aldersrogade 6C.
Tel 33 32 38 37.

Green Square
Strandlosvej 11B.
Tel 32 57 59 59.

Klassik
Bredgade 3.
Map 2 D5.
Tel 33 33 90 60.

Lysberg
Bredgade 77.
Map 2 E4.
Tel 33 14 47 87.

Royal Copenhagen
(See Royal Shopping)

SPECIALIST SHOPS

A.C. Perch's Thehandel
Kronprinsensgade 5.
Map 3 C1.
Tel 33 15 35 62.

Bering Flowers
Landemærket 12.
Map 1 C5.
Tel 33 15 26 11.

Meyers Bakery
Store Kongensgade 46.
Map 1 D5.
Tel 25 10 75 79.

Sømods Bolcher
Nørregade 36B.
Map 1 B5.
Tel 33 12 60 46.

Trianon Bakery
Hyskenstræde 8.
Map 3 C1.
Tel 33 15 66 82.

ENTERTAINMENT IN COPENHAGEN

Copenhagen has a vibrant cultural life, from world-class opera and ballet staged at the magnificent Operaen, to jazz clubs and street performance. Nightclubs range from small café-style venues to major nightspots, where live bands and international DJs play the latest sounds, and the gay scene is one of Europe's best. Festivals come in all sizes, especially during the summer months when the city seems to breathe

Roller-skating at Bakken

enjoyment. In July and August, locals make the most of the beaches, open-air swimming pools and sunbathing spots which open up along the harbour, including an urban beach on Amager island. Copenhagen is incredibly child-friendly and there is plenty to entertain young visitors, from the thrills and spills on offer at the ever-popular Tivoli amusement park to interactive fun at some of the country's top museums.

PRACTICAL INFORMATION

The first place to look for up-to-date information is the free magazine *Copenhagen This Week* (which despite its name comes out monthly) for the latest news on cultural events and club listings. It also has its own website: www.ctw.com.

BOOKING TICKETS

Tickets for theatre, opera, concerts, festivals and sport events can be booked via **Billetnet**, by phone, online, or at a post office. The **Royal Theatre/Opera Box Office** on Kongens Nytorv opens at 4pm for the sale of half-price tickets for that day's performances. Get there early, as queues can get long. Under-25s and over-65s are eligible for half-price tickets when booking for shows more than a week in advance.
Cinema tickets tend to be cheaper for matinee and weekday performances; these can be booked online at www.biobooking.dk.

OPERA AND CLASSICAL MUSIC

Opera fans should not miss a performance of the Royal Opera at the striking **Operaen** *(see p89)*, which also hosts classical music concerts. From early June until late August, **Det Kongelige Teater** (The Royal Theatre)'s open-air stage Ofelia Beach, on the waterfront outside Skuespilhuset, hosts free cultural events,

including opera performances by the Royal Danish Opera Academy. For eight days in late July and early August, the **Copenhagen Opera Festival** organizes shows at several venues across the city. Many events are free and take place outside, while others are produced specially for children. National broadcaster Danmarks Radio's world-class **DR Koncerthuset** houses a number of concert halls, the largest of which can seat 1,800 people.
Those who enjoy classical music will be thrilled by the concerts given at the **Tivoli Koncertsal**. Throughout the summer season, Danish and international conductors and soloists join the 80-strong Tivoli Symphony Orchestra for the **Tivoli Festival**'s varied programme. During the winter months, the orchestra becomes the Copenhagen Philharmonic.

Tivoli Koncertsal, home to the Tivoli Symphony Orchestra

Ballet performance at Det Kongelige Teater

For a less formal occasion, students from the Royal Danish Academy of Music give free concerts on Wednesday afternoons during spring and autumn in various venues. See www.onsdagskoncerter. dk for more details.

BALLET AND CONTEMPORARY DANCE

Det Kongelige Teater is home to the Royal Danish Ballet, whose season runs August–June, finishing with a free open-air performance in the grounds of Kastellet *(see p54)*.
The main venue for contemporary dance is **Dansescenen**, located in Northern Europe's largest centre for modern dance, the vast Dansehallerne complex, in the Carlsberg Brewery *(see p92)*. With a large stage (Store Carl) and the smaller Lille Carl, this venue is devoted to the best in Danish and international dance, as well as hosting a number of festivals to showcase young dance companies and choreographers.

Dansehallerne is also home to **Dansk Danseteater**, an experimental dance company founded in 1981 by the British

Jazz quintet playing at the Copenhagen Jazz House

dancer and choreographer Tim Rushton. Every August the company presents its popular festival Copenhagen Summer Dance, with free performances in the colonnaded courtyard of the Copenhagen City Police headquarters.

JAZZ CLUBS AND LIVE MUSIC

International performers are regulars at the atmospheric **Copenhagen Jazzhouse** and at the legendary **Jazzhus Montmartre**. Many bars host their own jazz sessions – like gritty **La Fontaine**, the oldest jazz venue in Copenhagen, which has live sessions every weekend. In July, the **Copenhagen Jazz Festival** fills the streets and venues all over the city, attracting some of the world's finest jazz musicians. Many of the 800 or so performances are free.

For blues fans, there is live music every night at **Mojo Blues Bar** and, in September, the **Copenhagen Blues Festival**.

For up-and-coming bands as well as international acts, **VEGA**, in Copenhagen's rejuvenated Vesterbro district, is a popular venue housed in a 1950s trade union building. The large hall (Store Vega) has seen many international bands, while the smaller room (Lille Vega) is ideal for more intimate, acoustic concerts. A great place to see the best young indie bands is **Loppen**, in alternative Christiania.

Last but by no means least is **Tivoli** *(see pp76–7)*, where

in summer, world-famous rock and pop acts perform on the open-air stage. Friday night rock concerts kick off at 10pm during the summer, and entrance is included in the Tivoli admission. Musicals also run in both summer and Christmas seasons.

NIGHTLIFE VENUES

Copenhagen's clubs start getting lively only after midnight, so many people head first to a pre-club bar, such as the trendy **Zoo Bar** or Ideal Bar in **VEGA**. **Rust**, in the vibrant Nørrebro district, has club nights from midweek on three floors; indie rock and hip hop dominate the live music, while in the basement DJs play indie, punk and electro. **Culture Box** is a purist techno club. The converted warehouses and cattle stalls of the former meat-packing district in Kødbyen come alive on weekend nights. The vast **KB3** attracts the hippest locals, as well as visiting DJs, to its dance nights, while **SIN CITY** is a two-floor club dedicated to hard rock and heavy metal.

For something completely different, head to **Wallmans Saloner**, where you can enjoy a seated dinner show with artists performing on different stages around the restaurant.

THEATRE

Most theatre in Copenhagen is performed in Danish, and while there are a number of English-language theatre companies, none have venues of their own. The best known

of these is **London Toast**, whose pre-Christmas pantomime in Tivoli's Glassalen is a Copenhagen tradition.

Most of the drama performed by the Royal Danish Theatre is now staged at the company's playhouse Skuespilhuset *(see p71)*. Housed in an 1807 listed building in the Latin Quarter, **Københavns Musikteater** is a lively venue for experimental musical theatre and avant-garde opera.

CINEMA

There are scores of cinemas in and around Copenhagen, ranging from art-house theatres to huge multiplexes. Most films are shown in their original language, with Danish subtitles.

To catch the latest blockbusters, the big **Cinemaxx**, part of the Fisketorvet shopping centre down by the harbour, shows all the major releases on ten screens. The **Imperial** is used for all the Danish premieres and charges a little extra for its luxurious seats. Around the corner, the **Dagmar** has a diverse programme and a pleasant atmosphere, while the independent **Empire Bio**, in a former locomotive factory, is popular with locals for its late night shows.

To get away from the mainstream, the long-established **Grand Teatret**, with its repertoire of European films, and **Cinemateket**, which is attached to the Danish Film Institute, are traditional art-house cinemas. For off-circuit and low-budget films, try **Vester Vov Vov**, in the Vesterbro district, or the tiny **Gloria**.

Entrance to Cinemaxx, one of Copenhagen's main cinemas

GAY AND LESBIAN

Copenhagen is a city with a long tradition of openness and acceptance: the city's first gay bar, **Centralhjørnet**, opened its doors in the 1930s and is still going strong. Famed for its annual Gay Pride Parade in August and for Mix, a well-established gay, lesbian, bi and transgender film festival in October, the city has a stream of other events year-round, including the Sankt Hans midsummer bonfire and beach party on Amager Island in June.

The city centre gay club, bar and restaurant scene is concentrated in quite a small area, so everything is pretty much within walking distance. **Club Cristopher** is Copenhagen's biggest gay club, with several dance floors, resident as well as visiting DJs and an open bar. **Jailhouse** is a popular concept bar and restaurant with booths kitted out as prison cells and staff dressed in police uniforms. On Friday evenings, DJs and a good atmosphere are available at the lounge-style **Oscar Bar & Café**. Young gay men favour **Masken Bar**, where the shows span live music and drag. **Mens Bar** is for the leather-clad contingent. For the really late night scene, head on to the aptly named **Never Mind**,

Tables on the pavement outside the Oscar Bar and Café

open daily until 6am, or the darker, dingier **Dunkel**, where closing time is when the manager feels like closing. **Café Intime** is a piano bar near Frederiksberg Have that attracts theatrical types.

For up-to-date listings of gay events in the city, see the **Copenhagen Gay Life** website.

BEACHES

Clean and spacious harbour swimming pools, with beaches and sports activities, are a great summer feature and only a short walk from the centre of Copenhagen. The harbour area has been revitalised with apartments, hotels and restaurants and the water really is clean enough for swimming. The pools are open from June until early September.

Havnebadet, just across the ramparts from Christianshavn at Islands Brygge, has five pools and a large grassy bathing "beach". The smaller **Copencabana** pool is by the Fisketorvet shopping centre and comes complete with sand beach and palm trees.

Further afield, the north end of **Bellevue Strand**, at Klampenborg, is a short train or bike ride from town. It's a gay-friendly place with a nudist area at the top end. **Amager Strandpark** (see pp96–7) on Amager Island is divided into two parts: an "urban" beach with a range of fitness activities, bars, food stalls, even a Bedouin tent; and a "wild" section with wide sandy beaches and small sand dunes. A lagoon between the island and the mainland has child-friendly shallow water.

CHILDREN'S ENTERTAINMENT

No child visiting Copenhagen should miss **Tivoli** amusement park (see pp76–7), which has enough rides and attractions to keep even the most demanding young person happy. **Bakken** (see p120) in a wooded area north of the city near Klampenborg, claims to be the oldest fun park in the world and has over 100 rides.

Miniature classic car ride in Tivoli Gardens

Zoologisk Have (see pp92–3) is the city's zoo and includes a mini zoo for smaller children and a large play area. **Danmarks Akvarium** (see p95) allows children to see weird and wonderful marine life up close.

Several museums in or near Strøget are especially suitable for children, including **Ripley's Believe It or Not!** (see p73), **Hans Christian Andersen's Wonderful World** and **Guinness World Records Museum** (see p69). These are all part of the same group, and it's possible to pay a joint entry price. There is also the **Experimentarium** (see pp94–5), a science-based museum with plenty of hands-on fun; or the chance to be dazzled by a 3D movie in the IMAX Space Theatre of the **Tycho Brahe Planetarium** (see p92). The **Nationalmuseet** (see pp84–5) has a separate children's wing, and families and children have their own exhibitions and guided tours at the **Statens Museum for Kunst** (see pp62–3).

Children's theatre is very popular in Denmark, with a number of international festivals held annually or bi-annually. Kids even have their own theatres, with child-size seats or centrally placed stages. **Zebu** in Amager has performances for kids aged one and upwards; most of them are virtually wordless.

Free puppet shows take place from June to mid-August at the **Marionet Teatret** at the foot of Kongens Have (see p58), a lovely green space in front of the fairy-tale Rosenborg Palace. There are plenty of other playgrounds, including many in natural settings, like the one in Naturcenter Vestamager (see p97). The harbour swimming pools (see Beaches) have areas reserved for kids and events during July's summer holidays.

DIRECTORY

BOOKING TICKETS

Billetnet
Tel 70 15 65 65.
www.billetnet.dk

Royal Theatre/ Opera Box Office
Kongens Nytorv. **Map** 4 D1. **www**.kglteater.dk

OPERA AND CLASSICAL MUSIC

Copenhagen Opera Festival
www.copenhagenopera festival.com/en

Det Kongelige Teater
August Bournonvilles Passage, Kongens Nytorv. **Map** 4 D1.
Tel 33 69 69 69.
www.kglteater.dk

DR Koncerthuset
Emil Holms Kanal 20, Ørestad.
Tel 35 20 62 62.
www.dr.dk/koncerthuset

Operaen
Ekvipagemestervej 10.
Map 2 F5.
Tel 33 69 69 69.
www.operahus.dk

Tivoli Festival
www.tivoli.dk/tivoli-festival

Tivoli Koncertsal
Vesterbrogade 3. **Map** 3 A2. *Tel 33 15 10 12.*
www.tivoli.dk

BALLET AND CONTEMPORARY DANCE

Dansescenen
Pasteursvej 24, 1.
Tel 33 29 10 10.
www.dansehallerne.dk

Dansk Danseteater
www.danskdanseteater.dk

Det Kongelige Teater
(See Opera and Classical Music)

JAZZ CLUBS AND LIVE MUSIC

Copenhagen Blues Festival
www.copenhagenblues festival.dk

Copenhagen Jazz Festival
www.jazz.dk

Copenhagen Jazz House
Niels Hemmingsens Gade 10. **Map** 3 C1.
Tel 33 15 47 00.
www.jazzhouse.dk

Jazzhus Montmartre
Store Regnegade 19A.
Map 1 C5. **www.** jazzhusmontmartre.dk

La Fontaine
Kompagnistræde 11.
Map 3 C1.
Tel 33 11 60 98.

Loppen
Bådsmandsstræde 43, Christianshavn. **Map** 4 E2.
Tel 32 57 84 22.
www.loppen.dk

Mojo Blues Bar
Løngangstræde 21. **Map** 3 B2. *Tel 33 11 64 53.*
www.mojo.dk

Tivoli
(See Opera and Classical Music)

VEGA
Enghavevej 40. *Tel 33 25 70 11.* **www**.vega.dk

NIGHTLIFE VENUES

Culture Box
Kronprinsensgade 54.
Map 1 C5.
Tel 33 32 50 50.
www.culture-box.com

KB3
Kødboderne 3, Kødbyen.
www.kb3.dk

Rust
Guldbergsgade 8. *Tel 35 24 52 00.* **www**.rust.dk

SIN CITY
I løkerboderne 18-22, Kødbyen.

VEGA
(See Jazz Clubs and Live Music)

Wallmans Saloner
Wallmans Cirkusbygningen, Jernbanegade 8. **Map** 3 A2. *Tel 33 16 37 00.*
www.wallmans.com

Zoo Bar
Kronprinsensgade 7.
Map 3 C1.
Tel 33 15 68 69.
www.zoobar.dk

THEATRE

Københavns Musikteater
Kronprinsensgade 7.
Map 3 C1.
Tel 33 32 55 56.
www.kobenhavns musikteater.dk

London Toast
www.londontoast.dk

CINEMAS

Cinemateket
Gothersgade 55.
Map 1 C5. *Tel 33 74 34 12.*
www.dfi.dk/filmhuset

Cinemaxx
Kalvebod Brygge 59.
Map 3 A5.
Tel 70 10 12 02.

Dagmar
Jernbanegade 2.
Tel 70 13 12 11.

Empire Bio
Guldbergsgade 29F.
Tel 35 36 00 36.
www.empirebio.dk

Gloria
Rådhuspladsen 59.
Tel 33 12 42 92.

Grand Teatret
Mikkel Bryggersgade 8.
Map 3 B2. *Tel 33 15 16 11.*
www.grandteatret.dk

Imperial
Ved Vesterport 4.
Tel 70 13 12 11.

Vester Vov Vov
Absalonsgade 5.
Tel 33 24 42 00.
www.vestervovvov.dk

GAY AND LESBIAN

Café Intime
Allegade 25, Frederiksberg.
Tel 38 34 19 58.

Centralhjørnet
Kattesundet 18. **Map** 3 B2.
Tel 33 11 85 49.
www.centralhjornet.dk

Club Christopher
Knabrostræde 3.
Map 3 B1.
www.clubchristopher.dk

Copenhagen Gay Life
www.copenhagen-gay-life.dk

Dunkel
Vester Voldgade 10.
Map 3 B2.

Jailhouse
Studiestræde 12.
Map 3 B1.
Tel 33 15 22 55.
www.jailhousecph.dk

Masken Bar
Studiestræde 33. **Map** 3 A1. *Tel 33 91 09 37.*
www.maskenbar.dk

Mens Bar
Teglgårdsstræde 3. **Map** 3 A1. *Tel 33 12 73 03.*
www.mensbar.dk

Never Mind
Nørre Voldgade 2.
Map 3 A1.
www.nevermindbar.dk

Oscar Bar & Café
Rådhuspladsen 77. **Map** 3 B2. *Tel 33 12 09 99.*
www.oscarbarcafe.dk

BEACHES

Bellevue Strand
Strandvejen 340, Klampenborg.

Copencabana
Kalvebod Brygge.
Map 3 A5.

Havnebadet
Islands Brygge. **Map** 3 C3.

CHILDREN'S ENTERTAINMENT

Hans Christian Andersen's Wonderful World
Rådhuspladsen 57.
Tel 33 32 31 31.
www.topattractions.dk

Marionet Teatret
www.marionetteatret.dk

Zebu
Øresundsvej 4, Amager.
www.zebu.nu

STREET FINDER

The map references given for all of Copenhagen's sights, hotels, restaurants, bars, shops and entertainment venues included in this guide refer to the maps in this section. All major sights, famous historic buildings, museums, galleries, railway, bus, metro and suburban train stations have been marked on the map. Other features are indicated by symbols explained in the key below. The names of streets and squares contained on the map are given in Danish. The word *gade* translates as street; *plads* means square, *allé* translates as avenue and *have* means park or garden.

KEY TO COPENHAGEN STREET FINDER

■ Place of interest	✚ A&E hospital
■ Other building	🚓 Police station
M Metro station	✝ Church
S S–tog station	✡ Synagogue
S Regional train station	⊠ Post office
R Central Station	═ Railway line
i Tourist information	▬ Pedestrianized street

1:11 500

SCALE OF MAPS 1–4

0 m	200
0 yards	200

Street Finder Index

A

A. F. Kriegers Vej 2 D1
Abildgårdsgade 1 B3
Adelgade 1 C5, 2 D4, D5
Admiralgade 3 C1, 4 D1
Ahlefeldtsgade 1 A5, B5
Amager Boulevard 3 C3, C4,
  4 D4, E4, F4
Amagerbrogade 4 E4, F4, F5
Amagerfælledvej 4 E3, E4, E5
Amagergade 4 E3
Amagertorv 3 C1
Amaliegade 2 E4, E5
Andreas Bjørns Gade 4 F2
Anker Heegårds Gade 3 B3
Arendalsgade 2 D2
Artillerivej 3 B5, C5, 4 D4, D5
Axel Heides Gade 3 A5, B5

B

Bådsmandsstræde 4 E2, F3
Badstuestræde 3 B1, C1
Bergensgade 2 D2, D3
Bergthorasgade 3 C4, C5
Bernstorffsgade 3 A2, A3, B3,
  B4
Blegdamsvej 1 A1, A2, A3, B1,
  B2
Blekingegade 4 F5
Borgerbo 4 E4, E5
Borgergade 2 D4, D5
Borgmester Jensens Allé 1 A1
Bornholmsgade 2 E4
Børsgade 4 D2
Bredgade 2 D5, E4, E5
Bremerholm 4 D1, D2
Brigadegården 4 F5
Brobergsgade 4 E2, F2
Brolæggerstræde 3 B1, C1
Bryggergade 3 B2
Bryghusgade 3 C3
Burmeistersgade 4 F2

C

Christian IX's Gade 1 C5
Christians Brygge 3 C3, 4 D2
Christianshavns Voldgade 4 E3,
  F3
Classensgade 1 C2, 2 D1, D2
Cort Adelers Gade 4 E1

D

D. Balfours Gade 4 D3
Dag Hammarskjölds Allé 1 C2,
  2 D2, D3
Dagøgade 4 D3
Dampfærgevej 2 E1, E2
Delfingade 2 D3
Dronningens Tværgade 2 D5
Dronningensgade 4 D3, E3
Dybensgade 4 D1

E

Eckersbergsgade 1 B3
Egilsgade 3 C4, C5, 4 D5
Elsdyrsgade 2 D3, D4
Esplanaden 2 E4, F4

F

Faksegade 1 C1
Falcks Gade 3 B3
Finlandsgade 4 E5, F5
Fiolstræde 1 B5, 3 B1
Fiskedamsgade 2 D1
Folke Bernadottes Allé 2 D3,
  E2
Forbindelsesvej 2 E2
Fortunstræde 3 C1, 4 D1
Fredensgade 1 A2, A3
Fredericiagade 2 D4, E4, E5
Frederik V. s Vej 1 A1, A2, B2
Frederiksbrogade 2 E2
Frederiksborggade 1 A4, A5,
  B5
Frederiksholms Kanal 3 C2

G

Gammel Strand 3 C1
Gammelmønt 1 C5
Gammeltoftsgade 1 B3, B4
Gefiongade 2 D1, E2
Gernersgade 2 D4
Gothersgade 1 A4, B4, B5, C5,
  2 D5
Grønningen 2 D3, E4
Gunløgsgade 3 C4, C5

H

H. C. Andersens Boulevard
  3 A1, A2, B2, B3, C3
Halfdansgade 3 B4, C4, C5
Hallandsgade 4 F5
Hallinsgade 1 B3, C3
Hambrosgade 3 B3, C3
Hammerensgade 2 E4
Hammerichsgade 3 A1, A2
Hannovergade 4 F4, F5
Hardanggade 2 D2
Hausergade 1 B5, C5
Havnegade 4 D2, E1, E2
Hedemannsgade 1 B2
Anker Heegårds Gade 3 B3
Henrik Harpestrengs Vej 1 A1,
  A2
Herluf Trolles Gade 4 D1, E1
Hestemøllestræde 3 B2
Holbergsgade 4 D1, E1
Hollænderdybet 4 E5, F4
Holmbladsvænge 4 F4
Holmens Kanal 4 D1, D2
Høyensgade 1 B3, C3
Hvitveldts Stræde 1 B5
Hyskenstræde 3 C1

I

Indiakaj 2 E2, F2
Ingerslevsgade 3 A3, A4
Irmingersgade 1 B2
Islands Brygge 3 A5, B4, B5,
  C3, C4

J

J. Kofods Gade 2 D4, E4
J.A. Schwartz Gade 1 B2, B3, C3
J. Holms Gade 4 F5
Jemtelandsgade 4 F4
Jens Juels Gade 1 B3
Jernbanegade 3 A2
Johan Semps Gade 4 D3
Juliane Maries Vej 1 A2

K

Kalkbrænderihavnsgade
  2 E1, E2
Kalvebod Brygge 3 A4, A5,
  B3, B4, C3
Kastelsvej 1 C2, 2 D2
Kattesundet 3 B1, B2
Klerkegade 2 D4
Klosterstræde 3 B1, C1
Knabrostræde 3 B1, C1, C2
Knippelsbrogade 4 D2
Købmagergade 1 B5, 3 C1
Kompagnistræde 3 B2, C1
Kongedybet 4 F4, F5
Krokodillegade 2 D3
Kronprinsengade 3 C1
Kronprinsessegade 1 C5, 2 D3,
  D4, D5
Krystalgade 3 B1
Kvæsthusbroen 2 E5

L

Laksegade 3 C1, 4 D1
Landemærket 1 B5, C5
Landgreven 2 D5
Langebrogade 3 C4, 4 D3
Langeliniekaj 2 F1, F2
Larsbjørnsstræde 3 B1
Larsens Plads 2 E5

Larslejsstræde 3 B1
Leifsgade 3 C4, C5
Lerfosgade 4 F5
Lille Kongensgade 4 D1
Linnesgade 1 A5, B5
Lipkesgade 2 D1, D2
Livjægergade 2 D1, D2
Løngangstræde 3 B2
Lønporten 1 C5
Løvstræde 3 C1
Lundingsgade 1 B2, B3

M

Magstræde 3 B2, C2
Markmandsgade 4 F4
Mikkel Vibes Gade 4 E3
Møntergade 1 C5

N

N. Hemmingsens Gade 3 C1
Nansensgade 1 A4, A5
Nicolai Eigtveds Gade 4 D2, D3
Niels Brocks Gade 3 B3
Niels Juels Gade 4 D1, D2
Nikolajgade 4 D1
Njalsgade 3 C4, 4 D4, D5, E5
Nordlandsgade 4 F4, F5
Nordre Frihavnsgade 1 C1
Norgesgade 4 E5, F4, F5
Nørre Farimagsgade 1 A4, A5,
  3 A1
Nørre Søgade 1 A4, A5
Nørre Voldgade 1 A5, B5
Nørregade 1 B5, 3 B1
Ny Kongensgade 3 B2, B3, C2
Ny Adelgade 2 D5
Ny Brogade 3 C1, C2
Ny Østergade 1 C5, 2 D5
Ny Vestergade 3 B2, C2
Nygade 3 B1
Nyhavn 4 D1, E1

O

Otto Mønsteds Gade 3 B3
Ole Suhrs Gade 1 B3, B4
Olfert Fischers Gade 2 D4
Olof Palme Gade 1 C3, D2
Olufsvej 1 B1, C1
Orlogsværftsvej 2 F5
Oslo Plads 2 D1
Overgaden neden Vandet 4 E2,
  E3
Overgaden oven Vandet 4 D3,
  E2, E3, F2

P

Pahusvej 2 E1
Pakhuskaj 2 F1, F2
Palægade 2 D5
Peder Skrams Gade 4 D1, E1
Peter Vedels Gade 4 E4
Pilestræde 3 C1
Præstøgade 2 D1
Prinsessegade 4 E2, E3, F2
Puggårdsgade 3 B3, C3
Pustervig 1 B5, C5

R

Rådhusstræde 3 B1, B2
Refshale Vej 4 F2
Rigensgade 1 C4, D4
Rømersgade 1 A5, B4, B5
Rørholmsgade 1 B3, B4
Rosenborggade 1 B5
Rosendalsgade 1 C1, C2
Rosengade 2 D4
Rosenvængets Sideallé 1 C1
Rosenvængets Hovedvej 2 D1
Rosenvængets Allé 1 C1, 2 D1
Ryesgade 1 A3, B2, C1
Rysensteensgade 3 B3, C3

S

Saabyesvej 2 D1, D2
Sankt Annæ Gade 4 E2, E3

Sankt Annæ Plads 2 D5, E5
Sankt Hans Gade 1 A3, A4
Sankt Pauls Gade 2 D4
Sankt Peders Stræde 3 A1, B1
Schleppegrellsgade 1 A3
Skovgårdsgade 1 B3, C3
Slotsholmsgade 4 D2
Slutterigade 3 B1, B2
Snaregade 3 C1, C2
Snorresgade 3 C4, C5
Sølvgade 1 B3, B4, C4, 2 D4
Søpassagen 1 A3, B3
Sortedam Dossering 1 A3, A4,
  B2, B3, C2
Staunings Plads 3 A1
Stockholmsgade 1 B3, C3,
  2 D3
Stoltenbergsgade 3 B3
Store Kannikestræde 3 B1
Store Kirkestræde 3 C1, 4 D1
Store Kongensgade 2 D3, D4,
  D5, E4
Store Mølle Vej 4 F4
Strandboulevarden 2 D1, D2
Strandgade 4 D2, D3, E2
Studiestræde 3 A1, A2, B1
Sturlasgade 3 B5, C5
Suensonsgade 2 D3, D4
Sundholmsvej 4 E5, F5
Syvens Allé 4 F4, F5

T

Thorshavnsgade 3 C4
Tietgensgade 3 A3, B3
Tøjhusgade 3 C2
Toldbodgade 2 E4, E5, 4 E1
Tordenskjoldsgade 4 D1, D2
Tornebuskegade 1 B5
Torvegade 4 D2, E2, E3
Trepkasgade 1 A2, B2
Trondhjemsgade 2 D2

U

Uplandsgade 4 F4
Upsalagade 1 C3

V

Ved Amagerport 4 E4
Ved Glyptoteket 3 B3
Ved Linden 4 E4, F4
Ved Sønderport 4 F4
Ved Stranden 3 C1, 4 D2
Vendersgade 1 A4, A5, B5
Vermlandsgade 4 E3, F3, F4
Vester Voldgade 3 A1, A2, B2,
  C3
Vesterbrogade 3 A2
Vestergade 3 A2, B1, B2
Vimmelskaftet 3 B1, C1
Vindebrogade 3 C1, C2
Visbygade 1 C2, C3, 2 D3
Vognmagergade 1 C5

W

W. Marstrands Gade 1 B3
Wildersgade 4 D3, E2, E3
Willemoesgade 1 C1, C2, 2 D1

Z

Zinnsgade 1 C2

Å

Åbenrå 1 B5, C5

Ø

Ørestad Boulevard 4 D4, D5
Østbanegade 2 D2, D3, E1, E2
Øster Allé 1 B1
Øster Farimagsgade 1 B3, B4,
  C2, C3
Øster Søgade 1 A4, B2, B3, C2
Øster Voldgade 1 B4, B5, C3,
  C4, 2 D3
Østerbrogade 1 C1, C2
Østergade 3 C1, 4 D1

DENMARK REGION BY REGION

DENMARK AT A GLANCE 114–115

NORTHWESTERN ZEALAND 116–151

SOUTHERN ZEALAND AND
THE ISLANDS 152–171

FUNEN 172–181

SOUTHERN AND CENTRAL JUTLAND
182–199

NORTHERN JUTLAND 200–215

BORNHOLM 216–227

GREENLAND AND THE FAROE ISLANDS
228–237

Denmark at a Glance

Denmark has a host of attractions for visitors. Small rural farms, rolling fields of wheat, lush woodlands and fine beaches are just some of the things that make the country especially popular with nature lovers. Those favouring outdoor activities will enjoy the many trails and cycle routes. Many of these are themed and are designed to take in some of the country's best historic churches, castles and palaces. For sightseers, there are Neolithic ruins, Viking remains and medieval villages to explore, while the various delights on offer at amusement parks such as Bakken or LEGOLAND® will not be lost on children.

NORTHERN JUTLAND
(See pp200–215)

SOUTHERN AND CENTRAL JUTLAND
(See pp182–199)

Northern Jutland *has some beautiful beaches, as well as fine buildings such as Voergård Slot. The works on display in the Skagens Museum perfectly capture the shimmering Nordic light found in this part of the country.*

Southern Jutland *is famous for towns such as Ribe, which survived flood and fire, and retains some of the best-preserved medieval architecture in Denmark. The level to which the waters of the Ribe Å River rose during a flood in 1634 are marked on a wooden column.*

Funen *has been nicknamed the "Garden of Denmark". The charm of this island resides mainly in its scenery, which includes flower-filled fields and meadows, ancient castles and half-timbered houses.*

◁ **Neo-Classical sculpture adorning Frederiksborg Slot's façade**

BORNHOLM
(See pp216–227)

Bornholm *is sometimes described as "Scandinavia in a nutshell" because it combines many typically Scandinavian features, such as rocky shores, picturesque villages and peaceful forests.*

Northwestern Zealand *is known for its royal castles and palaces. Among these is the magnificent Kronborg Slot on the Øresund coast, which was used by William Shakespeare as the setting for Hamlet. The castle now contains a museum.*

NORTHWESTERN ZEALAND
(See pp116–151)

Copenhagen *is Denmark's capital and its largest city. It has many sights, both modern and old, including the magnificent Marmorkirken, which offers splendid views from its grand dome. (See pages 46–111.)*

FUNEN
pp172–181)

SOUTHERN
ZEALAND AND
THE ISLANDS
(See pp152–171)

Southern Zealand *is a mix of farmland, woodland and glorious coastal scenery. There is much to see, including a 1,000-year-old Viking fortress at Trelleborg and the 12th-century Sankt Bendts Kirke, which is the oldest brick church in Denmark.*

0 km   30

0 miles   30

NORTHWESTERN ZEALAND

Zealand is the largest of the Danish islands and has an area of 7,500 sq km (2,895 sq miles). On its eastern shore lies Copenhagen (see pp46–107) – the country's capital city as well as its cultural and commercial centre. Away from the city, there is much to enjoy, from mighty castles and historic towns to sandy beaches, rural villages and beautiful countryside.

The island's scenery is typical of the lowland regions. Idyllic meadow scenery is broken here and there by beech forests and coastal fjords that cut deep into the land. Much of the region's wildlife can be seen around Arresø, Denmark's largest lake.

Most of the port towns were once Viking settlements. A reconstructed 10th–11th-century Viking camp can be visited in Trelleborg, while Viking ships can be seen at Roskilde's Viking Ship Museum. A visit to Sagnlandet Lejre, an experimental camp where Danish families volunteer to spend a week living in an Iron Age village, provides a glimpse into the past, as do the Viking plays staged at Frederikssund.

Northwestern Zealand has played an important part in the history of Denmark. Lejre was one of the first centres of Danish administration; later on this function was assumed by Roskilde, which in 1020 became a bishopric and the capital of Denmark. This lasted until 1443 when the role of the country's capital was taken over by Copenhagen. Traditionally, this area has been favoured by wealthy Danes and some of the most impressive royal castles can be found here including Kronborg, Fredensborg and Frederiksborg. In addition, there is a variety of more modest establishments worthy of a visit, such as Ermitagen, a royal hunting lodge a short way west of Klampenborg.

Hundested's popular beach

◁ | Neptune's Fountain, Frederiksborg Slot, symbolizing Denmark's power in the 17th century

Exploring Northwestern Zealand

Most visitors to Zealand never stray beyond the limits of Copenhagen. There are, however, many other parts of the island that are well worth exploring. The list of sacral buildings includes Roskilde Domkirke (Cathedral) and Vor Frue Kirke, in Kalundborg, a 12th-century church with five spires. The region also has several areas that are conducive to carefree holidays. The northern shores, washed by Kattegat's waters, are famous for their beautiful sandy beaches, while the forests, criss-crossed with a network of trails, are perfect for cyclists and hikers.

SEE ALSO

• **Where to Stay** pp247–9.

• **Where to Eat** pp274–6.

A statue of Esbern Snare, 12th-century founder of Kalundborg

GETTING AROUND

Denmark's capital, served by Copenhagen International Airport, is a good starting point for exploring Zealand. Central Station in Copenhagen is the island's main railway hub. Northwestern Zealand has a well-developed network of motorways and major roads, which make getting around by car straightforward.

ODSHERRED

Havnebjen 35

Høib

Sejerø

Sejerø Bugt

Asnæs

34 DRAGSHOLM

Hørve

RØSNÆS

Ulstrup 32

Saltbæk Vig

33

SVINNINGE

KALUNDBORG 31

Asnæs

Svebølle   Jyderup

NØRRE JERNLØSE MØLLE

Tissø

Gørlev

Stenlille

Høng

Dianalund

Bjerne

TRELLEBORG

30

SORØ 26

STORE BÆLT BRIDGE

29

27 TÅRNBORG

Slagelse

Odense 28 KORSØR

Næstved

KEY

▬▬▬	Motorway
▬ ▬ ▬	Motorway under construction
▬▬▬	Major road
▭▭▭	Minor road
▬▬▬	Scenic route
▬▬▬	Main railway
▬▬▬	Minor railway
▬▬▬	Regional border

The tall spires of Roskilde Domkirke

SIGHTS AT A GLANCE

Bakken ❷
Dragsholm ❸❹
Fredensborg Slot ❿
Frederiksborg Slot pp132–3 ⓬
Frederikssund ⓱
Frilandsmuseet ❸
Gilleleje ❾
Grønnesse Skov ⓭
Helsingør pp124–5 ❻
Holbæk ㉓
Hornbæk ❽
Hundested ⓮
Jægersborg Dyrehave ❶
Jægerspris Slot ⓰
Kalundborg ㉛
Korsør ㉘
Kronborg Slot pp126–7 ❼
Ledreborg Slot ㉒
Lejre ㉑

Louisiana Museum pp122–3 ❺
Nordskoven ⓯
Nørre Jernløse Mølle ㉕
Roskilde pp140–43 ⓴
Rungstedlund ❹
Røsnæs ㉜
Selsø Slot ⓲
Skibby ⓳
Sorø ㉖
Store Bælt Bridge ㉙
Svinninge ㉝
Tårnborg ㉗
Trelleborg ㉚
Tveje Merløse Kirke ㉔

Tours
Esrum Sø and Arresø ⓫
Odsherred ㉟

Stately Dutch Renaissance entrance to Frederiksborg Slot

Jægersborg Dyrehave ❶

Road map F4. 🚇 🚌

The beech forests and parkland covering an area between the motorway that runs from Copenhagen towards Helsingør and the shore of the Øresund (Sound) is one of the favourite places for weekend forays out of Copenhagen. This area, which is criss-crossed with paths and cycle routes, was established as a royal hunting ground in 1669. The park still supports a herd of some 2,000 deer. A good vantage point from which to look out for them is the Ermitagen hunting lodge at the centre of the park, which was built in 1736 for Christian VI.

Among the park's other attractions are Bakken amusement park *(see below)*, Kirsten Pils Kilde (a holy spring that was a pilgrimage destination in the 16th century) and, nearby, Bellevue (one of the area's best beaches). Horse-drawn carriages offer rides through the park and there is also a golf course and a horse racing track just to the south of Bakken.

Ermitagen hunting lodge

Bakken ❷

Road map F4. Ⓢ *Klampenborg.* **Tel** *39 63 35 44.* ◯ *May–Aug. Opening hours vary; consult the website before visiting.* 📷 **www**.bakken.dk

Bakken was founded in 1583 and is considered to be the world's oldest amusement park. Located just a short

One of the many rides to be enjoyed at Bakken

way out of Copenhagen, it is on the edge of the Jægersborg Dyrehave deer park.

The present amusement park has 100 or so rides, including roller-coasters and merry-go-rounds, as well as circus shows and a cabaret-style revue. There are 40 cafés and restaurants on site, although people can bring their own supplies for a picnic. Entrance to the park is free though rides must be paid for. Bakken opens on 1 May every year and closes on 31 August; both occasions are cause for a huge motorcycle parade up to the park from north Copenhagen.

Frilandsmuseet ❸

Road map F4. Kongevejen 100, 2800 Lyngby. 🚇 🚌 **Tel** *33 47 38 55.* ◯ *May–Oct: 10am–4pm Tue–Sun (Jul–mid-Aug: to 5pm).* **www**.frilandsmuseet.dk

This open-air museum, founded in 1897, contains virtually every kind of Danish country dwelling imaginable. Originally situated near Rosenberg Slot in Copenhagen, it was relocated to its present site in 1901 and is now run as part of the Nationalmuseet. Over 100 buildings are arranged into 40 groups and include many examples of rural architecture from cottages to grand manor houses, many of which are furnished and decorated in keeping with the period in which they were built. Visitors should allow a day to look round the collection, which includes

fishermen's cottages, windmills, peasant huts, a post mill (still with working sails) and a smithy (kitted out with irons and a hearth). Many of the staff dress in traditional costume and demonstrate such fading arts as turning clay pots and weaving cloth. The ticket also allows entry to Brede Værk, by the northern entrance of Frilandsmuseet. This textile mill, which closed in 1956, is now preserved as an industrial village complete with cottages, a school and the owner's country house.

A meticulously reconstructed house interior, Frilandsmuseet

Rungstedlund ❹

Road map F4. 2960 Rungsted Kyst. 🚇 🚌 **Tel** *45 57 10 57.* **Karen Blixen Museum** ◯ *May–Sep: 10am–5pm Tue–Sun; Oct–Apr: 1–4pm Wed–Fri, 11am–4pm Sat–Sun.* 📷 **www**.karen-blixen.dk

Made famous by Karen Blixen, author of *Out of Africa,* Rungstedlund is the author's birthplace and was where she grew up and wrote most of her works under the pen name Isak Dinesen.

Karen Blixen's house was built around 1500 and was first used as an inn. In 1879 her father bought the property. It is now maintained by a foundation established by the writer, and in 1991 was converted into a museum devoted to Blixen's life and work. The rooms remain little changed from the period when she lived here, and manuscripts, photographs and personal belongings are on display. Blixen's grave is in the surrounding park.

Karen Blixen

Karen Blixen was born in 1885. The most colourful period in the Danish writer's life was her stay in Africa. Blixen left for Kenya at the age of 28 with her Swedish husband, Baron Bror von Blixen-Finecke, to establish a coffee plantation. While in Kenya she wrote *Seven Gothic Tales*, a collection of stories that launched her career. Safari expeditions, the raptures and miseries of her affairs, the breakdown of her marriage and the eventual failure of the plantation are all themes of her best-known work, *Out of Africa*, which established her reputation. The author returned to Rungsted in 1931 and lived here until her death in 1962. Among Blixen's other famous stories is *Babette's Feast*, which was made into a film in 1987.

Karen Blixen's House
Only part of the original house is still standing; two wings burned down when Blixen was 13 years old.

Blixen's Grave
The park behind the house contains a beech tree, with a modest gravestone underneath. This is the final resting place of Karen Blixen, who died at the age of 77.

African Room
Displayed in the room are Masai shields and spears as well as other mementos brought back from Africa.

Karen Blixen
Despite suffering from cancer Blixen wrote right up to her death. Towards the end, unable to write herself, she dictated her thoughts to her secretary

The Film Version
The screen version of Out of Africa *stars Robert Redford and Meryl Streep. It was directed by Sydney Pollack (above) and departs markedly from the novel.*

Out of Africa
Out of Africa *was first published in 1937. It was originally written by the author in English and then translated by Blixen herself into Danish. The cover seen here is of the rare first Danish edition.*

Louisiana Museum ❺

This striking museum was established in 1958 to house a collection of modern Danish art. The museum's remit has expanded considerably since then and the collection now includes modern American and European paintings, graphic art and photography. The location and architecture are equally impressive. Light-filled galleries form a semi-circle round a 19th-century villa and open out onto a tranquil park filled with sculpture and offering stunning views of the Øresund. Among the many artists represented here are Giacometti, Henry Moore, Picasso and Warhol.

★ **Big Thumb (1968)**
The French artist César was fascinated by the shape of his thumb. This bronze image is 185 cm (73 inches) high.

Le Déjeuner sur l'Herbe (1961)
Picasso's painting is in homage to a famous work by Edouard Manet painted nearly 100 years earlier.

GALLERY GUIDE
Single-storey galleries are connected by a corridor to the south wing and underground galleries. Works are on rotation apart from a room devoted to Giacometti. A children's wing has workshops, art materials and computers for kids and their families.

Sculpture garden

Exit

★ **Vénus de Meudon (1956)**
This work by the French sculptor and painter Jean Arp depicts a woman's body reduced to its simplest form.

Asger Jorn Room
This gallery is dedicated to the abstract works of Asger Jorn (1914–73), an important figure in 20th-century Danish art.

Main entrance

KEY

▉	Exhibition space
▢	Cinema
▢	Giacometti collection
▢	Children's wing

Concert hall

VISITORS' CHECKLIST

Road map ⌐4.
Humlebæk Gl. Strandvej 13.
Tel 49 19 07 19. 🚉
⬭ 11am–10pm Tue–Fri,
11am–6pm Sat, Sun & hols. 🌐
www.louisiana.dk

Café
*On sunny days you can eat out-
side, enjoying coastal views and
the works in the sculpture garden.*

Marilyn Monroe (1967)
*Obsessed by the legendary
actress's suicide in 1962, Andy
Warhol set about immortalizing
the film star by endlessly duplicating her
image, using a silk-screen process to
transfer the picture onto canvas.*

The Graphics Wing,
opened in 1991, was
built underground to
protect its displays
from daylight.

Two Piece Reclining Figure No. 5 (1963–64)
*This Henry Moore bronze is in the sculpture
garden, in keeping with the artist's intention to
blend the female figure with the landscape.*

Ground floor

★ **South Wing**
*The south wing
of the museum
was added in
1982 and is
half buried in a
hillside facing the
Øresund. It houses
temporary and
special exhibitions.*

STAR EXHIBITS

★ Big Thumb

★ South Wing

★ Vénus de Meudon

Helsingør

Helsingør owes its prosperity to its location on the sound that links the North Sea with the Baltic. The town was a centre of international shipping during the 1400s, when Erik of Pomerania levied a tax on every ship passing through its local waters. In 1857 the dues were abolished, causing a temporary economic decline in the town's fortunes. This downturn was reversed in 1864 with the opening of a railway line and ferry services to Sweden. Today, most people visit Helsingør to see Kronborg Slot (*see pp126–7*), a late-16th-century castle that was used by William Shakespeare as the setting for *Hamlet*.

Exploring Helsingør

When sightseeing in Helsingør it is a good idea to start with a visit to the Carmelite Monastery and the Municipal Museum, and then continue with a walk along Biergegade promenade, turning occasionally into side streets (Stengade in particular). Further south is the tourist information centre in Havnepladsen and, a little further on, the ferry terminal.

Gothic cloisters surrounding the Karmeliterklosteret's courtyard

🔒 Karmeliterklosteret Sankt Mariæ Kirke

Sankt Anna Gade 38. ***Tel*** *49 21 17 74.* ◯ *mid-May–mid-Sep: 10am–3pm daily; mid-Sep–mid-May: 10am–2pm daily.* 📷 **www**.sctmariae.dk

This Gothic building once belonged to the Carmelites and was erected in the second half of the 15th century. It is considered to be one of the best-preserved medieval monasteries anywhere in Scandinavia and was described by H.C. Andersen as "one of the most beautiful spots in Denmark".

Among its many features are the chapterhouse with its barrel vault and the "Bird Room" decorated with ornithological frescoes. Christian II's mistress, Dyveke, who died in 1517, is believed to be buried in the grounds.

🏛 Helsingør Bymuseum

Sankt Anna Gade 36. ***Tel*** *49 28 18 00.* ◯ *noon–4pm Sun–Fri, 10am–2pm Sat.* 📷

The building that currently houses the town museum was erected by friars from the neighbouring monastery, who used it as a hospital for sailors arriving at the local harbour. Some of the instruments once used by the friars for brain surgery in the hospital are on display together with other exhibits relating to the town's past including a model of Kronborg Slot as it was in 1801. Visitors to the museum can also learn about the origin of the region's name: Øresund refers to the levy demanded by Erik of Pomerania which translates as "Penny Sound" ("øre" is the Danish penny, and "sund" means "sound").

Old apothecary on display in the town museum

🏛 Axeltorv

Helsingør's main square has a number of restaurants and bars. On Wednesday and Saturday mornings there is a colourful local market here that sells flowers, vegetables, fresh fish, handicrafts, cheese and souvenirs.

The statue in the centre depicts Erik of Pomerania – the Polish king and nephew of Margrethe I who occupied the throne of Denmark between 1397 and 1439. Following the break-up of the Kalmar Union and his subsequent dethronement in 1439 in favour of Christoffer III of Bavaria, the ex-monarch moved to the Swedish island of Gotland. Here, he began to occupy himself with piracy and he is sometimes referred to as "the last Baltic Viking".

In his old age Erik returned to Pomerania and is buried in the Polish town of Darlowo. One legend has it that Darlowo's castle still contains hidden treasure plundered from Denmark.

Monument to Erik of Pomerania in Axeltorv

🚮 Stengade

Helsingør's medieval quarter includes Stengade, a pedestrianized street that is linked by various alleyways to Axeltorv. Many of the colourful half-timbered houses once belonged to merchants and ferrymen and date from the 17th and 18th centuries. Oderns Gård, at Stengade No. 66, was built in 1459.

Statue of the Virgin Mary, Skt Olai's Kirke

🏠 Sankt Olai Kirke

Sankt Anna Gade 12. *Tel 49 21 04 43.* ⬜ *May–Aug: 10am–4pm Mon–Fri; Sep–Apr: 10am–2pm Mon–Fri.* 🈳

This building was consecrated around 1200 and served for centuries as a parish church. It was elevated to the rank of cathedral in 1961. Numerous elaborate epitaphs can be seen commemorating the many rich merchants and distinguished citizens of Helsingør who are buried here. The church's present-day appearance dates from 16th-century modifications when it also acquired its current furnishings. Among its most precious possessions are a 15th-century Gothic crucifix, a Renaissance pulpit (1568) and a carved wooden altar.

🏛 Museet for Søfart

Dok 1. *Tel 49 21 06 85.* ⬜ *Check website for opening hours prior to your visit.* 📶 🛇 📷 ⬜ www.maritime-museum.dk

Formerly located inside Kronborg Castle, the Danish Maritime Museum is now in purpose-built premises on the site of the old Helsingør shipyard. The building blends with the industrial landscape of the docks, but its modern architecture (featuring, among other things, suspended metal walkways) also provides a stark contrast to the old concrete quayside. The exhibition halls, many of them located underground, display artifacts related to the Danish naval fleet and the seafaring world in general. Many exhibits are interactive and child-friendly.

🐟 Øresundakvariet

Strandpromenaden 5. *Tel 49 21 37 72.* ⬜ *Jun–Aug: 10am–5pm daily; Sep–May: 10am–4pm Mon–Fri, 10am–5pm Sat & Sun.* 🈳 www.oresundsakvariet.ku.dk

In addition to a colourful collection of tropical fish from around the world, Helsingør's aquarium contains many species taken from the waters of the Øresund (Sound). These local varieties include Baltic jellyfish and seahorses.

A model ship at the Maritime Museum

HELSINGØR TOWN CENTRE

Axeltorv ③
Helsingør Bymuseum ②
Karmeliterklosteret ①
Museet for Søfart ⑥
Øresundakvariet ⑦
Sankt Olai Kirke ⑤
Stengade ④

0 m   300
0 yards   300

LAPPEN
STRANDPROMENADEN
STRAND ALLE
SANKT ANNA GADE
MARIENLYST ALLE
ALLEGADE
LUNDEGADE
KRONBORGVEJ
Øresundakvariet ⑦
Maritime Museum ⑥
KRONBORGVEJ
Kronborg Slot (see pp126–7)
MØLLEBAKKEN
Helsingør Kirkegård
Karmeliterklosteret ①
Axeltorv ③
Helsingør Bymuseum ②
Sankt Olai Kirke ⑤
HAVNEGADE
STENGADE
ILL. TVEDESVEJ
SUDERGADE
STJERNEGADE
BRAMSTRÆDE
FIOLGADE
STENGADE
TRÆKBANEN
STENGADE
STRANDG
JERNBANEVEJ
Helsingør Station ④
KONGEVEJEN
FÆRGEVEJ

Key to Symbols *see back flap*

Kronborg Slot ❼

Hamlet's "Castle of Elsinore" was originally
built by Erik of Pomerania in the early 15th
century. It was remodelled by Frederik II
and later by Christian IV but still retains an
eerie quality that makes it perfect for the
many productions of Shakespeare's play
performed here. Among the most impressive
rooms are the 62-m (203-ft) Great Hall, the
King's Chamber, which has a ceiling painted
by the Dutch artist Gerrit van Honthorst,
and the "Lille Sal" containing 16th-century
silk tapestries by the Flemish painter
Hans Knieper. The castle was added to
UNESCO's World Heritage List in 2000.

Exterior
*Originally
constructed
using red
brick, in
1580 the
castle was
remodelled on
the orders of
Frederik II
and faced
with attractive
sandstone.*

Trumpeter's Tower

Viking Chief
*The dungeons contain a sleeping
statue of Holger Danske, a Viking
chief. According to
legend he will
wake up should
Denmark find itself
in peril.*

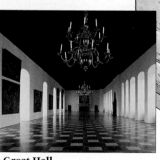

★ Great Hall
*Once the longest hall in
northern Europe, it was
completed in 1582 and is
decorated with paintings
from Rosenborg Slot. The
chandeliers date from the
17th century.*

STAR FEATURES

★ Chapel

★ Great Hall

★ "Lille Sal"

HAMLET

Shakespeare probably
never visited Kronborg, but
it is here that he set one of
his best-known plays. The
prototype for the fictional
Danish prince was Amlet,
a Viking king whose story
is recounted by the 12th-

century Danish chronicler Saxo Grammaticus in his *Historia
Danica* (Danish History). Shakespeare may have encountered
this classic tale of murder and revenge via Francois de
Belleforest's *Histoires Tragiques* (Tragic Histories), published
in 1570. A festival is held in the castle each year during which
Hamlet and other works by Shakespeare are performed.

King's Tower
Built during 1584–5, this was also known as the "Turner's Tower" because one of its rooms housed Frederik II's turnery containing lathes.

VISITORS' CHECKLIST

Road map F4.
Kronborgvej, DK 3000, Helsingør. **Tel** 49 21 30 78.
Fax 49 21 30 52.
◻ Apr, May, Sep & Oct: 11am–4pm daily; Jun–Aug: 10am–5:30pm daily; Nov–Mar: 11am–4pm Tue–Sun.
🖳 www.kronborg.dk

★ **"Lille Sal"**
The "small room" has seven tapestries depicting Danish kings with verses describing their various achievements.

The North Wing
was completed in 1585. Its western section contained the castle offices.

The Queen's Chambers at the corner of the north wing had direct access to the chapel, via the east wing.

Royal Chambers
These rooms contain ornate ceiling decorations and marble fireplaces. At one time the walls would have been lined with gold-embossed leather.

★ **Chapel**
The chapel has a beautiful altar, oak benches with intricately carved ends, a royal balcony and an organ dating from the early 18th century.

The Pigeon Tower
housed birds that were used for sending important royal messages.

Clean sandy beaches of Hornbæk

Hornbæk ❽

Road map F4. 🚌 🚆 ℹ️ *Vestre
Stejlebakke 2A.* **Tel** *49 70 47 47.*
www.visitnordsjaelland.com

The northern shore of
Zealand is famous for its
pleasant sandy beaches,
clean water and the small
town of Hornbæk, which has
for years been a favoured
resort. A large number of
visitors come from
Copenhagen, many
of whom have built
holiday homes here.
In summer the
resort fills with
holiday-makers
enjoying various
outdoor pursuits,
including sailing
and swimming.

Former Cistercian
monastery buildings

Environs
Esrum, situated southwest of
Hornbæk, is famous mainly
for its Cistercian monastery,
Esrum Kloster. Founded in
1151, it was regarded as
one of the most important
monasteries in Denmark
during the Middle Ages.
Its prominence was acknowledged even by the monar-
chy: in 1374 Queen Helvig,
wife of Valdemar IV, was
buried here. Even the fires
that plagued the establishment (in 1194 and 1204) did
not prevent the monastery
from becoming one of the
largest buildings in Scandinavia. During the Lutheran
Reformation in the 16th
century much of the church
was demolished and the

materials were used to build
Kronborg Slot *(see pp126–7).*
What remained of the buildings passed into the hands of
the monarch and the premises
were used first as a hunting
base and later as warehouses
before being turned into army
barracks. In the 20th century
they were used as offices, as
a post office and then as an
orphanage. During World
War II they became an air-
raid shelter and a fireproof
store for valuable documents
brought here from the
National Archives, and
for the Royal Library
collection.
   This chequered
history came to
an end when a
decision was
reached to
renovate the
ancient walls and
in 1997 the former monastery
opened to visitors. Its main
building now houses an
exhibition devoted to the
Cistercian order while the
vaults have been transformed
into a café. Also open to
visitors is the herb garden,
where medicinal plants are
grown and used, as they once
were when the monastery
flourished. Some of the plants
are used to produce a
flavoured beverage, which
is on sale in the shop.
   Not far from the monastery
is **Esrum Møllegard**, a 400-
year old mill. The mill was
first used to grind grain, and
later to generate electricity.
Today, it houses a centre for
environmental awareness.

Gilleleje ❾

Road map F4. 🚶 *6,000.* 🚆
ℹ️ *Hovedgade 6F.* **Tel** *48 30 01 74.*
www.visitnordsjaelland.com

The northernmost town in
Zealand is also one of the
oldest Danish fishing ports
and contains the island's
largest harbour. From
historical records it has been
established that the local
inhabitants were engaged in
fishing here as early as the
mid-14th century. Today,
Gilleleje is an attractive town
with thatched houses, a busy
harbour-side fishing auction
and a colourful main street
that has been turned into a
promenade. Rising above the
fisherman's cottages is the
town's church – Gilleleje
Kirke. During the German
occupation locals used the
church as a hiding place
for Danish Jews who were
then smuggled into neutral
Sweden aboard fishing boats
under cover of darkness.
   Other places of interest
include **Gilleleje Museum**,
devoted to the town's history,
and **Det Gamle Hus**, an old
fisherman's house that
illustrates the realities of
everyday life for a mid-19th-
century fishing family. A
coastal trail from the town
centre leads east to the
Nakkehoved Østre Fyr
lighthouse. Built in 1772, this
is one of a very few coal-
fuelled lighthouses in the
world to have survived to this
day. This historic building is
now open to visitors.

Nakkehoved Østre Fyr, a coal-fired
lighthouse near Gilleleje

Fishing boats in Gilleleje's harbour

Environs: The Gilbjergstien is a 2.5-km (1.5-mile) foot- and cycle path leading from Vesterbrogade, in Gilleleje, all the way to Gilbjergshoved, Zealand's northernmost point. The path offers splendid views across the water to Sweden from the cliffs. En route you can admire the Gilbjergstenen rock, which has a natural seat and back support, and a monument to the Danish philosopher Soren Kirkegaard.

🏛 Gilleleje Museum
Vesterbrogade 56. *Tel* 72 49 99 50.
◯ Jun–Aug: 1–4pm Wed–Mon;
Sep–May: 1–4pm Wed–Fri,
10am–2pm Sat. 🎫 includes a visit
to the lighthouse.

🏛 Det Gamle Hus
Hovedgade 49, Gilleleje.
Tel 48 30 16 31. 🎫

Fredensborg Slot ❿

Road map F4. *Tel* 33 40 31 87.
Palace, Chapel, Orangery and
Herb Garden ◯ Jul: 1–4:30pm
daily. 🎫 compulsory; every 15 mins
(duration about 35 mins). 🎫
Gardens ◯ 9am–5pm daily.
www.ses.dk

Frederik IV decided to build Fredensborg Castle in order to commemorate the 1720 peace treaty between Denmark and Sweden at the end of the Nordic Wars (Fredensborg means "Town of Peace"). The building was originally used as a hunting lodge. Nowadays

the castle is one of the main residences of the Danish royal family and is often used to receive VIPs from all over the world. According to tradition, guests who spend the night at the palace must sign their name on a glass pane using a diamond pen.

The original design was modelled on French and Italian castles and the long list of contributors who influenced its final shape includes renowned architects such as Niels Eigtved, Lauritz de Thurah and Caspar Frederik Harsdorf. The present-day complex consists of 28 separate buildings. At its centre is the Dome Hall (Kuppelsalen), surmounted by a dome crowned with a lantern. The magnificent room is encircled by a gallery, which divides the hall into two levels. It is used for formal royal family occasions and also for entertaining special guests.

One of the most interesting rooms in the palace is Havesalon, or the Garden Room, which features a wide door leading to the castle gardens. Its ceiling is

Fredensborg's gardens decorated
with numerous statues

decorated with a painting by Henrik Krock depicting Denmark and Norway begging the Olympian gods for help against Sweden.

Fredenborg Slot's ornate Chinese Dining Room (Kinesisk Spisesalon) is another notable room. It is decorated in yellow and red and houses a collection of Chinese porcelain.

The palace garden was established in the 1760s, and contains a lane decorated with a sculpted group of 70 figures, created by J.G. Grund, of fishermen and farmers from Norway and the Faroe Islands. Plants sensitive to cold, including a 250-year-old myrtle shrub, are shielded from low temperatures in a greenhouse built in 1995.

Fredensborg Slot, used as a residence by the Danish royal family

A Tour Around Esrum Sø and Arresø ⓫

These beautiful lakes are the two largest in Denmark and attract a great many visitors, especially in summer. Gribskov, on the west bank of Esrum Sø, is a forested area where marked paths and bicycle trails lead through thick clusters of ancient beech and spruce trees. Arresø, to the east of Esrum Sø, is Denmark's largest lake and reaches depths of 22 m (72 ft). Ospreys and cormorants can occasionally be spotted diving for fish. As well as being perfect for anglers, bathers and enthusiastic sailors, a tour around the area takes in lush farmland, ancient church ruins, picturesque towns and historic medieval villages.

Ramløse ③
Situated on Arresø's north bank *(above)*, the town's most interesting feature is its Dutch-style windmill (1908) that can be seen working on traditional "Mill Days".

Asserbo ②
Scenic ruins surrounded by a wind-blown forest are all that remains of this former fortress, built in 1100 on the orders of Bishop Absalon.

HUNDESTED

Arresø

Helsinge

Tulstrup

COPENH

Frederiksværk ①
Frederiksværk, built alongside a canal, is Denmark's oldest industrial town. A museum in a former gunpowder factory has exhibits on the town's industrial past.

Æbelholt Kloster ⑩
This 12th-century Augustinian abbey was once a hospital. Today, as well as viewing the ruins, visitors can examine the museum's collection of surgical instruments.

Esrum ⑤
The restored buildings of this former Cistertian monastery house a museum devoted to the community that lived here, giving visitors an idea of the monk's day-to-day life.

TIPS FOR DRIVERS

Length: about 100 km (62 miles). *Stopping-off points:* There is a large choice of restaurants and accommodation in Fredensborg.
www.visitdenmark.com
www.visitnordsjaelland.com

Annisse Nord ④
Annisse Nord is a sleepy village but was strategically important for the surrounding area in medieval times; at that time numerous watchtowers were erected along the fjord.

Fredensborg Slot ⑥
The castle gardens are arranged in a Baroque style and are open to the public all year round (*see p129*).

GILLELEJE

ELEJE

205

227

Esrum Sø

Gurre Sø

HELSINGØR

235

6

COPENHAGEN

9

8

6

227

6

7

19

19

COPENHAGEN

Fredensborg ⑦
This historic town has a long tradition of hunting and holds regular demonstrations of falconry.

Gribskov ⑨
Growing along the undulating western shoreline of Esrum Sø, Gribskov is the second largest forest in the country.

KEY

▬	Suggested route
▬	Scenic route
═	Other road
═	River, lake
☆	Viewpoint

0 km   2

0 miles   2

Nødebo ⑧
The tiny village of Nødebo is on the banks of Esrum Sø (*left*) and surrounded by Gribskov. The pretty village church is decorated with 15th-century frescoes.

Frederiksborg Slot ⑫

The first royal residence was constructed on this site by Frederik II in 1560. A fire in 1859 destroyed most of the castle, which may well have remained a ruin were it not for Carlsberg boss J.C. Jacobsen who restored the building and helped found a national history museum. The museum now takes up 80 or so of the palace rooms. Jacobsen also donated many of his own paintings which, along with others, are arranged chronologically to chart Denmark's history. Period furnishings and some magnificent architecture help to conjure up a feel for the country's past.

★ Slotskirken
From 1671 until 1840 the castle chapel was used to crown Denmark's monarchs. Its ebony altar dates from 1606 and is the work of Jakob Mores, a German goldsmith.

★ Riddersalen
The Knights' Hall has a carved wooden ceiling. The gilded ornaments, a 19th-century black marble fireplace and intricate tapestries add to the splendour.

Audienssalen
The Audience Chamber was completed in 1688. Among the paintings lining the walls is a portrait of a proud-looking Christian V, depicted as a Roman emperor surrounded by his children.

STAR FEATURES

★ Riddersalen

★ Slotskirken

Chapel Portal
The oak door, set within a sandstone portal in the shape of a triumphal arch, survived the fire of 1859 and looks as it would have done in Christian IV's day.

For hotels and restaurants in this region see pp247–9 and pp274–6

Queen Sophie's Room
During the reign of Christian IV this room was used by the king's mother. When the palace became a museum, it was hung with paintings associated with Frederik III.

VISITORS' CHECKLIST

Road map ⌐4. 3400 Hillerød, Slotsgade 1. **Tel** 48 26 04 39. ☐ Apr–Sep: 10am–5pm daily; Oct–Mar: 11am–3pm daily. 🅶
Baroque gardens
☐ 10am–sunset daily.
www.dnm.dk

The Royal Wing has a gallery of statues symbolizing the influence of planets on human life and is an excellent example of Dutch Mannerism.

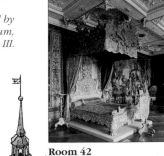

Room 42
This example of over-blown Baroque is typical of the taste associated with Denmark's era of absolute monarchy (see pp38–9). The bed with silk draperies was made in France in 1724.

Gardens
The castle gardens were established in the 1720s and restored in 1996. The carefully trimmed shrubs create a symmetrical pattern typical of a Baroque garden.

Room 46
All of the items in this room, such as this ornate wall clock, are in perfect accord with the colours and Rococo excess of the overall design.

Grønnesse Skov ⓭

Road map F4.

The ancient forest of
Grønnesse Skov is about
5 km (3 miles) east of
Hundested, on the shores
of Roskilde Fjord. Archaeological excavations indicate
that during the Neolithic era
this area was one of the more
important sites of early
culture in Zealand and the
site now attracts thousands
of visitors every year.

One of the most important
relics of Denmark's Neolithic
past is an extraordinary burial
chamber known as a dolmen.
It is one of many such tombs
in Denmark and consists of
a huge flat stone resting on
three chunky pillars. The
dolmen is referred to locally
as Carlssten ("Carl's Stone")
and is one of the biggest and
best preserved of its type
anywhere in Denmark. It
must be reached on foot but
the forest car park is only a
short distance away.

Prehistoric Carlssten, Grønnesse Skov

Hundested ⓮

Road map E4. 🚃 🛈 *Jernbanegade
8.* **Tel** *47 93 77 88.*
www.visitnordsjaelland.com

This small town lies on a
slender peninsula. Its name
translates literally as "dog's
place" and derives from a
species of local seal
commonly known as a sea
dog because of its canine-like
barking. The main reason
to come to Hundested is to
take a look around **Knud
Rasmussens Hus**, which is
situated on a high cliff close
to Spodsbjerg lighthouse. The
house was built in 1907 by
the intrepid Arctic explorer,
Knud Rasmussen, and now
houses a museum devoted to
his life and travels. Close by
is a monument to him erected
in 1936 made of stones
brought over from Greenland.

Environs
A short way northeast is
Kikhavn, the oldest fishing
village on the Halsnæs
peninsula, which dates back
to the 13th century. In the
18th century there were
many small farms here,
some of which were
partly destroyed by a storm
in 1793. A handful of
these have now been
reconstructed to form
an open-air museum.
Kikhaven is also the
starting point of a
footpath, **Halsnæsstien**,

**Knud Rasmussen's house, now a
popular museum**

that links the shores of
Isefjord and Kattegat.
Another place worth
visiting is **Lynæs**, just south
of Hundested. The local
church, built in 1901 from
huge granite blocks, serves
as a navigational guide for
returning fishermen. A
monument standing by the
church commemorates those
who lost their lives at sea.

🏛 **Knud Rasmussens Hus**
Tel *47 72 06 05.* ☐ *Apr–Oct:
11am–4pm Tue–Sun.* 🖼

**Kongeegen, believed to be the
oldest living oak tree in Europe**

Nordskoven ⓯

Road map F4.

The peninsula that
separates Roskilde Fjord
from Isefjord contains one
of Denmark's most beautiful
beech forests. The forest
has two sections, known
as Fællesskoven and Stude-
haven. Running between
them is a 15-km (9-mile)
long bicycle trail with views

KNUD RASMUSSEN

Knud Rasmussen was born in 1879. Half Inuit himself,
Rasmussen was fascinated by Inuit culture and language and
resolved to become a polar explorer at an early age. He
took part in his first scientific expedition in 1900 and soon
began organizing them himself. In 1910, together with Peter
Freuchen, he founded the Thule settlement in the north of
Greenland. Between 1921 and 1924 Rasmussen completed a
grand expedition from Greenland to the Bering Straight,
covering 18,000 km (11,185
miles) by dog-sleigh. From
each of his expeditions the
explorer brought back many
artifacts; most of these are
now in the Nationalmuseet
in Copenhagen *(see
pp84–5).* In the course of
his seventh expedition
Rasmussen fell seriously ill.
He died in 1933, aged 54.

**The explorer's house, full of
reminders of his expeditions**

Statue of a deer in front of Jægerspris Slot

over Roskilde Fjord. At its highest point, called Frederikshøj, is a hunting pavilion built by Frederik VII in 1875. A number of ancient trees can be found in the forest including three famous oaks: Kongeegen, Storkeegen and Snoegen, which have inspired many artists. Kongeegen, the most ancient of the three trees, is believed to be 1,500–1,900 years old. In 1973 its last bough broke away, leaving only the vast trunk, which has a circumference of 14 m (46 ft).

Jægerspris Slot ⑯

Road map F4. 🏰 *Jægerspris Slot, Slotsgården 20.* **Tel** *47 53 10 04.* ⏰ *Apr–Oct: 11am–4pm Tue–Sun.* 🌳 **Park** ⏰ *all year round.* **www.** kongfrederik.dk

This medieval castle, situated about 6 km (4 miles) west of Frederikssund, has been used by Danish royalty since the early 14th century and is now open to the public. The first royal building, known as Abrahamstrup, still exists although it has been swallowed by the north wing of the present complex. A life-size statue of a deer standing before the entrance to the castle is by Adelgund Vogt, a pupil of Bertel Thorvaldsen.

In the mid-19th century Frederik VII made the palace his summer residence. After his death in 1863 the monarch's widow, Countess Danner, turned part of the palace into a refuge for poor and unwanted girls. The centre became the first children's home in Denmark. A special exhibition illustrates the often austere way of life in an early 20th-century Danish orphanage.

Much of the house still retains its royal character, and visitors can take a look at magnificent rooms arranged by Frederik VII. There is also an exhibition of archaeological finds reflecting one of Frederik VII's abiding passions.

The gardens stretching to the rear of the castle include Zealand's largest collection of rhododendrons; standing among them are 54 obelisks with busts of famous Danish personages. The tomb of countess Danner is also in the castle gardens.

Frederikssund ⑰

Road map F4. 🏰 *17,000.* 🚉 🛈 *Havnegade 5A.* **Tel** *47 31 06 85.* 🚢 *Viking Festival (mid-Jun–early Jul).* **www.**visitfrederikssund.dk

This town was founded in 1655 on the orders of Frederik III. The choice of site was not accidental, as it overlooks the narrowest part of the Roskilde Fjord and was used for many years by boats crossing to the other side.

In the town centre is the **J.F. Willumsens Museum**. Willumsen (1863–1958), a prominent Danish Symbolist painter, donated his paintings, sculptures and drawings to Frederikssund on condition that a suitable building be erected to display them. The museum also contains works by other artists that were collected by Willumsen.

Frederikssund is primarily known, however, for its reconstructed **Viking Village**, located near the town's harbour. The village is open to visitors all year round but the best time to visit is during the summer Viking Festival, when events are held that involve the whole town. The most popular are the evening Viking plays that feature 200 actors, many of them local residents and children; the final night is celebrated with a grand banquet.

🏛 **J.F. Willumsens Museum**
Jenriksvej 4. **Tel** *47 31 07 73.* ⏰ *10am–5pm Tue–Sun.* 🚢

Danes dressed as Vikings during Frederikssund's summer festival

Selsø Slot, built in 1578

Selsø Slot ⑱

Road map F4. 🏠 Selsøvej 30A, 4050 Skibby. *Tel 52 17 20 60.* ⏰ *May–mid-Sep: 11am–4pm Tue–Sun.* 🈯 **www**.selsoe.dk

This property's history dates back to the 12th century. According to records, Bishop Absalon became interested in the site in about 1170 and by 1228 a sumptuous residence had been built here.

The present castle was built in 1578. It was reworked in 1734 and much of its original Renaissance style was replaced with Baroque details. The castle is now a museum and gives visitors an idea of what aristocratic life was like in the 1800s. The castle's stern, simple exterior hides a richer interior, including the "Grand Ballroom". With original marble panels and a decorated ceiling, it is used as a venue for classical music concerts. Wine-tasting sessions are held in the castle vaults. The castle church has an altarpiece dating from 1605.

The property owes much of its charm to its location on the banks of Selsø lake. A bird reserve established in the gardens is one of the premium places for bird-watching in Denmark. A viewing tower standing in the garden was built specifically for this purpose.

Skibby ⑲

Road map F4. 🚌 🏠 Havnegade 5A, 3600 Frederikssund. *Tel 47 31 06 85.* **www**.visitfrederikssund.dk

The main town of the peninsula between Roskilde Fjord and Isefjord, Skibby is known mainly for its early 12th-century church, which is decorated with some well-preserved frescoes. The oldest of these were found in 1855 in the Romanesque apses and date from the second half of the 12th century. Similar decorations can be found in other churches in the district, including some at nearby Dråby. In 1650 a manuscript, known as the *Skibby Chronicle*, was found buried behind the altar. The work, written in Latin, recounts the history of Denmark between 1046 and 1534. It is uncertain why the chronicle was found here. Its style points to the authorship of Paul Helgsen, a Carmelite monk and orator. Helgsen was a native of Helsingør, however, and since the work is unfinished, its discovery has provoked debate as to the fate of its author. Skibby's other claim to fame is as the location of Scandinavia's first nudist swimming pool.

Environs
Northeast of Skibby, in the town of Skuldelev, is a **doll museum** with a 6,000-strong collection. Also on display are antique baby carriages, dolls' prams and a working model railway from 1940 (runs from March to October).

Roskilde ⑳

See pp140–41.

Trying out a dugout canoe at Lejre's Stone Age village

Lejre ㉑

Road map F4. **Open-air museum** Slangealleen 2, 4320 Lejre. *Tel 46 48 08 78.* ⏰ *May, Jun & late Aug–mid-Sep: 10am–4pm Tue–Fri, 11am–5pm Sat & Sun; end Jun–late Aug: 10am–5pm daily.* 🈯 **www**.sagnlandet.dk

A reconstructed village that takes visitors back to the Iron Age is the main attraction of Lejre, which is situated 8 km (5 miles) to the southwest of Roskilde. In summer Sagnlandet Lejre ("Land of Legends") is populated by volunteer Danish families

Dråby Kirke, situated near Skibby

◁ Frederiksborg Slot and its surrounding gardens seen from the lake

Ledreborg Slot, surrounded by beautiful, well-kept gardens

who, in the name of research, dress in prehistoric furs and skins, use traditional tools and carry out all-but-forgotten chores such as chopping firewood and making clay pots.

The village is popular with children, especially in summer, when it is possible for them to take part in activities such as archery, dying clothes and paddling a dugout canoe. The centre also has a 19th-century cottage farm that re-creates the lives of Danish farmers of that period.

Lejre was one of the earliest centres of government in Denmark. Legend has it that it was the seat of a royal Stone-Age clan, the Skjoldungs, although the building shown to the visitors, once home of the supposed sovereign, is an 18th-century re-creation. It is quite likely, however, that the nearby grave-mound dates from the Stone Age period. The **Lejre Museum** has displays on the Skjoldung clan and artifacts from Viking times, as well as from the Stone and Iron ages.

fi Lejre Museum
Orehøjvej 4B. ☐ 11am–4pm Sat & Sun (Jul & Aug: 11am–4pm daily).

Ledreborg Slot ⑳

Road map F4. Ledreborg Alle 2, 4320 Lejre. **Tel** 46 48 00 38. ☐ only for events. **Park** ☐ 11am–4pm daily (all year round). 🖳 www.ledreborg-slot.dk

Elegant on the outside and opulent on the inside, Ledreborg Slot is one of the foremost examples of Baroque architecture in northern

Europe. It was built in 1739 on the orders of Count Johan Ludvig Holstein. In 1745 this exclusive residence acquired a chapel, which until 1899 served as a parish church.

The palace is closed to the public, but it is possible to explore the pleasant gardens that surround it. The neatly trimmed hedges make it one of the most enchanting Baroque gardens in the whole of Scandinavia. The grounds host a lifestyle exhibition in May and an outdoor chamber music concert in August.

Holbæk ㉓

Road map F4. 🏠 30,000. 🚉
🚹 Klosterstræde 18, 59 43 11 31.
www.visitholback.dk

An important port, Holbæk is also the main commercial town for the area. It serves as a good starting point for people wishing to visit Ørø island, which lies just 7 km (4 miles) away. The area has several bicycle trails, and Holbæk itself is popular with cyclists.

Holbæk was granted municipal privileges in the late 13th century, making it one of the oldest of Zealand's towns. At that time it was the site of a dynamic Dominican monastery, although the oldest surviving remains are those of a Franciscan monastery, which is located next to the Neo-Gothic Sankt Nicolaj Kirke in the medieval part of the town.

Not far from this church is **Holbæk Museum**, which consists of a dozen or so period houses dating from 1660 to 1867. Their interiors include typical items and furnishings from rural and urban dwellings of the 17th and 18th centuries. There is also a reconstructed grocery shop, café, toy shop and pottery exhibition. The tiny market square between the houses is a venue for numerous events staged during summer months, which often feature people dressed in period costumes.

Holbæk has some good local parks, such as Østre Anlæg and Bysøparken, which has a charming fountain. Just ouside the city is **Andelslandsbyen Nyvang**, an open-air museum that re-creates country life as it was from the 1870s until the 1950s.

fi Holbæk Museum
Klosterstræde 18. **Tel** 59 43 23 53.
☐ 10am–4pm Tue–Fri, noon–4pm Sun. 🖳 www.holbmus.dk

fi Andelslandsbyen Nyvang
Oldvejen 25. **Tel** 59 43 40 30.
☐ Apr–Oct: 10am–4pm Mon–Thu, 10am–5pm (4pm in Oct) Sat & Sun.

Period interior in Holbæk Museum

Roskilde ⑳

Founded in the 10th century by the Vikings, Roskilde was Denmark's first capital. In AD 980 Harald I (Bluetooth) built Zealand's first church here, making the town an important religious centre and from the 11th century it was a bishopric. In the Middle Ages Roskilde had a population of 10,000 and was one of the largest towns in northern Europe. When Erik of Pomerania moved the capital, the town lost much of its status but it flourishes today as a market centre for the region and is popular with visitors in summer who come to see the historic Viking ships and the ancient cathedral.

Exploring Roskilde
All of the town's attractions are within easy reach. The most prestigious streets, lined with shops and cafés, are Skomagergade and Algade. The Vikingeskibsmuseet (Viking Ship Museum) is by the harbour.

🏰 Roskilde Domkirke
See pp142–3.

Fountain in front of the town hall in Stændertorvet

🏛 Stændertorvet
This small square situated by the town's main promenade has for centuries been the heart of Roskilde. In the Middle Ages it was the site of fairs. Sankt Laurence, a Romanesque church, was demolished in the mid-16th century to provide more space for the growing market. A few remaining parts of the church can be seen today including the tower, which now adorns the town hall (built in 1884) and what remains of the church foundations. The foundations are open to the public and are in the town hall's vaults. In the square is a monument depicting, among others, Roar, the legendary father of Roskilde, who established Roskilde as homage to the two pagan gods, Thor and Odin.

🏰 Roskilde Palace
Stændertorvet 3.
Tel 46 31 65 65.
🕐 9am–7pm daily (to 8pm in summer). 🎫
Art Museum 🕐 11am–5pm Tue–Fri, noon–4pm Sat & Sun. www.samtidskunst.dk
Built in 1733 by the Danish architect Laurits de Thurah, this yellow Baroque palace is the former seat of Roskilde's bishops. It is linked to the neighbouring cathedral by the Arch of Absalon. Part of the palace houses the Museum of Contemporary Art (Museet for Samtidskunst), which organizes temporary exhibitions of Danish and foreign artists. Another wing is used by a local art association.

🏛 Roskilde Museum
Sankt Ols Gade 18. **Tel** 46 31 65 29.
🕐 11am–4pm daily. 🎫
www.roskildemuseum.dk
The municipal museum in Roskilde is an excellent place for anyone interested in the town's history. Its collection – including documents, photographs, archaeological finds and works of art – explains the region's past, from the Stone Age up to the present day (which is aptly symbolized by a display devoted to the prestigious rock festival organized every year in Roskilde since 1971). The museum also includes a building in Ringstedgade, named Brødrene Lützhøfts Købmandsgård, which is simply a shop furnished in a manner typical of a century or so ago, where potash soap and dried cod can be purchased.

Hussar's uniform, Roskilde Museum

🏰 Roskilde Kloster
Sankt Peder Stræde 8. **Tel** 46 35 02 19. 🕐 for tours only. 🎫 Easter & July: 11am & 2pm Wed (in Danish; book in advance for tours in English). 🎫 www.roskildekloster.dk
In the Middle Ages Roskilde had about 20 churches and monasteries, not counting the cathedral. Their sacral functions ceased as the Reformation swept through the country in 1536. This brick-built monastery, which stands in its own grounds, was built in 1560 and, in 1699, became Denmark's first refuge for unmarried mothers from well-to-do families. It has some fine interiors including a chapel, extensive library and a banqueting hall.

Brick monastery buildings of Roskilde Kloster

♣ Gråbrødre Kirkegård

The former cemetery, where prominent and wealthy citizens of the town were buried during the Middle Ages, is now used as a park and is located near the railway station. The station was built in 1847 to serve the Copenhagen–Roskilde line and is one of the oldest train stations in Denmark.

Roskilde Jars commemorating the city's 1,000-year anniversary

♞ Hestetorvet

The main landmark of the market square, used in medieval times for horse trading, are the three 5-m (16-ft) tall jars. These were put in place in 1998 as part of the town's millennium celebrations. Engraved on one of the jars are verses from a poem written by Henrik Nordbrandt, dedicated to Roskilde and to Margrete I. The jar's creator, Peter Brandes, intended them to symbolize life and death.

🏛 Vikingeskibsmuseet

Vindeboder 12. *Tel 46 30 02 53.*
◻ *Jul & Aug: 10am–5pm daily;
Sep–Jun: 10am–4pm daily.* 🖮
www.vikingeskibsmuseet.dk
About 1,000 years ago the boats now exhibited at the Viking Ship Museum were filled with stones and sunk in the fjord in order to block the passage of enemy ships. In 1962 five of the vessels were recovered. Although they had been underwater for so long, they are in remarkably good condition and give a good indication of Viking boat-building skills. The largest of them is a 30-m (98-ft) long warship with the capacity to carry a crew of 70 to 80 Vikings. The best preserved is a 14-m (46-ft) long merchant ship, which sailed around the Baltic and Danish sounds. The

Historic boat at Vikingeskibsmuseet

other ships are a deep-sea trader, a longship and a ferry. The museum also has an exhibition devoted to the Vikings and a working boatyard, where replicas of old Viking ships, including those in the museum, are built using traditional methods and materials. In summer it is possible to sail on a replica ship on the Roskilde Fjord. The museum also has a pleasant café, plus themed activities for children and adults.

> ### VISITORS' CHECKLIST
>
> **Road map** F4. 🚩 *50,000.*
> 🚉 🛈 *Stændertorvet 1.*
> *Tel 46 31 65 65.*
> 🎵 *Roskilde Rock Festival (late Jun–early Jul).*
> www.visitroskilde.com

ROSKILDE TOWN CENTRE

Gråbrødre Kirkegård ⑥
Hestetorvet ⑦
Roskilde Domkirke ①
Roskilde Kloster ⑤
Roskilde Museum ④
Roskilde Palace ③
Stændertorvet ②
Vikingeskibsmuseet ⑧

0 m   400
0 yards   400

Key to Symbols *see back flap*

Roskilde Domkirke

The twin towers of this magnificent brick cathedral, begun in the 12th century on the orders of Bishop Absalon, are a landmark of Roskilde. The cathedral is an organic mix of styles. For centuries it was used as the burial site of Danish monarchs, 38 of whom are interred here. The remains of Harald I (Bluetooth), a 10th-century Viking king, are said to be inside one of the columns to the side of the main altar. In view of its historic value the cathedral has been declared a UNESCO World Heritage Site.

★ Christian IV's Chapel
Christian IV supervised the construction of his own final resting place. The grand chapel contains a painting of the king in combat and a bronze statue by Bertel Thorvaldsen.

The South Tower has a unique clock with tiny moving figures including one of St Jørgen chasing a dragon.

St Birgitta's Chapel
As well as a wall painting of the four Fathers of the Church, the chapel contains various statues including St Christopher and Pope Lucius.

The storm bell is the oldest medieval bell in Denmark.

Main entrance

Pulpit
The pulpit was ordered by Christian IV in 1610. Its ornate carvings in marble, alabaster and sandstone were made by Hans Brokman of Copenhagen.

The Royal Column indicates the height of several Danish kings. Christian I is recorded as 2.06 m (6 ft 9 inches), although his skeleton is 1.88 m (6 ft 2 inches).

For hotels and restaurants in this region see pp247–9 and pp274–6

Stalls
Set near the altar these wooden pews are beautiful examples of Gothic carving.

VISITORS' CHECKLIST

Domkirkestræde 1. **Tel** *46 35 16 24.* 🔵 *Apr–Sep: 9am–5pm daily (from 12:30pm Sun & hols); Oct–Mar: 10am–4pm Tue–Sat, 12:30–4pm Sun & hols.* 🈲 **www**.roskildedomkirke.dk

Margrethe's Spire replaced a tower destroyed by fire in 1968.

★ Altarpiece
The altar, depicting scenes from the life of Christ, was produced in Antwerp in the 1500s. It is here quite by chance, having been confiscated while on board a ship bound for Gdansk.

Chapter House contains a crucifix made from two bells that melted in the 1968 fire.

★ Sarcophagus of Margrete I
The sarcophagus bearing an alabaster effigy of Margrete I as a young girl is considered to be the most beautiful sculpture in the cathedral.

Interior
The cathedral has been rebuilt several times, acquiring features typical of the styles that were currently in fashion. The last major works were carried out following a fire in 1968.

STAR FEATURES

★ Altarpiece

★ Christian IV's Chapel

★ Sarcophagus of Margrete I

Tveje Merløse Kirke ㉔

Road map E4. ⛪ Holbæk, Tveje Merløse 14. **Tel** 59 43 24 53.
◯ 8am–4pm daily.

Being a miniature version of Roskilde's original 12th-century cathedral, the church in Tveje Merløse, south of Holbæk, is one of the most interesting Romanesque sacral buildings in Denmark. Its most distinctive features are the two almost identical square towers. The history of the site as a place of worship is believed to date back to the Viking era; some records suggest it was used for worship even earlier than this, in the 3rd century.

The church's interior has an altarpiece by Joakim Skovgaard. At one time the church contained some colourful 13th-century frescoes depicting, among other things, the devil and the motif of God's Majesty, a typical medieval theme found particularly in the region of Øresund. These have been removed and are now on display in Copenhagen's Nationalmuseet (see pp84–5). A small cemetery is in the church grounds.

Nørre Jernløse Mølle ㉕

Road map E4.
Windmill Møllebakken 2, Regstrup. **Tel** 59 47 17 82. ◯ Apr–Oct: 10am–2pm 1st Sun of each month.
www.nrjernlosemolle.dk

The small village of Nørre Jernløse, located some 25 km (16 miles) west of Roskilde, has a 12th-century church containing 16th-century frescoes. The town is best known, however, for its 19th-century windmill, which is set on an sturdy octagonal base surrounded by a distinctive gallery.

The Dutch-style windmill was built in 1893 in Nørrevold, near Copenhagen, where it was known as Sankt Peders Mølle. When financial difficulties forced its owners to sell the mill it was bought by Niels Peter Rasmussen, a miller, who dismantled it and transported it in pieces on a horse cart to Jernløse, 70 km (43 miles) away. In 1899 the windmill was bought by Ole Martin Nielsen, whose family used and maintained it for the next 60 years. Finally, in 1979 the windmill was handed over to the parish of Jernløse.

Built on a stone base, the Nørre Jernløse mill has a timber structure with a shingled roof crowned with a wooden, onion-shaped cupola. Its sails were once cloth covered and could be operated directly from the gallery. The mill, which is no longer used to grind flour, now has an information centre where visitors can learn about the mill's history and about early methods of flour production.

Well in front of the monastery in Sorø

Sorø ㉖

Road map E5. ⛪ 7,000.
⛪ Storgade 15. **Tel** 57 82 10 12.
www.soroe.dk

Located on the banks of the Tuel and Sorø lakes, Sorø is one of the most beautiful towns in Zealand. In 1140 Bishop Absalon, the founder of Copenhagen, began to build a monastery here. When it was complete, the Klosterkirke was the largest building of its kind in Scandinavia and one of the first brick structures ever to be built in Denmark. This 70-m (230-ft) long Romanesque-Gothic church contains the remains of Bishop Absalon in a tomb at the rear of the main altar. The church also contains the sarcophagi of Christian II, Valdemar IV and Oluf III.

Attractions in Sorø include the **Sydvestsjællands Museum** (Museum of Southwest Zealand), which displays exhibits from the Stone Age right up to the present time. Next to the museum is the Bursers Apotekerhave (Apothecary Garden), with plants from

Dutch-style windmill in Nørre Jernløse

the herbarium of Joachim Burser, a pharmacist linked to the Danish royal family in the 1600s.

Sorø is perhaps best known for its Akademiet, which is set in a picturesque spot on Lake Sorø. This establishment, dedicated to the education of the sons of the nobility, was founded in 1623 by Christian IV in the monastery buildings left empty as a consequence of the Reformation. The Akademiet is surrounded by a park which contains a monument depicting the writer Ludwig Holberg, who bequeathed his considerable fortune and library to the school after his death in 1754. The school still operates though it is no longer reserved only for the country's nobility.

Environs

Tystrup-Bavelse is a national wildlife reserve with two connected freshwater lakes that attract a variety of birdlife; more than 20,000 water birds winter here. The forests contain many prehistoric grave-mounds, including **Kellerøddysen**, Denmark's largest megalithic stone formation, which is over 120 m (394 ft) in length. **Bjernede**, near Sorø, has the only surviving round church in Zealand. Constructed of stone and brick, it is quite unlike Bornholm's round churches *(see p221)* and was built around 1175 by Sune Ebbesøn, a provincial governor for Valdemar I (The Great).

🏛 **Sydvestsjællands Museum**
Storgade 17. **Tel** 57 83 40 63.
⏲ 1–4pm Tue–Thu & Sun,
11am–2pm Sat.

Tårnborg ㉗

Road map E5.

This ancient parish on the shores of Korsør bay, with the rising outline of a white 13th-century church, was once occupied by a castle and settlement. Tårnborg appeared

Distinct white exterior of the 13th-century church in Tårnborg

as a place name for the first time in a royal land survey completed in the first half of the 13th century, though it is likely that a stronghold existed at least one hundred years prior to this and that, together with the forts at Nyborg and Sprogø, it controlled the passage across the Store Bælt *(see pp146–7)*. From the 13th century it was also a major centre of commerce and in the 14th century Tårnborg forged links with neighbouring estates, helping to intensify foreign trade. The castle was demolished in the 15th century following a financial crisis.

Archaeological excavations suggest that Tårnborg's original stronghold measured about 30 m (98 ft) in diameter, with an 8-m (26-ft) high tower at its centre.

Bjernede Rundkirke – the only round church in Zealand

Korsør ㉘

Road map E5. 🚶 *20,000.* 🚉
ℹ *Nygade 7.* **Tel** *70 25 22 06.*
www.visitsydvestsjaelland.dk

The earliest records of this town date from 1241. The most prominent building in Korsør is a 13th-century fortress (Korsør Fæstning), which played a crucial role in the town gaining control of the Store Bælt. In 1658 the constantly enlarged fortress was captured by the Swedes, but returned to Danish control a year later. Its 25-m (82-ft) high tower now houses the **Korsør By-og Overfartsmuseet** (Town and Ferry Service Museum), which has a collection that includes models of ships that once sailed across the Store Bælt.

Clusters of historic buildings, mainly from the 18th century, can be seen in the environs of Algade, Slottensgade and Gavnegade. The Rococo mansion at No. 25 Algade dates from 1761 and was built by Rasmus Langeland, a shipowner. It was originally used as an inn for sailors who were waiting for the right conditions to cross the Store Bælt. Its front is adorned with allegories of the four seasons of the year. Inside is a small art museum displaying, among other things, sculptures by Harald Isenstein who died in 1980.

🏛 **Korsør By-og Overfartsmuseet**
Søbatteriet 7. **Tel** 58 37 47 55. ⏲
Apr–Dec: 11am–4pm Tue–Sun. 📷

Ancient cannons outside Korsør Fæstning (Fortress)

Storebælt Bridge 🏵

Until the late 20th century, the only way of travelling to Zealand was by air or ferry across the Storebælt (Great Belt). In 1998, after 12 years of construction work, the two biggest Danish islands – Zealand and Funen – were joined together. The link consists of two bridges with an artificial island in between. The journey time has now been cut to 10 minutes and the bridge is open 24 hours a day. Of the two bridges, the Østbro (Eastern) suspension bridge presents a more impressive sight. A toll charge of around 230–350 Dkr, depending on the size of your vehicle, is payable at the toll station on the Zealand side. Head to the yellow *Manuel* lanes for payment by credit card or cash.

VISITORS' CHECKLIST

Road map E5. *Tel* 70 15 10 15.
🖥 www.storebaelt.dk

These pylons, at 254 m (833 ft), are the highest man-made structures in Scandinavia.

85-m (279 ft) long cables

The bridge is 48.2 m (158 ft) wide.

Bridges
The Østbro is 7 km (4.4 miles) long and carries cars (trains run in a tunnel). The Vestbro is 6.6 km (4.1 miles) long and carries cars and trains.

Sprogø
This small island in the middle of the Storebælt is the junction where the Østbro motorway and the railway track meet.

THE STOREBÆLT

Langeskov
Slagelse
Trelleborg
Tamborg Kirke
Nyborg
Korsør
Skælskør

KEY
— Motorway
— Major road
— Other road

Agersø

Svendborg

0 km   15
0 miles   15

Tunnel
An 8-km (5-mile) long rail tunnel, measuring 7.7 m (25 ft) in diameter, descends 75 m (246 ft) below the surface. It is the second largest underwater tunnel in Europe.

A display of Viking archery in Trelleborg

Trelleborg 🅽

Road map E5. 7 km (4 miles) east of Slagelse. **Tower** Trelleborg Allé 4, 4200 Slagelse. ☐ *Jun–Aug: 10am–5pm Tue–Sun; Apr–May & Sep–Oct: 10am–4pm Tue–Sun.* 🔲 **www**.vikingeborg.dk

The best-preserved of Denmark's Viking fortresses was founded in the 10th century by Harald I (Bluetooth). At the height of its power it was manned by an estimated force of 1,000 warriors. Of the reconstructed buildings, the longhouse is the most impressive. It is built of rough oak beams and furnished with benches on which the Vikings slept.

Originally, there were 16 buildings in the main section of the fortress. Outside the fortress was a small cemetery, where archaeologists have counted about 150 graves.

In summer visitors can participate in fun and games. Some of the staff are dressed in Viking costume and are on hand to demonstrate such workaday jobs as grinding corn and sharpening tools. Daily workshops provide children with the opportunity to try their hand at archery and even dress up as Vikings.

A small museum exhibits finds excavated from the grounds such as jewellery and pottery. It also screens a 20-minute film about the history of Trelleborg.

Kalundborg 🅱

Road map E4. 🚶 *20,000.* 🚉
📍 *Klosterparkvej 7.* **Tel** *59 51 09 15.*
Museum *Adelgade 23.* **Tel** *59 51 21 41.* ☐ *May–Aug: 11am–5pm daily; Sep–Apr: 11am–4pm Sat & Sun.* 🔲 **www**.kalmus.dk *or* **www**. visitkalundborg.dk

Kalundborg is one of Zealand's oldest towns and was populated by the Vikings as early as the 9th century. The town was also once used as a base by pirates but in 1168 a castle was built here and control of the fjord's waters was assumed by the crown.

The ruins in Volden square are all that remains of the castle. Its builder was Esbern Snare, the brother of Bishop Absalon. Snare was also the creator of the well-preserved 12th-century Vor Frue Kirke (Church of Our Lady), which has five octagonal towers and a Byzantine design based on a Greek crucifix.

Kalundborg's medieval quarter surrounds the church and includes cobbled streets and 16th-century buildings. One of these now houses the town museum. Most of the exhibits are devoted to local history and include a collection of costumes and the skeletons of two beheaded Vikings. Standing in the museum courtyard is a model of Kalundborg, providing a view of the town's 17th-century layout.

Røsnæs 🅱

Road map D4. 📍 *Kalundborg.*

The Røsnæs peninsula, as well as the Asnæs peninsula that flanks the Kalundborg Fjord on the other side, were created by a continental glacier some 20,000 years ago. In the Middle Ages the Røsnæs peninsula, which thrusts into the Store Bælt, was covered with thick forest, making it one of the favourite areas for royal hunting trips. One hunt, in 1231, organized at the request of Valdemar the Victorious, ended in a bitter tragedy when a stray arrow killed the king's son (who was also named Valdemar).

The peninsula's tip is the westernmost point of Zealand and is marked by a lighthouse erected in 1845. The light from its lantern, mounted 25 m (82 ft) above sea level, can be seen up to 40 km (25 miles) away. A short way before the lighthouse, in the village of Ulstrup, is a Dutch-style windmill built in 1894. It was still being used in the 1950s to grind flour but is now purely a visitor attraction.

At the base of the Asnæs peninsula is Lerchenborg Slot, a Baroque castle built in 1753 by General Christian Lerche. H.C. Andersen stayed here in 1862 and some of the rooms contain items relating to the famous writer.

The unusual five-towered church in Kalundborg

Svinninge ⊛

Road map E4. 🚉 🛈 *Hovedgaden 7.* **Tel** *59 21 60 09.*

The main reason people come to this town, located at the base of the Odsherred peninsula, is to visit its model electric railway, which is one of the longest in Europe. **Svinninge Modeljernbane** is housed in a building measuring 8 m by 14 m (26 ft by 46 ft) and contains over 550 model railway coaches and nearly 90 locomotives. All of the rolling stock, as well as the convincing reconstructions of many Danish stations (including Svinninge, Hilbæk, Lisebro, Hjortholm and Egaa), are built to a scale of 1:87. The creators of this extraordinary display have meticulously and painstakingly recreated entire railway routes, including the link from Holbæk to Oxneholm.

The model railway was originally a private affair and was opened to the public after it was donated to the town by its original creator. The building of this impressive display involved a great deal of work by many people including model makers, carpenters, joiners and electricians. More than 80 m (262 ft) of cable were laid in order to supply current to over 2 km (1.3 miles) of track. Even today, the display continues to grow with new sections of track and locomotives being added yearly.

🏛 **Svinninge Modeljernbane**
Stationen 2, 4520 Svinninge.
Tel *59 21 60 09.* ⏱ *end Apr–end Oct: 10am–4pm daily.* 🖥 **www**.svmjk.dk

Section of the model railway in Svinninge

◁ **Sailing boats on one of Zealand's lakes**

Dragsholm Slot, seen from the courtyard

Dragsholm ⊛

Road map E4. Dragsholm Allé, 4534 Hørve. **Tel** *59 65 33 00.* 📷 *tours only: Jul: 1:30pm Tue (in English).* 🖥 **www**.dragsholm-slot.dk

The castle in Dragsholm was once a fortress and later a royal residence. It is now used as a luxurious hotel and restaurant, but has lost none of its historical grandeur.

Situated on the shores of Nekselø bay, at the foot of Zealand's third highest hill – Vejrhøj (121 m/ 397 ft above sea level) – Dragsholm Slot is one of Denmark's oldest and biggest castles. Its origins date back to the 12th and 13th centuries, when Roskilde's bishops decided to build themselves a seat, which would also serve as a military fortress. They occupied it until 1536 at which point the bishopric was moved to Copenhagen. Dragsholm was then taken over by the king who transformed it into a palace. Following a war with Sweden in the mid-17th century the castle was converted into a prison. The dungeon's most famous inmate was Lord James von Bothwell, the husband of Mary Queen of Scots,

Heraldic arms from Dragsholm Slot

who had sought sanctuary in Denmark after Mary's downfall. Instead he was imprisoned and languished here for five years. He eventually went mad and died in 1578. His tomb is in the castle chapel.

In the second half of the 17th century, during another war with Sweden, the castle was badly damaged. Extensive rebuilding work began in 1694 and gave the building its present distinct Baroque aspect. At that time the owners of the castle were Christian Adeler and his wife Henriette Margrete von Lente. The castle remained in the hands of the family until 1932. Since 1937 the property has been owned by the Bøttger family, who run it as a hotel and restaurant. The 1-m (3-ft) thick walls, high ceilings and sumptuously decorated interiors enhance the historic aura of the place. The most interesting rooms include the magnificent Banqueting Hall (Riddersalen) and Hunting Room (Jagtværelset).

The castle and its moat are surrounded by a large expanse of parkland that contains, among other plants, a collection of rhododendrons. Like all great castles, Dragsholm is reputed to be haunted. The three ghosts that are most frequently spotted are the White Lady, the Grey Lady and, of course, Lord von Bothwell.

Odsherred ㉟

Surrounded by the waters of the Kattegat, Isefjord and Sejerø bay, the Odsherred peninsula is one of the most popular holiday destinations in Denmark, visited annually by sunseekers and water sports enthusiasts. Its wide sandy beaches, the lure of the sea and the varied landscape also make this region popular with artists, some of whom have established galleries here.

Sjælland Sommerland ③
This amusement park (open mid-May–Sep only) provides a good day out for families with kids. Among the many attractions are a mini train, a roller coaster and giant water slides ending in splash pools.

Havnebyen ⑤
Cutters in the harbour and the aroma from the local smokehouses make this fishing village a memorable place.

Lumsås Mølle ④
This restored mill dates from the 19th century and is open to the public. Flour ground on site can still be bought.

Højby Sø ②
The banks of this small lake are inhabited by a wide variety of birds. The lake is also popular with anglers.

21
5
Overby *21* *Ebbeløkke* *Klint*
4
Stenstrup *Tengslemark*
Nyrup
Gudmindrup *2*
21 *1*
3 *VIG*

Gniben ⑥
The narrow strip of land stretching westwards has wide sandy beaches and is excellent for sunbathing. Gniben, situated furthest to the west, affords magnificent views of the sea.

0 km   2

0 miles   2

TIPS FOR DRIVERS

Length of route:
50 km (31 miles).
ℹ️ *Nykøbing SJ: Algade 43.*
Tel *59 91 08 88.*
www.visitodsherred.dk

KEY

▬ Suggested route

▬ Scenic route

═ Other road

☀️ Viewpoint

Højby ①
The interior of the local church is decorated with frescoes depicting, among others, Sankt Jørgen.

SOUTHERN ZEALAND AND THE ISLANDS

T*he lowlands of southern Zealand are characterized by cultivated fields and beautiful lakes. Many visitors see only Vordingborg and Køge, two towns that have played a significant part in Denmark's history, but the islands of Lolland, Falster and Møn to the south are attractive holiday destinations and offer miles of sandy beaches, woodland and awe-inspiring views of coastal cliffs.*

Southern Zealand (Sjælland) is an important region for the Danes. Vordingborg was the capital of the Valdemar dynasty and in the 12th century was used by Bishop Absalon as a staging post for his military expeditions to eastern Germany.

The market town of Ringsted, in central Zealand, was for many years the venue of the *landsting*, a regional government assembly that formed the basis of the present-day parliament. In 1677, Køge Bay was the scene of a major naval engagement in which the Danish Admiral Niels Juel became a national hero when he dealt a crushing blow to the Swedish fleet.

The islands to the south of Zealand are more rural in character. Lolland is Denmark's third biggest island (1,243 sq km/480 sq miles) and also its flattest (at its highest point it is a mere 22 m/72 ft above sea level). The island has some pretty beaches and is popular with hikers in summer. Falster is only slightly smaller and is visited mainly for its wide beaches. Møn is the smallest of the islands and the hardest to reach. The journey is worth it, however, as Møn has rustic scenery, spectacular white cliffs, good beaches and some interesting sights including Neolithic burial places and a number of medieval churches containing some spectacular frescoes.

Ducks near the shore of Søndersø, Maribo

◁ Spectacular chalk cliffs of Møns Klint

Exploring Southern Zealand and the Islands

The largest town in southern Zealand is Næstved, which has a number of historic buildings. However, Køge, Ringsted and Vordingborg have more to offer in the way of outstanding buildings. This part of Denmark is particularly attractive to families because it has a slow, relaxed pace and a number of child-friendly attractions such as BonBon-Land, Knuthenborg Safari Park on Lolland and, on Falster, a recreated medieval village. Falster benefits from some of Denmark's best beaches; Lolland has a popular resort complex.

Brick-built Holsted Kirke, Næstved

GETTING AROUND

Getting from southern Zealand to Falster and Lolland presents few problems thanks to the toll-free bridges. The main arterial road – the E47 motorway – runs from Copenhagen via southern Zealand to Falster and Rødbyhavn on Lolland. Most places are easily accessible from Copenhagen by train except for Møn, which has no railway.

KEY

═══	Motorway
▬▬	Major road
⋯⋯	Minor road
▬▬	Scenic route
┅┅	Main railway
▬▬	Minor railway
– –	Ferry route

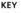

Tystrup Sø

GLUMS

Slagelse

157   22

Skælskør   265

❶ 🏛 Stigsnæs
AGERSØ

Omø

Smålandsfarvandet

Femø

Fejø

Horslunde
Købelevhaven   289

Tårs
🏛   Bandholm   ▨
NAKSKOV ❶❸   Søllested   ❶❷ SAFARI PAR
9   SAKSKØBI
275   MARIBO ❶❶
Søndersø
Lolland
E47   Holeby
LALANDIA ❶❹   Rødby   297
Rødbyhavn 🏛   ❶❺ TÅGERUP

SEE ALSO

• *Where to Stay* pp249–51.
• *Where to Eat* pp276–7.

0 km   10
0 miles   10

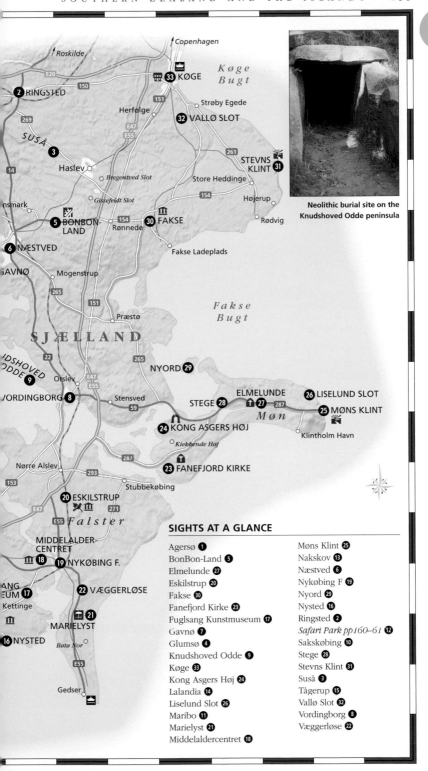

Neolithic burial site on the Knudshoved Odde peninsula

SIGHTS AT A GLANCE

Agersø ❶
BonBon-Land ❺
Elmelunde ㉗
Eskilstrup ⓴
Fakse ㉚
Fanefjord Kirke ㉓
Fuglsang Kunstmuseum ⓱
Gavnø ❼
Glumsø ❹
Knudshoved Odde ❾
Køge ㉝
Kong Asgers Høj ㉔
Lalandia ⓮
Liselund Slot ㉖
Maribo ⓫
Marielyst ㉑
Middelaldercentret ⓲

Møns Klint ㉕
Nakskov ⓭
Næstved ❻
Nykøbing F ⓳
Nyord ㉙
Nysted ⓰
Ringsted ❷
Safari Park pp160–61 ⓬
Sakskøbing ❿
Stege ㉘
Stevns Klint ㉛
Suså ❸
Tågerup ⓯
Vallø Slot ㉜
Vordingborg ❽
Væggerløse ㉒

Vaulted interior of Sankt Bendts Kirke, Ringsted

Agersø ❶

Road map E5. 🚢 www.agersoe.
com **Agersø Mølle Tel** 58 19 81 03.
⏲ Jul–early Aug: 2–4pm Fri–Sun. 🅿
www.agersoe-moelle.dk

A 15-minute ferry trip from
Stigsnæs, a small port 7 km
(4.3 miles) southwest of
Skælskør, takes visitors to
the lovely island of Agersø.
This strip of land is just
3 km (1.8 miles) wide and
7 km (4.3 miles) long, and
it is home to a community
of about 240 people.

Despite its small size,
Agersø has a lot to offer,
starting with the pretty
harbour, which plays host to
all manner of vessels, from
ferries and yachts to fishing
boats. There is also a comprehensive network of walking
and cycling routes starting
from the harbour and covering a length of 20 km (12.4
miles). The north of the island
features several unspoiled
beaches with good bathing.

The island's main attraction,
however, is probably the
Agersø Mølle, a mill built
in 1892. Farmers from the
surrounding areas would
come here to grind their corn.
Resting on a stone base, the
octagonal uppermill is made
of wood and covered with
shingle. The mill was in use
until 1959, when its owner,
a baker called Erik Thomsen,
gifted it to the people of
Agersø. A bench was placed
next to the mill in his honour.

Ringsted ❷

Road map E5. 🏘 18,000. 🚉
🚹 Nørregade 100. **Tel** 57 62 66 00.
www.visitringsted.dk

Owing to its location at the
crossroads of two trading
routes, Ringsted was once an
important market town. It
was the venue for regional
government assemblies –
the *landsting* – which took
decisions and passed laws on
major national issues. The
three stones standing in the
market square were used
hundreds of years ago by
members of the *landsting*.

Ringsted gained notoriety
in 1131 when Knud (Canute)
Laward, duke of southern
Zealand, was murdered in the
neighbouring woods by his
jealous cousin Magnus. He is
buried in Ringsted's Sankt
Bendts Kirke (St Benedict's
Church) along with a number
of Danish kings and queens.
Sankt Bendts Kirke was erected
in 1170 and is believed to be
the oldest brick church in
Scandinavia. Its main altarpiece dates from 1699; its
baptismal font is believed to
be 12th century and was for
a time used as a flower pot
in a local garden until it was
discovered quite by chance.
The magnificent frescoes were
painted in about 1300 and
include a series depicting Erik
IV (known as Ploughpenny
for his tax on ploughs).

In the 17th century it was
decided to open some of the
coffins. The items found in
them are on display in one of
the chapels. The Dagmar Cross,
dating from about AD 1000, is
a copy. The original is on display in the Nationalmuseet in
Copenhagen *(see pp84–5)*. The
famous cross once belonged
to Queen Dagmar, the first
wife of Valdemar II. Depicted
on its enamelled surface is a
beautiful figure of Christ with
his arms outstretched. On the
other side of the cross, Christ
is pictured with the Virgin
Mary flanked by John the
Baptist, St John and St Basil.

Suså ❸

Road map E5.

At nearly 90 km (56 miles)
long, Suså is one of Denmark's
longest rivers. From its source
near the town of Rønnede
it flows through two lakes,
Tystrup Sø and Bavelse Sø, to
end its journey in Karrebæk
Bay, near Næstved. The picturesque surroundings and
slow-flowing current make
the river particularly popular
with canoeists. Canoe trips
are usually taken over the
final stretch of the river,
where a canoe or a kayak can
be hired for an hour or two.
River traffic gets quite busy
in summer, and many large
family groups enjoy picnick-
ing along the river banks.

Near Haslev are two mag-
nificent properties. Gisselfeld
Kloster, completed in 1575, is
one of the finest Renaissance
castles in northern Europe
and is surrounded by gardens
containing about 400 species
of trees and shrubs. The castle
was often visited by Hans
Christian Andersen – it was
here that he got his idea for

Suså – Zealand's longest river

Canoeing on the Suså past the Gunderslev Kirke in Skelby

The Ugly Duckling. The grounds are open to the public for opera concerts, classic car shows and market days. On the latter, there are also guided tours of the house. Bregentved Slot, on the outskirts of Haslev, was erected in the 1650s; however, the property was substantially modified in the late 1880s.

Glumsø ❹

Road map E5. 🖳

Glumsø is a good base from which to embark upon a canoeing trip along the Suså. Located about 10 km (6 miles) south of Ringsted, its other main attraction is the **Dansk Cykel & Knallert Museum** (Museum of Bicycles and Motorbikes), which has a huge collection of two- and three-wheeled transportation, from vintage cycles to trendy modern scooters. Some bikes can even be ridden by visitors.

Environs

South of Glumsø, on the banks of the Suså, is **Skelby**. The main point of interest here is Gunderslev Kirke, a 12th-century church. Its sumptuously furnished interior was paid for by the former owners of the nearby Gunderslevholm estate.

🏛 **Dansk Cykel & Knallert Museum**
Sorøvej 8. **Tel** 57 64 77 94.
⏰ May–Sep: 11am–5pm Sat & Sun.
🖳 www.dckm.dk/cykelmuseum

BonBon-Land ❺

Road map E5. Holme-Ostrup, Gartnervej 2. **Tel** 55 53 07 00.
⏰ Apr–Oct. Opening hours vary; check the website before visiting. 🖳 children up to 90 cm (3 ft) tall are admitted free.
www.bonbonland.dk

This amusement park attracts large numbers of visitors in the summer. The entrance fee covers all the 100 or so attractions. The greatest thrill is undoubtedly provided by a ride on the giant roller coaster, which races along at speeds up to 70 km/h (43 mph) and rises to a height of 22 m (72 ft) before hurtling back down again. A similar surge of adrenaline can be felt when dropping from the 35-m (115-ft) high tower. Gentler amusement can be had on the park's merry-go-rounds or mini racetracks. The queues lengthen for the water slides when the temperature rises, as do those for a raft trip down some white-water rapids. BonBon-Land has lots of attractions for smaller children too, including an adventure playground. It is attractively situated in woodland a short walk from Holme-Ostrup train station; expect queues in the summer, especially at the snack bars.

Environs

Holmegaard Park, the former site of the historic Holmegaard glass factory, was founded by Countess Danneskiold-Samsøe of Gisselfeld Kloster *(see opposite)* in 1825, and was the first glassworks in Denmark. In the first half of the 20th century, designers like Jacob Bang brought Danish glass international recognition *(see p24)*, but the factory closed in 2008. The Holmegaard brand continues as part of Rosendahl, and the site has been converted into an outlet store and, during the summer months, an experience centre where children can enjoy glass, ceramic and even chocolate workshops. With shops selling hand-blown glass, ceramics and deli food items, this is also a great place to pick up souvenirs to take home. Outside of the summer holidays, the park is open as an outlet store only.

🌸 **Holmegaard Park**
Glasværksvej 54, Fensmark, Holmegaard. **Tel** 70 25 75 00.
⏰ Jul–mid-Aug: 10am–4pm daily; also Easter and Whitsun weekend.
🖳 www.holmegaardpark.dk

Children's attractions in BonBon-Land

Næstved ❻

Road map E5. 🏔 *40,700.* 🚉
ℹ️ *Havnen 1.* **Tel** *55 72 11 22.*
www.visitnaestved.com

Southern Zealand's largest
town, Næstved has been an
important centre of trade since
medieval times. The 15th-
century town hall in Axeltorv,
the main square, is one of the
oldest in Denmark. The town
has two Gothic churches. The
14th-century frescoes in Sankt
Peder Kirke (St Peter's Church)
depict Valdemar IV and his
wife Helveg kneeling in prayer.
Sankt Mortens is 13th century
and has a beautiful altarpiece
that was completed in 1667.

Other notable buildings
include Kompagnihuset, a half-
timbered guild hall (1493) and
Aposteluset (Apostles' House),
built in the early 16th century.
Its name derives from the
figures of Christ and his
12 disciples placed between
the windows.

Næstved's oldest building,
however, is Helligåndhuset
(House of the Holy Spirit),
which dates from the 1300s
and was used as a hospital and
almshouse. It now houses part
of the **Næstved Museum**, with
a collection of medieval and
contemporary woodcarvings.
Another annex of the museum,
in the Boderne houses near
Sankt Peder Kirke, displays
local handicraft from the
Holmegaard glass factory *(see
p157)* and nearby potteries
(dating 1839–1970). The
Løveapoteket (Pharmacy), on
Axeltorv, dates back to 1640 –
a herb garden is situated in

English-style castle garden in Gavnø

the courtyard. Munkebakken
Park (not far from Axeltorv)
contains statues of seven
monks which have been
carved out of tree trunks.

🏛 **Næstved Museum**
Ringstedgade 4. **Tel** *55 77 08 11.*
⬜ *10am–2pm Tue–Sat (to 6pm
Thu), 1–4pm Sun.*

Gavnø ❼

Road map E5. **Tel** *55 70 02 00.*
⬜ *daily. Apr & Aug–late Oct: 10am–
4pm; late Apr–late Jun: 10am–5pm;
late Jun–early Aug: 10am–6pm.* 📷
www.gavnoe.dk

Located a little way from
Næstved and linked to
Næstved by road, this tiny
island was used by pirates in
the 13th century. In the 14th
century Queen Margrethe I
established a convent here.
According to legend, the
convent was the
scene of a tragic
love affair in the
16th century
between Count
Henrik Hog and Ida
Baggsen. The boy's
father, who disap-
proved of the girl,
sent his son away,
while Ida was
forced to enter the
convent. When the
boy returned, the
lovers resumed their
affair. The couple
were discovered:
the nuns punished
the girl by burying

Former Benedictine abbey in Næstved

her alive; the count narrowly
escaped death and was
whisked abroad.

The remains of the convent
include a chapel dating from
1401. After the Reformation
the convent become a
privately owned manor
house. The current building is
18th century and is constructed
on the ruins of the convent. It
owes its Rococo appearance
to the Reedtz-Thott family,
who took control of the place
in 1755. The pride of the
house is its art collection,
which includes over 2,000
paintings. It is regarded as one
of the most important private
collections in Scandinavia.

The grounds themselves
look their best in spring when
there are displays of flowers
made from over half a million
plants, including tulips,
hyacinths and crocuses. The
gardens also have a butterfly
house containing specimens
imported from the Far East.

Vordingborg ❽

Road map F6. 🏔 *9,300.* 🚉
ℹ️ *Slotsruinen 1.* **Tel** *55 34 11 11.*
www.visitvordingborg.dk

Vordingborg is on the strait
between Zealand and Falster
that leads to the Baltic, and
was once Denmark's most
important town. It was the
royal residence of Valdemar I
(The Great) who came to the
throne in 1157 and built a
castle here, ushering in a
period of relative peace in the

country's history. In 1241 Valdemar II sanctioned the Jutland Code in Vordingborg, which gave Denmark its first written laws. Subsequent monarchs from the Valdemar dynasty also took a liking to the castle and enlarged it over the years. The final length of its defensive wall was 800 m (2,625 ft) and its imposing appearance was emphasized by nine mighty towers.

Most of the towers are now in ruins except for the 14th-century Gåsetårnet (Goose Tower). This 36-m (118-ft) high tower has walls that are 3.5 m (11.5 ft) thick in places. Its name dates back to 1368 when Valdemar IV placed a golden goose on top of the tower in order to express his belief that the Hanseatic League's declaration of war was no more threatening than the cackling of geese. Though it has been modified (the conical roof was added in 1871), Gåsetårnet is important as the only intact building to remain from the Valdemar era. The building opposite the tower houses the **Danmarks Borgcenter** (Danish Castle Centre), which has displays on the castle's history and the three kings who lived there.

Algade is Vordingborg's main street and has been pedestrianized. It leads to Vor Frue Kirke (Church of Our Lady), a 15th-century church which contains a Baroque altarpiece dating from 1642.

Environs
The **Kalvehave Labyrintpark** features several exciting outdoor mazes and an area with brain-teasers and puzzles.

🏛 **Tower & Danmarks Borgcenter**
⬜ Jun–Sep: 10am–5pm daily; Oct–May: 10am–4pm Tue–Sun. 📧
www.danmarksborgcenter.dk

🌿 **Kalvehave Labyrintpark**
Hovvejen 12, Kalvehave. **Tel** 55 34 47 71. ⬜ May & Jun: 10am–5pm Sat & Sun; Jul–mid-Aug: 10am–6pm daily; mid-Aug–early Sep: 10am–4pm daily; 13–21 Oct: 10am–5pm daily. 📧

Knudshoved Odde ❾

Road map E5. *The peninsula can be reached by car, from Oreby.* 📧

The narrow strip of the Knudshoved Odde peninsula is 20 km (12 miles) long and only 1 km (half a mile) at its widest point. The peninsula is owned by the Rosenfeldt Estate, which has managed to preserve this unique landscape. There are no towns or villages here, and the only road is closed to motor traffic after about 10 km (6 miles). This inaccessibility makes the Knudshoved Odde peninsula popular with people who wish to get away from it all and relax by indulging in simple activities such as sitting on the seashore, gathering blackberries and exploring the woods (which can be reached by foot from the car park halfway along the peninsula where the trail begins). The wood's marked walking trails are not taxing and range from a short stroll to one that is just under 4 km (2 miles).

Monument to Polish workers in Sakskøbing

The peninsula is also known for its Neolithic burial mounds. One of these historic graves, which was dug about 5,500 years ago, can be seen close to the car park. Excavations have established that its ancient occupant was provided with all possible necessities for the after-life, including plenty of food and drink.

Sakskøbing ❿

Road map E6. Lolland. 🏠 4,700. 🛈 Torvet 4. **Tel** 54 70 56 30 (Jun–Sep).

One of Lolland's oldest settlements, Sakskøbing has few historic remains other than a Romanesque church (13th century). However, in view of the town's location on the E47, the main road linking Zealand to Falster and Lolland, it is a popular stopping-off point. The town's most striking feature is a water tower that resembles a smiling face.

A distinctive landmark in the market square is the monument erected in 1939 for the Polish men and women who worked in the local fields. The town's links with Poland date back to the end of the 19th century when many Poles came here in search of work. Many settled permanently on the island and some local Catholic churches still celebrate mass in Polish.

The 14th-century Gåsetårnet in Vordingborg

Shores of the Knudshoved Odde peninsula

Safari Park ⑫

Knuthenborg Safari Park provides the
chance to see such exotic creatures
as zebras, camels, antelopes and
giraffes. The parkland itself has
been in the hands of the same
family since the 17th century. It
was landscaped in an English
style in the 19th century and
the first animals were transported by ship from Kenya
in 1969. Today there are
more than 1,000 animals.
The park's botanical garden
contains many rare trees and
shrubs, and there is an attractive
lake area that is ideal for picnics.

*Bandholm
Huset*

*Bandholm-
porten*

**AUSTRALIA
& REST OF
WORLD**

Exit

Egebæk Pla

ASIA

Knuthenborg

Skovridergarden

*Sko
P*

ASIA

Nordre Snapind

Søndre Snapind

Tiger Reser

★ Knuthenborg
*The house is surrounded by
English-style parkland and was
designed by Edward Milner. It
bears clear signs of a Victorian
influence. The main building is
still inhabited by the Knuth family
and closed to the public.*

★ Tiger Reserve
*The pride of the park
are the Siberian tigers,
the largest of all tigers.
They enjoy bathing,
which is unusual for
cats. The deep marks
visible on the trees have
been left by the tigers'
sharp claws.*

Statue of the Park's Founder
*Eggert Christoffer Knuth (1838–
74) was a great 19th-century
explorer. He brought back seeds
and cuttings from his many
voyages abroad. Many of these
were cultivated and some
are still growing in the park.*

STAR SIGHTS

★ Knuthenborg

★ Tiger Reserve

Zebras
The zebras are allowed to roam freely and mingle with other animals in the park. They can run at speeds of up to 60 km/h (40 mph) when startled.

VISITORS' CHECKLIST

Road map E6. Knuthenborg, Bandholm. Lolland. **Tel** *54 78 80 89.* ☐ *end Apr–early Sep: daily; early Sep–early Oct: Sat & Sun; for opening hours, visit the website.* 🖥 www.knuthenborg.dk

KEY

━━ Main route

━━ Car route only

═ Pedestrian route

Pheasant Woods

AMERICA

Bird Paradise

Deer Park

🅿
🚻

Swan Lake

Wolves Wood

🚻
🅿

...nthuset

Savannah

Limpopo House

🚻 ♿
🍴 ℹ 🅿

...key ...st

Safari Grill

AFRICA

Småland

Maglemer Slottet

Maglemer-porten

Giraffes
The giraffe can grow up to 5.5 m (18 ft) in height. The park's giraffes can sometimes be seen bending, with legs wide apart, to drink water.

Småland
This park for children features a water playground and a number of rides for "mini adventurers", including a train and a merry-go-round. Older kids can also have fun climbing rope bridges.

Entrance

0 m   250

0 yards   250

Cape Baboons
Easily recognized by their long faces, Cape baboons are located in the Monkey Forest area, where it is possible for visitors to help feed them.

Half-timbered houses in Maribo

Maribo ⓫

Road map E6. Lolland.
🚶 6,000. 🚉 🛈 Torvet 1, Det
Gamle Rådhus. **Tel** 54 78 04 96.
www.visitlolland-falster.com

Situated on the northern shore of Maribo Søndersø, the largest of four inland lakes, Maribo is Lolland's commercial centre. The town was founded in 1416 by Erik of Pomerania and soon acquired a Gothic cathedral. All that remains of an original convent and monastery complex are the cathedral's bells (that toll six times a day) and a gallery where the nuns used to pray. The convent was dissolved following the Reformation.

The cathedral is located a short way from Torvet, the town's main square, which contains a 19th-century Neo-Classical town hall and several half-timbered houses.

Maribo has two museums, which offer separate, as well as joint admission fees. The **Lolland-Falster Stiftsmuseet** has a collection of church art and displays relating to Polish workers. **Frilandsmuseet**, a short way southwest of Maribo, is an open-air museum with a number of period cottages, as well as other buildings, including a windmill and a smithy.

🏛 **Lolland-Falster**
Stiftsmuseet
Banegårdspladsen. **Tel** 54 84 44 00.
⭘ noon–4pm Wed–Sat. 🖼

🏛 **Frilandsmuseet**
Meinckesvej. **Tel** 54 84 44 00. ⭘
May–Sep: 10am–4pm Tue–Sun. 🖼

Safari Park ⓬

See pp160–61.

Nakskov ⓭

Road map E6. Lolland.
🚶 14,000. 🛈 Axeltorv
3. **Tel** 54 92 21 72.

Nakskov's origins date back to the 13th century. A reminder of its medieval past is the tower of Sankt Nikolai Kirke (Church), which rises above the old quarter. The oldest of Nakskov's houses are Dronningens Pakhus, a quayside warehouse that was built in 1590 and, at Tilegade 21, Den Gamle Smedje, a smithy where visitors can see a blacksmith working with 200-year-old tools.

Most of Denmark's sugar beet is grown on Lolland, and **Denmark's Sugar Museum** tells the story of the crop and the Polish immigrants who arrived to work in the fields.

There are 20 small islands in Nakskov Fjord, some of them inhabited. Post and other goods are still delivered using the **Postbåden**, a small boat that also welcomes tourists on its route (Jun–Aug). The route varies, but it always stops for a 1-hour lunch break at Albuen (The Elbow), an area with numerous natural attractions. It is well worth paying a little extra and bringing a bike; after cycling around one of the islands, you can catch another boat back to Nakskov. In addition to the daily morning excursions, there are also trips just before sundown.

Environs
Købelevhaven, about 6 km (4 miles) north of Nakskov, is a Japanese-style botanical garden. Established in 1975, it has a large rhododendron collection, a Japanese garden and some rare magnolia and Asian trees.

🏛 **Denmark's Sugar Museum**
Løjtoftevej 22. **Tel** 54 92 36 44.
⭘ Oct–May: 1–4pm Sat; Jun–Sep:
1–4pm Tue–Sun. 🖼
www.sukkermuseet.dk

Postbåden
Havnegade 2. **Tel** 54 93 12 36.
⭘ Jun–Aug: 9am daily. 🖼

🌷 **Købelevhaven**
Oddevej 116, Købelev. **Tel** 54 93 20
87. ⭘ May–Aug: 10am–5pm Tue–
Sun. 🖼 **www**.koebelevhaven.dk

Lalandia ⓮

Road map E6. Lolland. 🚌
🛈 Rødby, Lalandiacentret 1. **Tel** 54
61 05 00. 🖼 **www**.lalandia.dk

Many families come to Lalandia – Denmark's largest holiday centre – for a short break. The resort is on the southern coast of Lolland and offers numerous attractions to visitors. The local beach competes for children's attention with the aquapark where swimming pools and slides are surrounded by artificial lakes and tropical vegetation. Regardless of the outside temperature, the water in the pools never falls below 28° C (82° F). For sports enthusiasts, there are tennis courts, a golf course, mini-golf, and, in the case of bad weather, a vast leisure

Palm trees enliven the aquapark area at Lalandia

Display in Polakkasernen, Tågerup

complex that includes a gymnasium, bowling alleys, amusement arcades and indoor tennis.

Visitors to Lalandia can stay in apartments that sleep up to eight people. All of the apartments have their own bathrooms and kitchens. There are also numerous restaurants and bars spread around the holiday complex.

Tågerup ⑮

Road map E6. Lolland. 🚌

The main attraction of Tågerup, a small village situated a short way south of Maribo, is its Romanesque-Gothic church, which contains some fine 15th-century frescoes. At the entrance to the church is a runic stone. Many visitors are surprised to find a building displaying the Polish flag. This is **Polakkasernen**, or the Polish Barracks, and contains documents, fragments of diaries and various items left by Polish immigrants who from 1893 began arriving in Lolland in great numbers. Many Poles were on the move for political reasons as the Soviet Union had taken control of Poland. There were also economic reasons, however, and immigrants arrived from Poland between 1870 and 1920 in a bid to escape a feudal system that gave them few legal rights. Once they arrived, most Poles found employment as labourers in the local sugar-beet fields.

A short way from Polakkasernen is **Lungholm Gods**, an early 15th-century residence. The house is now used as a conference centre and spa. There are footpaths around it that are ideal for a pleasant ramble.

🏛 Polakkasernen
Højbygårsvej 34. **Tel** 54 82 23 30. ⬜ Easter, Whitsun, Jul–Aug: 2–4pm Tue–Sun. 📷

⚓ Lungholm Gods
Rødbyvej 24.

Nysted ⑯

Road map E6. Lolland.
🏛 1,500. 🚌

This small harbour town situated on the Rødsand bay was founded in the 13th century. Nysted's main historic monuments are a large Gothic church dating from the early 14th century, and a much later 17th-century tower. There are also a number of

half-timbered houses and a water tower, which now serves as a viewpoint.

Environs
Ålholm Slot (Castle) is on the outskirts of Nysted and dates from the 12th century. It was crown property for many years and the rooms contain many royal furnishings. In 1332 Christian II was held prisoner in the dungeons here on the orders of his half-brother. The castle is now in private hands and is not open to the public.

About 3 km (2 miles) north of Nysted is **Kettinge**, a small village with an old Dutch windmill and a church containing magnificent frescoes.

Fuglsang Kunstmuseum ⑰

Road map F6. Nystedvej 71, Toreby, Lolland. **Tel** 54 78 14 14. ⬜ Apr, Sep & Oct: 11am–4pm Tue–Sun; May–Aug: 10am–5pm daily; Nov–Mar: 11am–4pm Wed–Sun. 📷 ♿ **www**.fuglsangkunstmuseum.dk

Located in the grounds of Fuglsang Manor, between Nysted and Nykøbing F, this art museum was designed by the British architect Tony Fretton. The modern white building provides a stark contrast to the green rural landscape. Inside is a collection of Danish art from the 18th century onwards, with a focus on art from 1850 until 1950. Golden Age painters such as P.C. Skovgaard and Kristian Zahrtmann are represented, as are the Funen artists, painters from the Skagen School and the COBRA group.

Ålholm Slot seen from the water

Woman dressed in period costume at Middelaldercentret

Middelalder-centret ⑱

Road map F6. Lolland. 📍 *Sundby, Ved Hamborgskoven 2.* **Tel** *54 86 19 34.* ◯ *May & Sep: 10am–4pm Tue–Sun; Jun & Aug: 10am–4pm daily; Jul: 10am–5pm daily.* 📶 **www.** middelaldercentret.dk

Lolland's Middle Ages Centre is a recreated medieval settlement that provides an insight into what life was like in the 14th century. Crafts and games from medieval times are displayed and explained by staff wearing costumes from the period, while the local inn serves a range of "medieval" food. A replica sailing ship lies in the harbour and a huge wooden catapult is ready for firing. Jousting tournaments are a regular feature in summer, and visitors can also try their hand at archery. A marked walking trail in the nearby forest explains medieval customs and includes a site where

charcoal is made. Along the walk, visitors are warned about woodland spirits and are invited to throw a ghost-repelling stick at an appropriate spot – just in case.

The centre can easily be reached from Nykøbing F by crossing the bridge that connects Lolland and Falster.

Nykøbing F ⑲

Road map F6. Falster. 🏘 *16,500.* 🚉 🚌 ℹ *Langgade 2.* **Tel** *54 85 13 03.* **www.**visitlolland-falster.com

Falster's largest town and capital city was a busy commercial centre in medieval times and was granted municipal status in the early 13th century by Valdemar II. In order to distinguish it from two other Danish towns of the same name, this Nykøbing is followed by the letter F (standing for Falster).

Nykøbing F's main historic sight is a 15th-century brick church, which once formed part of a Franciscan monastery. Its richly decorated interior includes an eye-catching series of portraits of Queen Sophie (wife of Frederik II) together with her family, which were commissioned in 1627. Another notable sight is the half-timbered Czarens Hus (Tsar's House), which is one of the oldest buildings in town. In 1716 the Russian Tsar, Peter the Great, stopped here over night on his way

to Copenhagen. Today, the building is used as a restaurant and also houses a local history museum – **Falsters Minder**. Among the museum's exhibits are some reconstructed interiors including an 18th-century peasant cottage and a 19th-century burgher's house.

The most panoramic view of Nybøking F is from the early 20th-century yellow water tower. The town's **Guldborgsund Zoo** is a little way east of the train station and has a variety of animals including deer, monkeys and goats.

🏛 Falsters Minder
Langgade 2. **Tel** *54 84 44 00.* ◯ *11am–4pm Tue–Fri, 10am–3pm Sat (Jul–mid-Aug: 10am–4pm Mon–Sat).* 📶

🐾 Guldborgsund Zoo
Øster Alle 92. **Tel** *54 85 20 76.* ◯ *May–mid-Oct: 9am–5pm daily; mid-Oct–Apr: 10am–4pm daily.* 📶 **www.**guldborgsundzoo.dk

Eskilstrup ⑳

Road map F6. Falster.
🚉 🚌

Statue of a bear in Nykøbing F

This small town is situated a short distance from the E47 motorway and has two rather unusual museums.

The **Traktor-museum** is housed in a multi-storey brick building and contains over 200 tractors and engines dating from 1880 to 1960. Alongside a wide selection of vintage Fiats, Fords,

Nykøbing F, as seen from the river

◁ **Evening horse ride along the beach**

Beautiful white beaches around Marielyst

Volvos and Fergusons are rare Czechoslovakian and Romanian tractors. The oldest tractor in the museum is American and was built in 1917. There is also a steam traction engine built in England in 1889. Until 1925 it was still being used as a threshing machine. A number of small pedal-tractors are also provided for the amusement of children.

About 3 km (2 miles) from the town centre is the **Krokodille Zoo**. This is the largest collection of crocodiles in Europe and includes 21 of the 23 species of these sharp-toothed reptiles that exist worldwide. The smallest among them is the dwarf cayman, which grows up to 159 cm (62 inches) in length. At the other end of the scale, the zoo's giant Nile crocodile is called Samson and is currently the largest crocodile in Scandinavia.

As well as the many crocodiles, the zoo also contains a variety of other species including a green anaconda (the world's largest snake), turtles and a number of rare clouded leopards. The zoo donates a percentage of the admission price to an international programme of scientific research and protection associated with crocodiles living in the wild.

🏛 **Traktormuseum**
Nørregade 17B. *Tel* 54 43 70 07.
◻ Jun & Sep: 10am–4pm Tue–Fri, 10am–3pm Sat & Sun; Jul & Aug: 10am–5pm daily. 📷
www.traktormuseum.dk

🦎 **Krokodille Zoo**
Ovstrupvej 9. *Tel* 54 45 42 42.
◻ mid-Jun–Aug: 10am–5pm daily; Sep–mid-Jun: noon–4pm Tue–Sun. ⬤ Jan, Dec. 📷
www.krokodillezoo.dk

Marielyst ㉑

Road map F6. Falster. 🚌
ℹ Marielyst Strandpark 3. *Tel* 54 13 62 98. www.visitlolland-falster.com

Situated on the eastern end of the island, Marielyst gets its revenue mainly from its many summer visitors and is one of the foremost holiday resorts in the whole of Denmark. One of the main attractions is the fine white sand beach, which is a good length and easily accessible. It also benefits from clean and fairly shallow waters. The dunes running parallel to the coastline are an additional attraction and are fringed by an ancient beech forest.

There are plenty of shops, restaurants and bars. Along with camp sites, guesthouses and hotels the town also has about 6,000 summer cottages.

Environs
Just south of Marielyst is the **Bøtø Nor bird sanctuary** where a variety of birds can be spotted including cranes, ospreys and plovers.

Væggerløse ㉒

Road map F6. Falster. 🚌
The small town of Væggerløse, situated a little way south of Nykøbing F, has an 18th-century windmill, which now houses a glass-blowing workshop, and ceiling paintings from the late Middle Ages in the church. Another nearby attraction is the **Sports Car Museum**. Road signs direct drivers to a private farmstead where one of the buildings houses a collection of motor cars. Although not as large as the car museum found at Ålholm Slot near Nysted on Lolland (see p163), it is nevertheless worth visiting as it contains some interesting exhibits. Among the 65 vehicles on display are a 1917 Adler (which was once capable of reaching the giddy speed of 35 km/h/ 22 mph), as well as a Jaguar (which could travel as fast as 240 km/h/149 mph).

🏛 **Sports Car Museum**
Stovby Tværvej 11. *Tel* 54 17 75 89.
◻ 10am–5pm daily. 📷

A zoo keeper at the Krokodille Zoo picking eggs from a nest.

Frescoes in Fanefjord Kirke, painted in the mid-15th century

Fanefjord Kirke ㉓

Road map F6. Fanefjord Kirkevej 49, Askeby. ◻ *Jun–Aug: 8am–6pm daily; Sep–May: 8am–4pm daily.* **www**.fanefjordkirke.dk

The small church of Fanefjord stands on top of an isolated hillock surrounded by green fields. It provides an excellent viewpoint and from here it is possible to look out over the Baltic, Jes and the island of Falster. The Gothic church derives its name from the Fanefjord bay, whose waters come close to the building. The fjord was in turn named after Queen Fane, wife of King Grøn Jæger, local rulers in the late Stone Age.

Built about 1250, the church was at that time far too big for the needs of the 300 or so parishioners, but its builders took into account worshippers from ships anchoring in the bay as this was a busy harbour in the Middle Ages. According to records it was probably here that Bishop Absalon gathered his fleet before embarking on his raids against the Wends in eastern Germany.

Fanefjord Kirke is famous in Denmark for its frescoes. The oldest of them date from around 1350 and include an image of St Christopher carrying the infant Jesus. The later paintings date from the mid-15th century and include frescoes painted by the Elmelunde master, an artist about whom virtually nothing is known. His mark, which

looks like a man with long rabbit-like ears, can be seen on one of the ribs in the northeastern vault. A collection of votive ships hangs in the church. The oldest is a frigate hanging above the entrance which commemorates a tragic shipwreck off the north coast of Møn.

Kong Asgers Høj ㉔

Road map F6. Møn.

King Asgers mounds, located in a farmer's field near the village of Røddinge, are all that remain of Denmark's largest passage grave.

The Stone Age corridor consists of an 8-m (26-ft) long underground passage that leads to a large chamber, 10 m (33 ft) long by 2 m (6.5 ft) wide. It is dark inside, so it is wise to take a torch.

Corridor leading to the burial chamber of Kong Asgers Høj

Environs

A short way south of Kong Asgers Høj stands yet another burial mound – the **Klekkendehøj**, which has two entrances placed side by side. The chamber is 7 m (23 ft) long. The mound has been restored and is now illuminated.

At the south end of Møn is **Grønjægers Høj**, another highly unusual tomb that is estimated to be about 4,000 years old. The burial site is one of the largest dolmens in Denmark and consists of 134 weighty stones arranged in an oval shape. According to one local legend, the site is the final resting place of Queen Fane and her husband, Grøn Jæger.

Chalk crags of Møns Klint, rising from the waters of the Baltic

Møns Klint ㉕

Road map F6. Møn.

The white chalk cliffs soaring above the Baltic are one of Møn's main attractions. The cliffs are about 70 million years old and are formed mostly of calcareous shells. Stretching over a distance of about 7 km (4 miles), the crags reach 128 m (420 ft) in height to form a striking landscape. The highest point is near Dronningestolen (Queen's Throne). At one time these cliffs were mined for chalk but are now a legally protected zone. **Geocenter Møns Klint**, a visitors centre close to the cliffs, comprises geological exhibitions and hands-on activities. There is also a 3D cinema and café.

After a cliff-top hike many people head inland to explore Klinteskoven (Klint Forest), where about 20 types of orchid can be seen flowering from May to August.

Klintholm Havn is a port south of the cliffs. In the 19th century it was a private estate and later taken over by the local authorities. Small pleasure boats leave for 2-hour cruises from here and are a good way to take in the stunning coastal scenery.

One of Stege's quieter shopping streets

🏛 **Geocenter Møns Klint**
Stengårdsvej 8, Borre. **Tel** 55 86 36 00. ◯ Apr–Oct: 11am–5pm daily (Jul–mid-Aug: 10am–6pm). 🎫 ♿

Liselund Slot ㉖

Road map F6. Møn. **Palace** Langebjergvej 4. **Tel** 55 81 21 78. 🎫 May–Sep: 10:30am, 11am, 1:30pm & 2pm Wed–Sun. 🎫 free admission to the park. **www**.liselundslot.dk

The diminutive palace of Liselund was once crown property. A subsequent owner gave the building its present name in honour of his wife. The house is set in a large park, and its whitewashed walls are reflected in the waters of a small lake. The fairytale atmosphere is enhanced by the immaculate thatch on the building's roof (locals joke that this is the world's only thatched-roof palace). Liselund Ny Slot (New Castle), a 19th-century building in the midst of the estate, is now a hotel.

Sun dial at Liselund Slot

Elmelunde ㉗

Road map F6. Møn. 🚌 **Churches in Emelunde and Keldby** ◯ May–Sep: 8am–5pm daily; Oct–Apr: 8am–4pm daily. **www**.keldbyelmelundekirke.dk

Along with its famous cliffs, Møn boasts a number of churches with highly original frescoes. One of them can be

visited in Elmelunde; another in Keldby, a little to the west. Built around 1075, the church in Elmelunde is one of the oldest stone churches in Denmark. The frescoes date from the 14th and 15th centuries and were whitewashed during the Reformation. Ironically this only served to preserve the paintings from fading. They were restored in the 20th century under the guidance of Copenhagen's National-museet (National Museum). The frescoes depict scenes from the Old and New Testaments and include images of Christ and the saints as well as lively portrayals of demons and the flames of hell. Most of them are attributed to one artist, known simply as the Elmelunde Master. The paintings served to explain biblical stories to illiterate peasants and are characterized by their quirky static figures

Medieval fresco in Stege Kirke

with blank faces devoid of any emotion. More frescoes can be seen in Keldby Kirke, which also has a sumptuously carved 16th-century pulpit.

Stege ㉘

Road map F6. Møn. 🏚 4,000. 🚌 🛈 Storegade 2. **Tel** 55 86 04 00. **www**.visitvordingborg.dk

Møn's commercial centre, Stege grew up around a castle built in the 12th century and reached the height of its power in the Middle Ages, when it prospered thanks to a lucrative herring industry. A reminder of those days is Mølleporten (Mill Gate), which spans the main street of the town and once served as Stege's principal entrance. Ramparts belonging to the fortress walls are another medieval relic. **Empiregården**, Stege's museum, is a short way from Mølleporten and has local history exhibits.

Stege Kirke is in the town centre. This Romanesque church was built by Jakob Sunesen, who ruled Møn in the 13th century. Its ceiling frescoes were painted over during the Reformation and exposed again in the 19th century.

🏛 **Empiregården**
Storegade 75. **Tel** 55 81 40 67. ◯ 10am–4pm Tue–Sun. 🎫 **www**. empiregaarden.dk

Nyord island's meadows, with marshland beyond

Nyord ㉙

Road map F5.

Until the late 1980s, the only way to reach the small island of Nyord was by boat. A bridge, built in 1986, now links Nyord with Møn and has made the island more accessible and so increasingly popular with visitors. Nevertheless, both the island and the pretty hamlet of the same name have changed little since the 19th century. Nyord is particularly favoured by bird-watchers – its salt marshes attract massive flocks of birds, especially in spring and autumn, when the island is used as a stopping-off place for winged migrants. The most numerous among them include arctic terns, curlews and swans. The birds can be best viewed from an observation tower situated near the bridge.

Fakse ㉚

Road map F5. *Postvej 3, Fakse Ladeplads.* **Tel** 56 71 60 34. **www**.visitfaxe.dk

References to Fakse (also known as Faxe) can be found in late 13th-century records when it was an important area for limestone mining. Today the town is best known for its local brewery, Faxe Bryggeri, which produces over 130 million litres (28.6 million gallons) of beer each year.

The town's most historic building is the 15th-century Gothic church, which has a number of wall paintings dating from around 1500. **Geomuseum Faxe** has a collection of over 500 types of fossils including some 63 million-year-old remains of

plants and animals found in the Fakse Kalkbrud quarry about 2 km (1 mile) outside the town.

🏛 Geomuseum Faxe
Kulturhuset Kanten, Østervej 2. **Tel** 56 50 28 06. ⭕ Apr, May, Sep & Oct: 1–4:30pm Tue–Sun; Jun–Aug: 11am–4:30pm daily; Nov–Mar: 1–4:30pm Sat & Sun. ⚫ Mon in Jul.

Fakse's brewery, producing millions of gallons of beer a year

Stevns Klint ㉛

Road map F5. 🚶 *Rødvig, Havnevej 21.* **Tel** 56 50 64 64. **www**.visitstevns.dk

Although Denmark's most famous cliffs are found on Møn, the limestone peninsula of Stevns Klint is almost as impressive. The section between Rødvig, a small fishing port, and Gjorslev where there is a 15th-century Gothic castle is the most picturesque, especially when the sun glints against the white chalk surface.

The area was for centuries known for its limestone quarries, which supplied building material for the first castle built by Bishop

Absalon in Copenhagen; this castle became the nucleus of the royal residence, which in later times was given the name of Christiansborg Slot (see pp86–7). Large-scale limestone quarrying was abandoned in the 1940s.

The strip of coastal cliffs is about 15 km (9 miles) long, with the highest peaks rising to about 41 m (135 ft). The best viewpoint can be found next to the old church of Højerup (Højerup Kirke). Legend has it that this 13th-century edifice, built close to the cliff's edge, moves inland each Christmas Eve by the length of a cockerel's jump.

Another local myth recounts a story about a king of the cliffs who lives in a cave in a crag south of the church. The king of the cliffs failed, however, to save the church from the destructive forces of nature. Over the years, due to constant erosion, the sea has advanced closer and closer towards the church and in 1928 the presbytery collapsed and crashed into the water.

A short distance from the church is the small town of Højerup. Here, the **Stevns Museum** has a local-history collection that includes workshops, Stone-Age tools, antique toys and a collection of fire-fighting equipment from the past including pumps and fire engines. There is also an exhibition dealing with the geology of the local cliffs.

Limestone cliffs of Stevns Klint on Zealand's east coast

Environs

A few kilometres inland is **Store Heddinge**, with one of Zealand's best Romanesque churches. The 12th-century church is made from limestone excavated in the nearby quarries. Its octagonal shape probably made it easier to defend.

🏛 **Stevns Museum**
Højerup Bygade 38, 4660 Store Heddinge. **Tel** 56 50 28 06.
⏺ May, Jun, Aug, Sep: 11am–5pm Tue–Sun; Jul: 11am–5pm daily. 🖼

Vallø Slot, a moated 16th-century castle

Vallø Slot ㉜

Road map F5. **Tel** 56 26 05 00.
Castle 🔵 to visitors, but it is possible to explore the courtyard 10am–6pm daily. **Garden** 8am–sunset daily. 🖼

The secluded castle of Vallø is one of the most impressive Renaissance buildings in Denmark. As early as the 15th century the islet was surrounded by a moat and featured a complex of defensive buildings. The castle owes its present shape to the influence of two enterprising sisters, Mette and Birgitte Rosenkrantz, who in the 16th century owned the surrounding land. The sisters divided the estate in equal shares between themselves – the east part was managed by Birgitte, while the western section belonged to Mette.

In 1737 the castle was taken over by a trust that provided a home for unmarried daughters of noble birth during their later years.

The castle is closed to visitors. The large park is open, however, as is the former stable block, which houses a museum containing a mix of agricultural implements and equestrian accessories.

Køge ㉝

Road map F5. 🚶 40,000. 🚉 🚌
ℹ Vestergade 1. **Tel** 56 67 60 01.
www.visitkoege.com

One of Denmark's best-preserved medieval towns, Køge was granted a municipal charter in 1288 and grew quickly thanks to its large natural harbour at the mouth of a navigable river. Køge Bay entered the annals of Danish history in 1677, when the Danish fleet, led by Admiral Niels Juel, crushed a Swedish armada heading for Copenhagen. The battle and the victorious Admiral Juel are commemorated by a 9-m (30-ft) tall obelisk by the harbour.

The heart of the town is its market square, which contains a monument to Frederik VI. The town hall standing in the cobbled square is the longest-serving public building of its kind in Denmark. The cobbled streets leading from the market square are lined with half-timbered houses for which Køge is famous. The most interesting street in this respect is Kirkestræde. The small house at No. 20, with

Kirkestræde 10, now part of Køge library

only two windows, is the oldest half-timbered house in Denmark; the beam under its front door gives the year of construction as 1527.

Another impressive historic building is Sankt Nicolai Kirke, which dates from 1324. Its tower served for many years as a lighthouse and is now used as a viewpoint.

Køge Museum is located along Nørregade and occupies two early-17th-century buildings. Its exhibits include historic furniture, costumes and, as a reminder of the town's bloody past, the local executioner's sword. By the harbour is Kjøge Mini-by, an exact miniature version of Køge as it was in 1865.

🏛 **Køge Museum**
Nørregade 4. **Tel** 56 63 42 42.
⏺ Jun–Aug: 11am–5pm Tue–Sun; Sep–May: 1–5pm Mon–Fri & Sun, 11am–3pm Sat. 🖼

THE ARISTOCRATIC LADIES OF THE CASTLE

In 1737, Vallø's owner, Queen Sophie Magdalene, donated the castle to the Royal Vallø Foundation. From then on the castle become a home for unmarried women from noble families. The famously religious queen ensured the typically cloistral character of the place and promoted a lifestyle true to Christian principles. Initially it housed 12 women, some of whom were as young as 15. The convent was run by a prioress of high birth, and the mother superior was also descended from an aristocratic family. The male staff, an administrator, doctor and servants, lived opposite the castle. Some unmarried ladies still reside in Vallø Slot.

The imposing twin towers of Vallø Slot

FUNEN

Funen (Fyn in Danish) is Denmark's second largest island and occupies an area of about 3,000 sq km (1,158 sq miles). It has some of Denmark's best scenery including wide, sandy beaches, steep cliffs and lush pasture land and orchards. A number of neighbouring islands are considered to be part of Funen including Ærø and Tåsinge, which are themselves popular destinations.

Funen is separated from Zealand by the Store Bælt (Great Belt) and from Jutland by the Lille Bælt (Little Belt). Nearly half of Funen's inhabitants live in Odense, which is the island's capital, a lively cultural centre and the birthplace of Hans Christian Andersen. Aside from Odense there are no large towns on Funen and the island is sometimes described as the "garden of Denmark" because of the large amount of produce that grows in its fertile soil.

Thanks to the fact that the island has escaped most of Denmark's wars with other nations, Funen has an exceptionally high number of well-preserved historic buildings and palaces. The best-known of these is Egeskov Slot, a Renaissance castle encircled by a moat.

The relatively small distances, gently rolling landscape and the many interesting places to visit, make Funen an ideal area for cycling trips. The south-western part of the island features a range of wooded hills. The highest of these, rising to 126 m (413 ft), are found near the town of Faaborg. Central Funen is mostly flat and only becomes slightly undulated in the northeastern region. The south has most of the island's harbours and towns, while the northern and western parts are sparsely populated.

An archipelago of southern islets includes Langeland, Ærø and Tåsinge as well as a number of tiny islands inhabited only by birds. This area is popular with Danish yachtsmen and it is possible to explore the archipelago by joining an organized cruise on board a wooden sailing ship. Some of the islands can be reached by ferry.

The imposing façade of Egeskov Slot, one of Denmark's finest castles

◁ Cultivated fields typical of Funen's coastal region

Exploring Funen

Funen (Fyn in Danish) is known as the garden of
Denmark and for its windy roads and cosy half-
timbered houses. Throughout the centuries the Danish
aristocracy built their opulent residences on the
island, and Funen has over 120 beautifully
preserved mansions, castles and palaces.
The most impressive are Egeskov Slot
and, on Tåsinge, Valdemars Slot.
Funen's coastline is 11,000 km
(6,800 miles) long and has some
beautiful beaches. The lovely island
of Ærø is a picturesque place
with tiny villages and ancient farms.
Odense, Denmark's third-largest
city, is a university town and the
birthplace of Hans Christian Andersen.

Den Gamle Gaard, a merchant's house in Faaborg

KEY

━━━ Motorway

━━ Major road

═══ Minor road

── Scenic route

━━━ Main railway

── Minor railway

0 km   10

0 miles   10

SIGHTS AT A GLANCE

Assens ❶
Egeskov Slot ❻
Faaborg ❼
Hindsholm ❹
Kerteminde ❸
Langeland ❿
Marstal ⓫
Nyborg ❺
Odense pp178–9 ❷
Svendborg ❽
Tåsinge ❾
Ærøskøbing ⓬

Traditional wooden boat moored in Svendborg harbour

Imposing turrets and high walls of Egeskov Slot

GETTING AROUND

Funen is linked to Jutland and Zealand by two bridges. There is a frequent (almost hourly) rail service from Copenhagen and Jutland. The island's main transport artery is the E20 motorway running from east to west (a railway line runs roughly parallel to this). The most important roads that lead from Odense towards other major towns are the No. 9 road to Svendborg and the No. 43 to Faaborg. Ferries sail to Ærø, while Langeland can be reached via a bridge.

SEE ALSO

- **Where to Stay** pp251–3.
- **Where to Eat** pp277–9.

Quiet yacht marina in Assens

Assens ❶

Road map C5. ⛵ *15,000.* 🚌
ℹ️ *Willemoesgade 15A.* **Tel** *63 75 94 20.* **www**.visitassens.dk

Situated on the shores of the Store Bælt (Great Belt), Assens was for centuries a busy harbour for ferries on the route between Funen and Jutland. Following the construction of a bridge across the strait, far north of the town, it lost its importance. Assens contains numerous historic buildings including 18th- and 19th-century merchants' houses, as well as the 15th-century Vor Frue Kirke (Church of Our Lady).

The best-known citizen of Assens was Peter Willemoes (1783–1808), a war hero who, in 1801, fought against Admiral Nelson during the Napoleonic Wars and distinguished himself during Nelson's bombardment of Copenhagen. Willemoes' birthplace, **Willemoesgården**, now houses a museum of cultural history. A monument to Willemoes has been erected near the harbour. A house by the monument was once a sailors' kitchen.

Nearby is the Ernsts Samlinger exhibition in the house of a local silversmith, Frederik Ernst, which has Denmark's largest collection of antique silver and glass.

🏛 **Willemoesgården**
Østergade 36. **Tel** *64 71 31 90.*
⭕ *May–Sep, Easter & mid-Oct: 10am–4pm Tue–Sun; mid-Oct–Apr: 10am–4pm Wed & Sat.* 🖼

Odense ❷

See pp178–9.

Kerteminde ❸

Road map D5. ⛵ *5,500.* 🚌
ℹ️ *Hans Schacksvej 5.* **Tel** *65 32 11 21.* **www**.visitkerteminde.dk

Much of this pretty seaside town is clustered around the 15th-century Sankt Laurentius Kirke (Church). One of the town's main attractions is **Fjord&Bælt**, a sea-life centre built in 1997. A 50-m long tunnel with large windows allows visitors to walk beneath the fjord and enjoy the underwater view. The famous Danish painter Johannes Larsen (1867–1961) once lived in Kerteminde and the **Johannes Larsen Museum** contains many of his paintings.

Environs
Four kilometres (2 miles) southwest of Kerteminde is the **Ladbyskibet**, a 22-m (72-ft) long Viking ship that dates from the 10th century and was used as the tomb of a Viking chieftain.

Statue of St Laurentius, in Kerteminde

🛫 **Fjord&Bælt**
Margrethes Plads 1.
Tel *65 32 42 00.*
⭕ *Feb–Nov: 10am–4pm Mon–Fri, 10am–5pm Sat & Sun.* ⭕ *Jan, Dec.* 🖼
www.fjord-baelt.dk

🏛 **Johannes Larsen Museum**
Møllebakken 14.
Tel *65 32 11 77.* ⭕ *Jun–Aug: 10am–5pm daily; Mar–May, Sep & Oct: 10am–4pm Tue–Sun; Nov–Feb: 11am–4pm Tue–Sun.* 🖼

Hindsholm ❹

Road map D5. 🚌

Rising at the far end of the Hindsholm peninsula are 25-m (82-ft) high cliffs, which provide a splendid view over the coast and the island of Samsø. A little way inland is Marhøj knoll, a 2nd-century BC underground burial chamber.

The small town of Viby, north of Assens, has a 19th-century windmill and an Early-Gothic church. According to legend, Marks Stig, a hero of Danish folklore, was buried here in 1293. Before setting off for war, Marsk Stig is said to have left his wife in the care of the king, Erik Klipping. The king took the notion of "care" somewhat too far and when the knight returned he killed the king and was outlawed. Even his funeral had to be held in secrecy.

Crops growing on the Hindsholm peninsula

Royal painting and suits of armour in the Knights' Hall, Nyborg Slot

Nyborg ❺

Road map D5. 🎿 16,000. 🚆 🚌
ℹ️ Adelgade 3, 63 75 64 60.
www.visitnyborg.dk

The castle of **Nyborg Slot** was built around 1170 by Valdemar the Great's nephew as part of the fortifications that guarded the Store Bælt. For nearly 200 years the castle was the scene of the Danehof assemblies (an early form of Danish parliament). As a result, the city is considered to have been Denmark's capital from 1183 to 1413. The castle was also the venue of the signing, in 1282, of a coronation charter that laid down the duties of the king. Nyborg grew up around this fortress. Over the centuries the castle gradually fell into ruin; it was only after World War I that it was restored and turned into a museum. A number of rooms are open to the public including the royal chambers and the Danehof room. The castle ramparts and moat are now a park.

Nyborg Church, built in the late 14th century, has just one artifact from this time: a Gothic crucifix that is decorated to represent the Tree of Life.

During July and August, on Tuesdays at about 7pm, the Tappenstreg regiment marches through the streets of Nyborg. This regiment upholds an 18th-century tradition of checking whether all the town's entertainment venues have closed on time.

⚜️ **Nyborg Slot**
Slotsgade 11. **Tel** 65 31 02 07. ⭕
Apr, May, Sep & Oct: 10am–3pm
Tue–Sun; Jun–Aug: 10am–4pm
daily. 🏷️ www.museer-nyborg.dk

Egeskov Slot ❻

Road map D5. Egeskov Gade 18, Kværndrup. **Tel** 62 27 10 16. ⭕ May & Sep–early Oct: 10am–5pm daily; Jun–Aug: 10am–6pm daily (1 Jul–9 Aug: to 7pm). 🏷️ www.egeskov.dk

This magnificent castle was built in the mid-16th century and is one of Denmark's best-known sights. Egeskov means "oak forest" and the castle was built in the middle of a pond on a foundation of oak trees. The interior has some grand rooms containing antique furniture and paintings, and a hall full of hunting trophies that include elephant tusks and tiger heads.

Much of the grounds were laid out in the 18th century and include a garden adorned with various fountains, as well as a herb garden. Other additions to the layout are a bamboo maze and a vintage car museum.

Coat of arms from Egeskov Slot

Faaborg ❼

Road map D5. 🎿 8,000. 🚌
ℹ️ Torvet 19, 62 61 07 07.
www.visitfaaborg.dk

Faaborg is a picturesque place with cobbled streets and half-timbered houses. The market square contains the town's most famous monument, Ymerbrønden, produced by the Danish painter and sculptor Kai Nielsen in the early 1900s. Its main figure is Ymer, a giant who according to Nordic mythology was killed by Odin.

The view from the 15-m (49-ft) tall Klokketårnet (Clock Tower) embraces the bay. The tower is all that remains of a medieval church.

Den Gamle Gaard is a wealthy merchant's house that dates from 1725.

Faaborg Museum, designed by Carl Petersen, has a number of works by the "De Fynske Malere" group of Danish artists, which included the likes of Peter Hansen, Johannes Larsen and Fritz Syberg.

🏛️ **Den Gamle Gaard**
Holkegade 1. **Tel** 63 61 20 00.
⭕ Apr, May & Sep–mid-Oct:
11am–3pm Sat & Sun; Jun–Aug:
10am–4pm daily; Dec: 11am–3pm
daily. 🏷️ www.ohavsmuseet.dk

🏛️ **Faaborg Museum**
Grønnegade 75. **Tel** 62 61 06 45.
⭕ Nov–Mar: 11am–3pm Tue–Sun;
Apr–Oct: 10am–4pm daily. 🏷️
www.faaborgmuseum.dk

Collection of Danish art in Faaborg Museum

Odense ❷

The city's coat of arms

One of the oldest cities in Denmark, Odense derives its name from the Nordic god Odin who was worshipped by the Vikings. In medieval times it was an important centre of trade and from the 12th century on it was a major pilgrimage destination. Since the 19th century, when a canal was built linking Odense with the sea, the city has been a major port. Odense has a rich cultural life and plenty to see including a cathedral and a museum devoted to the city's most famous son, Hans Christian Andersen.

Exploring Odense

Most attractions lie within the boundaries of the medieval district. Getting around Odense is made easy by the Citypass, which entitles the holder to free travel, free admission to museums and cut-price tickets for boat cruises.

🏛 Brandts

Brandts Passage 37–43.
Mediemuseet *Tel* 65 20 70 10.
◯ 10am–5pm Tue, Wed & Fri–Sun; noon–9pm Thu. ● Mon (except for weeks 7, 8 & 42). 🖼
Museet for Fotokunst *Tel* 65 20 70 10. ◯ same as above. 🖼
Kunsthallen Brandts *Tel* 65 20 70 10. ◯ same as above. 🖼
For more than fifty years Brandt's textile factory was the biggest company in Odense. After its closure in 1977 it stood empty for a number of years until it was renovated and transformed into a cultural centre. Today it houses museums, a cinema, art galleries, shops, restaurants and cafés. The **Mediemuseet** has displays on the history of print production and the latest electronic media. The **Museet for**

Art gallery in Brandts

Fotokunst exhibits works by Danish and international photographers, while the **Kunsthallen Brandts** shows contemporary art, craft, design and performance.

Childhood home of Hans Christian Andersen

🏛 H.C. Andersens Barndomshjem

Munkemøllestræde 3–5. *Tel* 65 51 46 01. ◯ Jan–Jun & Sep–Dec: 11am–3pm Tue–Sun; Jul & Aug: 10am–4pm daily. 🖼 www.museum.odense.dk
The Andersen family moved to this small house close to the cathedral when Hans was two years old. Andersen lived here until the age of 14. The museum has only a few rooms, furnished with basic period household objects, but manages to conjure up what life was like for a poor Danish family in the early 19th century.

⛪ Sankt Knuds Kirke

Klosterbakken 2. *Tel* 66 12 03 92. ◯ Apr–Oct: 10am–5pm daily; Nov–Mar: 10am–4pm daily. www.odense-domkirke.dk
Odense cathedral is named after Canute (Knud) II, who ruled Denmark from 1080–86. The king's skeleton is on public display in a glass

16th-century cathedral altarpiece by Claus Berg

case down in the basement. The present cathedral is one of Denmark's most beautiful examples of Gothic architecture. It stands on the site of an earlier Romanesque structure, which was destroyed by fire in 1248. The cathedral's ornate gilded altar is a masterpiece of 16th-century craftsmanship by Claus Berg of Lübeck. The triptych is 5 m (16 ft) high and includes nearly 300 intricately carved figures within its design.

🏛 Flakhaven

Flakhaven derives its name from an old Danish word meaning an area surrounded by meadows and gardens. For centuries the square was used as a market venue and attracted merchants and farmers from all over Funen. The main building standing in the square is the Rådhus (city hall), which has a west wing dating from the 19th century. The remainder of the building is 20th century. Guided tours are available on Tuesdays and Thursdays in the summer and include access to the Wedding Room, the Town Council Chamber and a wall commemorating citizens who have made major contributions to the city's history.

🏛 Fyns Kunstmuseum

Jernbanegade 13. *Tel* 65 51 46 01. ◯ 10am–4pm Tue–Sun. 🖼 www.museum.odense.dk
This museum has a very large collection of Danish art, though only a fraction of it is on display at any one time. The Classicist building is adorned on the outside with a frieze depicting scenes from Danish history and mythology. The interior is

crammed with paintings, etchings and sculptures by Danish artists spanning a period of 250 years. One section contains works by local Funen artists, collectively known as Fynboerne.

🏛 H.C. Andersens Hus

Bangs Boder 29.
Tel 65 51 46 01.
⬜ Jan–Jun & Sep–Dec: 10am–4pm Tue–Sun; Jul & Aug: 10am–5pm daily.
🖥 www.museum.odense.dk

Bust from Fyns Kunstmuseum

Denmark's most famous writer was born in this house in 1805. It is now a museum, and it was greatly extended and modernized to celebrate the 200th anniversary of Andersen's birth. The exhibition includes a recreation of the author's study and numerous items belonging to Andersen, including his notes and letters. There is even an old rope – apparently Andersen was terrified by the thought of a fire and carried this with him wherever he went in readiness for an emergency evacuation. Hanging on one of the walls is a world map

indicating the countries in which Andersen's tales have been published in translation. A special collection includes copies of his works in 120 languages.

Close to the museum is Fyrtøjet, a children's cultural centre based on Andersen's stories.

🏛 Carl Nielsen Museet

Claus Bergs Gade 11. **Tel** 65 51 46 01. ⬜ May–Aug: 11am–3pm Wed–Sun; Sep–Apr: 3–7pm Thu & Fri, 11am–3pm Sat & Sun.

This museum, devoted to the famous Danish composer Carl Nielsen (1865–1931), was opened in 1988 to celebrate

VISITORS' CHECKLIST

Road map D5.
👥 185,000. 🚌 🚆
ℹ City Hall, 63 75 75 20.
@ otb@visitodense.com
www.visitodense.com

the town's millennium. The exhibits, donated by the descendents of the composer, are all associated with Nielsen, who is mainly known for his operas, symphonies and violin concertos. In addition to handwritten scores of the artist's compositions, the collection includes Nielsen's piano and works by his wife, the sculptor Anne Marie Brodersen.

City hall façade, crowned with an allegorical statue of Justice

ODENSE CITY CENTRE

Brandts ①
Carl Nielsen Museet ⑦
Flakhaven ④
Fyns Kunstmuseum ⑤
H.C. Andersens Barndomshjem ②
H.C. Andersens Hus ⑥
Sankt Knuds Kirke ③

🚌 Bus Station
🚆 Train Station

Key to Symbols see back flap

Svendborg ⑧

Road map D5. 🏘 *30,000.* 🚆 🚌
ℹ️ *Centrumpladsen 4.* **Tel** *62 23 57
00.* 🎏 *Fyn Rundt Regatta (Jul).*
www.visitsvendborg.dk

Funen's second largest town,
Svendborg is a busy port and
has strong links with shipbuilding. In the 19th century
its boatyards produced half
of all Danish vessels.

Most of Svendborg's sights
are within easy reach of
Torvet, the market square.
Closest to hand is the 13th-
century Vor Frue Kirke, which
has a carillon consisting of
27 bells. Sankt Nicolai Kirke
is slightly older, though also
13th century. A short distance
west of Vor Frue Kirke is
Anne Hvides Gård, a half-
timbered building dating from
1560. **SAK Kunstbygningen**
(SAK Art Exhibitions) displays
works by the Danish sculptor
Kai Nielsen (1882–1924), who
was born in Svendborg. Other
museums in town include
Naturama, a natural history
museum, and **Forsorgs-
museet**, built in 1872 as a
"poor farm". In 1906 there
were 450 such institutions in
Denmark; this, the only extant
one, houses a museum telling
the story of the country's poor.

🏛 **SAK Kunstbygningen**
Vestergade 27. **Tel** *62 22 44 70.*
⭕ *11am–4pm Tue–Sat.* 🎟

🏛 **Forsorgsmuseet**
Viebæltegård Gruppemøllevej 13.
Tel *62 21 02 61.* ⭕ *May–Oct:
10am–4pm daily; mid-Feb–Apr:
10am–2pm Tue–Sun.* 🎟 🔊 🚻 🛍
🏠 **www**.svendborgmuseum.dk

Kattesund, a scenic alley in
Svendborg

An elegant apartment in Valdemars Slot, Tåsinge

Tåsinge ⑨

Road map D6. 🏘 *2,500.* 🚌

The island of Tåsinge is linked
by bridge to Funen and
Langeland. The major local
attraction is **Valdemars Slot**,
built by Christian IV for his
favourite son Valdemar and
completed in 1644.

The castle's architect was
Hans van Steenwinckel, who
was also responsible for
Rosenborg Slot in Copenhagen
(see pp60–61). In 1670s the
king gave the castle to Admiral
Niels Juel in recognition of his
successful command of the
Danish fleet during the Battle
of Køge Bay. The castle has
remained in the hands of the
Juel family ever since. The
royal apartments, the reception rooms and the kitchens
are open to the public. In the
attic there is a collection of
items including trophies from
African safaris. The domestic
quarters, arranged around a
lake, house a small museum.

Environs
Near the castle, heading for
Svendborg, is the fishing port
of **Troense**. Its most attractive
street, Grønnegade, is lined
with half-timbered houses.
In Bregninge, the **Tåsinge
Museum** illustrates life at sea;
it also tells of the ill-fated love
affair between circus performer
Elvira Madigan and Swedish
lieutenant Sixten Sparre.

⚓ **Valdemars Slot**
Troense. **Tel** *62 22 61 06.*
⭕ *Apr–Oct: 10am–5pm, days
vary; see website for details.* 🎟
www.valdemarsslot.dk

🏛 **Tåsinge Museum**
Kirkebakken 1, Bregninge.
Tel *62 22 71 44.*
⭕ *Jun–Aug: 10am–4pm Tue–Sun;
at other times by appointment
(groups only).* 🎟 🖼
www.taasinge-museum.dk

Statue of Hans Christian Ørsted
in Rudkøbing

Langeland ⑩

Road map D6. 🏘 *13,000.* 🚢 🚌
ℹ️ *Rudkøbing Torvet 5.* **Tel** *62 51
35 05.* **www**.langeland.dk

Langeland is positioned off
the southeast coast of Funen
and can be reached by bridge
or from Lolland by ferry. The
island has a number of good
beaches and marked cycling
paths. Windmills are dotted
here and there, along with
quaint hamlets and farms.

Rudkøbing is the capital
and the island's only sizeable
town. Its most famous citizen
was Hans Christian Ørsted
(1777–1851), a physicist who
made major advances in the

field of electromagnetism. The house in which the scientist was born is known as **Det Gamle Apotek** (The Old Pharmacy) and has been arranged to re-create an 18th-century pharmacist's shop and herb garden. In front of it stands a statue of Ørsted. From here it is only a short distance to the market square, which contains a 19th-century town hall and a much older church with an inscription giving its year of founding as 1105.

About 10 km (6 miles) north of Rudkøbing is **Tranekær**, whose main attraction is Tranekær Slot, a pink-coloured castle that dates from around 1200. The castle is normally closed to visitors, but there are some guided tours in July, and the grounds can also be visited. Part of the estate now serves as a botanical garden which has a number of rare trees including some Californian sequoias. An open-air gallery exhibits sculptures and installations by Danish and international artists. About 30 km (18 miles) south of Rudkøbing is the **Koldkrigsmuseum** (Cold War Museum), where you can explore a submarine, a minesweeper and a bunker.

ⅲ Det Gamle Apotek
Brogade 15, Rudkøbing. **Tel** 63 51 63 00. ☐ for guided tours (Jul).

ⅲ Koldkrigsmuseum
Vognsbjergvej 4B, Bagenkop. **Tel** 62 56 27 00. ☐ Apr–Oct: 10am–5pm daily (Apr & Oct: to 4pm). **www**.langelandsfortet.dk

Colourful façade of Tranekær Slot, Langeland

Picturesque 17th-century houses in Ærøskøbing

Marstal ⓫

Road map D6. Ærø. 🏠 1,500. ⛴ 🚌 🛈 Havnegade 5. **Tel** 62 52 13 00. ☐ mid-Jun–Aug: 9am–3:30pm Mon–Sat.

Marstal is the largest town on the island of Ærø. Its history has long been associated with the sea and in the 18th century it was a busy port with about 300 ships arriving here every year.

The **Søfartmuseum** (Maritime Museum) occupies four buildings near the harbour and contains many items connected with the sea including model schooners and seafaring paintings.

The dependence of the local population on the sea is also apparent in the local church on Kirkestræde, which was built in 1738. The altarpiece in the church depicts Christ calming the rough waves, and hanging in several places within the building are votive sailing ships. Outside in the cemetery there are numerous gravestones of local sailors. The church clock was created by Jens Olsen, who also produced the World Clock in the Rådhus in Copenhagen (*see p74*).

Exhibit from Marstal's Søfartmuseum

ⅲ Søfartmuseum
Prinsensgade 1. **Tel** 62 53 23 31. ☐ Nov–Apr: 10am–4pm Mon–Fri, 11am–3pm Sat; May, Sep & Oct: 10am–4pm daily; Jun: 9am–5pm daily; Jul & Aug: 9am–6pm daily.

Ærøskøbing ⓬

Road map D6. Ærø. 🏠 800. ⛴ 🚌 🛈 Havnen 4. **Tel** 62 52 13 00.

Many of the 17th-century houses lining the cobbled streets are a reminder of a time when Ærøskøbing was a prosperous merchant town. The oldest house dates from 1645 and can be found at Søndergade 36. The town's most picturesque dwelling is Dukkehuset (Dolls' House) at Smedegade 37. Also in Smedegade is **Flaske-Peters Samling**, a museum devoted to Peter Jacobsen, who first went to sea at the age of 16. Known as "Bottle Peter", he created about 1,700 ships-in-a-bottle before he died in 1960. Also in the museum is a cross he made for his own grave. **Ærø Museum** has displays on the history of the island and its people, including a collection of 19th-century paintings.

ⅲ Flaske-Peters Samling
Smedegade 22. **Tel** 62 52 29 50. ☐ early Apr–mid-Jun & mid-Aug–mid-Oct: 10am–4pm daily; mid-Jun–mid-Aug: 10am–5pm daily; mid-Oct–early Apr: 1–3pm Tue–Fri, 10am–noon Sat.

ⅲ Ærø Museum
Brogade 3–5. **Tel** 62 52 29 50. ☐ early Apr–mid-Jun: 11am–3pm daily; mid-Jun–mid-Sep: 10am–4pm daily; mid-Oct–early Apr: 10am–1pm Mon–Fri & Sun, noon–3pm Sat.

SOUTHERN AND CENTRAL JUTLAND

*A*s well as the scenic lowlands and undulating hills and meadows found on the eastern side of central Jutland, this region has much to recommend it. Attractions include beautifully preserved medieval towns, traditional hamlets, parks, castles and ancient Viking burial grounds. In addition, no one travelling with children should miss a trip to LEGOLAND®.

Jutland derives its name from the Jutes, a Germanic tribe that once inhabited this peninsula. When the Vikings, who occupied the islands to the east, began to encroach on this territory, the mixing of the two tribes gave rise to the Danes as a distinct people.

After Denmark's defeat during the Schleswig Wars in 1864, Jutland was occupied by Prussia, and subsequently, as part of Schleswig, remained under German control. It was not until a plebiscite in 1920 that it once more became part of the kingdom of Denmark. After the final resolution of this Danish-German border dispute, many families decided to remain on the "other" side. The expatriate minorities are still active on both sides of the border.

On the islands of Fanø and Rømø the influence of the nearby Netherlands can be seen in the tiles decorating some of the houses. The Wadden Sea around these islands is well worth exploring on a seal or oyster safari. The milder east coast features wealthy borough towns with fine museums.

The top attraction for families with children is LEGOLAND®, where millions of plastic LEGO® bricks are used to create Denmark's best-known amusement park. The cities of Aarhus and Silkeborg offer a more cultural approach.

Carved Viking figures and replica Viking ship in Vejle Fjord

◁ Farmhouses set amid the undulating fields of Jutland

Exploring Southern and Central Jutland

Jutland is the only part of Denmark that is not an island. The bottom section of the peninsula is cut across by a 69-km (43-mile) long national border with Germany. The most popular attraction of southern and central Jutland is LEGOLAND®. However, this region has much more to offer, including four national parks; several historically significant centres – such as Ribe, Denmark's oldest town, and Jelling, which is famous for its ancient burial mounds; and the delightfully arty town of Silkeborg, splendidly located in the heart of a Lake District. Aarhus, Denmark's second city, is famous for its nightlife, fuelled by the students at its university.

GETTING AROUND

Jutland is almost three times larger than the rest of Denmark put together and distances between towns can be significant. The E45 runs from the German border all the way to northern Jutland along the eastern coast of the peninsula, connecting to Esbjerg from Kolding, and to Silkeborg and Herning from Aarhus. The fastest route from Copenhagen is the E20, which joins with the E45 at Fredericia. It is also possible to take a ferry to either Aarhus or Ebeltoft. Esbjerg's harbour handles ferry traffic from the UK.

SEE ALSO

• *Where to Stay* pp253–5.
• *Where to Eat* pp279–81.

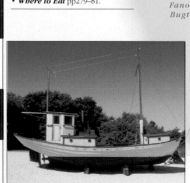

Restored cutter in front of Esbjerg's maritime museum

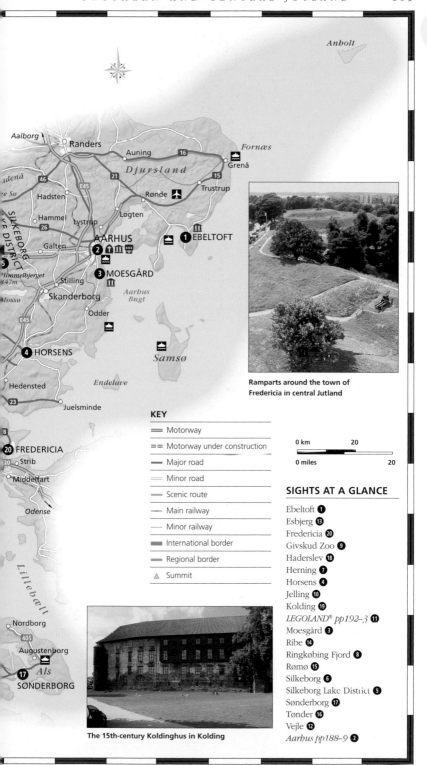

Anholt

Aalborg
Randers
Auning
Fornæs
16
Grenå
Djursland
udenå
46
E45
21
15
e Sø
Hadsten
Trustrup
Rønde
Hammel
Lystrup
26
Logten
SILKEBORG
LAKE DISTRICT
AARHUS
2
1 EBELTOFT
Galten
3 MOESGÅRD
5
Himmelbjerget
147m
Stilling
Skanderborg
Aarhus Bugt
Mosso
Odder
E45
4 HORSENS
Samsø
Hedensted
Endelave
23
Juelsminde

Ramparts around the town of Fredericia in central Jutland

KEY

═══ Motorway

══ Motorway under construction

─── Major road

⋯⋯ Minor road

─── Scenic route

⌐⌐ Main railway

─── Minor railway

▬▬ International border

─── Regional border

△ Summit

| 0 km | 20 |
| 0 miles | 20 |

SIGHTS AT A GLANCE

Ebeltoft **1**

Esbjerg **13**

Fredericia **20**

Givskud Zoo **9**

Haderslev **18**

Herning **7**

Horsens **4**

Jelling **10**

Kolding **19**

LEGOLAND® pp192–3 **11**

Moesgård **3**

Ribe **14**

Ringkøbing Fjord **8**

Rømø **15**

Silkeborg **6**

Silkeborg Lake District **5**

Sønderborg **17**

Tønder **16**

Vejle **12**

Aarhus pp188–9 **2**

8
20 FREDERICIA
20 Strib
Middelfart
Odense
Lillebælt
Nordborg
405
Augustenborg
17 *Als*
SØNDERBORG

The 15th-century Koldinghus in Kolding

Aarhus ❷

See pp188–9.

Moesgård ❸

Road map D4. *7 km (4 miles) south of Aarhus.* **Tel** *87 16 10 16.* 🎭 *Vikingetræf (Jul).* **www**.moesmus.dk

Formerly located in a manor house, Moesgård is a large prehistoric museum that is due to reopen to the public in purpose-built premises in 2014–15. Situated on a hill known as Hill of the Elves, a short drive south of Aarhus, the museum has several highlights, ranging from its collection of runic stones, the largest in Scandinavia, to a hoard of votive offerings – swords, axes, shields and other items – found at Illerup Ådal, near Skanderborg, and dating to about 200 AD. Its star exhibit, however, is the Grauballe Man. This mummified body, discovered in 1952 in a bog, had been preserved thanks to a combination of acids and iron in the soil. He is believed to have been about 40 years old when he died in 80 BC. A slash across his throat indicates that he was probably murdered.

Each year in late July, Moesgård becomes the venue for a lively and entertaining Viking festival, Vikingtræf, which features battles, a Viking marketplace and Icelandic horses performing.

Lichtenberg Palace, Horsens, once a residence for the tsar's family

Horsens ❹

Road map C4. *38 km (24 miles) south of Aarhus.* 🚶 *50,000.* 🚉 🚌 🛈 *Fussingsvej 8.* **Tel** *75 60 21 20.* 🎭 *Medieval Festival (late Aug).* **www**.visithorsens.dk

Horsens is the birthplace of Vitus Bering (1681–1741), the explorer who discovered Alaska and the straits that separate it from Siberia (these were subsequently named after him). The guns from Bering's ship now stand in the town's main park. Mementos from his expeditions are on display in **Horsens Museum**.

The Danish Romanesque Vor Frelsers Kirke (Our Saviour's Church) is 13th century. Nearby, Lichtenberg Palace was used by the tsar's family after they fled Russia. The **Horsens Kunst Museum** has contemporary Danish art.

🏛 **Horsens Museum**
Sundvej 1A. **Tel** *76 29 23 50.* 🕐 *Jul–Aug: 10am–4pm daily; Sep–Jun: 11am–4pm Tue–Sun.* 🈲

🏛 **Horsens Kunst Museum**
Carolinelundsvej 2. **Tel** *76 29 23 70.* 🕐 *Jul & Aug: 10am–4pm daily (to 5pm Sat & Sun); Sep–Jun: 11am–4pm Tue–Sun (to 5pm Sat & Sun).* 🈲 **www**.horsenskunstmuseum.com

Fregatten Jylland in Ebeltoft, now serving as a museum

Ebeltoft ❶

Road map D3. 🚶 *7,500.* 🚌 🛈 *S.A. Jensens Vej 3.* **Tel** *86 34 14 00.*

Boasting the smallest *rådhus* (town hall) in Denmark, Ebeltoft, part of the Mols Bjerge national park, is over 700 years old. Many of the town's cobbled streets, including Adelgade, are lined with half-timbered houses from the 17th century.

In the harbour is **Fregatten Jylland**, a large restored wooden ship that took part in the Battle of Helgoland in 1864. Groups of visitors can arrange overnight stays on board, sleeping in a hammock and experiencing the life of a sailor. A large museum annex focuses on maritime history.

The nearby **Glasmuseet** has many items of contemporary glass art on display, including pieces by Dale Chihuly and Harvey Littleton.

Bell from
Fregatten Jylland

🏛 **Fregatten Jylland**
S.A. Jensen Vej 2–4. **Tel** *86 34 10 99.* 🕐 *Jan–Mar, Nov & Dec: 11am–3pm daily; Apr–Aug: 10am–5pm daily; Sep & Oct: 11am–4pm daily; during school holidays: 10am–6pm.* 🈲 **www**.fregatten-jylland.dk

🏛 **Glasmuseet**
Strandvejen 8. **Tel** *86 34 17 99.* 🕐 *Jan–Mar, Nov & Dec: 10am–4pm Tue–Sun; Apr–Jun, Sep & Oct: 10am–5pm Tue–Sun; Jul & Aug: 10am–6pm Tue–Sun.* 🈲 **www**.glasmuseet.dk

Reconstructed burial chamber at Moesgård

Silkeborg harbour, in Denmark's Lake District

Silkeborg Lake District ❺

Road map C4.

The stretch between Silkeborg and Skanderborg and the area slightly to the north of it is a land of lakes and hills known as Søhøjlandet. Here, visitors find Jutland's largest lake – the Mossø, as well as Denmark's longest river, the Gudenå (176 km/109 miles). The Lake District also has some of the country's highest peaks. In summer it is a favourite destination for canoeists and cyclists, as well as hikers, all of whom make the most of the lakeland scenery.

Gjern has a vintage car museum (with about 70 models, the oldest dating from the early 20th century), while Tange Sø boasts **Elmuseet**, an electricity museum situated next to the country's largest power station.

Other places worth visiting include the church in Veng, which was built around 1100 and is thought to be the oldest monastery in Denmark, and, on the shores of Mossø, the ruins of Øm Kloster, the best preserved Cistercian monastery in Denmark.

Silkeborg ❻

Road map C4. 🏠 *42,000.* 🚆 🚌
🛈 *Åhavevej 2A.* **Tel** *86 82 19 11.*
🎵 *Jazz Festival (Jun), Country Music Festival (Aug).* **www**.silkeborg.com

Silkeborg owes much of its past prosperity to the paper factory, built in 1846, that was at one time powered by the local river.

Silkeborg's **Culture Museum** occupies a former manor built in 1767. Most visitors head straight for the Tollund Man, one of the best-preserved prehistoric bodies in the world.

The city is also famous for its art galleries, such as **Silkeborg Bad**, which focuses on contemporary art, and **Museum Jorn**, with works by the Danish artist Asger Jorn and other members of the COBRA movement.

In summer a 19th-century paddle steamer travels the 15 km (9 miles) to Himmelbjerget, where a 25-m (82-ft) high tower offers great views.

Tollund Man

🏛 **Culture Museum**
Hovedgårdsvej 7. **Tel** *86 82 14 99.*
⭘ *10am–5pm daily.* 📷

🏛 **Museum Jorn**
Gudenåvej 7–9. **Tel** *86 82 53 88.*
⭘ *10am–5pm Tue–Sun.* 📷 ♿ 📷

🏛 **Silkeborg Bad**
Gjessøvej 40. **Tel** *86 81 63 29.*
⭘ *noon–4pm Tue–Fri, 11am–5pm Sat & Sun (May–Sep): 10am–5pm Tue–Sun).* 📷

Herning ❼

Road map C4. 🏠 *30,000.*
🚆 🚌 🛈 *Østergade 21.*
Tel *96 27 22 22.*
www.visitherning.dk

The town of Herning was established in the late 19th century following the arrival of the railway. The **Herning Museum** tells the story of the town as well as the history and archaeology of the region. The **Herning Kunstmuseum** (Art Museum), exhibits works by artists such as Carl-Henning Pedersen, a representative of the COBRA movement. Housed in a building designed by the US architect Steven Holl, **Heart** is a museum of Danish and international contemporary art. The **Danmarks Fotomuseum** has an extensive collection of cameras and interesting photographic displays.

🏛 **Herning Museum**
Museumgade 32. **Tel** *96 26 19 00.*
⭘ *10am–4:30pm Tue–Fri, 11am–4:30pm Sat & Sun (Jul: also Mon).* 📷

🏛 **Herning Kunstmuseum**
Birk Centerpark 3. **Tel** *97 12 10 33.*
⭘ *10am–5pm Tue–Fri, noon–5pm Sat & Sun (May–Oct: 10am–5pm Tue–Sun; Jul: also Mon).* 📷

🏛 **Heart**
Birk Centerpark 8. **Tel** *97 12 10 33.*
⭘ *10am–5pm Tue–Sun.* 📷

🏛 **Danmarks Fotomuseum**
Museumsgade 28. **Tel** *97 22 53 22.*
⭘ *noon–4:30pm Tue–Sun (Jul: 11am–4:30pm daily).* 📷

One of Herning's tranquil streets

Aarhus ❷

Denmark's second-largest city dates back to Viking times. It was originally named Aros, meaning "at the mouth of the river", and due to its location on Jutland's eastern coast it became a major seaport. After the Reformation Aarhus grew into an important trading centre, and the 19th century saw the development of the harbour. A university was founded here in 1928, and today Aarhus boasts a vibrant cultural life, with some fine museums and venues, as well as lively cafés and bars. The city is also a major centre for wind energy and the home of many wind turbine manufacturers.

Town panorama from the Rådhus tower

Exploring Aarhus
Most of the town's attractions are concentrated within a fairly small area; the only site located more than 1 km (0.6 mile) away is Den Gamle By. Sightseeing is made easier by the Aarhus Pass, which gives free admission to museums and free use of public transport.

▥ Musikhuset
Thomas Jensens Allé 2.
Tel 89 40 40 40. ◯ *11am–9pm daily.* **www**.musikhusetaarhus.dk
The city's concert hall opened in 1982 and is one of Denmark's foremost cultural centres. The glass-fronted building is home to the prestigious Jutland Opera Company and Aarhus Symphony Orchestra, which holds concerts most Thursday evenings. The building is worth visiting if only to see its vast glazed hall, planted with luxuriant palm trees. The centre features its own café, which often has concerts, and a restaurant, the Richter, named after Johan Richter, the main architect of the building.

▥ Rådhus
Rådhuspladsen. **Tel** 87 31 50 10. ▨
The modern city hall was designed by Arne Jacobsen and Erik Møller and completed in 1941. The building is a prime example of Danish Modernism. It is clad on the outside with dark Norwegian marble and topped with a rectangular clock tower, which affords a good view of the city. The interior has a lighter feel. The large council chamber and Civic Room are worth seeking out.

The modernist Rådhus, designed by Arne Jacobsen

▥ ARoS Kunstmuseum
Aros Allé 2. **Tel** 87 30 66 00.
◯ *10am–5pm Tue, Fri–Sun, 10am–10pm Wed & Thu.*
▨ ▧ ▥ **www**.aros.dk
This gallery is housed in a ten-storey building topped by a circular rainbow-coloured walkway; designed by Olafur Eliasson, *Your Rainbow Panorama* offers breathtaking views of the city. The art collection presents works spanning from the Danish Golden Age to the present day.

▥ Vikingemuseet
Sankt Clemens Torv. ◯ *10am–4pm Mon–Wed, Fri, 10am–5:30pm Thu.*
www.vikingemuseet.dk
In a building across from the cathedral, next to the Nordea Bank, is a museum devoted to the Viking era. The prime exhibit is a section of archaeological excavation that was conducted in Clemens Torv. Fragments of the original Viking ramparts, discovered in 1964, are on display along with items dating from 900 to 1400 including a skeleton, a reconstructed house, wood-working tools, pottery, and runic stones. Similar discoveries at nearby Store Torv have confirmed the importance of Aarhus as a major centre of Viking culture.

▥ Domkirke
Store Torv. **Tel** 86 20 54 00.
◯ *May–Sep: 9:30am–4pm Mon–Fri; Oct–Dec: 10am–3pm Mon–Sat.*
www.aarhus-domkirke.dk
Aarhus's main place of worship is at the heart of the city's oldest district. The cathedral was built in 1201 but destroyed by fire in the 14th century. It was rebuilt in the late 15th century in a Gothic style, and is easily Denmark's longest cathedral with a nave that spans nearly 100 m (328 ft). Until the end of the 16th century most of the cathedral walls were covered with frescoes. During the Reformation these were whitewashed over, but many have since been restored. The five-panel altarpiece dates from 1479 and is the work of Bernt Notke of Lübeck. The Baroque pipe organ dates from 1730.

For hotels and restaurants in this region see pp253–5 and pp279–81

🏛 Kvindemuseet

Domkirkeplads 5. *Tel 86 18 64 70.* ⬜ 10am–4pm daily (to 8pm Sat). 🖼 www. kvindemuseet.dk

The Women's Museum has made a name for itself with its imaginative temporary exhibitions relating to women's issues – past and present. Since 1984 the museum has been collecting objects, photographs and documents illustrating the many changes that have taken place over the centuries in the lives of women in Danish society.

Figure from Bernt Notke's altarpiece

🔒 Vor Frue Kirke

Frue Kirkeplads. *Tel 86 12 12 43.* ⬜ May–Aug: 10am–4pm Mon–Fri; Sep–Apr: 10am–2pm Mon–Fri, 10am–noon Sat. www. aarhusvorfrue.dk

Vor Frue Kirke is a complex of three churches in a former Dominican monastery. The oldest section of this complex is the 11th-century Romanesque stone crypt. The highlight here is a replica of an early crucifix featuring a Christ with Viking plaits. The star adornment inside

VISITORS' CHECKLIST

Road map D4. 🚗 255,000. 🚉 🚌 ℹ *Banegårdspladsen 20, 8000 Aarhus C. Tel 87 31 50 10.* 🎷 *Aarhus International Jazz Festival (2nd half of Jul), Aarhus Festuge/Cultural Week (1st week Sep).* www.visitaarhus.com

the church is a 16th-century wooden altarpiece carved by Claus Berg.

🏛 Den Gamle By

Viborgvej 2. *Tel 86 12 31 88.* ⬜ *Opening hours vary; check the website or call the museum prior to your visit.* 🖼 www.dengamleby.dk

This open-air museum consists of 80 or so buildings – including shops, a mayor's house, a school, a post office and a windmill – re-creating a typical Danish town the way it would have looked in the 19th century, at the time of Hans Christian Andersen. The atmosphere is especially vibrant during the Living History season (Easter–Dec), when actors play key characters in the town, such as the vicar and the town crier. Two separate sections re-create life in the 1920s and the 1970s.

The 11th-century crypt of Vor Frue Kirke

AARHUS CITY CENTRE

ARoS Kunstmuseum ③
Domkirke ⑤
Kvindemuseet ⑥
Musikhuset ①
Rådhus ②
Vikingemuseet ④
Vor Frue Kirke ⑦

0 m   200
0 yards   200

Key to Symbols *see back flap*

Harbour with Ringkøbing Fjord in the background

Ringkøbing Fjord ❽

Road map B4. 🛈 *Ringkøbing, Torvet 22; Hvide Sande, Nørregade 2B.* **Tel** *70 22 70 01.* 🎭 *Sand Sculpture Festival (Søndervig, mid-Jun–Nov).* **www**.visitvest.dk

A thin strip of land some 35 km (22 miles) long separates Ringkøbing Fjord from the North Sea. This sandy spit is about 1 km (half a mile) wide and has many summer cottages tucked among the dunes. The only water access between the sea and Ringkøbing Fjord is through a channel and lock in the town of Hvide Sande. Ringkøbing Fjord is popular with windsurfers and the calm waters of the bay are suitable for novices; the North Sea, on the other side of the spit, offers more challenging conditions.

On the bay's northern shore is **Ringkøbing**, the largest town in this region. Ringkøbing was once a sea-port but over the centuries the entrance from the bay to the sea shifted southwards and the town became an inland harbour. Standing in Torvet, the town's main square, are some of the most historic buildings including Hotel Ringkøbing, a timbered building that dates from 1600. The local **museum** has alternating exhibitions.

The locality includes many attractions. **Fiskeriets Hus** (House of Fisheries) at Hvide Sande contains an aquarium with fish and shellfish from the North Sea and fjord waters as well as displays on the area's fishing industry. A paved footpath, suitable for wheelchair users, leads from the museum to **Troldbjerg**, Hvide Sande's main viewpoint. The mast at the top was once used by sailors to warn them about water levels. Another good view is from the 60-m (197-ft) high lighthouse on the Nørre Lyngvig dune, 5 km (3 miles) north of Hvide Sande.

A different kind of scenery can be found on the southern shores of Ringkøbing Fjord, where the marshes form **Tipperne Nature Reserve**, one of Denmark's most important sites for waterfowl. Access is restricted to a few hours on Friday or Sunday mornings so as not to disturb the migrating birds. The reserve contains an observation tower.

Bust of Jacob Hansen, Givskud Zoo's founder

🏛 **Ringkøbing Museum**
Herningvej 4. **Tel** *97 32 16 15.* ◯ *11am–5pm Mon–Fri, 10am–3pm Sat & Sun.* 🎭 www.levendehistorie.dk

🐟 **Fiskeriets Hus**
Nørregade 2B, Hvide Sande. **Tel** *97 31 26 10.* ◯ *10am–5pm daily (Nov–Easter: to 4pm).* 🎭 www.fiskerietshus.dk

Givskud Zoo ❾

Road map C4. **Løveparken Givskud Zoo Tel** *75 73 02 22.* ◯ *late Apr–mid-Oct: from 10am daily. Closing times vary; check the website for details.* 🎭 **www**.givskudzoo.dk

A short way north of Jelling is Givskud Zoo (sometimes referred to as Løveparken), home to the largest pride of lions in Scandinavia. When the park was established in 1969 the pride had 29 members; today it has over 40. In addition to the lions, Givskud has about 900 other animals representing 70 species. Givskud is part-zoo, part-safari park, and many of the animals are left to wander freely within their allocated areas. Car drivers can travel along marked routes. Visitors on foot can enjoy a safari by bus. The lions are the most popular sight, but there is no denying the appeal of the giraffes, zebras, buffalos, ostriches and other species that inhabit the park. One of the zoo's other attractions is the Western Lowland gorillas enclosure; the family of apes was brought over from Copenhagen's zoo in 2001.

Fenced-off areas provide children with the opportunity to stroke some of the park's more domesticated animals or have fun feeding the camels.

Small herd of zebra wandering freely in Givskud Zoo

Ancient burial mound in Jelling

Givskud Zoo is not only a family attraction but also a major scientific establishment. A third of the species at the park are endangered. One of Givskud's programmes resulted in deer and antelope reared at the park being re-introduced into the wilds of Pakistan in the late 1980s.

Jelling ⑩

Road map C4. 👥 *2,500.* 🚌
ℹ️ *Gormsgade 23.* **Tel** *75 87 23 50.*
🎭 *Viking Fair (Aug).*
www.visitvejle.com

For the Danes Jelling is a special place: this unassuming village served as the royal seat of Gorm the Old, a 10th-century Viking who conquered Jutland and then Funen and Zealand to create a new state. The dynasty he established has ruled Denmark continuously to this day.

Although few traces are left of the old royal castle, **Jelling Kirke** and the two burial mounds beyond it have revealed much of Denmark's ancient history. The church was built in about 1100, but it is now known that the site was occupied far earlier than this by at least three wooden churches. The first of these was, according to legend, built by Gorm's son, Harald Bluetooth, who came to the throne around 958 and adopted Christianity a short time afterwards. For a long time it was believed that the two knolls outside the church contained the remains of Denmark's first ruler, but when they were excavated in the 19th century nothing was found. In the late 1970s, however, archaeologists began a series of digs inside Jelling Kirke and found the remains of the three earlier wooden churches, along with Viking jewellery and human bones. Forensic examinations, conducted at Copenhagen's Nationalmuseet, concluded that the bones could indeed be those of Gorm and in the year 2000, in the presence of the current royal family, the remains were reburied under the floor of Jelling Kirke. Today the place is marked with a silver sign. Close to the church are two runic stones. The larger one, known as the "Danes' baptism certificate", was erected in 965 by Harald in memory of his parents – Gorm and Thyra. Still visible on the stone is a picture of Christ – the oldest representation of Christ in Scandinavia. The stone's inscription proclaims that "Harald king

Runic stone in Jelling

ordered this monument to be erected to Gorm his father and Thyra his mother for the glory of Denmark", and that he converted the Danes to Christianity. This inscription is considered to be the first written record in which the word "Denmark" appears. In 1994 the entire complex was declared a UNESCO World Heritage Site. The landscape is undergoing renovation to display future archaeological finds in as authentic a setting as possible.

Kongernes Jelling, an exhibition centre opposite the church is devoted to the history of the Vikings and the establishment of the Danish monarchy.

The atmosphere of Jelling can best be enjoyed during the annual Viking Fair. This weekend-long event is popular with many Danes, some of whom take it as an opportunity to dress up as Vikings and parade through the streets of the town. Another reminder of Denmark's past can be found at Fårup lake where a full-scale replica of a Viking ship takes visitors on cruises of the lake.

🔒 **Jelling Kirke**
🕐 *8am–5pm Mon–Sat, noon–5pm Sun.*
🏛 **Kongernes Jelling**
Gormsgade 23. **Tel** *41 20 63 31.*
🕐 *Jun–Aug: 10am–5pm Tue–Sun; Sep–May: noon–4pm Tue–Sun.* 🖼
www.natmus.dk

Runic writing including the oldest record of the name "Denmark"

LEGOLAND® ⑪

LEGO® bricks, known and loved by children throughout the world, were invented in the 1930s by Danish toymaker Ole Kirk Christiansen. This popular amusement park was opened in 1968. Its attractions include amazingly detailed miniature versions of cities, as well as famous landmarks, constructed entirely from plastic LEGO® bricks. In addition there are thrilling rides, miniature trains and water chutes.

DUPLO® Land is for the youngest children.

Atlantis by SEA LIFE ™
At this underwater attraction, visitors are able to get up close and personal with sharks and tropical fish. There are also submarines and shipwrecks.

★ **Toyota Traffic School**
Children aged 7 to 13 can learn to drive here. This is one of the park's most popular attractions, so book ahead.

LEGO® Train
Miniland can be explored aboard a train or viewed from a revolving platform that gradually ascends to the top of a tower.

Entrance

LEGO® Studios
Musical Fountain
DUPLO® Playhouses
DUPLO® Express
LEGONDOL®
Monorail
Hotel LEGOLAND®
LEGO® Cano
Mine Train
P B
LEGOTOP®
Timber R
LEGO® Safari
The Lightho
Caterpil
Frog Hopper
Mini Boats

★ **Miniland**
Over 20 million LEGO® bricks were used to construct famous buildings, airports, trains and even entire cities.

The Dragon
Shaped like its namesake, this roller coaster hurtles through the majestic King's Castle and is great fun for children and adults alike.

★ Polar Land
Hop aboard the hair-raising Polar X-plorer, a roller coaster that travels through a frozen polar landscape filled with LEGO® animals.

Ice Pilots School

Polar X-plorer

Knight's Kingdom

X-treme Racers

Penguin Bay

Jungle Racers

Falck Fire Brigade

Pirate Carousel

Pirate Wave Breaker

Pirate Water Falls

0 m   20
0 yards   20

Vikings River Splash
is an aquatic roller coaster ride sending rafts splashing down wild water rapids and waterfalls through a world of dragons and Vikings.

The Temple
Re-creating a large Egyptian archaeological dig, The Temple allows young visitors to go on an exciting treasure hunt.

Pirate Splash Battle
Board a pirate ship and take your position behind a water cannon. See how long you can stay dry in this playful re-creation of a sea battle.

STAR SIGHTS

★ Miniland

★ Toyota Traffic School

★ Polar Land

Vindmølle, a Vejle landmark with a flour milling museum

Vejle ⑫

Road map B4. 🏛 55,000. 🚗 🚌
ℹ️ *Banegårdspladsen 6.* **Tel** 75 81 19 25. **www**.visitvejle.com

The fjord town of Vejle is famous for being the place where the beech trees (Denmark's national tree) are first to burst into leaf and announce the arrival of spring. Vejle makes a good base for visiting LEGOLAND® *(see pp192–3)* and the burial mounds at Jelling *(see p191)*. Its main point of interest is Sankt Nicolai Kirke, a Gothic church dating from the 13th century. A curiosity of the church, though they can't be seen, are the 23 skulls hidden in its walls, which belonged to 23 robbers executed in 1630.

Rådhustorvet, Vejle's main square, contains the town hall. It stands on the site of a Dominican monastery and its medieval bell can be heard ringing each day from the tower. The **Vejle Museum** is spread over a number of locations in town. A modern interactive venue displays the mummified body of a woman known as Queen Gunhild. The body was found in 1835 in a peat bog; forensic tests have revealed that the woman lived during the Iron Age, around 450 BC. The exhibition in Den Smidtske Gard, an early 19th-century burgher's residence, covers 800 years of Vejle's history. On the edge of town, Vejle Vindmølle is also part

of the museum. Built in 1890 and operational until 1960, the windmill houses an exhibition devoted to flour milling.

While in Vejle it is also possible to visit the Ecolarium, a centre that aims to raise awareness of environmental issues and the potential of alternative energy, and Ravninge Broen, a Viking-era bridge in Ravninge Enge (Meadows) exhibition centre.

🏛 **Vejle Museum**
Tel 76 81 31 00. ◻ *see the website.*
www.vejleegnensmuseer.dk

Esbjerg ⑬

Road map B5. 🏛 83,000. 🚗 🚌 ✈
ℹ️ *Skolegade 33.* **Tel** 75 12 55 99. 🎵 *Rock Festival (mid-Jun); Esbjerg Festival Week (mid-Aug), Chamber Music (Aug).* **www**.visitesbjerg.com

In 1868, the former fishing village of Esbjerg began to develop into a harbour from which Jutland's farmers and producers could export goods. Today it is one of Denmark's largest commercial ports and a centre for North Sea oil operations.

Despite lacking a medieval district, Esbjerg has several places worth visiting. For years the town's main symbol was its **Vandtårnet** (Water Tower), which was erected in 1897.

Seals, a favourite sight at Esbjerg's aquarium

Today, it serves as an observation platform, from which there is a panoramic view of the town. Close to the tower is the Musikhuset (Concert Hall) designed by Jørn Utzon and built in 1997.

Esbjerg Museum presents an historical portrait of the town and also has a large collection of amber. The **Fiskeri-og Søfartsmuseet** (The Fisheries and Maritime Museum), 4 km (2 miles) northwest of Esbjerg's centre, contains a large aquarium and various marine-related displays. Most of the sea life in the aquarium comes from the North Sea. Its most popular inhabitants are the seals. This vast museum complex also features a collection of navigation instruments and model vessels, a number of fishing boats placed outside the building and a reconstructed coastal lifeboat station. Outside the museum grounds, on the seashore, are four 9-m (30-ft) tall snow-white stylised figures of seated men, which are entitled *Man Meets the Sea* and were created by Svend Wiig Hansen to mark the city's centennial in 1995.

The maritime theme continues in Esbjerg harbour where the 20th-century **Horns Rev Lightship** is moored.

Exhibition room in Esbjerg's Fiskeri-og Søfartsmuseet

🏛 Vandtårnet
Havnegade 22. **Tel** 76 16 39 39. ◯
Jun–mid-Sep: 10am–4pm daily. 🖼

🏛 Esbjerg Museum
Torvegade 45. **Tel** 76 16 39
39. ◯ 10am–4pm Tue–Sun. 🖼

🏛 Fiskeri-og Søfartsmuseet
Saltvandsakvariet Tarphagevej 2–6.
Tel 76 12 20 00 ◯ Sep–Jun:
10am–5pm daily; Jul–Aug:
10am–6pm daily. 🖼

🏛 Horns Rev Lightship
Tel 21 62 11 04. ◯ May–Aug:
11am–4pm Mon–Fri. 🖼

Ribe ⓮

Road map B5. 🏚 18,000. 🚃 🚌
🛈 Torvet 3, 75 42 15 00.
www.visitribe.com

Scandinavia's oldest town is
also one of the best preserved
and contains many fine buildings including a medieval
cathedral and a 16th-century
schoolhouse. The medieval
centre features a maze of
cobbled streets lined with
crooked, half-timbered houses
with beautifully painted and
ornamented doors.

Ribe was once a seaport.
With the passage of time the
mouth of the river that flows
through it became silted up,
and now the town is quite a
way from the seashore.

In 856 the missionary
Ansgar, known locally as the
Apostle of Scandinavia, built
a small wooden
church here. In
the 10th century
Ribe became a
bishopric, and
in the mid-12th
century it acquired
an impressive
cathedral, which
still stands today.
Ribe Domkirke
is built of a soft
porous rock called
tufa that was
quarried near
Cologne. The most
prominent entrance,
used by the bishops,
is on the south side
of the church. This entrance
features a 13th-century "Cat's
Head" doorway that got its
name from the knocker made
in the shape of a lion's head.
Another feature of the portal
is the pediment portraying

Nave of Ribe Domkirke

Jesus and Mary – positioned
at their feet are the images
of Valdemar II and his wife
Dagmar, who died in child-
birth in 1212. To this day at
noon and 3pm the cathedral
bells chime the tune of a folk
song dedicated to the queen.
The most notable features of
the church's interior are the
16th-century frescoes and
the modern mosaics by Carl-
Henning Pedersen. The left
wing of the transept contains
a marble floor slab from the
tomb of Christoffer I, who
died in 1259 and is laid in the
adjacent sarcophagus. It is
thought to be the oldest royal
tombstone in Scandinavia.
Stunning views of the flat
lands and the Wadden Sea
can be had from the top
of the 14th-century tower.
Det Gamle Rådhus,
opposite the cathe-
dral's southeast
corner, was built
in 1496. The town
hall's museum
has a small
collection of tor-
ture instruments
and executioners'
swords. From here
it is not far to the
river, where the
Stormflodssøjlen
(Flood Column)
indicates the floods that
have submerged the town.

**The night watchman
in Ribe**

Ribe has two Viking muse-
ums. Standing opposite the
railway station on Odin square
is **Ribes Vikinger**, where the
market town atmosphere of

late 8th-century Ribe
is re-created. The
Vikingecenter, 3 km
(2 miles) south of the
town centre, is an
open-air museum that
offers a portrait of Ribe
during the Viking era.

Ribe Kunstmuseum,
the local art gallery,
houses a collection of
Danish art from 1750
until 1950, including
examples from the
Skagen School and the
Danish Golden Age.

Environs
At the **Vadehavscentret**
(Wadden Sea Centre),
you can learn more
about the Wadden Sea
and arrange safari tours.

🛕 Ribe Domkirke
Torvet. **Tel** 75 42 06 19. ◯ daily.
Oct–Apr: 11am–3pm (Apr & Oct: to
4pm); May–Sep: 10am–5pm (Jul–
mid-Aug: to 5:30pm).

🏛 Det Gamle Rådhus
Von Støckens Plads. **Tel** 76 16 88
10. ◯ Jun–Aug 1–3pm daily. 🖼

🏛 Ribes Vikinger
Odin Plads 1. **Tel** 76 16 39 60.
◯ Jul–Aug: 10am–6pm (until 9pm
Wed) daily; Sep–Oct & Apr–Jun:
10am–4pm daily; Nov–Mar:
10am–4pm Tue–Sun. 🖼

🏛 Ribe Vikingecenter
Lustrupvej 4. **Tel** 75 41 16 11.
◯ May–Jun, Sep: 10am–3:30pm,
Jul–Aug: 11am–5pm. 🖼

🏛 Ribe Kunstmuseum
Sankt Nicolaigade 10. **Tel** 75 42 03
62. ◯ 11am–4pm Tue–Sun. 🖼

🏛 Vadehavscentret
Okholmvej 5, Vester Vedsted.
Tel 75 44 61 61. ◯ mid-Feb–Nov:
10am–4pm daily (May–Sep: to 5pm).

**Half-timbered houses, adding to the
charm of Ribe**

Palisade by Rømø dyke

Rømø ⑮

Road map B5. 👥 *750.* 🚌
ℹ️ *Nørre Frankel 1.* **Tel** *74 75 51 30.*
www.romo.dk

The largest Danish island
in the North Sea, Rømø
was a prosperous whaling
base in the 18th century. Its
western shores are fringed
with wide stretches of beach.
The island is connected to
Jutland by a causeway that
passes through marshland
rich in birdlife.

In the village of **Toftum**
is the Kommandørgården
(Captain's House), which
dates from 1748. The house,
which now serves as a
museum, has a thatched
roof and some original
interior decor, including
wall coverings consisting
of 4,000 Dutch tiles. Close
by is an 18th-century school.
A short distance further
north, in the hamlet
of **Juvre**, is a whale
jawbone fence con-
structed in 1772. In
Kirkeby, next to the
walls that surround
the Late-Gothic
church, are whalers'
gravestones that were
brought back from
Greenland. The
histories of captains
and their families
have been carved
by local artists.

The main point of
interest at the south
end of the island is
Havneby, which has
a labyrinth park. A
ferry goes from here
to the tranquil island
of Sylt, in Germany,
just to the southwest.

Tønder ⑯

Road map B5. 👥 *8,200.* 🚉 🚌 ℹ️
Torvet 1. **Tel** *74 72 12 20.* 🎭 *Tønder
Festival (Aug).* **www**.visittonder.dk

In the Middle Ages Tønder
was a major fishing port.
During subsequent centuries
it became the centre of a lace-
making industry, which is
now commemorated by a
lace-makers' festival held
every three years.
Examples of fine
lace and the sophis-
ticated tools used in
its production are on
display in the **Tønder
Museum**. In the 17th
and 18th centuries
Tønder also pro-
duced ceramics that
were used as wall
tiles, some of which
can be seen in the
museum. The Tønder
Museum is part of the

Doorway of a house in Østergade, Tønder

Museum of Southern Jutland,
which shows a collection of
modern art, including chairs
by Hans J. Wegner.

Tønder's town centre is a
pleasant place to explore and
the narrow streets contain
many houses with decorative
doorways and picturesque
gables and window shutters.
The best-known house is
Det Gamle Apotek (The Old
Pharmacy), at Østergade 1,
which has a Baroque door-
way dating from 1671. The
market square contains a
16th-century Rådhus (town
hall). Also in the square is
the 16th-century Kristkirken,
which has some fine
paintings and carvings.

🏛 **Tønder Museum &
Museum of Southern Jutland**
Kongevejen 51. **Tel** *74 72 89 89.*
◻ *Jun–Aug: 10am–5pm daily;
Sep–May: 10am–5pm Tue–Sun.* 🎟
www.museum-sonderjylland.dk

**Font in Haderslev
Domkirke**

Sønderborg ⑰

Road map C5. Als. 👥
30,000. 🚉 🚌 ℹ️ *Rådhus-
torvet 7.* **Tel** *74 42 35 55.*
www.visitsonderborg.com

Sønderborg, meaning
"South Castle", is on
the island of Als. It
owes its name to a
castle fortress built by
Valdemar I in 1170. Over the
centuries the castle served a
variety of purposes. Christian II
was held prisoner here for 17
years in the early 16th century.
Later on it was used in turns
as a warehouse, a hospital, a
prison and military barracks.

The town's turbulent history
is brought to life at the
Historiecenter Dybbøl Banke,
situated near Sønderborg,
close to the village of Dybbøl.
In the spring of 1864 this area
was the scene of a fierce battle
between Danish and Prussian
forces. Dybbøl Mølle, a windmill that was damaged during
the fighting, is now regarded
as a national symbol. As a
result of Denmark's defeat,
Sønderborg was destroyed
and southern Jutland incorporated into Prussia and later
into Germany (the territory
was returned in 1920).

Environs

About 16 km (10 miles) to the west is the royal castle of **Gråsten**; the garden can be visited when the queen is not in residence.

♠ Sønderborg Castle
Sønderbro 1. *Tel* 74 42 25 39. ○
10am–4pm daily (May–Sep: to 5pm; Nov–Mar: 1–4pm Tue–Sun).

🏛 Historiecenter Dybbøl Banke
Dybbøl Banke 16. *Tel* 74 48 90 00. ○ *early Apr–mid-Oct: 10am–5pm daily.*

Haderslev ⓲

Road map C5. 🏘 *21,000.* 🚌
🄸 *Nørregade 52, 73 54 56 30.*
www.visithaderslev.dk

The present-day capital of southern Jutland is situated between a narrow fjord and a lake that was formed by the construction of a dam. A market town in the 13th century, Haderslev contains many period buildings.

During the Reformation Haderslev was a major centre of Protestantism and in 1526 it became the site of the first Protestant theological college. The town's main place of worship, Haderslev Domkirke, was built in the 13th century but has been remodelled many times. It boasts a magnificent altarpiece featuring a 14th-century crucifix and alabaster statues of the apostles.

The most enchanting of the town's buildings are found on

Interior of the 13th-century cathedral in Haderslev

Courtyard at Koldinghus castle

Torvet, a square flanked by half-timbered houses. The nearby **Haderslev Museum** has exhibits on the archaeological history of the area, a local-history collection and its own mini open-air museum.

🏛 Haderslev Museum
Dalgade 7. *Tel* 74 52 75 66. ○ *Jun–Aug: 10am–4pm Tue–Sun; Sep–May: 1–4pm Tue–Sun.*

Kolding ⓳

Road map C5. 🏘 *56,000.*
🚊 🚌 🄸 *Akseltorv 8.*
Tel 76 33 21 00.
www.visitkolding.dk

Kolding's most important historic building is Koldinghus – a mighty castle that has a distinctive square tower with a flat roof (called the Heroes' Tower). The first fortress on this site was built in 1268, but the oldest surviving walls date from about 1440. More of the castle's history can be learned at the **Museet på Koldinghus**, which also hosts temporary exhibitions on decorative art and design. Kolding's main square is Akseltorv, which contains the beautiful Renaissance Borchs Gård dating from 1595. The **Kunstmuseet Trapholt** on the town's eastern outskirts has a large collection of Danish modern art.

Coat of arms on gate in Fredericia

Every August, an outdoor concert by the National Opera Ensemble draws large crowds to the hill of Skamlingsbanken.

🏛 Museet på Koldinghus
Markdanersgade 11.
Tel 76 33 81 00 ○
10am–5pm daily.
www.koldinghus.dk

🏛 Kunstmuseet Trapholt
Æblehaven 23. *Tel* 76 30 05 30. ○ *10am–5pm daily (to 8pm Wed).*

Fredericia ⓴

Road map C5. 🏘 *36,000.* 🚊 🚌
🄸 *Vendersgade 30D. Tel* 72 11 35 11. **www** visitfredericia.dk

Frederik III decided to build Fredericia on this strategic section of the Lille Bælt (Little Belt) – the narrowest point between Jutland and Funen – in 1650. In 1657 the fortress town was captured by the Swedes who slaughtered the entire garrison stationed here. In 1849, during the Schleswig conflict, it was the scene of a battle between the Danes and the Prussian army. The Landsoldaten monument by the Prince's Gate commemorates that event. The town ramparts remain from the original fortress. The best section is by Danmarksgade, where the grassy embankments reach 15 m (49 ft) in height. The nearby water tower dates from 1909 and provides the best view of the surrounding area. **Fredericia Museum** has displays relating to the town's military and civilian history. Madsby Park, a short way outside the old town, contains a miniature version of Fredericia.

🏛 Fredericia Museum
Jernbanegade 10. *Tel* 72 10 69 80. ○ *noon–4pm Tue–Sun (mid-Jun– mid-Aug: daily).* ● *Jan.*

Man Meets the Sea, sculpture outside Esbjerg ▷

NORTHERN JUTLAND

*V*isitors to northern Jutland can enjoy beautiful, pristine scenery and peace in this region of farmland and fields, heathland and dunes. The university town of Aalborg is the area's only large city, but in the summer months, the seaside resorts of Skagen and Lokken-Blokhus can also get very busy. There are a number of places to visit, including a Viking burial ground at Lindholm Høje.

The least populated and the wildest part of this region is its northern end, which is shaped by its proximity to the sea. This area provides excellent nesting grounds for a variety of birds. On the northwestern side, facing Skagerrak, the scenery is dominated by dunes, which display the clear effects of frequent sea breezes that shift the sand by up to 10 m (33 ft) each year.

Many visitors embark on trips to Grenen, Denmark's northernmost point, which is washed over by the waters of the Baltic and the North Sea. This area is sometimes referred to as the "Land of Light" and enjoys more hours of sunshine than anywhere else in Denmark. The extraordinary light has long been appreciated by artists, who came here in search of inspiration in the 19th century. Many settled around Skagen, which became a magnet for prominent painters and writers who formed the Skagen School.

Another distinct feature of northern Jutland's landscape are its heathlands. As recently as the mid-19th century they covered one third of this region; now they can be seen only here and there. Northern Jutland also boasts Rold Skov, Denmark's largest forest. Numerous coves make up the Limfjord straits, where you can find traditional inns and little wooden ferries.

The most important of the area's historic sights are the Lindholm Høje prehistoric burial ground and the 1,000-year-old Viking fortress at Fyrkat, which includes a replica Viking farmstead.

Some of Denmark's best beaches can also be found in northern Jutland and there are many holiday cottages and camp sites in the area.

Renaissance manor in Voergård

◁ Lindholm Høje – the largest Viking burial ground in Scandinavia

Exploring Northern Jutland

Aalborg makes a good base for exploring this part of the country, while smaller towns such as Thisted, Løgstør, Mariager or Skagen can also serve as good jumping-off points. When heading north, it is best to travel by car, since many of the most attractive areas are some distance from each other, and there may be problems with finding suitable public transport. Even when travelling by car it pays to allow plenty of time as many roads are fairly minor and pass through villages. The advantage of travelling on these minor routes is that the scenery is varied and offers a portrait of Denmark quite different from any seen from motorways.

Viking enthusiast sharpening a blade in the village of Fyrkat

View of the cathedral from the shore of the lake in Viborg

SIGHTS AT A GLANCE

Frederikshavn **4**
Fyrkat **17**
Fårup **1**
Gammel Estrup **19**
Grenen **3**
Hirtshals **2**
Hjerl Hedes
  Frilandsmuseum **11**
Holstebro **10**
Kongenshus Mindepark **12**
  Limfjorden pp210–11 **9**
Lindholm Høje **7**
Mariager **16**
Mønsted **13**
Randers **18**
Rebild Bakker **15**
Sæby **5**
Viborg **14**
Voergård Slot **6**
Aalborg pp208–9 **8**

GETTING AROUND

The major transport artery of the region is the E45 motorway, running from the German border to Frederikshavn. The larger towns of the region are all accessible by train. The main ferry harbours are in Frederikshavn and Hirtshals.

GRENEN **3**

Skagen

Ålbæk Bugt

HIRTSHALS **2**

Ålbæk

597

40

55

Hjørring

Sindal

35

4 FREDERIKSHAVN

Tårs

585

Løkken

Vrå

553

Ør Vrå

E39

5 SÆBY

FÅRUP **1**

543

585

541

Læsø

Brønderslev

180

6 VOERGÅRD SLOT

Pandrup

Hjallerup

E45

Aabybro

Asaa

11

55

Vodskov

Brovst

7 LINDHOLM HØJE

KEY

AALBORG **8**

583

▰▰▰	Motorway
▬▬	Major road
▭▭▭	Minor road
▬▬	Scenic route
⊷⊶	Main railway
⎯⎯	Minor railway
▬▬	Regional border

Nibe

595

Hals

Svenstrup

NORDJYLLAND

Aalborg Bugt

187

Støvring

E45

Aars

Skørping

13

REBILD BAKKER **15**

541

29

507

Aalestrup

Hadsund

Hobro

541

FYRKAT **17**

16 MARIAGER

180

507

3

16

GAMMEL ESTRUP

547

IBORG

RANDERS **18**

19

503

Langå

Auning

erringbro

525

46

Grenå

Gudenå

E45

21

26

Rosenbolm Slot

arhus

Aarhus

Hornslet

SEE ALSO

• *Where to Stay* pp256–8.
• *Where to Eat* pp281–3.

Former Carmelite monastery in Sæby

Fårup Sommerland, a vast amusement park

Fårup ❶

Road map C2. Pirupvejen 147.
Tel 98 88 16 00. ◯ May & early
Sep: from 10am Sat & Sun; early
Jun–late Aug: from 10am daily.
Always consult the website before
visiting. 🖳 www.faarup
sommerland.dk

Fårup Sommerland is an
amusement park set amid
forests and heathlands,
between Saltum and Blokhus.
The park's history is linked
with the Krageland family
of merchants, who ran a
wholesale business in
Aalborg. In June 1975 Fårup
opened its doors for the first
time. Among the thrills and
spills on offer are water
chutes, white-water rafting
and roller coasters. In addition, there are gentler attractions for younger visitors.

Hirtshals ❷

Road map C1. 🏘 15,000. 🚢 🚌
ℹ Nørregade 40. **Tel** 98 94 22 20.
www.visithirtshals.dk

Towards the end of the 19th
century Hirtshals was no
more than a small fishing
hamlet; now it is one
of Jutland's major
ports. Regular ferry
links with the
Norwegian towns
of Kristiansand,
Oslo and Moss make
this small town an
important bridge
with Denmark's
Scandinavian neigh-
bours on the other
side of Kattegat.

The town has a thriving fishing harbour and every day, at
7am, it becomes the venue for
auctioning the night's catch.

The greatest attraction is
the **Nordsøen Oceanarium**, a
sea-life centre that is situated
about 1 km (half a mile) east
of the town centre. Since it
opened in 1984, the oceanarium has attracted thousands
of visitors every year. Its
vast tank contains 4.5 million
litres (990,000 gallons) of
sea water, making it one of
Europe's biggest aquariums.
The aquarium includes an
amphitheatre that looks
onto a huge glass pane that
is 8 m (26 ft) high and 41 cm
(16 in) thick. The fish include
schools of herring and mackerel as well as sharks. A diver
enters the tank every day
at 1pm (and also at 4pm in
summer) to feed the fish.

As well as the aquarium,
the Nordsøen Oceanarium
has numerous displays that
explain about the issues
surrounding fishing in the
North Sea and the ecology of
the region. Outside is a seal
pool, which has regular feed
times at 11am and 3pm.

Hirtshals also offers an
extensive network of walking

and cycling trails, including
one leading to a 57-m
(187-ft) tall lighthouse and
also to Husmoderstrand –
a beach with many safe
places for children to
play and swim.

Hirtshals Museum is in a
former fishermen's cottage
that dates from 1880. This
has an exhibition of everyday
objects illustrating the
significance of the sea to
the local population in the
early 20th century.

🐟 **Nordsøen Oceanarium**
Willemoesvej. **Tel** 98 94 41 88.
◯ Jan–Mar & Nov: 9am–4pm
daily (to 5pm Sat, Sun & hols);
Apr–Jun, Sep & Oct: 9am–5pm
daily; Jul & Aug: 9am–6pm daily.
🖳 http://nordsoenoceanarium.dk

Grenen, where the Baltic meets
with the North Sea

Grenen ❸

Road map D1. 🚌 ℹ Vestre
Strandvej 10, Skagen. **Tel** 98 44 13
77. **www**.skagen-tourist.dk

Grenen is the northernmost
point of Denmark. Standing
by the car park, from
which a 2-km (1-mile) trail
leads to the point, is the
Skagen Odde Naturcenter.
Designed by the Danish
architect Jørn Utzon, the
centre aims to enable visitors
to appreciate the natural
environment of this region
through a series of
imaginative displays utilizing
sand, water, wind and light.

The environs of Grenen
consist of vast sand dunes,
here and there overgrown
with heather. This wild
landscape captivated the
Danish writer Holger
Drachmann (1846–1908) to
such an extent that he made
it his wish to be buried in
the sands of Grenen. His
grave can be found on
one of the nearby dunes.

Aquarium at Nordsøen Oceanarium, Hirtshals

Skagen Artists

The former fishing port of Skagen is now a fashionable resort, full of brightly painted yellow houses and a good number of restaurants and shops. The town's character is accurately represented by its coat of arms, which features a painter's palette in the shape of a flounder. In the late 19th century many artists flocked here in order to "paint the light" and formed what is now known as the Skagen School. Its members included the writer Holger Drachmann, and painters Anna and Michael Ancher, Peder Severin Krøyer, Lautitz Tuxen, Carl Locher, Christian Krogh and Oskar Bjørck. The Skagens Museum exhibits many of their works and it is also possible to visit the former home of the Anchers and that of Drachmann.

The extraordinary light, *produced by the reflection of the sun's rays in the waters surrounding Skagen and the dunes, was the inspiration for the 19th-century artists arriving here from all over Denmark, as well as from Sweden and Norway.*

The Skagens Museum *houses a huge collection of works. Most of the paintings are of local scenes and all of the Skagen School of artists are well represented.*

The fishing harbour *is crowded with cutters as Skagen is still one of the major centres of fishing in northern Denmark, although much of the town's income now derives from tourism.*

Brøndums Hotel, *founded by Erik Brøndum in 1859, is charmingly old-fashioned. The hotel was popular with artists, who often met in the bar at night. The Skagens Museum is located in the grounds.*

The Skagen artists' work *is often characterized by vibrant seascapes and naturalistic portraits. The painting above, by P.S. Krøyer, depicts Anna Ancher and the artist's wife, Marie.*

Michael Ancher *lived for four years in Brøndums Hotel. Ancher married Anna Brøndum, step-sister of the hotel's owner, who was herself a talented artist. This 1886 portrait of Ancher is by P.S. Krøyer.*

Frederikshavn

Road map D1. 🏠 30,000. 🚊
🚢 🚌 ℹ️ Skandiatorv 1. **Tel** 98 42
32 66. 🎭 Tordenskiold Festival (Jun).
www.frederikshavn-tourist.dk

The main international
ferry port of Jutland has a
number of historical sights.
The Krudttårnet (Gunpowder
Tower) is all that remains of a
17th-century citadel that once
guarded the port. Today the
tower houses a small military
museum. Frederikshavn Kirke
dates from the 19th century
and contains a painting by
Michael Ancher, one of the
best-known of the Skagen
School (see p205). The
Bangsbo-Museet is about
3 km (2 miles) south of the
centre. This 18th-century
manor house has an eclectic
collection that includes
objects relating to the town's
history and the Danish
Resistance during World War
II. There is also a display of
artifacts made from human
hair. Perhaps the best exhibit
is a reconstructed 12th-
century Viking merchant ship.

Opulent dining room in Voesgård Slot

🏛 **Bangsbo-Museet**
Dronning Margrethes Vej 6. **Tel** 98
42 31 11. ⬜ 10am–5pm Tue–Sun.
🖥 **www**.bangsbo.com

Sæby ❺

Road map D1. 🏠 18,000. 🚊 🚌
ℹ️ Krystalgade 3. **Tel** 98 46 12 44.
www.visitsaeby.dk or **www**.saeby-
tourist.dk

The town skyline is dominated
by the tower of Vor Frue Kirke
(Church of Our Lady), which

once formed part of a 15th-
century Carmelite monastery.
The church is richly decorated
with frescoes. Its beautiful
Late-Gothic altarpiece dates
from around 1520. Next to the
church is the grave of Peter
Jakob Larssøn, a 19th-century
buccaneer who went on to
become Sæby's mayor.
Sæby has a compact centre
with half-timbered houses and
an attractive harbour. In
summer a trumpeter heralds
the end of each day, which is
followed by the ceremonial
lowering of a flag. **Sæby
Museum**, housed in the 17th-
century Ørums Consul's House,
contains a 1920s schoolroom
and a violinmaker's workshop.

Environs
A short distance north of
town is **Sæbygård**, a
beautifully preserved 16th-
century manor house set
in a small beech forest.

🏛 **Sæby Museum**
Algade 1–3. **Tel** 98 46 10 77.
⬜ Jun–Aug: 10am–4pm Tue–Sun;
Sep–May: 10am–4pm Tue–Fri. 🖥

Voergård Slot ❻

Road map D2. Voergård 6,
Dronninglund. **Tel** 98 86 71 08.
⬜ Easter: 11am–4pm; May–mid-Jun:
1–4pm Sat, 11am–4pm Sun & hols;
mid-Jun–Aug: 11am–5pm daily; Sep–
early Oct: 1–4pm Sat, 11am–4pm Sun;
autumn hols: 1–4pm. 🖼 compulsory.
🖥 **www**.voergaardslot.dk

This Renaissance castle is one
of Denmark's most stylish
buildings. Its splendid portal
was intended originally for
the royal castle of Fredensborg.
Initially the estate was part of
a religious complex, but after
the Reformation it passed into
private hands. The main wing
has a large collection of paintings that includes works by
Raphael, Goya, Rubens and
Fragonard. Also on display are
many fine pieces of furniture
and porcelain (including a dinner set made for Napoleon I).

Lindholm Høje ❼

Road map C2. **Burial ground** ⬜
until dusk. **Museum** Vendilavej 11.
Tel 99 31 74 40. ⬜ Apr–Oct: 10am–
5pm daily; Nov–Mar: 10am–4pm
Tue–Sun. 🖥 **www**.nordjyllands
historiskemuseum.dk

Denmark's largest Iron Age and
Viking burial ground has survived so well due to a thick
layer of sand that blew over
it. The sand deposit kept the
site hidden until 1952, when
archaeologists unearthed
nearly 700 graves. The oldest
ones are triangular; others are
circular. The Viking-era graves
have been made to resemble
ships. Other finds discovered

Half-timbered house in one of Sæby's picturesque streets

in the vicinity indicate that between the 7th and 11th centuries this was an important Viking trade centre. Lindholm Høje comes to life each year during the last week of June, when a Viking festival is held here. Throughout the rest of the year it is possible to visit a museum and try Viking-era food in its restaurant.

Village house in Hjerl Hedes Frilandsmuseum

Aalborg ❽

See pp208–9.

Limfjorden ❾

See pp210–11.

Holstebro ❿

Road map B3. 🏘 *31,000.* 🚉 🚌
🛈 *Jeppe Schous Gade 14. Tel 96 11 70 86.* **www**.visitholstebro.dk

The earliest records of Holstebro can be found in 13th-century documents. The town was often plagued by fire, however, and has few historic sights. Continuing a centuries-old tradition the town bells chime every day at 10pm reminding citizens to put out fires for the night.

In front of the mid-19th-century town hall in the centre of town is a sculpture by Alberto Giacometti. The nearby Neo-Gothic church is 20th century and contains the remains of a 16th-century altar.

The **Holstebro Kunstmuseum** has a sizeable collection of paintings (including works by Picasso and Matisse), as well as sculpture and ceramics, mainly by

contemporary Danish artists. It also houses interesting temporary exhibitions.

Environs
The **Strandingsmuseet St George**, 45 km (28 miles) to the west of Holstebro, tells the story of a shipwreck that took place in 1811.

🏛 **Holstebro Kunstmuseum**
Museumsvej 2. *Tel 97 42 45 18.*
⬚ *Jul–Aug: 11am–5pm Tue–Sun; Sep–Jun: noon–4pm Tue–Fri, 11am–5pm Sat–Sun.* 📷

🏛 **Strandingsmuseet St George**
Vesterhausgade 1E, Thorsminde. *Tel 97 49 33 66.* ⬚ *Jan–Mar: 11am–4pm daily; Apr–Oct: 10am–5pm daily; Nov: 11am–3pm daily.* 📷

Hjerl Hedes Frilandsmuseum ⓫

Road map B3. Hjerl Hedevej 14.
Tel 97 44 80 60. ⬚ *Opening hours vary; consult the website for details.*
📷 🚹 **www**.hjerlhede.dk

A short distance northeast of Holstebro is an open-air museum that re-creates the development of a Danish

Façade of the Holstebro Kunstmuseum

village from 1500 to 1900. The collection of buildings includes an inn, a school, a smithy and a dairy. In summer, men and women wear period clothes and demonstrate traditional skills such as weaving and bread-making.

Kongenshus Mindepark heathland reserve

Kongenshus Mindepark ⓬

Road map C3. Vestre Skivevej 142, Daugbjerg, Viborg. *Tel 86 66 13 78.*
⬚ *all year round.* 📷 **www**. kongenshus.dk

A small section of Denmark's uncultivated heathland, of which just 800 sq km (309 sq miles) remains, can be explored at Kongenhus Mindepark. For many years early pioneers attempted to cultivate this windswept and inhospitable area. In the 18th century an army officer from Mecklenburg leased the land from Frederik V, intending it for cultivation. Assisted by the king's generosity, he built a house, which he named Kongenshus (King's House). However, after 12 years the officer abandoned the project and returned to Germany. The house is now a hotel; next to it is a visitors centre.

Aalborg ●

North Jutland's capital city is situated on the south bank of the Limfjorden. It was founded by the Vikings in the 10th century and rapidly acquired a strategic significance as a hub of trade and transport. It prospered in the 17th century thanks to a thriving herring industry and many of its finest buildings date from this time. Aalborg remains a commercial centre and is the seat of the regional government and a

Satyr sticking out its tongue toward city hall

university town. The local industry includes the country's leading producer of Danish schnapps, *akvavit*.

Coat of arms from Jens Bangs Stenhus

Panoramic view of Aalborg, capital of northern Jutland

Exploring Aalborg

Most of the historic buildings in Aalborg are clustered around the compact medieval quarter. Jomfru Ane Gade has restaurants and bars and is the centre of the city's nightlife.

⛪ Vor Frue Kirke

Niels Ebbesens Gade. ☐ *9am–2pm Mon–Fri, 9am–noon Sat.*
www.vorfrue.dk
The Church of Our Lady dates back to the 12th century. In the 16th and 17th centuries it was the main place of Christian worship in Aalborg. The west portal deserves a closer look.

♣ Aalborghus Slot

Slotspladsen 1. ☐ *8am–9pm daily.*
Dungeons ☐ *May–Sep: 8am–3pm Mon–Fri.* **Underground passages**
☐ *8am–9pm daily.*
This modestly sized half-timbered castle was built on the orders of Christian III and completed in 1555. The dank castle dungeons and underground passages leading off them make for an eerie walk.

⛫ Utzon Center

Slotspladsen 4. **Tel** *76 90 50 00.*
☐ *10am–5pm Tue–Sun.*
www.utzoncenter.dk
The Utzon Center, a power-house of architectural and design exhibitions, was created by the late Jørn Utzon, in collaboration with his son Kim. Utzon, the man responsible for the Sydney Opera House, grew up in Aalborg. The centre also features a library and an auditorium. It is located by the waterfront, next to the harbour pool, where you can go for a swim.

🏛 Jens Bangs Stenhus

Østerågade 9. ● *to the public.*
A Dutch Renaissance-style house, this five-storey edifice, decorated with gargoyles and floral ornaments, was built in 1624 for Jens Bang, a wealthy merchant. Its façade facing the Rådhus (city hall) includes a stone figure of a satyr sticking its tongue out – this was intended to symbolize the owner's attitude towards the city's councillors who refused to admit him into their ranks. The cellars house a wine bar that serves traditional Danish food.

🏛 Rådhuset

Gammel Torv 2. ● *to the public.*
The yellow-painted Baroque city hall was completed in 1762 and stands on the site of a demolished Gothic town hall. The motto written above the main door translates as "Wisdom and Determination" and was used by Frederik V, who was on the throne when the city hall was built.

Soldiers preparing for a parade, Aalborghus Slot

For hotels and restaurants in this region see pp256–8 and pp281–3

🏛 Budolfi Domkirke

Algade 40. **Tel** 98 12 46 70.
🕐 Jun–Aug: 9am–4pm Mon–Fri,
9am–2pm Sat; Sep–May: 9am–3pm
Mon–Fri, 9am–noon Sat.

With a distinctive Baroque
cupola, this white-plastered
Gothic cathedral from around
1400 is an important Aalborg
landmark. Among the notable
interior features are portraits
of wealthy merchants, a gilded
Baroque altarpiece and
16th-century frescoes. The
church's patron, St Budolfi,
is the patron saint of sailors
whose cult was propagated
by English missionaries.

**Delightfully simple interior of
Budolfi Domkirke**

🏛 Historiske Museum

Algade 48. **Tel** 99 31 74 00.
🕐 10am–5pm Tue–Sun. 🚫 www.
nordjyllandshistoriskemuseum.dk
Just west of the cathedral is
the local history museum. Its
varied collection includes
archaeological finds from
Lindholm Høje (see pp206–7)
and rare glassware and
ancient coins. The museum's
star exhibits include a
reconstructed drawing room
from an early 17th-century
merchant's house. Most
interesting of all, perhaps, is
the skeleton of a 40-year-old
female discovered in a peat
bog who died around AD 400.

🏛 Helligåndsklostret

Kloster Jordet 1, C.W. Obels Plads.
Tel 98 12 02 05. 🕐 late Jun–mid-
Aug: 2pm Mon–Fri. 🚫
This convent was founded in
1431 and is one of the best
preserved buildings of its
type in Scandinavia. The only
original part is the west wing;
the north and the east wings
are 16th century. Guided
tours allow visitors to look at
the frescoes in the hospital
chapel, step into the refectory
with its starry vault and listen
to the story of a nun who was
buried alive for having a
relationship with a monk.

Helligåndsklostret

🏛 Kunsten Museum of Modern Art Aalborg

Kong Christians Allé 50.
Tel 99 82 41 00. 🕐 10am–5pm
Tue–Sun. 🚫 www.
nordjyllandskunstmuseum.dk
Designed by Alvar Aalto in
conjunction with Danish
architect Jean-Jacques Baruël,
this striking museum has a
great collection of Danish
and European modern art.

**AALBORG
HISTORIC CENTRE**

Budolfi Domkirke ⑥
Helligåndsklostret ⑧
Historiske Museum ⑦
Jens Bangs Stenhus ④
Rådhuset ⑤
Utzon Center ③
Vor Frue Kirke ①
Aalborghus Slot ②

0 m   200

0 yards   200

Key to Symbols see back flap

Limfjorden ⑨

Limfjorden is Denmark's largest body of inland water. Although narrow inlets connect it to both the Kattegat and the North Sea, Limfjorden resembles a lake. In summer, ferries offer trips to the smaller islands and other areas. Just how significant this area was at one time can be deduced from the many Bronze Age burial mounds, churches and castles. The shape of the island of Mors resembles Jutland. According to legend, when God created Jutland he first built a model. It was so good that he placed it at the centre of Limfjorden. The Hanklit Cliffs on the northern tip of Mors have particularly stunning views.

★ **Jesperhus Park**
This park is planted with half a million flowers. Some are planted to form figures of animals found in the park zoo, such as a crocodile.

Spit
A narrow 10-km (6-mile) spit leads from Thyborøn to Harboøre. The west side is flanked by the fjord, the eastern side by the North Sea.

Hanstholm

Thisted

Snedsted

Agger

Hurup

Thyborøn

Agerø Mors

Harboøre

Nykøbing Mors

Jesperhus

Nissum Bredning

Spøttrup

Lemvig

Venø

Venø Bugt

Struer

Hjerl Hede

0 km ___ 10
0 miles ___ 5

RINGKØBING

HOLSTEBRO

★ **Spøttrup Borg**
Protected against attack by a moat and high ramparts, this medieval castle has changed little since it was built in 1500.

Hjerl Hedes Frilandsmuseum
Among the many historic buildings at this open-air museum are an inn, a smithy, a dairy, a school, a vicarage and a grocer's shop.

Fjerritslev
Situated between the fjord and the North Sea, Fjerritslev is surrounded by beautiful scenery. The town brewery, a red-brick building, has been preserved as a museum.

VISITORS' CHECKLIST

Road map C2
Thisted 🚉 🚌 🛈 *Store Torv 6.*
***Tel** 97 92 56 04.*
Nykøbing Mors 🚉 ⛴ 🚌
🛈 *Havnen 4. **Tel** 97 72 04 88.*
www.visitmors.dk
www.visitthy.dk
www.visitskive.dk

Aalborg
Northern Jutland's capital city has many interesting sights, including the superb Kunsten Museum of Modern Art (see p209).

Nibe
This idyllic Limfjord town used to be famous for its herring markets, which would supply fish for the royal table.

Lovns Bredning
This section of Limfjorden, which has some enchanting coves, is a protected area because of the rich diversity of birdlife found here.

KEY

▬	Motorway
▭	Major road
═	Other road
═	River
⁂	Viewpoint

STAR SIGHTS

★ Jesperhus Park

★ Spøttrup Borg

Mønsted's limestone mine

Mønsted ⑬

Road map C3. Mønsted Kalkgruber, Kalkværksvej 8. **Tel** 86 64 60 11. ◯ Apr–Oct: 10am–5pm daily. 🖾 **www**.monsted-kalkgruber.dk

As far back as the 10th century the area around Mønsted was famous as a centre of limestone mining. The mine, which was still in operation in the 20th century, is now an unusual local attraction. Although only 2 km (1 mile) of the entire 60 km (37 miles) of its tunnels are open, a walk through the underground maze is an unforgettable experience. Visitors can wander at their own pace through the galleries, but they must wear safety helmets. For those who prefer more comfort, there is a mine train, which travels into the pit, past limestone columns and underground lakes. In view of the mine's steady humidity and temperature, which stays at 8° C (46° C), some of the caves situated 35 m (115 ft) below the surface are used for ripening cheese.

Viborg ⑭

Road map C3. 🏠 35,000. 🚉 🚌 ⓘ Nytorv 9. **Tel** 87 87 88 88. 🎏 Marching Festival (Jun). **www**.visitviborg.dk

Viborg is scenically located on the shores of two lakes. Its history dates back to the 8th century and it became one of Denmark's bishoprics in 1060. The 12th-century cathedral was used for coronation ceremonies by the Danish monarchy until the 17th century. The present twin-towered **Domkirke** (cathedral) was completed in 1876. This huge granite building has some valuable relics as well as a crypt dating from 1130, which is all that remains of the original cathedral. Other features include a gilded altarpiece and a vast 15th-century candelabra. The cathedral's frescoes form an illustrated Bible and were created by the Danish artist Joakim Skovgaard (1901–

Figures from Viborg's Domkirke

06). Other works by the artist can be seen in the **Skovgaard Museet**, which is next to the cathedral. The **Viborg Museum** contains a variety of exhibits relating to the town's history, including some items that date from the Viking era. Viborg's city hall, located on the outskirts of the town, in the middle of a park, is a modern and fully sustainable building designed by the architect Henning Larsen.

🛈 **Domkirke**
Domkirkepladsen, Sankt Mogensgade 4. **Tel** 87 25 52 50. ◯ Jan–Mar: 11am–3pm Mon–Sat, noon–3pm Sun; Apr–Sep: 11am–4pm Mon–Sat, noon–4pm Sun; Oct–Dec: 11am–3pm Tue–Sat, noon–4pm Sun. 🖾

🏛 **Skovgaard Museet**
Domkirkstræde 4. **Tel** 86 62 39 75. ◯ Jun–Aug: 10am–5pm Tue–Sun; Sep–May: 11am–4pm Tue–Sun. 🖾

🏛 **Viborg Museum**
Hjultorvet 4. **Tel** 87 87 38 38. ◯ mid-Jun–Aug: 11am–5pm Tue–Sun; Sep–mid-Jun: 1–4pm Tue–Fri, 11am–5pm Sat & Sun. 🖾

Rebild Bakker ⑮

Map C3. 🛈 Rebild-Skørping Turistbureau, Sverrig Gårdsvej 4. **Tel** 99 88 90 00. **www**.visitrebild.dk

Rebild is part of Rold Skov, the largest forest in Denmark. In 1912, after fund-raising among the Danish expatriate community in the USA, a section of it was purchased and turned into this park. Covering 77 sq km (30 sq miles), an array of wildlife lives in the park, including foxes, deer, squirrels, martens, badgers and numerous birds. Close to Rebild Park is the **Fiddlers Museum**, where every Sunday afternoon visitors are encouraged to participate in a lively square dance. The museum also explores the way in which the surrounding forest has shaped the economy of the area and the lives of the local people by looking at various forest trades, including hunting and poaching.

🏛 **Fiddlers Museum**
Cimbrervej 2. **Tel** 98 39 16 04. ◯ Oct–Apr: 1–5pm Sun; May–Aug: 10am–5pm daily; Sep: 11am–4pm daily. 🖾 💻 🛈

Mariager ⑯

Road map D3. 🏠 2,500. 🚌 ⓘ Torvet 1B, 70 27 13 77. **www**.visitmariager.dk

In the Middle Ages Mariager was a major centre of pilgrimages, owing to the nunnery that was established here in 1410. Today, it is a quiet fjord town, with cobbled streets and picturesque houses engulfed in roses. The main reminder of the convent is the church standing on a wooded hill.

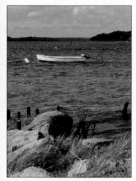

Banks of Limfjorden, near Mariager

Though it is much smaller than the original 14th-century building it is possible to imagine what the convent would have been like from a scale model in **Mariager Museum**, which is housed in an 18th-century merchant's house.

At **Danmarks Saltcenter** visitors can learn about methods of salt production, make their own crystals and take a bath in Denmark's version of the Dead Sea, which has pools filled with warm water so salty that it's quite impossible to dive beneath the surface. Bring a swimsuit.

🏛 **Mariager Museum**
Kirkegade 4A. *Tel* 98 54 12 87.
◯ mid-May–mid-Sep: 1–5pm daily.

🏛 **Danmarks Saltcenter**
Ny Havnevej 6. *Tel* 98 54 18 16.
◯ 10am–4pm daily (to 5pm Sat, Sun & hols). 🖼

Fyrkat ⓱

Road map C3. Fyrkatvej 37B, Hobro. *Tel* 99 82 41 75. ◯ May: 10am–4pm daily; Jun–Aug: 10am–5pm daily; Sep: 10am–3pm daily. 🖼 www.nordmus.dk

In 1950 the remains of a Viking settlement dating from around AD 980 were discovered in fields 3 km (2 miles) from the town of Hobro. A modern visitor centre has since been built around the site.

The entire settlement was surrounded by ramparts 120 m (394 ft) in diameter. The entry gates to the fortress, aligned strictly with the points of the compass, were linked with each other by two intersecting streets. An ancient burial site containing 30 graves was discovered outside the main camp. A Viking-style farmstead north of the settlement re-creates many aspects of Viking life. Visitors can try on a Viking tunic and bake bread over an open fire.

Randers ⓲

Road map D3. 🏘 60,000. 🚊 🚌
ℹ Rådhustorvet 4 *Tel* 86 42 44 77.
www.visitranders.com

Jutland's fourth largest city was already a major market town in the Middle Ages. Its most important historic sight is the 15th-century Sankt Morten's Kirke. Hanging inside is a model of a ship dating from 1632. The three-storey Paaskesønnernes Gård nearby is late 15th century and one of the city's oldest houses. The most popular attraction is **Randers Regnskov**, an unusual tropical zoo that houses 200 animal species and 450 species of plants in a tropical rain forest environment. Here, regardless of the time of the year, the temperature remains at a constant 25° C (77° F), accompanied by very high humidity. Among the many animals kept at the zoo are crocodiles, gibbons, colourful butterflies, tapirs and snakes. There is also an area focusing on old breeds of Danish farm animals.

Small bag of salt from Danmarks Saltcenter

🦎 **Randers Regnskov**
Tørvebryggen 11.
Tel 87 10 99 99. ◯ 10am–4pm Mon–Fri, 10am–5pm Sat & Sun.
🖼 www.regnskoven.dk

Gammel Estrup ⓳

Road map C3. Randersvej 2–4.
Tel 86 48 30 01. ◯ Opening hours vary; check the website prior to your visit. 🖼 www.gammelestrup.dk

One of the region's major attractions is the Gammel Estrup estate, near the village of Auning on the Djursland peninsula. The estate's 15th-century manor house is partially surrounded by a moat and now houses a museum. Its interiors, complete with period furniture, paintings and tapestries, include reception rooms, bedrooms, a chapel and an alchemist's cellar. An agricultural museum, the Dansk Landbrugsmuseum, focuses on Denmark's agricultural past and includes farm machinery and tools.

Environs
Rosenholm Slot, near Hornslet, is a 16th-century castle built on a small island in the middle of a lake. It was here that Count Rosenkrantz, immortalized in Shakespeare's *Hamlet*, lived.

Façade of Gammel Estrup's manor house

BORNHOLM

ar out in the Baltic, the idyllic island of Bornholm has an atmosphere all of its own. For years it remained relatively unknown to outsiders but the beauty of the island's sprawling beaches, its rugged coastal cliffs and distinctive architecture have made it a popular holiday destination. Tourism remains a low-key affair, however, and the villages and towns have changed little over the years.

Bornholmers are proud of their ancestry and have their own flag and, among the older generation, a distinctive dialect that is as unique to the island as the *rundkirke* (round churches) that are found here.

The discovery of ancient burial mounds and engravings suggest that the island was inhabited by 3000 BC. At one time Bornholm was an important centre for trade, and coins have been unearthed from as far afield as Rome and the Near East. The name "Bornholm" appeared for the first time in AD 890 at a time when the island was inhabited by the Vikings.

From the mid 12th century much of Bornholm became the property of the Archbishop of the city of Lund, which at that time belonged to Denmark. For a period in the 17th century it was controlled by Sweden but the islanders' strong allegiance to Denmark resulted in a rapid withdrawal of Swedish forces. Following the surrender of Germany in May 1945 Bornholm was occupied by the Soviets until the Danish army established a permanent garrison.

Today, Bornholm has a thriving fishing industry and no visitor should leave without sampling its smoked herring, known as *røget bornholmer*.

A wide variety of natural habitats is found here ranging from secluded forests and pasture land to rugged cliffs and long, sandy beaches. Another of the island's assets is its climate, with mild winters and Denmark's highest percentage of sunny days. The local flora features many species typical of the Mediterranean, including orchids, figs, grapes and mulberry trees.

Svaneke's yacht marina

◁ **Entrance to NaturBornholm in Aakirkeby, one of Bornholm's few modern landmarks**

Exploring Bornholm

Bornholm has some good cycle paths and
exploring by bicycle is both convenient and
enjoyable. The northern shore is marked by
steep cliffs while sandy beaches are the main
feature of the south and southeast coasts.
Bornholm is known for its round
churches and for the atmospheric ruins
at Hammershus Slot. Rønne, the
island's main town, has some
well-preserved quarters, as do
many of the smaller harbour
ports. Children will enjoy a visit
to Joboland Park, which includes
an aquapark and a small zoo,
and Østerlars' history centre
where they can see what life was
like in a medieval village.

**Modern power-generating windmills
north of Hasle**

**One of Bornholm's fortified 12th-
century round churches**

SEE ALSO

• *Where to Stay* pp258–60.

• *Where to Eat* pp283–4.

SIGHTS AT A GLANCE

Allinge ➋
Gudhjem ⑫
Hammershus Slot ➊
Hasle ➍
Joboland ➓
Nyker ➎
Nylars ➐
Olsker ➌
Rønne ➏
Svaneke ➒
Aakirkeby ➑
Østerlars Kirke ⑪

0 km   2

0 miles   2

For additional map symbols *see back flap*

The scenic coast of Bornholm

GETTING THERE

Bornholm's airport is 5 km (3 miles) southeast of Rønne. A flight from Copenhagen takes half an hour. Many visitors arrive by ferry. The journey from Køge takes six to seven hours (overnight ferries are an option). As an alternative, visitors can take a three-hour train to Ystad in Sweden, and pick up a ferry from there to Rønne. Buses are also available from Copenhagen to Ystad and cost a little less.

KEY

— Major road

===== Minor road

— Scenic route

– – Ferry route

Christiansø 19 km (12 miles)

🏠 GUDHJEM **12**

Melsted

🏛 **11** ØSTERLARS KIRKE

158

Bølshavn   Listed

Østermarie

ORNHOLM   🔁 **10** **9** SVANEKE

JOBOLAND

Almindingen

Ibsker   Årsdale

🏛 AKIRKEBY   38   *Øle Å*

Bodilsker   Neksø

158

Balka

Pedersker   Povlsker   Snogebæk

derne

Dueodde

One of Rønne's many colourful half-timbered houses

Picturesque ruins of Hammershus Slot

Hammershus Slot ❶

Castle ☐ all year round.
Hammershus Exhibition
Langebjergvej 26, Allinge. ☐ mid-
Apr–mid-Oct: 10am–4pm daily;
Jun–Aug: 10am–5pm daily. 🖼️

The atmospheric ruins of
Hammershus Slot are the
largest in northern Europe
and stand on a 70-m (230-ft)
high cliff. The castle was built
in the 13th century on the
orders of the Archbishop of
Lund. Legend has it that
Hammershus was originally to
be built at a different site, but
the walls erected during the
day vanished each night. A
change of location was
thought necessary and
horses were let loose; the
spot where they finally
stopped was chosen as
the new site.

The entrance to the
castle leads over a stone
bridge that was once a
draw-bridge. The ruins
also include what remains
of a brewery, a cistern, a
granary and a bakery.

The impressive square
tower, Manteltårnet, was
used in the Middle Ages
for storing the country's
tax records and later
served as the quarters
of the castle
commander and also
as a prison. In 1660
Leonora Christina,
daughter of Christian IV,
and her husband
were imprisoned
in the tower,
accused of
collaboration
with the Swedes.

**Granite obelisk at
Allinge Cemetery**

Technological improvements
in artillery eventually
diminished the castle's
defensive capabilities as its
walls became vulnerable
to attack from powerful
cannons. It was abandoned
in 1743 and much of the
castle was used as building
material for local homes. An
exhibition includes a model
of Hammershus Slot as it was
at the peak of its might.

Allinge ❷

🏠 2,000. 🚌 ℹ️ Kirkegade 4.
Tel 56 48 64 48.

Allinge and nearby
Sandvig, 2 km (1 mile)
to the northwest, are treated
as one town though the
two have slightly different
characters. Allinge has the
majority of commercial
facilities while Sandvig is
quieter, with walking trails
and neatly-tended gardens.
Allinge's church is mostly
19th century, although the
church itself grew out of
a chapel erected five
centuries earlier. Inside
is a painting that once
adorned the chapel
in Hammershus Slot as
well as tombstones
of the castle's past
commanders. On the
outskirts of Allinge
there is a well-kept
cemetery for Russian
soldiers, with a granite
obelisk proudly
displaying the
Soviet star at the
top. This is a
reminder of the
Red Army, who

occupied Bornholm from the
end of World War II until
March 1946.

On the outskirts of Allinge
is Madsebakke Helleristininger
– the biggest and the most
precious set of rock paintings
to be found in the whole of
Denmark. These simple
enigmatic Bronze Age
drawings, depicting ships,
boats and the outlines of feet,
are thought to be 4,000 years
old. Another local curiosity is
the Moseløkken quarry,
where between May and
September visitors can learn
all about the excavation of
granite on Bornholm and
even have a go at splitting
a piece themselves.

**12th-century three-storey round
church in Olsker**

Olsker ❸

🏠 1,700. 🚌

The village of Olsker, south
of Allinge, has one of the
best known of Bornholm's
distinctive round churches.
Historians once believed they
were of pagan origin. This
hypothesis has now been
discarded and the current
theory is that they were
intended for defensive
purposes, as well as being
used for storage. This three-
storey granite building is the
slenderest of Bornholm's four
round churches and has nine
windows. It was erected in the
mid-12th century in honour of
St Olaf, a Norwegian king who
died in 1031, and who is
revered in Denmark. The hill
on which the church stands
affords a beautiful view of the
surrounding countryside.

For hotels and restaurants in this region see pp258–60 and pp283–4

Round Churches

Bornholm's four sparkling-white *rundkirke* (round churches) are each dedicated to a different saint. They were built between 1150 and 1200 at a time when pirate attacks were a constant threat to the island and have 2-m (7-ft) thick granite walls. Apart from the one at Nyker, all are three-storey buildings. The bottom level was used mainly for worship.

The first floor served as a supply warehouse and also stored the church's valuables and donations received from the faithful. In times of danger the first floor also provided shelter for women and children, while the third, top level was used for surveillance and was an ideal place from which to shoot and throw stones at the advancing enemy.

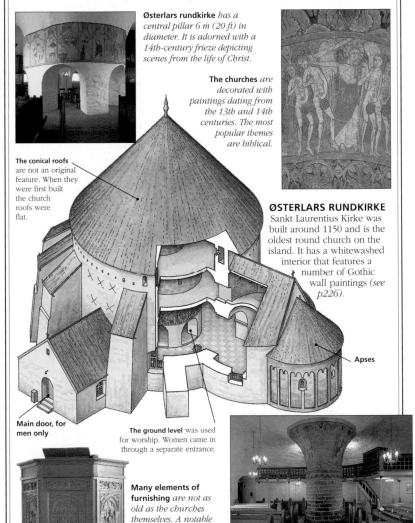

Østerlars rundkirke *has a central pillar 6 m (20 ft) in diameter. It is adorned with a 14th-century frieze depicting scenes from the life of Christ.*

The churches *are decorated with paintings dating from the 13th and 14th centuries. The most popular themes are biblical.*

ØSTERLARS RUNDKIRKE
Sankt Laurentius Kirke was built around 1150 and is the oldest round church on the island. It has a whitewashed interior that features a number of Gothic wall paintings *(see p226).*

The conical roofs are not an original feature. When they were first built the church roofs were flat.

Apses

Main door, for men only

The ground level was used for worship. Women came in through a separate entrance.

Many elements of furnishing *are not as old as the churches themselves. A notable feature of Olsker's church is its richly ornamented 16th-century pulpit.*

Top floors *were accessed by a stairway leading through narrow passages knocked out of the thick walls.*

Hasle ❹

🏠 1,800. 🚌 ℹ️ Havnegade 1.
Tel 56 96 44 81. **www**.hasle.dk

One of Bornholm's oldest towns, Hasle is mentioned in records as early as 1149. The herring industry has long been the town's main source of revenue although many locals were once also employed in excavating brown coal until the mine closed in 1946. The town is popular with visitors, many of whom come to sample the herring from local smoke-houses, which can be found thanks to their conspicuous chimneys. Many of these houses also function as museums, where visitors can watch the smoking process. The Silderøgerierne Museum is probably the best of these and contains an exhibition illustrating the history of Hasle as well as the surrounding area.

In the centre of town stands an interesting 15th-century church with a lovely two-winged altarpiece made in Lübeck in 1520. According to one local story the altar was a gift from a sailor who miraculously escaped from a sinking ship.

A monument in the town square commemorates Peder Olsen, Jens Kofoed and Poul Anker who became the local heroes of an uprising against the Swedes that erupted in Bornholm in 1658.

On the outskirts of the town, on the road leading towards Rønne, is a huge runic stone – the largest one on the island.

Nykirke's pillar with scenes from the Stations of the Cross

Nyker ❺

🏠 800. 🚌

The smallest of Bornholm's historic round churches *(see p221)* is in Nyker. It is only two storeys high and lacks external buttresses. In keeping with its name (Nykirke or New Church) it is also the most recently built of the churches. A Latin inscription found on the Late-Gothic chalice kept in the church proclaims that the church is dedicated to All Saints. Other items to look out for include the frescoes that decorate the main pillar of the church, which depict the Stations of the Cross, and a stone laid in the portico with a Resurrection scene that dates from 1648. Another interesting object is an 18th-century tablet carved with the names of the local inhabitants who died during two plagues that devastated the area in 1618 and 1654.

Rønne ❻

🏠 15,000. 🚆 ⛴️ ℹ️ Nordre Kystvej 3. **Tel** 56 95 95 00. 🛒 Wed, Sat. **www**.bornholm.info

One third of Bornholm's population live in Rønne. The town has grown up around a natural harbour and two of the first buildings that can be seen when approaching from the sea are the 19th-century lighthouse and Sankt Nicolai Kirke.

Rønne has two main squares – Store Torv and Lille Torv (Big Market and Little Market). Store Torv was originally used for military parades but is now the venue for a twice-weekly market.

The Tinghus at Store Torv 1 dates from 1834 and was once used as the town hall, court-house and jail. A number of picturesque cobbled streets lead off from Store Torv and many of the early 19th-century houses are still standing, despite a series of bombing raids carried out by the Soviets in May 1945. One of Rønne's most unusual buildings is in Vimmelskaftet – its width allows for one window only. Standing at the corner of Østergade and Theaterstræde is the restored Rønne Theatre, one of the oldest theatres in Denmark, dating from 1823. **Bornholms Museum** has a good local-history section that includes archaeological finds, a small collection of paintings and a selection of 6th-century golden tablets known as *goldgubber*. Over 2,000 of these tablets engraved with small figures have been found on the island.

Distinctive white chimneys of a smokehouse in Hasle

Harbourside smithy in Rønne

The **Forsvarsmuseet** (Military Museum) is housed in a citadel south of the town centre that was built around 1650. The defensive tower houses a large collection of weapons, ammunition, uniforms and one of the oldest cannons in Denmark.

Bornholms Museum
Sankt Mortensgade 29.
Tel 56 95 07 35. ☐ Jan–mid-May & mid-Oct–Dec: 1–4pm Mon–Fri, 11am–3pm Sat; mid-May–Jun & Sep–mid-Oct: 10am–5pm Mon–Sat; Jul & Aug: 10am–5pm daily. ⊠

Forsvarsmuseet
Arsenalvej 8. *Tel* 56 95 65 83.
☐ mid-May–Sep: 10am–4pm Tue–Sat. ⊠

Nylars ⓐ

Situated some 7 km (4 miles) east of Rønne, Nylars Rundkirke is one of Bornholm's four well-preserved round churches *(see p221)*. It was built in 1150 and is dedicated to St Nicholas, the patron saint of sailors. To climb the stairs to the upper levels it is necessary to squeeze through narrow passages knocked through thick walls. For invaders trying to reach the upper floor this presented a big obstacle. The frescoes that adorn the distinctive pillar that rises through all three levels of the building depict biblical scenes including Adam and Eve's expulsion from the Garden of Eden.

Aakirkeby ⓑ

🚶 *2,000.* 🚌 🛈 *Torvet 30.* *Tel* 56 97 37 20.

During the Middle Ages this was the most important town on the island and the seat of Bornholm's church and the lay authorities. As a result, the 12th-century Aekirke is Bornholm's largest church. The Romanesque building contains a number of treasures including a 13th-century baptismal font and an early 17th-century pulpit. Climbing to the top of the church's high bell tower affords great views of the town. Aakirkeby's latest attraction is **NaturBornholm**, a state-of-the-art natural history museum situated on the southern outskirts of town. A trip to the museum takes visitors back 2,000 years and provides an

Denmark's national emblem, Åkirke

entertaining and informative way to learn about the flora and fauna of the island. Behind this centre is a gigantic natural fault in the bedrock created some 400 million years ago, which marks the geological boundary between the continental plates of Europe and Scandinavia.

NaturBornholm
Grønningen 30. *Tel* 56 94 04 00.
☐ Apr–Oct: 10am–5pm. ⊠
www.naturbornholm.dk

Svaneke ⓒ

🚶 *1,200.* 🚌 🛈 *Havnebryggen 2.* *Tel* 56 49 70 79. 🚢 *Sat.*

In the 1970s this appealing town won the European Gold Medal preservation award and Svaneke continues to maintain its unspoilt historic character. A short distance south of the town centre is Svaneke Kirke. A majestic swan adorns the spire of this 14th-century church (Svaneke translates as "Swan Corner"), and the image of a swan is also included in the town emblem.

In the local glass factory, Pernille Bulow, visitors can watch as skilled workers produce glassware. As well as being known as one of the most photogenic towns on Bornholm, Svaneke is also famous for its windmills. These can be seen standing by each of the town's exit roads. The best preserved is the Årsdale Mølle (1877) on the road leading to Nexø. The mill is open to visitors and also sells its own flour.

Horse-drawn tram in Svaneke, a popular way to see the town

Joboland ⑩

3 km (2 miles) from Svaneke,
Højevejen 4. **Tel** 56 49 60 76.
⬭ early May–Jun & mid-Aug–late
Aug: 11am–5pm Tue–Thu, Sat & Sun;
Jul–early Aug: 10am–6:30pm daily;
early Aug–mid-Aug: 11am–5pm
daily. 🖳 www.joboland.dk

This amusement park has
enough entertainment to last
an entire day. Its greatest
attraction is the aquapark
with pools of water kept at a
constant 25° C (77° F). The
aquapark contains five water
slides and a 125-m (410-ft)
long Wild River, which
adventurous visitors can ride
on a rubber tyre. It is also
possible to sail a boat, whizz
down a "death slide" and
walk across a rope bridge.
During high season the park
lays on additional shows and
games for children, such as
treasure hunts. Joboland also
has its own small zoo with a
variety of animals including
peacocks, goats, monkeys
and exotic birds.

Climbing frames at Joboland amusement park

**Østerlars Kirke, the largest of the
island's round churches**

Østerlars Kirke ⑪

Gudhjemvej 28. **Tel** 56 49 82 64.
⬭ mid-Apr–mid-Oct: 9am–5pm
Mon–Sat (Jul & Aug: 1–5pm Sun). 🖳

The largest of Bornholm's
round churches *(see p221)* is
Østerlars Kirke, which is scenically located in the middle
of wheat fields. The church
dates from 1150 and is dedicated to Sankt Laurentius
(St Laurence). The sturdy
buttresses and conical roof
are later additions. Inside,

the central pillar is decorated
with 14th-century frescoes.
A rune stone at the entrance
dates from 1070 and bears
the inscription: "Edmund
and his brother erected this
stone to the memory of their
father Sigmund. May Christ,
St Michael and St Mary help
his soul."

Near the church is Middelaldercenter, a re-created village
where staff in medieval dress
work in the smithy, grind
corn and tend sheep. There
are daily demonstrations
of medieval skills such as
making clay pots and archery.

🏛 **Middelaldercenter**
Stangevej 1. **Tel** 56 49 83 19. ⬭
May & Sep: 11am–3pm Mon–Fri;
Jun & Aug: 10am–5pm Mon–Fri; Jul:
10am–5pm Mon–Sat. 🖳 www.
bornholmsmiddelaldercenter.dk

Gudhjem ⑫

🚶 900. 🚌 🅸 Åbogade 9.
Tel 56 48 64 48.

The village of Gudhjem ("God's
Home") is built on a steep hill
overlooking the sea. The picturesque harbour, cobbled
streets and brightly painted

half-timbered houses with red-
tiled roofs make it a popular
spot with visitors in summer.

The village has long been
associated with the fishing
industry and in 1893 Gudhjem
acquired the first proper
smokehouse in Bornholm.
The famous "Sun over Gud-
hjem", a herring smoked in
its skin and served with egg
yolk, is well worth trying.

In the centre of the village
is a late 19th-century church.
Close by are the remains of
a much older chapel dating
from the 13th century. The
Oluf Høst Museet has a large
selection of paintings by the
Bornholm artist Oluf Høst who
died in 1966. The collection is
housed in the artist's home,
which he built in 1929. An old
railway station houses the
Gudhjem Museum, which has
displays on local history.

🏛 **Oluf Høst Museet**
Løkkegade 35. **Tel** 56 48 50 38. ⬭
early May–end Sep: 11am–5pm daily.
⬤ early May–mid-Jun: Mon. 🖳

🏛 **Gudhjem Museum**
Stationsvej 1. **Tel** 56 48 54 62.
⬭ 10am–5pm Mon–Sat, 2–5pm
Sun. 🖳

Half-timbered houses in Gudhjem

◁ **Sankt Nicolai Kirke towering over Rønne's harbour**

Cycling on Bornholm

The best way to explore Bornholm is by bicycle and cycle groups are a common sight. The island has 235 km (146 miles) of well signposted cycling routes, many of which connect to the main towns. The routes provide an ideal way to enjoy Bornholm's meadows, fields and forests. Most are far away from busy roads. Rønne, Allinge, and Gudhjem are good places to start. An English language brochure entitled *Bicycle Routes on Bornholm* is available at tourist information centres. Be aware that cycling on Bornholm requires a reasonable level of fitness as there are numerous hills.

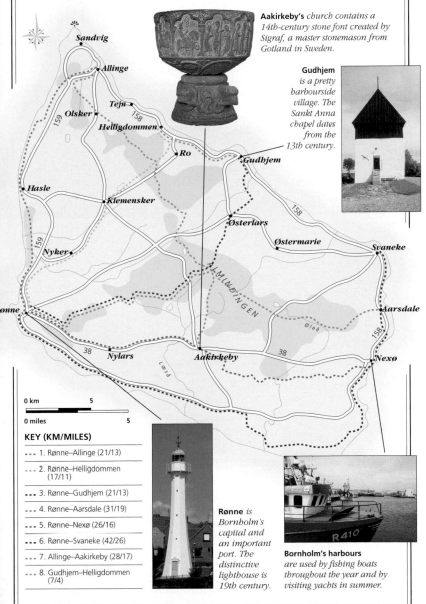

Aakirkeby's *church contains a 14th-century stone font created by Sigraf, a master stonemason from Gotland in Sweden.*

Gudhjem *is a pretty harbourside village. The Sankt Anna chapel dates from the 13th century.*

KEY (KM/MILES)

- **‑ ‑ ‑** 1. Rønne–Allinge (21/13)
- **‑ ‑ ‑** 2. Rønne–Helligdommen (17/11)
- **‑ ‑ ‑** 3. Rønne–Gudhjem (21/13)
- **‑ ‑ ‑** 4. Rønne–Aarsdale (31/19)
- **‑ ‑ ‑** 5. Rønne–Nexø (26/16)
- **‑ ‑ ‑** 6. Rønne–Svaneke (42/26)
- **‑ ‑ ‑** 7. Allinge–Aakirkeby (28/17)
- **‑ ‑ ‑** 8. Gudhjem–Helligdommen (7/4)

Rønne *is Bornholm's capital and an important port. The distinctive lighthouse is 19th century.*

Bornholm's harbours *are used by fishing boats throughout the year and by visiting yachts in summer.*

GREENLAND AND THE FAROE ISLANDS

These two far-flung territories of Denmark offer spectacular adventure and some of the world's most stunning scenery. Greenland's vast frozen glaciers and wondrous northern lights, and the remote settlements and varied birdlife on the Faroe Islands, are ideal for visitors attracted by solitude and natural beauty.

Denmark's two distant island territories enjoy a particular status. Greenland was granted home rule in 1979; the Faroe Islands in 1948. Both have their own government but due to the fact that Denmark retains responsibility for matters such as defence, both are represented in the Danish parliament.

Native Greenlanders share a common heritage with the Inuit of Alaska and northern Canada. Denmark's links with the island began in the 10th century when Viking settlers arrived here and began trading with the Greenlanders. The island was named by Erik the Red, a Viking chief who reached the southern end of Greenland around AD 985.

Early settlers on the Faroe Islands were from Norway. When Norway came under Danish rule in the 14th century the islands also became part of Denmark. Denmark ceded Norway to Sweden in 1814 under the Treaty of Kiel but the Faroes continued under the Danish crown until demands for independence led to eventual home rule. The local name for the Faroes is Føroyar, which translates as "sheep island". The Faroes are aptly named and there are currently almost twice as many sheep as people.

Both Greenland and the Faroe Islands are perfect for nature lovers. A boat tour through parts of Greenland, for instance, takes visitors through crystal-clear waters teeming with marine life including seals and whales. Dog-sled tours across frozen lakes are possible during the winter. The Faroe Islands are a paradise for hikers and ramblers and have a huge variety of birdlife.

Typical Faroe Islands scenery with rocky islets jutting out into the sea

◁ Distinctive houses in Qaqortoq's harbour, Greenland

Exploring Greenland

Greenland is the world's largest island (assuming Australia is a continent) and has a total area of 2,175,600 sq km (840,000 sq miles) and 40,000 km (25,000 miles) of coast. About 80 per cent of the land mass is covered by a huge ice-sheet that is up to 3 km (2 miles) thick. Despite its great size, the island has a population of just 57,000, the majority of whom are descended from a mixture of Inuits and European immigrants. For much of the year Greenland is a vast frozen wilderness. During spring and summer, however, the southern coastal regions thaw and the temperature can rise to as much as 21° C (70° F). Most of the towns and villages have both Inuit and Danish names.

Greenlander family in colourful
Inuit costumes

Midnight sun during summer months

Lincoln Sea

Knud Rasmussen Land

6 QAANAAQ (THULE)

Savissivik

Qimusseriarsuaq

Baffin Bay

Upernavik

UUMMANNAQ (UMANAK) **5**

Disko Øer

Qeqertarsuaq (Godhavn)

Aasiaat (Egedesminde)

4 ILULISSAT (JAKOBSHA...

Sisimiut (Holsteinsborg)

3 KANGERLUSSUAQ (SØNDRE STRØMFJORD)

Maniitsoq

Labrador Sea

NUUK (GODTHÅB) **2**

Paamiut (Frederikshåb)

Ivittuut

Narsarsuaq

QAQORTOQ **1** (JULIANEHÅB)

Kap Fe...

Greenland huskies, bred north of the Arctic Circle

GETTING THERE & AROUND

Kangerlussuaq, just north of the Arctic Circle, has Greenland's main international airport. It lies 370 km (230 miles) north of Nuuk and serves traffic from Copenhagen, Iceland and Canada. From Copenhagen and Keflavik in Iceland it is possible to fly to the southern town of Narsarsuaq.

All domestic inland services are handled by Greenlandair. These flights tend to be expensive. Travel by ferry is possible all year round, although sailing times are vulnerable to adverse weather conditions.

SIGHTS AT A GLANCE

Ilulissat (Jakobshavn) ❹
Kangerlussuaq (Søndre Strømfjord) ❸
Nuuk (Godthåb) ❷
Qaanaaq (Thule) ❻
Qaqortoq (Julianehåb) ❶
Tasiilaq (Ammassalik) ❼
Uummannaq ❺

KEY

Green areas

Permafrost

Kap Morris Jesup

Nord

Kong Frederik VIII Land

GREENLAND SEA

Danmarks Havn

Daneborg

Ymers Øer

Traill Øer

Scoresby Land

Kong Christian X Land

Ittoqqortoormiit (Scoresbysund)

Kong Christian IX Land

Aputiteeq

Arctic Circle

TASIILAQ (AMMASSALIK) ❼

ATLANTIC OCEAN

SEE ALSO

• **Where to Stay** pp260–61.

• **Where to Eat** pp284–5.

0 km	200
0 miles	200

Glacier near the small town of Ilulissat

The 19th-century church of St Saviour in Nuuk

Qaqortoq (Julianehåb) ①

🏛 3,300. 🚉 (+299) 64 24 44. www.sagalands.com

The town of Qaqortoq was established in 1775. Traces of earlier, 10th-century Viking settlers can be seen in nearby Hvalsey where the remains of a local settlement and church are the best-preserved Nordic ruins in Greenland.

Other local attractions include the hot springs in Uunartoq and the research station in Upernaviarsuk which grows the only apple trees in Greenland.

Qaqortoq participates in Greenland's Stone and Man programme, an open-air sculpture project that uses natural rock formations as base material for a variety of abstract shapes and figures.

Nuuk (Godthåb) ②

🏛 14,800. 🚉 Ilivinnguaq 1, Postbox 2291. **Tel** (+299) 31 32 18. www.tupilaktravel.gl

Greenland's capital was founded in 1728 by Hans Egede, a Danish missionary who established a year-round trading post here. Nuuk is the largest and oldest town on the island and the seat of Greenland's government. Egede's monument is on a hill, close to the cathedral.

More information about the history of Nuuk can be found at the **National Museum**, which has a collection of

Inuit costumes as well as other Greenland artifacts.

According to some traditions Santa Claus lives in Nuuk and even has his own box number (2412 Nuuk Post Office). Next to the post office is a huge letterbox for Santa's letters.

The best time to visit is summer – in June humpback whales can be seen in the bay.

🏛 **National Museum**
Hans Egedesvej 8. **Tel** (+299) 32 26 11. ◯ mid-Jun–mid-Sep: 10am–4pm daily; mid-Sep–mid-Jun: 10am–4pm Tue–Sun. 🖼 www.natmus.gl

Kangerlussuaq (Søndre Strømfjord) ③

🏛 600. 🚉 World of Greenland – Arctic Circle, P.O. Box 1009. **Tel** (+299) 84 16 48. www.wogac.com

Situated near the fjord of the same name, Kanger-lussuaq was until 1992 home to Blue West 8, a US base. A museum, located in the former HQ building, contains memorabilia from the base's history including a replica of the commander's hut.

This area is an excellent venue for hiking, biking, camping and fishing and is inhabited by large herds of reindeer as well as musk ox, arctic foxes and polar hares. A popular day-trip destination

Gently sloping green coastline near Kangerlussuaq

is to Russells Glacier, an ice cap some 25 km (16 miles) away. Rising about 10 km (6 miles) from Kangerlussuaq is Sugarloaf Mountain, which has a wonderful view of the inland ice from its peak.

Ilulissat (Jakobshavn) ❹

🏠 *4,500.* ℹ️ *Destination Avannaa, Fredericap aqq 7A.* **Tel** *(+299) 94 33 37.* **www**.northgreenland.com

The town of Ilulissat looks out over Disko Bay, which is full of floating icebergs. It has been calculated that almost 10 per cent of the icebergs floating on Greenland's waters come from the nearby 40 km (25-mile) long glacial fjord, where the ice can be up to 1,100 m (3,600 ft) thick. The glacier can be reached by boat from Ilulissat.

The most famous inhabitant of Ilulissat was the polar explorer Knud Rasmussen. His former house contains objects associated with Inuit art and the everyday life of Greenlanders.

Other museums include the Museum of Hunting and Fishing and the so-called Cold Museum (it has no heating), which has a selection of tools and machinery from a former trading settlement.

Uummannaq ❺

🏠 *1,300.* ℹ️ *c/o Hotel Uummannaq Box 202.* **Tel** *(+299) 95 15 18.* **www**.icecaphotels.gl

Despite its location 600 km (373 miles) north of the Arctic Circle, this place enjoys more days of summer sunshine than anywhere else in Greenland. Such favourable conditions have for a long time been a magnet for hunters and whalers. The charm of this town, situated on a small island, is due in part to its colourful houses set on a rocky shore against the backdrop of the 1,175-m (3,855-ft) high Hjertetjeldet ("Heart Shaped") mountain. The old stone cottages with turf roofs date from 1925.

Children dressed in traditional Inuit costumes

The nearby museum, housed in a late 19th-century hospital, contains hunting implements, kayaks and a display devoted to German scientist Alfred Wegener's expedition across the inland ice in 1930 on propeller-driven sledges.

Nearby is the Inuit village of Qilaqitsoq, where some mummified bodies were discovered in a cave in 1972. The mummies can be seen in Nuuk's National Museum.

In winter it is possible to take a dog-sled trip across the frozen fjord.

Qaanaaq (Thule) ❻

🏠 *700.* ℹ️ *P.O. Box 75.* **Tel** *(+299) 97 14 73.* **www**.turistqaanaaq.gl

Greenland's northernmost town was built in the 1950s. Its inhabitants follow a traditional way of life hunting for seals, walruses and polar bears. Visitors can participate in hunts, which involve sleeping in igloos and travelling by sled. Hunts such

as these are an important means of survival in this area and not for the squeamish.

About 500 km (311 miles) from Qaanaaq is the vast North and East Greenland National Park. The park is mostly covered by an inland ice cap and contains musk ox, polar bears and, in summer, walruses. Permission to enter must be obtained from the Expedition Office of the Government of Greenland *(exp@nanoq.gl)*.

Tasiilaq (Ammassalik) ❼

🏠 *1,900.* ℹ️ *P.O. Box 506, Skæven Ujuaap Aqqutaa B 48.* **Tel** *(+299) 98 12 43 or 98 15 43.* **www**. eastgreenland.com

Situated on the shores of a fjord, surrounded by high mountains, Tasiilaq is one of eastern Greenland's larger towns. The first Europeans arrived here about 100 years ago, and tourism is becoming increasingly important. From here, visitors can go whale watching, visit the nearby "Valley of Flowers" (in summer this is a splendid opportunity to enjoy the Arctic flora) or climb the mound that towers over the town (it was raised in 1944 to celebrate the 50th anniversary of Tasiilaq), from which there are some stunning views.

The town's other points of interest include a modern church decorated with Greenland artifacts. The oldest of Tasiilaq's houses dates from 1894 and was built by a Danish missionary.

Uummannaq, built on the rocks of a small island

Exploring the Faroe Islands

This cluster of 18 islands, sandwiched between the Atlantic and the Norwegian Sea, is home to about 49,000 people, almost half of whom live in the capital Tórshavn on Streymoy. The Faroes have a total area of 1,399 sq km (540 sq miles) and are 450 km (280 miles) from the Shetland Islands and 1,500 km (900 miles) from Copenhagen. Many of the islands are interlinked by a network of tunnels and causeways. The Faroes are perfect for ramblers, and marked trails cover many routes. This is rough terrain and the right equipment, including maps and a compass, should always be carried. The island's seafaring past is evident in the busy harbours, while the town museums have displays on island customs and folklore. Sea cruises are an ideal way to explore the Faroes.

Garden gate made from a ship's wheel

Rugged cliffs on the tiny island of Koltur

KEY

=== Minor road

┝╍╍┥ Tunnel

Viðareiði
Múli
Viðoy
Fugloy
adalur
Kirkja
Kunoy
Hvannasund
Svinoy
Kunoy
SOY
Svinoy
Klaksvik
Borðoy
Leirvik

Saltangará
Toftir

ÓRSHAVN
Nólsoy
Nólsoy
bøur

oy
Skálavik

Dalur

ra Dímun

Litla Dímun

Sumba

Steel sheep sculpture on the outskirts of Tórshavn

GETTING THERE & AROUND

The Faroe Islands Smyril Line ferry service operates regularly between Tórsholm, the island's capital, and Hanstholm in northern Jutland. In summer there are additional services from Bergen in Norway, Lerwick on the Shetlands and Seyðisfjörður in Iceland. Atlantic Airways and Air Iceland serve routes from Copenhagen in Denmark. Atlantic Airways also flies from Oslo in Norway. From April to September twice-weekly routes operate from London and Aberdeen. The Faroe Islands' international airport is near the town of Sørvágur, on the island of Vágar, about 70 km (43 miles) from Tórshavn. A bus connects the airport with Tórshavn. Most of the towns and villages are connected by road, while local ferries cater for the more outlying settlements.

SEE ALSO

• *Where to Stay* p261.

• *Where to Eat* p285.

0 km   10

0 miles   10

SIGHTS AT A GLANCE

Eysturoy ⑥
Kalsoy ⑦
Mykines ④
Streymoy ②
Sud-uroy ⑤
Tórshavn ①
Vágar ③

Fishing boats in Klaksvik's harbour

Brightly coloured houses lining Tórshavn harbour

Tórshavn ❶

👥 19,000. 🚢 🚌
ℹ️ Niels Finsens Gøta 13, Tórshavn.
Tel (+298) 31 57 88.

The Faroe Islands' capital is a lively and picturesque place with a well preserved old centre, although much of the town is fairly modern. Tórshavn was granted municipal status in 1909, but its history stretches back much further.

In the 11th century Tórshavn became a venue for annual Viking gatherings known as the Althings, an early form of the Faroese parliament. The meetings were held in summer and were used to settle quarrels and to trade. A permanent settlement developed around the annual event, and eventually became Tórshavn.

Some of the Faroes' earliest inhabitants were Irish friars, and Tórshavn's oldest building is the 15th-century Munkastovan, or Monks' House, which is one of the few buildings to survive a fire in 1673.

The ruins of Skansin Fort, which was built in 1580 to defend the village from pirates, can still be seen to this day. The fort acquired its present shape in 1780 and was used by British troops during World War II. Today, it provides a good viewpoint for surveying the town's busy

FAROE ISLANDS WEBSITES

www.faroeislands.com
www.visit-faroeislands.com

harbour, which is crammed with fishing boats, ferries and pleasure craft.

Føroya Fornminnissavn (Historical Museum) has a wide-ranging collection tracing the Faroes' seafaring history, including boats and fishing equipment, as well as religious artifacts and items dating back to the Viking era.

🏛 **Føroya Fornminnissavn**
Brekkutún 6, Hoyvík. **Tel** (+298) 34 05 00. ☐ mid-May–mid-Sep: 10am–5pm daily (from 2pm Sat & Sun); mid-Sep–mid-May: 2–5pm Sun. 📷 www.natmus.fo

Streymoy ❷

👥 22,000. 🚢 🚌 ℹ️ Vaglið, P.O. Box 379, Tórshavn. **Tel** (+298) 30 24 25.

The largest of the Faroe Islands has a varied terrain and is criss-crossed by ancient paths that were used to travel between settlements.

Saksun is a small village on the shores of an inlet that leads into Pollur lake – a fine spot to fish for trout and salmon.

The **Dúvugarðar Museum**, located in an old turf-roofed farmhouse, has exhibits on island life from medieval times to the 1800s.

Traces of a group of 8th-century Irish friars have been found in the village of Kirkjubøur, at the south end of Streymoy. Written records show that Kirkjubøur was a busy place in medieval times. A reminder of those days is the 12th-century church of St Olaf, the archipelago's oldest historic site.

Southwest from Tórshavn are the Vestmannabjørg (Bird Cliffs) where hundreds of sea birds inhabit the 640-m (2,100-ft) high cliff face.

🏛 **Dúvugarðar Museum**
FO436, Saksun. **Tel** (+298) 21 07 00. ☐ mid-Jun–mid-Aug: 2–5pm Fri–Wed (or on request). 📷

Vágar ❸

👥 2,800. ✈️ 🚌 ℹ️ At the airport. **Tel** (+298) 35 33 00.

The Faroe Islands' modern airport is on Vágar and was originally used as a landing strip by the RAF. This mountainous island has some of the region's most stunning sights including the 313-m (1,027-ft) tall needle rock called "Trollukonufingur" ("Troll Woman's Finger"). Lake Sorvagsvatn is a little way from Midvagur, Vágar's largest town, and is a great place for fishing. Sandavagur, a nearby village, is the birthplace of Venceslaus Ulricus Hammershaimb (b. 1819), creator of the Faroese alphabet.

House hugging the cliff on Streymoy

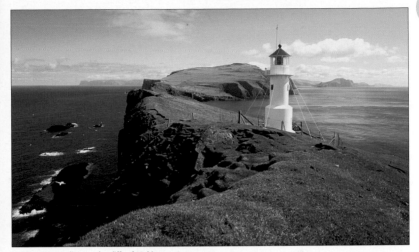

Lighthouse standing on the cliffs of Mykines

Mykines ④

🚶 20. ⛴

On this tiny island of only 10 sq km (4 sq miles), the inhabitants are vastly outnumbered by the birds, including thousands of puffins. All the islanders live in the same village, which is a pretty place with colourful houses topped by turf roofs. This is one of the hardest islands to reach but the trip is worth it, especially for keen hikers. Mykineshólmur, a tiny islet, is a good spot from which to view gannets, as well as large colonies of puffins. It is connected to the island by a footbridge that has been built 24-m (79-ft) above the sea.

Suðuroy ⑤

🚶 5,000. ⛴ 🛈 *Kunningarstovan á Tvøroyri, Tvøråvegur 37, Tvøroyri.* **Tel** *(+298) 61 10 80.* **www**.visitsuduroy.fo

The largest town on Suðuroy, the Faroes' southernmost island, is Tvøroyri, which has a population of 1,800. The little village of Famjin, on the west coast, is more historically important, however, as its church contains the original Faroe Islands' flag. The red-and-blue cross on a white background was designed by two students and accepted as the national ensign in 1940. A short hike above the village is Kirkjuvatn ("Church Lake"), one of the Faroes' largest lakes.

The village of Sandvik, at the northern end of the island, has an isolated and expansive beach. In AD 1000 Sigmund Bresterson, an early Norwegian settler and hero of the Faroe Sagas, was murdered here while preaching Christianity. On the way from Sanvik to Hvalba are two stones that, according to legend, were brought here by Bresterson. Passing between them is believed to be unlucky and can spell misfortune or even death.

Eysturoy ⑥

🚶 11,000. 🛈 *Kunningarstovan í Runavík, Heiðavegur, P.O. Box 200, Saltangará.* **Tel** *(+298) 41 70 60.* **www**.visiteysturoy.fo

The second largest island of the archipelago is connected to Streymoy by a road bridge, which is often jokingly described by locals as the only bridge across the Atlantic.

Eysturoy has a number of unique features. At 882 m (2,894 ft), Slættaratindur is the Faroes' highest point. The summit can easily be reached by climbing the mountain's eastern ridge – the views from the peak are breathtaking.

Close to Fuglafjørður are the Varmakelda hot springs. Their water remains at a constant 18° C (64.4° F) and is believed to have medicinal properties. Further north is the village of Oynadarfjordur. Just beyond its shore are the Rinkusteinar, or rocking stones, two huge blocks that constantly rock, moved by the motion of the sea. At nearby Gjøgv there is a 200-m (656-ft) long gorge that with time has eroded to become a sea-filled bay.

Goat on one of the islands' rural smallholdings

Kalsoy ⑦

🚶 140. ⛴

Nicknamed the "flute" because of its elongated shape, this rugged island is ideal for hikes. Many walkers head towards Kap Kallur, at the island's northern tip, where the lighthouse makes an excellent point from which to view the cliffs. Puffins are a frequent sight. The sea stacks at Eysturoy's northern tip can be seen on a clear day.

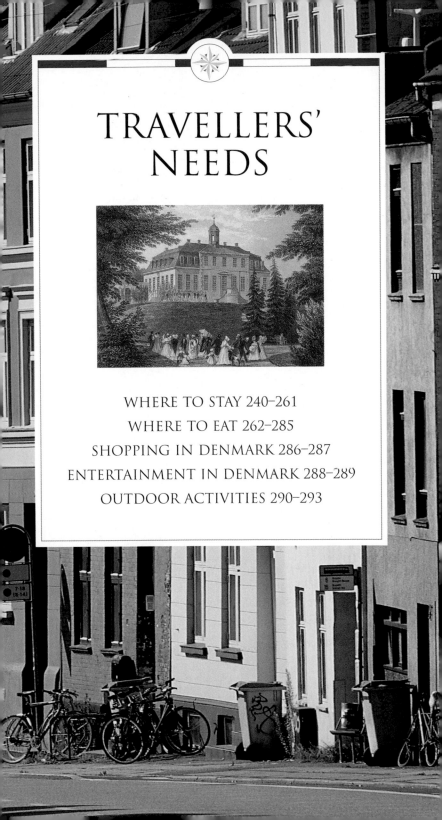

TRAVELLERS'
NEEDS

WHERE TO STAY 240–261
WHERE TO EAT 262–285
SHOPPING IN DENMARK 286–287
ENTERTAINMENT IN DENMARK 288–289
OUTDOOR ACTIVITIES 290–293

WHERE TO STAY

Holiday accommodation in Denmark is of a high standard and provides visitors with plenty of options. The choice ranges from luxury hotels and apartments to roadside inns, budget hotels, family hostels, private homes and camp sites. Information is readily available from tourist offices and on the Internet. Some of Denmark's hotels can be expensive, however. For those on a tight budget,

Copenhagen hotel porter

staying on a camp site or in one of the country's well-run hostels provides a cheaper alternative. Those seeking something a little different might choose to stay in an historic castle or on one of the farms taking part in Denmark's agritourism scheme. Visitors to Greenland can even choose to stay in an igloo. Whatever your preference, Danish accommodation has a reputation for professionalism and a warm welcome is generally assured.

Main entrance to a hotel in Sandvig, Bornholm

CHOOSING A HOTEL

Travellers in Denmark have a wide choice of hotel accommodation. Information is readily available and details of hotels found in brochures and on websites is generally both up to date and accurate. Many of Denmark's hotels are 3-star establishments, and are aimed at holiday-makers as well as business travellers. The majority of three-star hotels offer rooms with a private bathroom, telephone and TV. Be clear when booking a room if a bath is specifically required, as some hotels have showers rather than baths in rooms. Visitors may be able to use their laptops as rooms often have Internet access but it is wise to enquire. The cheaper hotels tend to be

rather plain but even these are generally clean and well run. An all-you-can-eat breakfast, consisting of pastries, bread, cereal, coffee/tea and fruit, is often included in the price of a room.

When planning a journey to Denmark by car, take into account the cost of parking in town centres. It is worth finding out in advance whether the hotel has its own car park or off-street parking. Hotels on Greenland and the Faroe Islands are not plentiful. Those that do exist can be fairly costly.

Pension sign in Elmehøj, Møn

HOW TO BOOK

During peak season, hotels are often booked up in Denmark so it pays to reserve a room in advance. Hotel accommodation can be

booked via the Internet at www.danishotels.dk or www.visitdenmark.dk. Many individual hotels in Denmark also have their own websites. Alternatively, bookings can be made by telephone, fax or e-mail. It may also be worth contacting a travel agent, as they often have details about special offers or schemes. Local tourist offices can also provide accommodation lists in their towns.

HOTEL PRICES

Hotel prices in Denmark can be rather high. There are many hotels at the lower end of the scale, however, which charge about 600 to 700 Dkr per night; the most expensive ones may quote up to 10,000 Dkr for a luxury suite. The majority of room prices fall into the 900–1,400 Dkr bracket. During summer and at weekends when business visitors are scarce, many hotels offer discounted rates.

ADDITIONAL COSTS

Some hotels and hostels belonging to the Green Key association add an "ecological tax" of 35 Dkr (or a certain percentage of the bill) to the price of an overnight stay. This scheme, which began in 1994, ensures that the hotel has fulfilled certain ecological criteria, such as using low-energy light bulbs, low-water consumption toilets and environmentally friendly cleaning products.

◁ **Colourful houses lining a street in Århus, central Jutland**

A guest room in the Admiral Hotel, Copenhagen *(see p244)*

CHAIN HOTELS

The majority of hotels in Denmark belong to large hotel chains including First & Clarion, Hilton, Radisson and Scandic. Some chains, such as Best Western, have their own schemes whereby visitors can get discounts at weekends or during the holiday period. It is best to book in advance for these, though deals can sometimes be struck on the spot.

HISTORIC HOUSES

A small number of Denmark's manor houses and palaces offer accommodation. These historic buildings are run by **Danske Slotte & Herregaarde** (The Danish Association of Castles and Manor Houses), and they are usually located in the countryside, surrounded by nature. The venues are undeniably romantic, but they can be rather expensive.

INNS

Outside larger towns, it is possible to stop for a night in an inn, known as *kro* in Denmark. The variety on offer ranges from modern roadside inns to meticulously restored period houses. Those with an interesting historic background are known as *privilegeret kro*. Some country inns have retained much of their 18th or 19th-century rusticity; others are downright luxurious. Many *kro* offer a family atmosphere, and it is not unusual for inns to be used for family gatherings and big occasions.

CAMP SITES

Denmark has more than 565 camp sites. Of these, as many as 100 are open all year round, providing relatively inexpensive accommodation, often in

Camp site on Hindsholm peninsula, Funen

areas of outstanding natural beauty. All are rated by the **Dansk Camping Union** using a system of stars from one to five. Prices depend on the number of stars, which reflect not only comfort and a site's attractiveness, but

also specific facilities, such as whether the site has a playground and the distance to the nearest grocery store. The cost generally includes a charge for pitching a tent or parking a caravan, plus a charge for each occupant. One-star sites will have little more than basic facilities, such as fresh drinking water and toilets. Sites rated three stars and above will have a TV room, on-site shop and a café or restaurant. Whatever the rating and the amenities on offer, it is rare to find a Danish camp site that is not efficiently run.

Roughly 400 of Denmark's camp sites also feature chalet accommodation, or cabins that can sleep four to six. Many cabins have cooking facilities, but visitors usually have to supply their own linen and towels. Most cabins do not have private washing or toilet facilities.

A comprehensive database available at *www.danske campingpladser.dk* allows a search according to location and facilities.

Anyone wishing to camp in Denmark will need a Visitor's Pass. These annual permits are readily available and can be purchased on the spot at any of the official camp sites.

Pitching a tent in areas not designated as camp sites is not encouraged, and anyone caught camping in a field or on the beach without permission may be fined.

Distinctive architecture of the Royal Holstebro, Jutland *(see p256)*

Historic hotel room in Liselund Slot, Møn

HOSTELS

All of Denmark's 95 or so hostels or *vandrehjem* are incorporated into the **Danhostel** association, which registers its hostels in five categories marked (as in the case of hotels and camp sites) by stars. Along with communal dormitories, most hostels have private "family" rooms, which usually sleep four to six and must be booked well in advance. Blankets and pillows are usually provided, but it is generally the case that visitors supply their own bed linen and towels (though these are available for a fee). In all hostels it is possible to buy breakfast; many also offer dinner, charging half-price for children up to the age of 12. Most hostels have kitchen facilities, where guests can prepare their own meals, although plates and cutlery are rarely provided.

The prices of family rooms can vary, but the maximum price of a bed in a communal dormitory is fixed each year for the entire country. Prices for an overnight stay vary between high and low seasons. From September until May a place in a provincial hostel must be booked at least three days in advance. During peak season all hostels should be booked as early as possible and couples wishing to rent a private room during this period may be asked to pay for all the beds in the room.

It is not necessary to have a Youth Hostel Association (YHA) card to stay at a hostel, but card-holders enjoy reduced rates. For visits that exceed five days it is worthwhile buying a membership.

Danhostel's website has telephone numbers and website addresses for all of its hostels, where additional information can be found.

BED & BREAKFASTS

Denmark's bed and breakfasts offer good quality and value, and usually charge about 250 Dkr per person per night. Many can be booked from local tourist offices. Alternatively, a list is available from **Dansk Bed & Breakfast**. Some Danish B&Bs quote a price that only includes accommodation. Breakfast usually costs extra, or it may not be available at all.

DISABLED TRAVELLERS

Many hotels can accommodate disabled guests. The majority of multi-storey hotels have lifts. VisitDenmark, the tourist board *(see p297)*, has a leaflet entitled *Access in Denmark – a travel guide*, which has information on disabled access to hotels. The Scandic chain of hotels employs a disability ambassador to ensure its hotels provide suitable accommodation for guests with special needs. Their Aarhus hotel has no fewer than 22 specially designed rooms.

TRAVELLING WITH CHILDREN

Taking children on holiday to Denmark is not a problem. Many hotels and hostels, particularly establishments aimed at holiday-makers, offer family rooms for three to four people. Hotels belonging to the Scandic group are also ready to receive young guests; many of these have playrooms. Hotel restaurants not only provide high chairs for babies and toddlers, but also offer special menus that will satisfy all but the most picky children.

Sign advertising one of Denmark's bed & breakfasts

COTTAGES AND HOLIDAY CENTRES

Cottages are available to rent – usually on a weekly basis (from Saturday to Saturday). Many of them are let out by private owners but managed by professional rental agencies. Others are run purely as commercial ventures. Either way, a cottage must be booked well in advance. Many

Entrance to one of Denmark's converted manor houses

Youth Hostel dormitory

FARM HOLIDAYS AND HOME EXCHANGES

Spending time on a farm is becoming an increasingly popular activity in Denmark. There are now more than 100 Danish farms where a stay is possible, and most are far away from busy resorts. Such rural retreats provide a chance to relax in pastoral surroundings and, in some cases, to muck in with the chores. Farm stays can be booked via **Landsforeningen for Landboturisme**. A holiday of this sort can be arranged in several ways. You can choose B&B or full-board accommodation. Cottages, a simple apartment with a kitchen, or a room can be rented. Alternatively, visitors can pitch a tent or park a caravan on farm land. Some farms offer theme holidays that may include angling, cookery courses or environmental studies.

Another possibility is to travel from farm to farm by bicycle or car. Regardless of what type of vacation is on offer, visitors can be sure of a clean room and warm rural atmosphere. Prices start from 200 Dkr per adult (for bed and breakfast).

A home exchange allows participants to swap their home with that of a family in Denmark, offering an authentic Danish experience. Visit **Home Link** for information.

companies are able to handle bookings nationwide.

Holiday centres, which have purpose-built accommodation, children's playgrounds, swimming pools and other family-friendly amenities, have lots of space for children to play. Prices vary widely.

DIRECTORY

INFORMATION ON ACCOMMODATION & RESERVATIONS

www.hotel.dk

www.visitdenmark.com

INFORMATION ON ACCOMMODATION & RESERVATIONS IN COPENHAGEN

Copenhagen Right Now Information and Booking Service
Vesterbrogade 4A.
Tel 70 22 24 42.
Fax 70 22 24 52.
www.visitcopen
hagen.com

HISTORIC HOUSES

Danske Slotte & Herregaarde
L. Sct. Mikkelsgade 7, 1,
8800 Viborg.
Tel 86 60 38 44.
Fax 86 60 38 31.
www.slotte-
herregaarde.dk

INNS

Danske Kroer & Hoteller
Vejlevej 16,
8700 Horsens.
Tel 75 64 87 00.
Fax 75 64 87 20.
www.smalldanishhotels.
com

CAMP SITES

Campingrådet
Mosedalvej 15,
DK-2500 Valby.
Tel 39 27 88 44.
Fax 39 27 80 44.
www.camping
raadet.dk

Dansk Camping Union
Korsdalsvej 135
2605 Brøndby.
Tel 33 21 06 00.
www.dcu.dk

DK-CAMP 2002
Industrivej 5,
Bredballe,
7120 Vejle Ø.
Tel 75 71 29 62.
Fax 75 71 29 66.
www.dk-camp.dk

FDM Camping
Firskovvej 32.
2800 Kgs. Lyngby.
Tel 45 27 07 07.
www.fdmcamping.dk

HOSTELS

Danhostel Danmarks Vandrehjem
Vesterbrogade 39,
1620 Copenhagen V.
Tel 33 31 36 12.
www.danhostel.dk

B&BS

Dansk B&B
Sankt Peders Stræde 41,
1453 Copenhagen K.
Tel 39 61 04 05.
www.bedand
breakfast.dk

HOLIDAY CENTRES

Danland & DanCenter
Lyngbyvej 20,
2100 Copenhagen Ø.
Tel 33 63 02 00.
Fax 70 13 70 71.
www.danland.dk

Dansk Folkeferie
Hedegaardsvej 88,
2300 Copenhagen.
www.folkeferie.dk

COTTAGES

Dansommer
Voldbjergvej 16,
8240 Risskov.
Tel 86 17 61 22.
Fax 86 17 68 55.
www.dansommer.dk

Novasol
Rygårds Alle 104,
2900 Hellerup.
Tel 70 42 44 24.
www.novasol.co.uk

Sol & Strand
Ilsigvej 21, Hune,
9492 Blokhus.
Tel 99 44 44 44.
Fax 99 44 44 45.
www.sologstrand.com

FARM HOLIDAYS AND HOME EXCHANGES

Home Link
www.homelink.org

Landsforeningen for Landboturisme
Føllevej 5, 8410 Ronde.
www.bonde
gaardsferie.dk

Choosing a Hotel

The hotels in this guide have been selected across a wide price range for facilities, good value, and location. All rooms have an ensuite bathroom and TV unless otherwise stated. The hotels are listed by area. For Copenhagen map references, *see pp106–111*. For regional map references, *see inside back cover*.

PRICE CATEGORIES
Price categories are for a standard double room with bath or shower per night in high season including breakfast, tax and service.
Ⓚ Under 600 Dkr
ⓀⓀ 600–1,000 Dkr
ⓀⓀⓀ 1,000–1,500 Dkr
ⓀⓀⓀⓀ 1,500–2,000 Dkr
ⓀⓀⓀⓀⓀ Over 2,000 Dkr

COPENHAGEN

NORTH COPENHAGEN Clarion Hotel Neptun
ⓀⓀⓀ
Sankt Annae Plads 14–20, 1250 **Tel** *33 96 20 00* **Fax** *33 96 20 66* **Rooms** *133* **Map** *2 D5*

This is a top-notch hotel attractively located near to the royal palace and close to the bars and restaurants of Nyhavn. Many of the rooms look onto a quiet internal courtyard, and while the bathrooms are a little small they are clean and there is never any want for hot water. **www.choicehotels.dk**

NORTH COPENHAGEN Copenhagen Admiral
ⓀⓀⓀ
Toldbodgade 24–8, 1253 **Tel** *33 74 14 14* **Fax** *33 74 14 16* **Rooms** *366* **Map** *2 E4*

This 1780's-era warehouse has been turned into a modern hotel that is swimming in nautical and maritime detail. No two rooms are alike, but they do all boast mod cons and portal-style windows, and many look out to the sea. Despite the inviting atmosphere, it sees few tourists and exists mostly as a business hotel. **www.admiralhotel.dk**

NORTH COPENHAGEN First Hotel Esplanaden
ⓀⓀⓀ
Bredgade 78, 1260 **Tel** *33 48 10 00* **Fax** *33 48 10 66* **Rooms** *117* **Map** *2 D5*

An ornate, period building featuring the lavish design typical of First Hotels offerings, but with somewhat small rooms. Though the Esplanaden is a bit of a hike from the city centre, it is set in quiet green surroundings, the staff are very friendly and efficient and the breakfasts are large. **www.firsthotels.com**

NORTH COPENHAGEN Christian IV
ⓀⓀⓀⓀ
Dronningens Tværgade 45, 1302 **Tel** *33 32 10 44* **Fax** *33 32 07 06* **Rooms** *42* **Map** *4 D3*

A central, unassuming hotel that is situated away from the hustle and bustle of the city centre yet still well placed for Nyhavn. The rooms all have a refined, Scandinavian look and feel. They serve excellent continental breakfasts, hire out cycles and offer free wi-fi in the rooms. **www.hotelchristianiv.dk**

NORTH COPENHAGEN Phoenix
ⓀⓀⓀⓀ
Bredgade 37, 1260 **Tel** *33 95 95 00* **Fax** *33 33 98 33* **Rooms** *206* **Map** *2 D5*

The Phoenix is housed in an 18th-century building close to Amalienborg Slot and Nyhavn. The lavish, elegant rooms proffer silk bedspreads, original art on the walls, Louis XIV furniture and gold fixtures in the large marble bathrooms. The staff are very welcoming. Enquire about cheaper weekend rates. **www.phoenixcopenhagen.com**

NORTH COPENHAGEN Scandic Front
ⓀⓀⓀⓀ
Sankt Annae Plads 21, 1022 **Tel** *33 13 34 00* **Fax** *33 11 77 07* **Rooms** *132* **Map** *2 D5*

Scandic Front is one of Copenhagen's most exclusive boutique hotels. All the rooms are lavish in their comforts, with deep beige and brown accents, Barcelona chairs, and flat-screen TVs, as well as tiled bathrooms with vanity mirrors. Breakfast is included, and guests can enjoy free coffee throughout the day. **www.scandichotels.com**

CENTRAL COPENHAGEN Danhostel Copenhagen City
Ⓚ
H.C. Andersens Boulevard 50, 1553 **Tel** *33 11 85 85* **Fax** *33 11 85 88* **Rooms** *192* **Map** *3 A1*

Do not be deceived by the anonymous high-rise exterior: the interior furnishings and sleekly-styled rooms would put most mid-level hotels to shame. Many of the rooms have superb views over the city. Facilities include an Internet café, comfortable TV lounge, laundry and large kitchen. **www.danhostelcopenhagencity.dk**

CENTRAL COPENHAGEN Bed and Breakfast Bonvie
ⓀⓀ
Frederiksberggade 25 C, 2nd Floor, 1459 **Tel** *33 93 63 73* **Fax** *33 93 63 73* **Rooms** *4* **Map** *3 B1*

This family-style guesthouse, set along Strøget, is one of Copenhagen's most central budget hotels. Rooms are decorated in an eclectic homely style but can suffer from street noise. Ensuite rooms cost extra. Guests can sit in the small courtyard and there is a washing machine available for their use. **www.bbbonvie.dk**

CENTRAL COPENHAGEN Jørgensen
ⓀⓀ
Rømersgade 11, 1362 **Tel** *33 13 81 86* **Fax** *33 15 51 05* **Rooms** *37* **Map** *1 A5*

Denmark's first gay-friendly hotel. Just minutes from Nørreport station, this is an excellent place from which to explore the city. The rooms are simply furnished, and the staff are very friendly. There are also a number of inexpensive, cramped dormitory-style rooms. Laundry available next door. **www.hoteljoergensen.dk**

Key to Symbols *see back cover flap*

CENTRAL COPENHAGEN Sømandshjemmet "Bethel"

Nyhavn 22, 1051 **Tel** *33 13 03 70* **Rooms** *30*   **Map** *4 D1*

This neo-Gothic building was once a popular stopping-off point for merchants on their way out to the high seas. The decor is traditional Scandinavian and the rooms, though at times a bit on the small side, are well equipped. Several of the larger corner rooms have excellent views to the harbour. **www.hotel-bethel.dk**

CENTRAL COPENHAGEN Copenhagen Strand

Havnegade 37, 1058 **Tel** *33 48 99 00* **Fax** *33 48 99 01* **Rooms** *174*   **Map** *4 D2*

Set in an original harbourside warehouse, with a vague maritime atmosphere throughout the hotel lobby. The Strand's rooms are uninspiring but comfortable. However, many of them look right across the water to Christianshavn. Ask about cheaper weekend rates. **www.copenhagenstrand.dk**

CENTRAL COPENHAGEN Hotel Fox

Jarmers Plads 3, 1551 **Tel** *33 95 77 55* **Fax** *33 14 30 33* **Rooms** *61*   **Map** *3 A1*

Easily one of the most unusual hotels in the city, the Fox was fashioned by a group of graphic designers, street artists and illustrators. Their off-the-wall creations range from the ultra-minimalist (floor-to-ceiling white formica) to the fantastical (walls covered in outlandish murals). Friendly reception and a great restaurant to boot. **www.hotelfox.dk**

CENTRAL COPENHAGEN Opera

Tordenskjoldsgade 15, 1055 **Tel** *33 47 83 00* **Fax** *33 47 83 01* **Rooms** *91*   **Map** *4 D1*

The location of the Opera, next to the Royal Theatre, accounts for the large number of Danish and international actors who have stayed here over the years. The rooms, though sometimes on the small side, are decorated in impeccable, elegant English style. At weekends there is a sizeable discount on the standard rate. **www.hotelopera.dk**

CENTRAL COPENHAGEN The Square

Rådhuspladsen 14, 1550 **Tel** *33 38 12 00* **Fax** *33 38 12 01* **Rooms** *267*   **Map** *3 A2*

The entire place epitomises all there is to love about Denmark: sleek design, efficient service, friendly reception but with high prices to match. The superbly designed rooms are to die for, with some of the most comfortable beds in the entire city, and some of them with very fetching views. Breakfast available. **www.thesquare.dk**

CENTRAL COPENHAGEN Alexandra

H.C. Andersens Boulevard 8, 1553 **Tel** *33 74 44 44* **Fax** *33 74 44 88* **Rooms** *61*   **Map** *3 A1*

Housed in what were once fashionable city apartments built in 1910, this chic retro hotel has a stylish and upmarket decor, with plenty of attention to detail. The walls are hung with original artworks and much of the furniture is classic Danish design, including pieces by Arne Jacobsen. **www.hotel-alexandra.dk**

CENTRAL COPENHAGEN Ascot

Studiestræde 61, 1554 **Tel** *33 12 60 00* **Fax** *33 14 60 40* **Rooms** *190*   **Map** *3 A1*

The wall reliefs of men and women bathing are a reminder that this building was once a public baths. The bathrooms, rather appropriately, are prodigious and luxurious. Though the hotel has been extensively renovated, it does manage to maintain an old-world atmosphere. **www.ascothotel.dk**

CENTRAL COPENHAGEN DGI-byens Hotel

Tietgensgade 65, 1704 **Tel** *33 29 80 50* **Rooms** *104*   **Map** *3 A3*

Situated within a massive sporting complex just south of Halmtorvet, DGI-byens' rooms are homages to chic Scandinavian design, featuring bleached oak flooring and leather sofas. Guests get free access to the massive pool and discounted spa treatments. Parking is available for a fee. **www.dgi-byen.dk/hotel**

CENTRAL COPENHAGEN First Hotel Kong Frederik

25 Vester Voldgade, 1552 **Tel** *33 12 59 02* **Fax** *33 37 06 30* **Rooms** *110*   **Map** *3 A1*

The Kong Frederik, now part of the First Hotels group, retains its classic English townhouse style in modern monochrome tones. The hotel's original, bookish theme is inspired by Danish writers who have stayed at the hotel. It has an excellent Italian restaurant and a very central location just off Rådhuspladsen. **www.firsthotels.com**

CENTRAL COPENHAGEN Grand Hotel Copenhagen

Vesterbrogade 9, 1620 **Tel** *33 27 69 00* **Fax** *33 27 69 01* **Rooms** *161*   **Map** *3 A2*

The bright, smallish rooms here bring a touch of modern style to this classic Copenhagen hotel, which dates from 1890. The more upmarket rooms have leather reading chairs, mahogany writing desks, large windows and all mod cons. Wi-Fi access is available throughout. **www.grandhotel.dk**

CENTRAL COPENHAGEN Ibsens

Vendersgade 23, 1363 **Tel** *33 13 19 13* **Fax** *33 13 19 16* **Rooms** *118*   **Map** *1 A4*

Set within a classic French-style apartment building, this hotel has classic, old-world, individually styled rooms, ranging from modern Scandinavian to classical English, though all are modestly decorated. The hotel is hidden away in a narrow café-lined street close to Nansensgade – great for a night out. **www.ibsenshotel.dk**

CENTRAL COPENHAGEN First Hotel Skt Petri

Krystalgade 22, 1172 **Tel** *33 45 91 00* **Fax** *33 45 91 10* **Rooms** *268*   **Map** *3 B1*

Super-chic colourful establishment offering rooms which are impeccably designed by top Danish architects. The rooms on the upper floor have great views over to the nearby Latin Quarter, at a supplement. There is a trendy café, cocktail bar and parking (for a fee). **www.firsthotels.com**

CENTRAL COPENHAGEN Hotel D'Angleterre

Kongens Nytorv 34, 1022 **Tel** *33 12 00 95* **Fax** *33 12 11 18* **Rooms** *123*

Map 4 D1

One of the most respected hotels in Copenhagen, the D'Angleterre has been in business for more than 250 years and remains the choice for visiting dignitaries. The rooms are very large, classic in decor, and filled with every amenity you could want. The queen's official residence is just around the corner. **www.dangleterre.com**

CENTRAL COPENHAGEN Radisson Blu Royal Hotel

Hammerichsgade 1, 1611 **Tel** *33 42 60 00* **Rooms** *260*

Map 3 A1

This is the original designer hotel. The entire place, inside and out, was designed in 1960 by Arne Jacobsen, including Swan and Egg chairs, a spiral staircase and anodized doorknobs. The comfortable rooms have Internet access, a sophisticated decor and all modern amenities. **www.radissonblu.com/royalhotel-copenhagen**

SOUTH COPENHAGEN Carstens Guest House

Christians Brygge 28, 5th Floor, 1559 **Tel** *33 14 91 07* **Rooms** *5*

Map 3 C3

Chipper, gay-friendly bed and breakfast that has woodsy rooms set in two separate apartment buildings. The staff will cook a full breakfast for you, if you book in advance. The rooftop terrace is good for evening drinks. There are also shared, dormitory-style rooms in the loft, a Finnish sauna and laundry facilities. **www.carstensguesthouse.dk**

SOUTH COPENHAGEN Hotel Danmark

Vester Voldgade 89, 1552 **Tel** *33 11 48 06* **Fax** *33 14 36 30* **Rooms** *88*

Map 3 A1

A stone's throw from Rådhuspladsen and the shopping neighbourhood of Strøget, this is an ideal location for a short break in the capital. The building is late 18th century and the rooms are on the small side though all have good beds and some boast small French balconies. Weekends are quite a bit cheaper. **www.hotel-danmark.dk**

SOUTH COPENHAGEN Radisson Blu Scandinavia

Amager Boulevard 70, 2300 **Tel** *33 96 50 00* **Fax** *33 96 55 00* **Rooms** *542*

Map 3 C3

The largest hotel in Denmark, with 26 floors. Most rooms have views of the city. The fitness centre features a huge indoor pool and squash courts, and there are four restaurants – Danish, Italian, Japanese and Thai – on the ground floor, along with Copenhagen's only casino. Free parking. **www.radissonblu.com/scandinaviahotel-copenhagen**

FURTHER AFIELD Løven

Vesterbrogade 30, 1st Floor, 1620 **Tel** *33 79 67 20* **Fax** *33 79 67 30* **Rooms** *67*

The Løven is located on the lively Vestbrogade. Its bright rooms are simply furnished and without TVs; some have hard-wood floors. A few have private facilities, while others share. You can use a guest kitchen for preparing meals. With double and multiple-occupancy rooms, this is definitely one of the better bargains in this area. **www.loevenhotel.dk**

FURTHER AFIELD Sleep-In Heaven

Struenseegade 7, 2200 **Tel** *35 35 46 48* **Rooms** *76 beds*

The small beds at this basement hostel might not offer a heavenly night's sleep but they do attract a variety of students, boho types and backpackers. As it gets crowded, especially in summer, be prepared to wake up early to get a hot shower. Free Internet access, a bar, no curfew, breakfast and bed linen extra. **www.sleepinheaven.com**

FURTHER AFIELD Andersen Hotel

Helgolandsgade 12, 1653 **Tel** *33 31 46 10* **Rooms** *73*

Map 3 A3

This brightly coloured, reasonably priced boutique hotel is situated just minutes away from Copenhagen's Central Station. Rooms come in three price classes – Cool, Brilliant and Wonderful – and one night's stay is valid for 24 hours from the time you check in. Cycle hire and free Wi-Fi available. **www.andersen-hotel.dk**

FURTHER AFIELD City Hotel Nebo

Istedgade 6–8, 1650 **Tel** *33 21 12 17* **Fax** *33 23 47 74* **Rooms** *84*

Located right next to the train station, this ecumenical hotel is an affordable option for this part of town. There are three different price levels of room, though all have their own private shower and toilet. The cheapest rooms are great for budget travellers who wish to avoid staying in a youth hostel. **www.nebo.dk**

FURTHER AFIELD Danhostel Ishøj Strand

Ishøj Strandvej 13, 2635 **Tel** *43 53 50 15* **Fax** *43 53 50 45* **Rooms** *40*

This huge hostel lies south of Copenhagen, but the S-Bane E line train takes you within a kilometre of it. It is ideal for families, offering jungle gyms, table tennis, miniature golf and bike rental, as well as being close to a sandy beach for swimming, sunbathing and windsurfing. The dormitory beds are cheaper. **www.ishojhostel.dk**

FURTHER AFIELD Sct Thomas

Frederiksberg Allé 7, 1621 **Tel** *33 21 64 64* **Fax** *33 25 64 60* **Rooms** *50*

The small, tranquil Sct Thomas is a well-run modern hotel offering excellent value for money. The rooms are modestly decorated (with the exception of flat-screen TVs), and those with shared facilities are somewhat cheaper. The 250S bus from the airport stops right outside. **www.hotelsctthomas.dk**

FURTHER AFIELD Tiffany

Halmtorvet 1, 1700 **Tel** *33 21 80 50* **Fax** *33 21 87 50* **Rooms** *29*

The Tiffany is on a little square in Vesterbro just half a block from the train station. The spacious rooms have every amenity imaginable, including microwaves, dining tables for four and fetching tiled bathrooms. The service is remarkably friendly. Breakfast is included. **www.hoteltiffany.dk**

Key to Price Guide *see p244* **Key to Symbols** *see back cover flap*

FURTHER AFIELD Adina Apartment Hotel Copenhagen
Amerika Plads 7, 2100 **Tel** *39 69 10 00* **Fax** *88 19 36 99* **Rooms** *128*
Map 2 E1

Adina Apartment Hotel is a four-star establishment just minutes away from the Little Mermaid monument. With its modern design and vibrant colour scheme, it offers the perfect home-away-from-home experience for both business and leisure guests. Facilities include an indoor pool, Jacuzzi, sauna and gym. **www.adina.eu**

FURTHER AFIELD Ansgar
Colbjørnsensgade 29, 1652 **Tel** *33 21 21 96* **Fax** *33 21 61 91* **Rooms** *81*
Map 3 A3

Set immediately opposite the train station, this tourist-class hotel has rooms with fairly predictable Ikea-style furnishings, but all are bright and have TV, phone and Wi-Fi Internet access. The bathrooms are small. Free indoor parking is available to guests. There are great discounts to be had during low season. **www.ansgarhotel.dk**

FURTHER AFIELD Avenue
Åboulevard 29, 1960 **Tel** *35 37 31 11* **Fax** *35 37 31 33* **Rooms** *68*

Originally built in 1898, the Avenue always gets glowing reviews from guests, who admire its ability to combine cutting-edge Danish interior design with a cosy ambience. The bright rooms are very stylish, and there is an excellent breakfast buffet. A short walk from the city centre. **www.avenuehotel.dk**

FURTHER AFIELD Bertrams Hotel Guldsmeden
Vesterbrogade 107, 1620 **Tel** *33 25 04 05* **Fax** *33 25 04 02* **Rooms** *47*

The lofty, elegant rooms of this gable-roofed boutique hotel are furnished in French-colonial style and feature lavish trimmings such as Oriental carpets, canopied beds and sumptuous linens. The Bertrams offers surprising luxury for this part of town and a great organic breakfast. **www.bertramshotel.dk**

FURTHER AFIELD STAY Apartment Hotel
Islands Brygge 79A, 2200 **Tel** *72 44 44 34* **Rooms** *180*

In an attractive building renovated by Danish designers, STAY provides guests with space and independence in two- and three-room serviced apartments with superb views of the waterfront. No breakfast, but the building houses an Italian restaurant, an organic supermarket and a gourmet bakery. **www.staycopenhagen.dk**

FURTHER AFIELD Hotel Kong Arthur
Nørre Søgade 11, 1370 **Tel** *33 11 12 12* **Fax** *33 32 61 30* **Rooms** *155*
Map 1 A5

This former orphanage is on a small lake just by Rosenborg Slot. The smallish rooms have classic, turn-of-the-century Scandinavian decor with a good number of antique furnishings. Breakfast is taken in a sunroom that looks onto a quaint courtyard. There are several restaurants, a spa, free parking and frequent special offers. **www.kongarthur.dk**

FURTHER AFIELD Marriott
Kalvebod Brygge 5, 1560 **Tel** *88 33 99 00* **Fax** *88 33 99 99* **Rooms** *401*
Map 3 A4

This 11-storey, high-class chain hotel offers superb views of the city and harbour. The rooms, while plush enough, are in classic international Marriott style which can, at times, veer towards the uninspiring. However, if you want to be guaranteed a safe and welcoming stay, this is your place. **www.copenhagenmarriott.dk**

FURTHER AFIELD Radisson Blu Falconer Hotel
Falkoner Alle 9, 2000 **Tel** *38 15 80 01* **Fax** *38 15 80 02* **Rooms** *166*

A favourite with businessmen, this hotel makes a nice stop if you are looking to stay further from the city. A bright and airy lobby leads to clean, if slightly dated rooms. Service can be unreliable. The fitness centre has massage rooms and a sauna. Good weekend rates, especially if you book online. **www.radissonblu.com/falconerhotel-copenhagen**

FURTHER AFIELD Skovshoved Hotel
Strandvejen 267, 2920 **Tel** *39 64 00 28* **Fax** *39 64 06 72* **Rooms** *22*

A short drive outside the city, in leafy Charlottenlund village, this hotel has been around since 1660, but a design overhaul has earned it a coveted spot on the "hip hotels" circuit. The rooms are very modern and have views over the Øresund; there is even a private bathing jetty, not to mention a superb restaurant. **www.skovshovedhotel.dk**

NORTHWESTERN ZEALAND

BIRKERØD Hotel Birkerød
Birkerød Kongevej 102–104, 3460 **Tel** *45 81 44 30* **Fax** *45 82 30 29* **Rooms** *29*
Map F4

A good-value hotel convenient for Copenhagen as well as Northwestern Zealand, the Birkerød is bright with uninspired rooms. The reception, however, is very friendly and the whole place is set in lovely grounds just minutes from a forest and rolling hills. Facilities include tennis courts. **www.hotelbirkerod.dk**

ESKEBJERG Myrehøj Bed and Breakfast
Vilhelmshøjvej 1, 4593 **Tel** *59 29 00 26* **Fax** *59 29 00 28* **Rooms** *13*
Map E4

Set in a farmhouse built in 1686, the grounds of this modest B&B feature an orchard, flower gardens and a large outdoor terrace. The lovely rooms are done up in a variety of styles and many feel quite dainty, with light colours and simple cast iron or shaven-wood furniture. The beach is a fair walk away. **www.myrehoj.dk**

FREDERIKSSUND Villa Bakkely

Roskildevej 109, 3600 **Tel** *30 63 45 10* **Rooms** *7*

Map *F4*

A small bed and breakfast with seven distinctive rooms, all of which have large double beds and flatscreen TVs. None have en-suite facilities, but there is a cosy breakfast café, terrace, and a beautiful old garden. A good option if you want to get a bit outside of Frederikssund, which tends to be busy in high season. **www.villabakkely.dk**

GILLELEJE Gilleleje Badehotel

Hulsøvej 15, 3250 **Tel** *48 30 13 47* **Fax** *48 36 04 69* **Rooms** *24*

Map *F4*

This splendid beach hotel was built in 1895 for wealthy, weekending Copenhageners. It has since been given a bright maritime makeover which succeeds in being contemporary. The best part: downstairs you will find a sauna, steam room and Jacuzzi – perfect after a dip in the sea. **www.gillelejebadehotel.dk**

HELSINGØR Danhostel Helsingør Vandrerhjem

Ndr Strandvej 24, 3000 **Tel** *49 28 49 49* **Fax** *49 28 49 39* **Rooms** *38*

Map *F4*

A few steps away from its own small, private beach, this youth hostel occupies some great real estate. The old villa consists primarily of double and triple rooms, though there are a few very spacious dormitory-style rooms as well. Reception is professionally run and there is wireless Internet access throughout. **www.helsingorhostel.dk**

HELSINGØR Madam Sprunck Hotel and Restaurant

Bramstræde 5, 3000 **Tel** *49 21 05 91* **Fax** *49 49 26 01* **Rooms** *37*

Map *F4*

The building itself is one of the town's oldest and is centrally located. The Hamlet is also very close to the train station. Some of the rooms have been renovated in rich, deep colours; others still have very cramped bathrooms. Its proximity to Helsingør's nightclubs means that weekends can be noisy. **www.hotelhamlet.dk**

HELSINGØR Hotel & Casino Marienlyst

Nordre Strandvej 2, 3000 **Tel** *49 21 40 00* **Rooms** *222*

Map *F4*

This massive establishment was Denmark's first official seaside resort. Situated right on the shores of the Kattegat, there are views straight to the Sound or to Kronborg Castle. The rooms are beautifully furnished. You can find excellent discounts if you want to stay for more than just a night or two. Onsite casino. **www.marienlyst.dk**

HOLBÆK Holbæk Vandrerhjem

Ahlgade 1B, 4300 **Tel** *59 44 29 19* **Fax** *59 43 94 85* **Rooms** *26*

Map *F4*

An outstanding hostel option that never ever feels like a hostel, with Oriental rugs, Alpine-style rooms and the friendliest of staff. This place makes other Danish hostels green with envy. The ground-floor restaurant is one of the best places to eat in town, and there is an authentic Turkish bathhouse. **www.sidesporet.dk/vandrerhjem**

HORNBÆK Ewaldsgården

Johannes Ewaldsvej 5, 3100 **Tel** *49 70 00 82* **Fax** *49 70 00 82* **Rooms** *12*

Map *F4*

This 150-year-old guesthouse is set around a cobblestone courtyard. The rooms are bright and spacious with large comfortable beds, and there is such a perfectly rustic ambience throughout the hallways and living rooms that it almost feels as though you are in an old ethnographic museum. Open Jun–mid-Aug only. **www.ewaldsgaarden.dk**

HORNBÆK Havreholm Slot

Klosterrisvej 4, 3100 **Tel** *49 75 86 00* **Fax** *49 75 80 23* **Rooms** *26*

Map *F4*

Situated amongst sprawling lawns bordered by woodlands and looking onto a pristine lake, this bright modern-meets-classic hotel has spacious well-equipped rooms. There are numerous sports activities available, including golf, tennis, and swimming in the pool or lake. There is also an excellent terrace restaurant. **www.havreholm.dk**

HORNBÆK Hotel Bretagne

Sauntevej 18, 3100 **Tel** *49 70 16 66* **Fax** *49 25 65 04* **Rooms** *26*

Map *F4*

This one-time hospital has outstanding views over the Hornbæk lake, the Kattegat and the surrounding forest. Today the Bretagne boasts pastel-coloured rooms with wireless Internet and cooking facilities, though there is also a hotel restaurant. **www.hotelbretagne.dk**

HUNDESTED Hundested Kro

Nørregade 10, 3390 **Tel** *47 93 75 38* **Fax** *47 93 78 61* **Rooms** *46*

Map *F4*

Most of the rooms at this much-loved inn are very elegant, though be sure to ask for one with views to the Isefjorden. Facilities include a pool and sauna, and it is just a short distance from the beach. The inn restaurant is well known for serving excellent food and there is also a lively bar. **www.hundested-kro.dk**

HØRVE Dragsholm Slot

Dragsholm Allé, 4534 **Tel** *59 65 33 00* **Fax** *59 65 30 33* **Rooms** *36*

Map *E4*

Finding more luxury and class than is offered by this establishment would be tough. Set in a 13th-century castle built to defend the town, the rooms here are unique, with a distinctive antique feel to them. The Dragsholm is popular for weddings, so check ahead of time to be sure you are not next door to some newlyweds. **www.dragsholm-slot.dk**

KORSØR Svenstrupgård Feriecenter

Svenstrup Strandvej 3, 4220 **Tel** *58 38 15 19* **Rooms** *38*

Map *E5*

Located in the middle of the forest on the water's edge, the rooms in this rustic holiday centre are spacious and feel new, while featuring exposed beams and vaulted brick ceilings. There are also cheaper dormitory rooms, a common sitting room and communal kitchen that guests can use. Ideal for outdoor enthusiasts. **www.svenstrupgaard.dk**

NYKØBING S Anneberg Vandrerhjem ⊗
Egebjergvej 162, 4500 **Tel** *41 86 55 44* **Rooms** *13* **Map** *E4*

This gorgeous youth hostel is set within a 17th-century estate that from the outside looks like it should be lived in by royalty. The rooms are clean and tasteful, though undeniably hostel-like, and the grounds lead to a private beach. Families are welcomed. **www.annebergvandrerhjem.dk**

ROSKILDE Roskilde Vandrerhjem 🚻 ⊗⊗
Vindeboder 7, 4000 **Tel** *46 35 21 84* **Rooms** *40* **Map** *F4*

Situated in the harbour next to the Viking Ship Museum, the Vandrerhjem is a 15-minute walk from the centre of town. This spectacular youth hostel feels more like a minimalist design hotel with a maritime ambience than a regular hostel. It is clean and very well run. There are good offers for families. **www.rova.dk**

ROSKILDE Scandic Hotel Roskilde 🛏️🍴📺🚻 ⊗⊗
Søndre Ringvej 33, 4000 **Tel** *46 32 46 32* **Fax** *46 32 02 32* **Rooms** *98* **Map** *F4*

Part of the reliable Scandic chain, this hotel has many facilities, including a sauna and solarium. The rooms are comfortable and furnished in a traditional style, though they can feel quite bland at times. Located outside of town on the ring road, the Scandic is best if you have a vehicle. **www.scandic-hotels.com/roskilde**

ROSKILDE Prindsen 🛏️🍴🚻 ⊗⊗⊗
Algade 13, 4000 **Tel** *46 30 91 00* **Fax** *46 30 91 50* **Rooms** *76* **Map** *F4*

Excellently located on a pedestrianized street between the train station and the Domkirke, this historic hotel dates from 1875, though an inn has stood here since 1695. The Prindsen offers classic elegance and high levels of service. Ask for one of the quieter rooms facing the courtyard. Good weekend rates. **www.prindsen.dk**

SKIBBY Hotel Frederikssund ⊗
Ved Diget 7–9, Skuldelev Strand, 4050 **Tel** *47 50 40 42* **Rooms** *9* **Map** *F4*

This affordable, family-run bed and breakfast is located on a farm not far from Skibby. Rooms are simply decorated but do include a flat-screen TV and Internet. Skuldelev harbour is just a few minutes' walk from the guesthouse, and guests can rent a sailboat. There is also an outside barbecue. **www.hotelfrederikssund.dk**

SORØ Hotel Postgården 🍴🚻 ⊗⊗
Storgade 25, 4180 **Tel** *57 83 22 22* **Rooms** *18* **Map** *E5*

The Danish writer Ludvig Holberg composed a number of his stories here. Centrally located right on the main street in Sorø, the rooms at this classy hotel are elegant and smart and the reception friendly and helpful. There is also a great pan-Asian restaurant just next door. **www.hotelpostgaarden.dk**

TISVILDELEJE Kildegaard 📋🍴🚻 ⊗⊗
Hovedgaden 52, 3220 **Tel** *48 70 71 53* **Fax** *48 70 72 19* **Rooms** *27* **Map** *F4*

This tiny family guesthouse has quaint little rooms which have hardly changed since the place was established in 1904. Some of the original furnishings are still present. The leafy garden out back is a great place to spend a quiet sunny afternoon and there is a bathing beach nearby. **www.kildegaard-tisvildeleje.dk**

TISVILDELEJE Sankt Helene 🍴🚻 ⊗⊗
Bygmarken 30, 3320 **Tel** *48 70 98 50* **Rooms** *93* **Map** *F4*

A modern resort complex close to the train station and a short walk from the beach and town, Sankt Helene comprises private hostel rooms, self-contained apartments and more basic cabins. There are farm animals and several playgrounds for children of all ages in the complex's extensive grounds. **www.helene.dk/en**

TISVILDELEJE Strand Hotel 🍴🚻 ⊗⊗⊗
Hovedgade 75, 3220 **Tel** *48 70 71 19* **Rooms** *24* **Map** *F4*

This gorgeous *fin-de-siècle* building was originally the town's general store. Today it is a modern hotel featuring a colourful interior with colonial influences; all rooms are individually decorated. The Strand has, however, retained a number of older features, such as exposed beams and traditional wicker chairs. **www.strand-hotel.dk**

SOUTHERN ZEALAND AND THE ISLANDS

KØGE Central Hotellet ⊗⊗
Vestergade 3, 4600 **Tel** *56 65 06 96* **Fax** *56 66 02 07* **Rooms** *12* **Map** *F5*

The rooms at this small comfortable hotel, situated right next to the tourist office, are basic. The perfectly acceptable doubles are fairly priced (especially if you don't mind sharing the bathroom), and the location is right in the middle of town. The cheery reception is run by helpful locals who have plenty of recommendations. **www.centralhotellet.dk**

KØGE Hvide Hus 🛏️🍴📺🚻 ⊗⊗⊗
Strandvejen 111, 4600 **Tel** *56 65 36 90* **Fax** *56 66 33 14* **Rooms** *126* **Map** *F5*

Popular with business conferences and weekend golfers, Hvide Hus offers basic rooms with design features such as minimalist lighting and boutique textiles. This, combined with expansive grounds inhabited by wandering flamingoes and the fact that the beach is nearby, make this a real find. **www.hotelhvidehus.dk**

MARIBO Hotel Maribo Søpark

Vestergade 29, 4930 **Tel** *54 78 10 11* **Fax** *54 78 05 22* **Rooms** *107*

Map E6

This superb hotel enjoys an exceptionally lovely location. Its spacious rooms are elegantly furnished, and many have balconies looking onto the beautiful Maribo Sø lake. In addition to a wellness centre and spa, the Søpark also has a fantastic restaurant and an outdoor swimming pool. **www.maribo-soepark.dk**

MARIELYST Hotel Nørrevang

Marielyst Strandvej 32, 4873 **Tel** *54 13 62 62* **Rooms** *80*

Map F6

Set in a 19th-century landscape in the centre of town, this is by far the nicest place to stay in Marielyst. It is close to the beach but an indoor/outdoor swimming pool is great for cooling off during the day. A number of the rooms are set within chalet-style duplex buildings with lofted beds. Attracts a fair share of large groups. **www.norrevang.dk**

MØN Møns Klint Youth Hostel

Langebjergvej 1, 4791 **Tel** *55 81 20 30* **Fax** *55 81 28 18* **Rooms** *29*

Map F6

This efficiently run hostel is set on the quiet Hunosøen lake, where guests can go fishing. Rooms are large and have a rustic feel to them, and it is not uncommon to have an entire room to yourself. The hostel is just 15 minutes by foot to the chalk cliffs of Møns Klint. Horse-riding is available next door. **www.danhostel.dk/moen**

MØN Bakkegaard Gæstgiveri 16

Busenevej 64, 4791 **Tel** *55 81 93 01* **Fax** *55 81 94 01* **Rooms** *12*

Map F6

Set in a large farmhouse on sprawling lawns towards the eastern half of Møn (a 20-minute walk from the stunning chalk cliffs of Møns Klint), this B&B offers pleasant and sparsely decorated rooms. Breakfast is taken in a sunroom or in a covered gazebo on the lawn, from which you can see the Baltic. Dinner on request. **www.bakkegaarden64.dk**

MØN Liselund ny Slot

Langebjergvej 6, 4791 **Tel** *55 81 20 81* **Fax** *55 81 21 91* **Rooms** *17*

Map F6

This tiny thatched castle is a unexpected gem. Each room is named after one of H.C. Andersen's fairy tales and retains original wall panelling and ceiling frescoes, plus old wooden planks for floors and private baths. For a particularly memorable stay there is the tower honeymoon suite with panoramic views. **www.liselundslot.dk**

NAKSKOV Hotel Harmonien

Nybrogade 2, 4900 **Tel** *54 95 91 90* **Fax** *54 95 91 30* **Rooms** *33*

Map E6

Situated close to the sights of central Nakskov, the spacious, minimalist rooms and suites are elegantly decorated in whites, blues and light greys, with dark wooden furniture and large bathrooms. There is also a spa and wellness centre. Probably Nakskov's best hotel option. **www.hotel-harmonien.dk**

NÆSTVED Hotel Kirstine

Købmagergade 20, 4700 **Tel** *55 77 47 00* **Fax** *55 72 11 53* **Rooms** *31*

Map E5

Long ago, Næstved's mayors lived within the walls of this 18th-century brick and timber building. The top-class hotel that now occupies the premises makes good use of this history, with classical rooms with antique furnishings. The Kirstine also offers several budget rooms which they do not advertise. **www.hotelkirstine.dk**

NÆSTVED Hotel Vinhuset

Sct Peders Kirkeplads 4, 4700 **Tel** *55 72 08 07* **Fax** *55 72 03 35* **Rooms** *56*

Map E5

This hotel, in a classic 1778 building, offers all modern conveniences while retaining its antique charm. The rooms are individually decorated in rich colours and a few feature canopy beds. There is a beautiful, old cellar restaurant, as well as a modern bar on site. **www.hotelvinhuset.dk**

NYSTED The Cottage

Skansevej 19, 4880 **Tel** *54 87 18 87* **Fax** *54 87 18 78* **Rooms** *16*

Map E6

This charming half-timbered property on the outskirts of Nysted was built in 1908 to house governors of a nearby English school. It became a hotel in 1970 and was enlarged in the 1980s. The traditional ensuite rooms open out on to a small terrace, and there's also minigolf and an excellent restaurant. **www.cottage.dk**

PRÆSTØ Kirsebærkroen

Kirsebærvej 1, 4720 **Tel** *55 99 39 55* **Rooms** *7*

Map F5

Run by a friendly elderly Danish couple, this one-time farmstead features nicely decorated rooms, each with minibar and TV, all set in quiet grounds close to a beach on Præstø fjord. Each room has an adjoining patio with table and chairs – ideal for relaxing in the picturesque surroundings. Some rooms have kitchenettes. **www.kirsebaerkroen.dk**

RINGSTED Scandic Hotel Ringsted

Nørretorv 57, 4100 **Tel** *57 61 93 00* **Fax** *57 67 02 07* **Rooms** *75*

Map E5

A four-storey hotel south of the town centre with comfortable, simply decorated rooms. This chain is popular with business travellers. High standards throughout with generous breakfast buffet, however for dinner it is recommended to head into town. You can even borrow the hotel's bicycles. **www.scandic-hotels.dk/ringsted**

RINGSTED Sørup Herregård

Sørupvej 26, 4100 **Tel** *57 64 30 02* **Fax** *57 64 31 73* **Rooms** *102*

Map E5

Set in an old manor house, this hotel overlooks a small lake and even has its own landing stage. The rooms are particularly well furnished, with dark hardwood floors, fine linens, all mod cons and great views of the hillside. There is also an indoor pool, sauna and terrace restaurant. **www.sorup.dk**

Key to Price Guide see p244 **Key to Symbols** see back cover flap

RØDVIG STEVNS Rødvig Kro og Badehotel

Østersøvej 8, 4673 **Tel** *56 50 60 98* **Rooms** *16* **Map** *F5*

An old, atmospheric family-run inn with particularly fetching views out to the Baltic and to the Stevns Klint cliffs. The tidy rooms come in a variety of sizes, but all are impeccably decorated with modern furnishings and comfortable beds. The hotel restaurant is worth trying, and in summer guests can eat outside. **www.roedvigkro.dk**

SAKSKØBING Otel Våbensted

Krårup Møllevej 6, 4990 **Tel** *54 70 63 63* **Rooms** *15* **Map** *E6*

This pleasant hotel, with its inviting rustic ambiance, is a good place to stay in an otherwise uneventful part of Lolland. The rooms are elegantly simple, some with private bathrooms, and the staff are uncharacteristically animated. There is also a large garden. Breakfast available. **www.otelvaabensted.dk**

VORDINGBORG Hotel Kong Valdemar

Algade 101, 4760 **Tel** *55 34 30 95* **Rooms** *60* **Map** *F6*

Located opposite the ruins of Vordingborg castle, the Valdemar may lack style but it certainly makes up for it in the friendliness of its reception. By far the most central hotel in Vordingborg and there is a decent restaurant and Internet access. **www.hotelkongvaldemar.dk**

FUNEN

ASSENS Marcussens

Strandgade 22, 5610 **Tel** *64 71 10 89* **Rooms** *33* **Map** *C5*

Located in the old merchant's town of Assens, this is an ideal place to soak up the small-town atmosphere that Funen is known for. The hotel is set just off a pedestrianised street and though most of the rooms feel somewhat dated, many do boast views of the water. There is also a pleasant terrace for meals. **www.marcussens.dk**

FAABORG Fåborg Vandrerhjem

Grønnegade 73, 5600 **Tel** *62 61 12 03* **Rooms** *18* **Map** *D5*

A superb youth hostel that feels as if you have stepped into an old museum, with creaky floors, uneven window panes, and subdued matte colours that call to mind homesteads of the early 19th century. It could not be more central too, placed equidistant from the ferry terminal, train station and town square. **www.danhostel.dk/faaborg**

FAABORG Hotel Fåborg

Torvet 13–15, 5600 **Tel** *62 61 02 45* **Rooms** *21* **Map** *D5*

Originally built in 1916, this gorgeous Gothic-style brick renovation of an old warehouse sits right on Fåborg's central square. All the rooms, soft and somewhat dainty in their colouring and furniture, have private facilities. The Mediterranean-style restaurant downstairs is one of the best spots to eat in town. **www.hotelfaaborg.dk**

FAABORG Hvedholm Slot

Hvedholm Alle 1, 5600 **Tel** *63 60 10 20* **Fax** *63 60 10 29* **Rooms** *42* **Map** *D5*

Hvedholm is an imposing castle that has been in the same family since 1570. The rooms have chandeliers, canopy beds, and plenty of regal ambience. The excellent restaurant specialises in game and fish dishes, and there is a wine cellar beneath it, which offers tastings every Saturday afternoon. **www.slotshotel.dk**

KERTEMINDE Danhostel Kerteminde

Skovvej 46, 5300 **Tel** *65 32 39 29* **Rooms** *30* **Map** *D5*

A good budget option set in a wooded area and only a few minutes' walk from the town beach. The bucolic, cabin-like rooms hardly feel like a youth hostel, though the many visiting youth groups will be enough of a reminder. About a 10 minute walk the town centre. **www.dkhostel.dk**

KERTEMINDE Tornøes Hotel

Strandgade 2, 5300 **Tel** *65 32 16 05* **Fax** *65 32 48 40* **Rooms** *38* **Map** *D5*

This brick building, originally built in 1643, is set right on the harbourside. The bright rooms are of a high standard, and the best ones feature canopy beds and views out to Kerteminde fjord. The hotel succeeds in retaining a very old-world feel and there is a good restaurant. **www.tornoeshotel.dk**

MARSTAL Hotel Marstal

Dronningestræde 1A, 5960 **Tel** *62 53 13 52* **Rooms** *18* **Map** *D6*

Located in an old harbour town at the easternmost point of the island of Ærø, this classic hotel has a number of plain but clean, bright and comfortable rooms offering sea views and private access to an enclosed garden. The hotel restaurant is the best in town, serving fine seafood in an English pub setting. **www.hotelmarstal.dk**

MIDDELFART Toldboden Bed & Breakfast

Brogade 1, 5500 **Tel** *64 41 47 37* **Rooms** *3* **Map** *C5*

This small bed-and-breakfast is just across from the harbour in the old quarter of Middelfart. The three colourful rooms all have sea views, as does the spacious balcony. There are two clean bathrooms shared between the rooms, and a large kitchen is also available for guests. **www.toldboden-bb.dk**

MIDDELFART Hindsgavl Slot

Hindsgavl Allé 7, 5500 **Tel** *64 41 88 00* **Rooms** *120*

Map *C5*

Occupying a medieval castle and its former stables, this hotel enjoys a magnificent lakeside location. The rooms feature quilted beds, window sashes, small crystal chandeliers and elegant trimmings. Verdant grounds and a gourmet restaurant add to its attractions, making it a choice stay for this part of Funen. **www.hindsgavl.dk**

NYBORG Villa Gulle

Østervoldgade 44, 5800 **Tel** *65 30 11 88* **Rooms** *23*

Map *D5*

Located close to Nyborg's harbour, Villa Gulle is a small, old-fashioned guesthouse with period furnishings and chintz wallpaper. Almost all rooms are ensuite, with flat-screen TVs and free Internet access. Breakfast is included, and full-board accommodation is also offered. **www.villa-gulle.dk**

NYBORG Hotel Hesselet

Christianslundsvej 119, 5800 **Tel** *65 31 30 29* **Fax** *65 31 29 58* **Rooms** *59*

Map *D5*

Located north of the city on the edge of a beech forest, the stylish, spacious, and individually decorated rooms of this grand old hotel are typified by wooden furniture and luxurious bathrooms with granite floors and double washbasins. There is also an indoor pool, sauna, two tennis courts and free cycle hire for guests. **www.hesselet.dk**

ODENSE Best Western Hotel Knudsens Gaard

Hunderupgade 2, 5230 **Tel** *63 11 43 11* **Fax** *63 11 43 01* **Rooms** *77*

Map *D5*

Part of the Best Western chain, the Knudsens Gaard is situated close to Ring Road 2, in Odense's southern suburbs. Its attractive half-timbered buildings are collected around a charming courtyard. The hotel features all modern facilities, and central Odense is only 10 minutes away by bus. **www.knudsensgaard.dk**

ODENSE Cabinn Odense

Ostre Stationsvej 7, 5000 **Tel** *63 14 57 00* **Fax** *63 14 57 01* **Rooms** *201*

Map *D5*

Ideal for short stays, this hotel is a good budget option with a great location, close to the train station and the city centre. Designed to be like ship cabins, the rooms are clean and comfortable. Breakfast (available at an additional cost) is served on the upper floor, which has views over the city. Free Wi-Fi and friendly staff. **www.cabinn.com**

ODENSE City Hotel Odense

Hans Mules Gade 5, 5000 **Tel** *66 12 12 58* **Fax** *66 12 93 64* **Rooms** *43*

Map *D5*

This centrally located establishment, close to the train station, is popular with businessmen. The rooms are comfortable enough, with all mod cons, though quite bland in their decor; an alternative might be one of the hotel's five apartment-style rooms. Great roof terrace for breakfast. **www.cityhotelodense.eu**

ODENSE Clarion Collection Hotel Plaza

Østre Stationsvej 24, 5000 **Tel** *66 11 77 45* **Fax** *66 14 41 45* **Rooms** *68*

Map *D5*

The Plaza is located on the edge of the Kongs Haven park in an old building that, from certain angles, resembles a castle. The rooms here are rather endearing, with classical furniture and a vague air of glamour. Copious breakfasts, large common areas, Wi-Fi Internet and friendly staff. **www.millinghotels.dk**

ODENSE Domir

Hans Tausensgade 19, 5000 **Tel** *66 12 14 27* **Fax** *66 12 13 14* **Rooms** *38*

Map *D5*

Quiet and independently run, the Domir is simply and elegantly decorated with friendly low-key service. Here you will find very comfortable beds, TV and a phone in every room, although a few of the rooms are on the small side ask to take a look first. The owners also run the smaller, less expensive Ydes next door. **www.domir.dk**

ODENSE Hotel Ansgar

Østre Stationsvej 32, 5000 **Tel** *66 11 96 93* **Fax** *66 11 96 75* **Rooms** *74*

Map *D5*

The rooms here boast plenty of classical charm thanks to their Italian-style chairs and window sashes. Catering to business and leisure travellers alike, the Ansgar also features a bar and restaurant, which offers a very good lunchtime buffet. **www.millinghotels.dk**

ODENSE Motel Ansgarhus

Kirkegårds Allé 17–21, 5000 **Tel** *66 12 88 00* **Fax** *66 12 88 65* **Rooms** *16*

Map *D5*

Just 5 minutes southeast of the city centre, this quaint family-run hotel is in a very desirable location next to the Å river. The rooms are small but cheery and there is wireless Internet access throughout. Nearby you can take a river boat all the way down to the Fynske Landsby open-air museum or to Odense Zoo. **www.ansgarhus.dk**

ODENSE Odense City Hostel

Østre Stationsvej 31, 5000 **Tel** *63 11 04 25* **Rooms** *39*

Map *D5*

Situated in the same complex as the train station, this spacious and bright hostel is the most central and inexpensive place in town. The reception is very friendly and hands out brochures on activities in and around town. Wireless Internet access included. **www.cityhostel.dk**

ODENSE Radisson Blu H.C. Andersen

Claus Bergs Gade 7, 5000 **Tel** *66 14 78 00* **Fax** *66 14 78 90* **Rooms** *145*

Map *D5*

Located in a pretty cobblestone district, only minutes from the Andersen museums, this plush hotel has been around since the early 1980s. The decor features furniture by top Danish designers, such as Arne Jacobsen. Wireless Internet connection is available free of charge. **www.radissonblu.com/hotel-odense**

Key to Price Guide *see p244* **Key to Symbols** *see back cover flap*

RUDKØBING Rudkøbing Skudehavn

Skudehavnen 21, 5900 **Tel** *62 51 46 00* **Fax** *62 51 49 40* **Rooms** *24*

Map *D6*

Down at Langeland's largest marina, a ten minute walk from the centre of Rudkøbing, this Swedish-style hotel has spacious chalet-style rooms. Each room has its own bathroom. Nearby you will find an excellent selection of restaurants and shops. **www.rudkobingskudehavn.dk**

SVENDBORG Ærø Hotel

Brogade 1, 5700 **Tel** *62 21 07 60* **Fax** *63 20 30 51* **Rooms** *33*

Map *D5*

Svendborg's oldest hotel, dating from 1870, is placed in a charismatic old building just across from the ferry harbour. The modern rooms are very well equipped and have an old-world, somewhat sumptuous feel to them. The hotel's Restaurant 5 serves modern Danish cuisine. **www.hotel-aeroe.dk**

ÆRØSKØBING Pension Vestergade 44

Vestergade 44, 5970 **Tel** *62 52 22 98* **Rooms** *8*

Map *D6*

This British-run guesthouse is set along one of Ærøskøbing's many atmospheric cobblestone streets and has lots of charm and some very comfortable, quite exquisite rooms. There is a pretty garden out back for taking meals, including afternoon English tea, in the fresh island air. **www.vestergade44.com**

SOUTHERN AND CENTRAL JUTLAND

BILLUND Hotel Propellen

Nordmarksvej 3, 7190 **Tel** *75 33 81 33* **Fax** *75 35 33 62* **Rooms** *94*

Map *C4*

This cosy three-storey hotel is a no-frills establishment with efficient friendly service. The rooms are cheery and comfortable and there are plenty of activities available such as table tennis and swimming. For children the hotel has its own playroom and outdoor playground. **www.propellen.dk**

BILLUND Legoland

Aastvej 10, 7190 **Tel** *75 33 12 44* **Fax** *75 35 38 10* **Rooms** *199*

Map *C4*

Set up mainly for visitors to LEGOLAND®, this hotel is connected to the park by an overhead walkway and the price for the first night includes two days admission to the attraction. Some of the rooms provide a view of the entire park and all of them have wireless Internet access. **www.hotellegoland.dk**

EBELTOFT Ebeltoft Park

Vibæk Strandvej 4, 8400 **Tel** *86 34 32 22* **Fax** *86 34 49 41* **Rooms** *71*

Map *D3*

Just opposite a white-sand beach and about 1 km (0.6 mile) from the centre of town, this hotel provides an ideal stay in a comfortable environment. Rooms are modestly decorated and have a TV and private bathroom. The nearby ferry terminal offers links with Zealand. Wireless Internet access is available. **www.ebeltoftparkhotel.dk**

EBELTOFT Hotel Ebeltoft Strand

Nordre Strandvej 3, 8400 **Tel** *86 34 33 00* **Fax** *86 34 46 36* **Rooms** *72*

Map *D3*

This modern beachfront hotel is surrounded by stunning scenery. Each of the brightly coloured rooms has a view over the enchanting Ebeltoft Vig cove. Facilities include a sauna. This is a popular area for surfers. Internet access available. **www.ebeltoftstrand.dk**

ESBJERG Scandic Olympic Esbjerg

Strandbygade 3, 6700 **Tel** *75 18 11 88* **Fax** *75 18 11 08* **Rooms** *147*

Map *B5*

Centrally located in the heart of the city, this modern hotel offers clean, well-maintained accommodation. The comfortable rooms are decorated in cool hues of white and blue with modern wooden furnishings. All the rooms have free wireless Internet. **www.scandichotels.com**

FANØ Sønderho Kro

Kropladsen 11, 6720 **Tel** *75 16 40 09* **Rooms** *13*

Map *B5*

Nestled behind the sand dunes in the heart of Sønderho, this 18th-century thatched inn has a pleasant atmosphere and four-poster beds. The rooms are individually furnished and enjoy views over the marshland and the sea. The French-Danish restaurant, one of the best on the island, attracts gourmets from afar. **www.sonderhokro.dk**

FREDERICIA Kronprinds Frederik

Vestre Ringvej 96, 7000 **Tel** *75 91 00 00* **Rooms** *78*

Map *C5*

This comfortable hotel is located in the recreational area of Madsby Enge, not far from Fredericia and the local beach. Next to the Kronprinds Frederik is the large Subtropical Waterland tourist attraction, where admission is free for guests of the hotel. **www.hkf.dk**

FREDERICIA Kryb-i-ly-Kro Best Western

Kolding Landevej 160, 7000 **Tel** *75 56 25 55* **Fax** *75 56 45 14* **Rooms** *77*

Map *C5*

Built in 1610, this cosy inn has plenty of character. Its name means "take shelter". Situated in peaceful surroundings, this popular and highly regarded establishment is within an hour's drive of Givskud Safari Park and LEGOLAND®. The facilities include an indoor swimming pool and sauna. **www.krybily.dk**

GRENÅ Helnan Marina

🍴 🏨   Ⓚ Ⓚ Ⓚ

Kystvej 32, 8500 **Tel** *86 32 25 00* **Fax** *86 32 62 05* **Rooms** *79*   *Map D3*

This modern hotel, located opposite a delightful and child-friendly sandy beach, is immersed in a verdant landscape. There are running trails in the nearby forest and a wellness centre on site that has a sauna, Jacuzzi, steam room and offers aromatherapy. Room rates include breakfast. **www.helnan.info**

HERNING Østergaards Hotel

📶 🍴 🛗   Ⓚ Ⓚ

Silkeborgvej 94, 7400 **Tel** *97 12 45 55* **Fax** *97 12 01 52* **Rooms** *84*   *Map C4*

Located in Central Jylland in quiet and peaceful surroundings, this modern hotel offers rooms with contemporary furnishings. It is popular with both businesspeople (thanks to its fully equipped conference centre) and those looking to unwind. Several golf courses are located in the vicinity. **www.oestergaardshotel.dk**

HORSENS Scandic Bygholm Park

🍴 🏨 🛗   Ⓚ Ⓚ

Schüttesvej 6, 8700 **Tel** *75 62 23 33* **Fax** *75 61 31 05* **Rooms** *142*   *Map C4*

Located in the beautiful Bygholm Park, this modernized manor house dates back to 1775. The hotel overlooks Bygholm Lake and visitor attractions in the area include the Museum of Art. All the rooms feature wireless Internet access. **www.scandichotels.com**

HORSENS Best Western Hotel Danica

📶 🍴 🏨 🛗   Ⓚ Ⓚ Ⓚ

Ove Jensens Allé 28, 8700 **Tel** *75 61 60 22* **Fax** *75 61 66 63* **Rooms** *39*   *Map C4*

This modern and comfortable hotel is situated in the town centre close to the town hall. The rooms are tastefully decorated and equipped with all modern amenities. The hotel restaurant is well worth a visit as it has received widespread recognition for its gourmet menu. Internet access is available. **www.hoteldanica.dk**

KOLDING Saxildhus Hotel

📶 🍴 🛗   Ⓚ Ⓚ Ⓚ

Jernbanegade 39, Banegårdspladsen, 6000 **Tel** *75 52 12 00* **Fax** *75 53 53 10* **Rooms** *87*   *Map C5*

Situated in the centre of Kolding, opposite the train station, this international establishment exudes an air of nostalgia and history. The beautifully decorated rooms have been refurbished respecting the original character of the building. The rooms facing the main street can be slightly noisy. **www.saxildhus.dk**

KOLDING Comwell Kolding

📶 🍴 🛗   Ⓚ Ⓚ Ⓚ

Skovbrynet 1, 6000 **Tel** *76 34 11 00* **Fax** *76 34 12 00* **Rooms** *180*   *Map C5*

The Comwell Kolding is a modern hotel equidistant from the town centre and Koldinghus Castle. It lies adjacent to a small lake and is decorated in contemporary Danish style. All the rooms are bright and cheerful. Facilities include internet access and an indoor swimming pool. **www.comwell.com**

RIBE Weis Stue

🍴   Ⓚ

Torvet 2, 6760 **Tel** *75 42 07 00* **Fax** *75 41 17 95* **Rooms** *8*   *Map B5*

An atmospheric inn-style hotel situated in the heart of Ribe not far from the town's famous 12th-century cathedral. The hotel building is half-timbered and dates back to the year 1600. The rooms are small and cosy with shared bathroom facilities. **www.weisstue.dk**

RIBE Dagmar

🍴 🛗   Ⓚ Ⓚ Ⓚ

Torvet 1, 6760 **Tel** *75 42 00 33* **Fax** *75 42 36 52* **Rooms** *48*   *Map B5*

Denmark's oldest hotel, built in 1581, the Dagmar is in a charming half-timbered building which has been gently restored over the years. Low ceilings, windows with deep sills and sloping floors take you back in time. The individually decorated rooms are stylish with canopy beds. Internet access in the lobby. **www.hoteldagmar.dk**

RINGKØBING Fjordgården

🍴 🛗   Ⓚ Ⓚ

Vesterkær 28, 6950 **Tel** *97 32 14 00* **Fax** *97 32 47 60* **Rooms** *98*   *Map B4*

A modern hotel located a short walk from the town centre, where, on summer evenings, Ringkøbing's night-watchmen sing in the streets. The rooms are a good size with pleasant sea and country views. Free wireless Internet access and indoor swimming pool available. **www.hotelfjordgaarden.dk**

RØMØ Havneby Kro

🍴   Ⓚ Ⓚ

Skansen 3, 6792 **Tel** *74 75 75 35* **Rooms** *9*   *Map B5*

This charming inn is situated close to the harbour, and the rooms offer views over the Wadden Sea. However, if you want to swim, the beach is about 4 km (2.5 miles) away. For those without a car, there are buses to the mainland. An ideal place to escape to. **www.havneby-kro.dk**

SABRO Hotel Nilles Kro

🍴 🛗   Ⓚ Ⓚ

Hadstenvej 209, 8471 **Tel** *86 94 88 99* **Fax** *86 94 80 89* **Rooms** *25*   *Map D3*

Built in 1954, this charming little inn is surrounded by magnificent countryside, but it is still close to the Moesgård Museum, Tivoli Friheden, golf courses and beaches. The Nilles Kro has a restaurant that serves typical Danish specialities. **www.nilleskro.dk**

SILKEBORG Radisson Blu

📶 🍴 🛗   Ⓚ Ⓚ

Papirfabrikken 12, 8600 **Tel** *88 82 22 22* **Fax** *88 82 22 23* **Rooms** *100*   *Map C4*

Silkeborg's old paper mill has been remodelled into this modern hotel. Located in the centre of town, near the harbour and the Aqua Aquarium, it overlooks the Remstrup River. The interior is bright, and all the expected facilities are available. **www.radissonblu.com**

Key to Price Guide *see p244* **Key to Symbols** *see back cover flap*

SILKEBORG Dania
🌊 ⅰ 🅿️ ⓚⓚⓚ

Torvet 5, 8600 **Tel** *86 82 01 11* **Fax** *86 80 20 04* **Rooms** *47* **Map** *C4*

Located in the town square and built in 1848, the Dania provides panoramic views of the lake. The rooms are uncluttered with modern decor and many of them have been named after personalities who have stayed at the hotel: Hans Christian Andersen stayed for several years! **www.hoteldania.dk**

SKANDERBORG Skanderborghus
ⅰ 🅿️ ⓚⓚ

Dyrehaven 3, 8660 **Tel** *86 52 09 55* **Fax** *86 52 18 01* **Rooms** *46* **Map** *C4*

Situated in the centre of Skanderborg Dyrehave, this lakeside hotel is surrounded by some breathtaking natural scenery, visible from all the hotel's rooms. The interiors are bright and airy. It is possible to charter a boat, the "Dagmar", that passes just outside the hotel from May to September. **www.hotelskanderborghus.dk**

SØNDERBORG Scandic Hotel
ⅰ 🍴 🅿️ ⓚⓚ

Ellegårdvej 27, 6400 **Tel** *74 42 26 00* **Fax** *74 42 76 00* **Rooms** *102* **Map** *C6*

This modern hotel has high ceilings and bright, airy rooms. It is close to attractions such as Sønderborg castle, the Sommerland Syd amusement park and Danfoss Universe, a science-focused theme park. It offers a playroom for children and free wireless Internet access. **www.scandichotels.dk**

SØNDERBORG Comwell Sønderborg
🌊 ⅰ 🍴 🅿️ ⓚⓚⓚ

Rosengade 2, 6400 **Tel** *74 42 19 00* **Rooms** *95* **Map** *C6*

This splendid hotel is not far from the picturesque town centre of Sonderborg, just across from the castle and very close to the beach. The rooms are bright and comfortable and the staff are renowned for their personable professional service. The facilites include Internet access and an indoor swimming pool. **www.comwell.dk**

TØNDER Schackenborg Slotskro
ⅰ 🅿️ ⓚⓚⓚ

Slotsgaden 42, Møgeltønder, 6270 **Tel** *74 73 83 83* **Fax** *74 73 83 11* **Rooms** *25* **Map** *B6*

An elegant hotel with an enchanting atmosphere, the Slotskro stands close to the ducal palace of Schackenborg where Prince Joachim has lived since 1995. Many of the hotel rooms were decorated under the supervision of his former wife, the Countess of Frederiksborg, Alexandra Manley. Wireless Internet is available. **www.slotskro.dk**

VEJLE BB Hotel
🌊 ⓚⓚ

Orla Lehmannsgade 5, 7100 **Tel** *70 22 55 30* **Fax** *75 72 05 39* **Rooms** *32* **Map** *C4*

Vejle's oldest hotel is now part of the BB self-service chain, which means online bookings only and no reception. The "key" to your room comes in the form of a code on your invoice. Rooms are comfortable and bright, with a relaxed atmosphere. Wireless Internet is available, and breakfast is included in the price. **www.bbhotels.dk**

VEJLE Hotel Australia
🌊 ⅰ 🅿️ ⓚⓚ

Dæmningen 6, 7100 **Tel** *76 40 60 00* **Fax** *76 40 60 01* **Rooms** *102* **Map** *C4*

Located in the heart of Vejle with panoramic views of the harbour and the town, this modern high-rise is the tallest building in the area. The rooms are spacious and clean. The service is efficient and the hotel is conveniently placed close to all the shops and restaurants. **www.hotelvejle.dk**

AARHUS Cab Inn Aarhus
🌊 ⓚⓚ

Kannikegade 14, 8000 **Tel** *86 75 70 00* **Fax** *86 75 71 00* **Rooms** *192* **Map** *D4*

Conveniently situated right in the heart of Aarhus, the Cab Inn has been designed with the budget-conscious traveller in mind. The petite rooms are modelled on ship cabins and the hotel's facilities are all shared. There is a café located on the premises. **www.cabinn.dk**

AARHUS Best Western Hotel Ritz
🌊 ⅰ ⓚⓚⓚ

Banegårdspladsen 12, 8000 **Tel** *86 13 44 44* **Fax** *86 13 45 87* **Rooms** *67* **Map** *D4*

Built in 1932 near to the town's Musikhuset (concert hall), theatres and restaurants, Best Western's Ritz has been redecorated and carefully refurbished in keeping with the original architecture. The hotel houses an elegant restaurant called MASH (Modern American Steak House). Internet access is available in the lobby. **www.hotelritz.dk**

AARHUS Guldsmeden
ⓚⓚⓚ

Guldsmedgade 40, 8000 **Tel** *86 13 45 50* **Fax** *86 13 76 76* **Rooms** *27* **Map** *D4*

This small hotel is discreetly positioned among the winding lanes close to the canal. It offers a warm and homely atmosphere. The rooms vary in size but are all simply decorated with references from around the world and rustic furniture. All the art is by Knud Weinert. Free wireless Internet available. **www.hotelguldsmeden.dk**

AARHUS Helnan Marselis Hotel
🌊 ⅰ 🍴 🅿️ ⓚⓚⓚⓚ

Strandvejen 25, 8000 **Tel** *86 14 44 11* **Fax** *86 14 44 20* **Rooms** *162* **Map** *D4*

Created by the famous architects Friis & Molkte in 1967, this hotel has been cleverly designed to offer a view of Aarhus Bay from every room. About 3 km (2 miles) from the town centre, the Marselis is next to the beach, with several golf courses nearby. The interiors display the simple lines of Scandinavian design. **www.marselis.dk**

AARHUS Hotel Royal
🌊 ⅰ ⓚⓚⓚⓚ

Store Torv 4, 8000 **Tel** *86 12 00 11* **Fax** *86 76 04 04* **Rooms** *66* **Map** *D4*

Situated in the heart of Aarhus, this famous hotel is next to the cathedral in the Latin Quarter. Built in 1838, it has been sensitively restored. The walls are decorated with fascinating art pieces. Past guests have included such names as Madonna, George Michael and David Beckham. A casino is on site. **www.hotelroyal.dk**

NORTHERN JUTLAND

DRONNINGLUND Dronninglund 🔲 🔲 ⓀⓀ
Slotsgade 78, 9330 **Tel** *98 84 15 33* **Fax** *98 84 40 50* **Rooms** *72* **Map** *D2*

Located amid the picturesque countryside of Ostvendsyssel, close to Dronninglund Castle, this simple provincial hotel offers comfortable, bright surroundings and a family-friendly atmosphere. White sandy beaches are a short car or bike ride away. The hotel also has its own indoor swimming pool. **www.dronninglundhotel.dk**

FARSØ Himmerland Golf & Spa Resort 🔲 🔲 🔲 🔲 ⓀⓀⓀ
Centervej 1, Gatten, 9640 **Tel** *96 49 61 00* **Fax** *98 66 14 56* **Rooms** *60* **Map** *C2*

A golfer's paradise: this hotel has two international golf courses, a golf simulator and a three-par course on site. Surrounded by a lovely wooded area and overlooking a lake, it has modern rooms, all with Internet access. For the non-golfer there are bowling facilities, an indoor swimming pool and a spa centre. **www.himmerlandgolf.dk**

FARUP Purhus Kro 🔲 🔲 ⓀⓀ
Præstevejen 6, 8990 **Tel** *86 45 28 55* **Fax** *86 45 22 08* **Rooms** *21* **Map** *C3*

A cosy and family-friendly inn built in 1752, the Purhus Kro has modern and comfortable rooms. There is a lake and lovely gardens in the grounds as well as a playground for children. Disabled facilities are available and there is free Internet access in all rooms. **www.purhus-kro.dk**

FREDERIKSHAVN BB Hotel 🔲 ⓀⓀ
Margrethevej 5–7, 9900 **Fax** *98 42 90 91* **Rooms** *18* **Map** *D1*

This simple and affordable self-service hotel is close to Frederikshavn's famous Palm Beach. Features include hypo-allergenic bed linen, private bathrooms, flat-screen TVs and free Internet access. A self-service breakfast is included in the price. Booking online only. **www.bbhotels.dk**

FREDERIKSHAVN Best Western Hotel Herman Bang 🔲 ⓀⓀ
Tordenskjoldsgade 3, 9900 **Tel** *98 42 21 66* **Rooms** *53* **Map** *D1*

Dating from 1882, this is the oldest hotel in Frederikshavn. Its location on the town's pedestrian street is ideal for both the ferry terminal and the train station. The Herman Bang has doubles and suites, as well as family rooms, and there's also a budget-priced B&B annex just across the road. **www.hermanbang.dk**

FREDERIKSHAVN Jutlandia 🔲 🔲 🔲 ⓀⓀ
Havnepladsen 1, 9900 **Tel** *98 42 42 00* **Fax** *98 42 38 72* **Rooms** *95* **Map** *D1*

An elegant hotel, centrally located and overlooking the harbour, the Jutlandia is occasionally used by the Danish royal family. The rooms feature simple modern decor and the service is impeccable. The Jutlandia is close to both shops and ferries. Internet available in the lobby. Superb restaurant. **www.hotel-jutlandia.dk**

FREDERIKSHAVN Scandic The Reef 🔲 🔲 🔲 ⓀⓀ
Tordenskjoldsgade 14, 9900 **Tel** *98 43 32 33* **Fax** *98 43 33 11* **Rooms** *210* **Map** *D1*

Conveniently situated in the middle of town, this well-equipped hotel offers comfortable rooms all with wireless Internet access. Downstairs there is a large heated swimming pool. The hotel is close to local attractions such as Bangsbro Museum and the Frederikshavn Kirke (church). **www.scandic-hotels.com**

HANSTHOLM Montra Hotel Hanstholm 🔲 🔲 🔲 ⓀⓀⓀ
Chr. Hansensvej 2, 7730 **Tel** *97 96 10 44* **Fax** *97 96 25 84* **Rooms** *76* **Map** *B2*

Surrounded by sand, water and woods, on the edge of Thy National Park, the Hanstholm is in a small paradise all of its own. The rooms are bright and simply decorated, most of them with a balcony or terrace attached. It is ideal for families and has its own playground and indoor swimming pool. **www.hotelhanstholm.dk**

HIRTSHALS Skaga 🔲 🔲 🔲 🔲 ⓀⓀⓀ
Willemoesvej 1, 9850 **Tel** *98 94 55 00* **Fax** *98 94 55 55* **Rooms** *108* **Map** *C1*

The Skaga is situated along the E39 motorway, close to the Color Lines ferry terminal (for ships to Norway and Iceland). Facilities include a conference centre, indoor pool, solarium, sauna, bar and nightclub. Families are well-placed for the North Sea Centre, bowling alley, woodland and excellent beaches. **www.skagahotel.dk**

HOLSTEBRO Best Western Hotel Schaumburg 🔲 🔲 ⓀⓀⓀ
Nørregade 26, 7500 **Tel** *97 42 31 11* **Fax** *97 42 72 82* **Rooms** *57* **Map** *B3*

Now thoroughly modernised, the Schaumburg has a copy of Copenhagen's Little Mermaid statue in the front hall. It offers all the facilities you would expect from Best Western, and some of the rooms have views of the town's old city hall. The price includes free admission to the nearby Holstebro Badeland waterpark. **www.hotel-schaumburg.dk**

HOLSTEBRO Royal Holstebro 🔲 ⓀⓀⓀ
Den Røde Plads 10, 7500 **Tel** *97 40 23 33* **Rooms** *40* **Map** *B3*

Located in the heart of the town, this hotel is topped by a striking glass pyramid. The well-equipped rooms have wireless Internet and overlook the Musikteater (concert hall). For golf enthusiasts, the beautiful Holstebro Golfklub course is 15 km (9 miles) away. A complimentary breakfast is served in the hotel's Cafe Royal. **www.hotel-royal.dk**

Key to Price Guide *see p244* **Key to Symbols** *see back cover flap*

NYKØBING MORS Pakhuset Hotel & Restaurant

Havnen 1, 7900 **Tel** *97 72 33 00* **Fax** *97 72 52 33* **Rooms** *18*

Map *B2*

This pleasant hotel is located in an old warehouse on the harbour front and combines original 19th-century features with modern Danish design. In summer, the harbour is abuzz with activity and the hotel is a popular place to stay, so do reserve in good time. American Express is not accepted. **www.phr.dk**

NYKØBING MORS Sallingsund Færgekro

Sallingsundvej 104, 7900 **Tel** *97 72 00 88* **Fax** *97 72 25 40* **Rooms** *40*

Map *B2*

Set amid the landscape typical of the Limfjorden, this historic ferry inn offers reasonably priced accommodation and a wealth of packages – from extended weekend deals to gourmet and wine breaks. In addition to the hotel, there are also camping facilities and seven luxury cabins. **www.sfkro.dk**

RANDERS Scandic Hotel Kongens Ege

Gl. Hadsundvej 2, 8900 **Tel** *86 43 03 00* **Fax** *86 43 22 73* **Rooms** *130*

Map *D3*

High on a hilltop overlooking the town, the Kongens Ege offers modern comfortable rooms with stunning views of the city centre, Randers Fjord and the surrounding park. It is only a 5 minute drive from the city centre. All rooms have free wireless Internet access. **www.scandichotels.com/KongensEge**

RANDERS Randers

Torvegade 11, 8900 **Tel** *86 42 34 22* **Fax** *86 40 15 86* **Rooms** *79*

Map *D3*

With the reputation of being one of Denmark's best (and oldest) hotels, the Randers has spacious and stylish rooms with all the amenities you would expect and a pleasant old-world atmosphere. It is close to the railway station and within short walking distance of a fitness centre. **www.hotel-randers.dk**

SKAGEN Color Hotel Skagen

Gl. Landevej 39, 9990 **Tel** *98 44 22 33* **Fax** *98 44 21 34* **Rooms** *152*

Map *D1*

This pleasant, rather formal hotel is located in quiet surroundings between old Skagen and the maritime centre. The rooms are spacious with large windows which make the most of Skagen's famous natural light. On site amenities include an outdoor swimming pool. Close to Den Tilsandede Kirke (The Sand-buried Church). **www.skagenhotel.dk**

SKAGEN Plesner

Holstvej 8, 9990 **Tel** *98 44 68 44* **Fax** *98 44 36 86* **Rooms** *16*

Map *D1*

With unpolished wooden floor boards, muted decor, and the famously comfortable Hästens beds in all rooms, the Plesner makes for a real haven of luxurious peace in this remote outpost of the country. Close to the beach and the countryside, yet plumb in the centre of town. Fabulous light and airy restaurant, too. **www.hotelplesner.dk**

SKAGEN Ruths Hotel

Hans Ruths Vej 1, 9990 **Tel** *98 44 11 24* **Fax** *98 45 08 75* **Rooms** *52*

Map *D1*

This atmospheric establishment is in the old part of Skagen and close to the beach. Built in the late 19th century, it has been completely modernized and the rooms are spacious and light, all with Internet access. There is an indoor pool. The hotel's gourmet restaurant, run by head chef Michel Michaud, is worth visiting. **www.ruths-hotel.dk**

SKIVE Best Western Hotel Gl. Skivehus

Søndre Boulevard 1, 7800 **Tel** *97 52 11 44* **Fax** *97 52 81 68* **Rooms** *56*

Map *C3*

Located in the heart of Skive, this modern family-run hotel is in a grand former manor house overlooking the river Karup; the hotel owns the fishing rights to this stretch of river, and some visitors come specifically to enjoy this activity. The rooms are clean, simple and uncluttered. Close to the park, beach and golf courses. **www.skivehus.dk**

SKØRPING Comwell Rebild Bakker

Rebildvej 36, 9520 **Tel** *98 39 12 22* **Fax** *98 39 24 55* **Rooms** *151*

Map *C2*

This modern low-rise hotel and conference centre is nestled in between the hills and unspoiled nature at the edge of the Rebild Bakker National Park. All the rooms are well equipped and have stunning views of the countryside. Local attractions include the limestone caves at Thingbæk and a golf course. **www.comwell.dk**

SÆBY Stiholt

Trafikcenter Sæby Syd 1, 9300 **Tel** *96 89 66 69* **Fax** *96 89 66 67* **Rooms** *10*

Map *D1*

Although situated next to a petrol station, this modest and inexpensive hotel is an excellent stopping-off place for travellers on their way to Skagen. All the rooms are light and airy and there is a tourist office within the hotel. It is also only a 3-km (2-mile) drive to the beach. **www.tcss.dk**

SÆBY Hotel Viking

Frederikshavnsvej 70-72, 9300 **Tel** *98 46 17 00* **Fax** *98 46 24 93* **Rooms** *86*

Map *D1*

A comfortable family-friendly hotel, about 1.5 km (1 mile) from the town and a short stroll from a sandy beach. The rooms are bright with all the usual modern amenities. The Viking also has a courtyard garden, with a playground for children, and is known for its good food and wellness centre. Nearby is the "Old Water Mill". **www.hotelviking.dk**

VIBORG Best Western Palads

Sct. Mathiasgade 5, 8800 **Tel** *86 62 37 00* **Fax** *86 62 40 46* **Rooms** *100*

Map *C3*

Centrally located and in one of the town's most beautiful buildings, this grand hotel combines tradition with comfort. Hotel guests have free access to Viborg Vandland, an indoor water complex with fitness facilities, as well as free Internet access and parking. **www.hotelpalads.dk**

AALBORG Best Western Scheelsminde   🟦🟦   ⓦⓦ
Scheelsmindevej 35, 9100 **Tel** *98 18 32 33* **Fax** *98 18 33 34* **Rooms** *96*   **Map** *D2*

Built in 1808, this was once one of the most beautiful manor houses in Denmark. Converted into a hotel and then extensively restored, the rooms feature under-floor heating in the bathrooms. It is worth checking out the restaurant with its exceptional wine cellar. There is also an indoor swimming pool, sauna and spa. **www.scheelsminde.dk**

AALBORG Hotel Aalborg Sømandshjem   🟦🟦🟦   ⓦⓦ
Østerbro 27, 9000 **Tel** *98 12 19 00* **Fax** *98 11 76 97* **Rooms** *55*   **Map** *D2*

This is a family-friendly economy hotel located just opposite Nordkraft, Aalborg's cultural centre, and only a 5-minute walk to the main shopping streets. There are also many restaurants in the area. The rooms are comfortable and simply decorated. Parking available. **www.hotel-aalborg.com**

AALBORG Hotel Hvide Hus   🟦🟦🟦   ⓦⓦ
Vesterbro 2, 9000 **Tel** *98 13 84 00* **Fax** *98 13 51 22* **Rooms** *198*   **Map** *D2*

This 16-floor hotel sits surrounded by the lovely Kilde Park, in the city centre. The rooms are bright with balconies and large windows, and the staff are efficient and friendly. Modern, sleek design is throughout and amenities include top-notch business facilities and a panoramic restaurant. Breakfast included. **www.hotelhvidehus.dk**

AALBORG Hotel Scandic   🟦🟦🟦   ⓦⓦ
Hadsundvej 200, 9220 **Tel** *98 15 45 00* **Fax** *98 15 55 88* **Rooms** *101*   **Map** *D2*

In a rather unpromising block some 5 km (3 miles) away from the centre of Aalborg, the rooms of the Scandic are light, inviting, and feature wireless Internet access. In the summer, there are well-organised facilities including a children's playroom. **www.scandic-hotels.dk**

AALBORG Helnan Phønix Hotel   🟦🟦🟦🟦   ⓦⓦⓦ
Vesterbro 77, 9000 **Tel** *98 12 00 11* **Fax** *98 10 10 20* **Rooms** *210*   **Map** *D2*

A major feature of the town, this historic hotel was built in 1783 as a palace to Brigadier William Von Halling and converted into a hotel in 1853. Located in the heart of Aalborg, the hotel provides classic hospitality in an elegant setting. Rooms are warmly decorated. **www.helnan.dk**

AALBORG Radisson Blu Limfjord   🟦🟦🟦🟦   ⓦⓦⓦ
Ved Stranden 14, 9000 **Tel** *98 16 43 33* **Fax** *98 16 17 47* **Rooms** *188*   **Map** *D2*

Located in the heart of Aalborg, the rooms are comfortably furnished and most of them offer fabulous views over the city and Limfjord. The hotel is just opposite a famous street lined with cafés, Jomfru Anne Gade. Casino Aalborg is located at the hotel. Free wireless Internet access is available. **www.radissonblu.com/hotel-aalborg**

BORNHOLM

ALLINGE Byskrivergården Hotel Garni   ⓦⓦ
Løsebækgade 3, 3770 **Tel** *56 48 08 86* **Fax** *56 48 18 86* **Rooms** *20*

Set in a converted 18th-century farmhouse on the Baltic, this is one of the most cherished overnight spots on this part of the island. The cosy rooms are in the converted stables. The dining room/lounge looks out from the top floor to the water – a perfect place to enjoy the complimentary breakfasts. Small beach nearby. **www.byskrivergaarden.dk**

ALLINGE Danchels Hus   ⓦⓦ
Havnegade 38, 3770 **Tel** *56 48 22 18* **Fax** *56 48 22 18* **Rooms** *4*

The rooms at this small Swedish-run guesthouse have stylish furniture and chintzy decorations. Two of them have sea views, and room No.2 is especially atmospheric. There is also an apartment available by the week. Set in its own grounds, you can take a pleasant stroll from the door of your room right down to the water. **www.danchelshus.dk**

ALLINGE Hotel Romantik   🟦   ⓦⓦ
Strandvejen 68, 3770 **Tel** *56 48 03 44* **Fax** *56 48 06 44* **Rooms** *50*

In the 19th century this was Bornholm' best-known hotel and it is still popular today. Many of the neat rooms have sea views from their small-ish windows. All have telephone and satellite TV. The Romantik also offers some larger apartment-style rooms with Jacuzzis and self-catering apartments. Complimentary breakfast. **www.hotel-romantik.dk**

ALLINGE Strandhotel Abildgaard   🟦🟦🟦   ⓦⓦ
Tejnvej 100, 3770 **Tel** *56 48 09 55* **Fax** *56 48 08 35* **Rooms** *85*

An all-inclusive hotel offering full board for its guests, the Abildgaard is popular with tour groups. The large family rooms include an interconnecting annex, and all rooms come with kitchenettes. There is a good-sized heated pool, though you're only minutes away from one of north Bornholm's best beaches. **www.hotel-abildgaard.dk**

ALLINGE Friheden   🟦   ⓦⓦⓦ
Tejnvej 80, 3770 **Tel** *56 48 04 25* **Fax** *56 48 16 65* **Rooms** *44*

Set in the coastal hamlet of Sandkås, this upmarket hotel features a health centre with spa treatments, a sauna and pool. A dozen of the rooms have views out to the water, and some have small terraces. There are also family rooms, apartments and self-contained cottages. Bicycles for hire and complimentary breakfast. **www.hotelfriheden.dk**

Key to Price Guide *see p244* **Key to Symbols** *see back cover flap*

CHRISTIANSØ Christiansø Gæstgiveri

Christiansø, 3760 **Tel** *56 46 20 15* **Fax** *56 46 20 86* **Rooms** *6*

Set on the idyllic tiny island of Christansø, with one boat a day to Bornholm, the rooms in this 18th-century ex-garrison all have bathrooms, large beds, creaky floorboards, and views to the harbour. The owner is an affable irreverent Dane who ensures only scrumptious meals are served in the restaurant. **www.christiansoekro.dk**

DUEODDE Dueodde Vandrehjem

Skrokkegårdsvejen 17, 3730 **Tel** *56 48 81 19* **Fax** *56 48 81 12* **Rooms** *36*

Dueodde Vandrehjem is located in a beautiful forest area right by the beach. In high season, four- to eight-person bedrooms are available, but camping is also possible. The hostel features an indoor swimming pool and spa area, and plenty of activities like table tennis and ball games. Open May–Sep. **www.dueodde.dk**

DUEODDE Dueodde Badehotel

Sirenevej 2, 3730 **Tel** *56 95 85 66* **Fax** *56 95 34 66* **Rooms** *52*

This modern holiday complex has sleek rooms with brushed oak flooring and balconies that look onto a garden, as well as larger apartment-style suites and flats. The facilities include a sauna, tennis courts, a small shop and a café. They usually rent by the week, but it is possible to get one- or two-night stays too. **www.teambornholm.dk/dueodde**

GUDHJEM Gudhjem Vandrerhjem

Løkkegade 7, 3760 **Tel** *56 48 50 35* **Fax** *56 48 56 35* **Rooms** *37*

This harbourside hostel is in a weathered old building that was once the town's general store. The rooms have exposed wood beam ceilings and half-timbered walls, and there are common toilets and kitchen facilities. Cycle hire also available. **www.danhostel-gudhjem.dk**

GUDHJEM Stammershalle Badehotel

Sdr. Strandvej 128, Stammershalle, 3760 **Tel** *56 48 42 10* **Fax** *56 48 42 11* **Rooms** *17*

A small, old-fashioned spa hotel overlooking the coast on the road between Allinge and Gudhjem. The building dates from 1911 and its grounds once housed a small private zoo; the white rooms, many with sea views, are classically decorated. The hotel restaurant is one of the best on Bornholm. **www.stammershalle-badehotel.dk**

GUDHJEM Jantzen's Hotel

Brøddegade 33, 3760 **Tel** *56 48 50 17* **Rooms** *16*

Founded in the 1870's, this hotel is one of the oldest on Bornholm. Many of the rooms have small, cast iron balconies that look out to the water. In summer you can enjoy a sumptuous breakfast buffet outside in the attractive back courtyard. The perfect romantic hide-away. **www.jantzenshotel.dk**

GUDHJEM Melsted Badehotel

Melstedvej 27, 3760 **Tel** *56 48 51 00* **Fax** *56 48 55 84* **Rooms** *18*

This hotel consists of several small buildings set on a sprawling lawn a stone's throw from the Baltic. The dainty rooms are all done in bright whites with very comfortable Swedish beds. TVs and phones are nowhere to be seen ensuring blissful peace. Three apartments are also available. **www.melsted-badehotel.dk**

NEXØ Hotel Balka Strand

Boulevarden 9A, 3730 **Tel** *56 49 49 49* **Rooms** *95*

A large, four-star hotel with modern interiors and a good restaurant, the Balka Strand is very family friendly. It is only a short walk from a nature reserve and beautiful bathing beaches (though the hotel has its own outdoor pool and sauna). **www.hotelbalkastrand.dk**

NEXØ Strand Hotel Balka Søbad

Vestre Strandvej 25, 3730 **Tel** *56 49 22 25* **Fax** *56 49 22 33* **Rooms** *106*

One of the few hotels on Bornholm with its own bathing beach (and a pool to boot), the modern rooms here come with balconies and feature extra fold-out beds, making them great for families. The Balka Søbad is also placed right by several walking and cycling paths that lead to Nexø. Cycle hire is available. **www.hotel-balkasoebad.dk**

RØNNE BB-Hotel Rønne

Store Torv 17, 1, 3700 **Tel** *70 22 55 30* **Rooms** *21*

This B&B offers fairly priced rooms right on the main square in Rønne, close to restaurants, shops and public transport for the entire island of Bornholm. The rooms are small but well designed, and the kitchen offers free access to coffee and tea 24 hours a day. Parking is available, and there is a golf course nearby. **www.bbhotelronne.dk**

RØNNE Danhostel Rønne

Arsenalvej 12, 3700 **Tel** *56 95 13 40* **Fax** *56 95 01 32* **Rooms** *29*

Danhostel Rønne is within walking distance of the ferry and only a stone's throw away from the beach and the forest. It is furnished in a homely style and offers different activities – both indoors and outdoors – like table tennis, mini golf and a children's playground. **www.danhostel-roenne.dk**

RØNNE Hotel Skovly

Nyker Strandvej 40, 3700 **Tel** *56 95 07 84* **Fax** *56 95 48 23* **Rooms** *29*

Lying next to a babbling brook and within a protected forest several kilometres north of Rønne, this is one of the town's hidden gems. Each of the rustic, apartment-style rooms has its own terrace. There is a beach nearby where you can swim and fish. Breakfast is included. **www.hotel-skovly.dk**

RØNNE Griffen

Ndr Kystvej 34, 3700 **Tel** *56 90 42 44* **Fax** *56 90 42 45* **Rooms** *142*

This lovely modern hotel is on the Baltic shoreline and offers large rooms with sofas, desks, and balconies. Half of the rooms have a view to the sea; the other half look onto a cobblestone street of old Rønne. All have wireless Internet. The Griffen also has a restaurant, an indoor pool and spa, and a small private beach. **www.hotelgriffen.dk**

RØNNE Radisson Blu Fredensborg

Strandvejen 116, 3700 **Tel** *56 90 44 44* **Fax** *56 90 44 43* **Rooms** *72*

From the outside, this modern establishment does not promise much, but inside everything is business class. Rooms are meticulously decorated in modern Scandinavian style; all have wireless Internet and small balconies or terraces with views out to the Baltic. There is also a private beach. Complimentary breakfast. **www.ronne.radissonsas.com**

SANDVIG Hotel Hammersø

Hammershusvej 86, 3770 **Tel** *56 48 03 64* **Fax** *56 48 10 90* **Rooms** *40*

Located on the edge of the tranquil Hammersø (Denmark's only mountain lake), this hotel complex offers breakfast and half-board accommodation. It has a heated outdoor swimming pool and a sunny terrace with table tennis tables. Several of the rooms have small balconies with pretty views. **www.hotel-hammersoe.dk**

SANDVIG Hotel Pepita

Langebjergvej 1, 3770 **Tel** *56 48 04 51* **Fax** *56 48 18 51* **Rooms** *36*

A yellow, half-timbered farmhouse dating from the 16th century houses the Pepita, one of Sandvig's more modern hotels. Some of the rooms overlook the terrace, others the sea, and there is a very popular *à la carte* restaurant on-site as well. **www.pepita.dk**

SVANEKE Hotel Østersøen

Havnebryggen 5, 3740 **Tel** *56 95 85 66* **Fax** *56 95 34 66* **Rooms** *21*

Open year-round, this hotel located right on the harbour is housed in a former merchant's estate. The individual apartment-style accommodation opens onto a gorgeous courtyard with a heated pool. Rooms are full of character, with exposed beams. **www.oestersoen.dk**

SVANEKE Siemsens Gård

Havnebryggen 9, 3740 **Tel** *56 49 61 49* **Rooms** *49*

The Siemsens Gård has Ikea-styled rooms set within an old merchant's house dating from the 17th century. Most of the rooms have cooking facilities, views to the sea (or, alternatively, to a garden), and private access to the terrace and lawns. The hotel's restaurant is a great place to try out the local *smørrebrød*. **www.siemsens.dk**

ÅKIRKEBY Danhostel Boderne

Bodernevej 28, 3720 **Tel** *56 97 49 50* **Fax** *56 97 49 48* **Rooms** *20*

A short drive from Åkirkeby, this family-friendly hostel is set in a large rural farmhouse lying among the conifers on Bornholm's southern coast. Most rooms are en-suite. The hostel offers bicycles for hire, Internet access, a television room and childrens' playground. Close to some sandy beaches. **www.rosengaarden.dk**

GREENLAND

ILULISSAT Hotel Icefiord

Box 458, 3952 Ilulissat **Tel** *94 44 80* **Fax** *94 40 95* **Rooms** *31*

Delightful rooms abound at this wonderful hotel in an old wooden building. Several rooms, including two deluxe suites, have stunning sea views, and there is a lounge with a fireplace and a terrace from which you can watch the icebergs in Disko Bay. Price includes transport to the airport. Wireless Internet in the rooms. **www.hotelicefiord.gl**

KANGERLUSSUAQ Polar Lodge

Mitaarfiit Aqq – P.O. Box 1009, 3910 Kangerlussuaq **Tel** *84 16 48* **Fax** *84 16 19* **Rooms** *16*

Located close to Kangerlussuaq Airport, Polar Lodge offers accommodation in former air-base buildings. Rooms are slightly bland, but they are clean and modern, with shared bathroom facilities. There is a kitchen for guests to use, and Wi-Fi is available for a small fee. **www.wogac.com**

KANGERLUSSUAQ Hotel Kangerlussuaq

P.O. Box 1006, 3910 Kangerlussuaq **Tel** *84 11 80* **Fax** *84 12 84* **Rooms** *70*

Conveniently located at the town's airport, this modern facility is a great base for exploring the region, though it tends to fill up with business groups and tours. Attached to the hotel is a smaller annex with cheaper rooms available (shared bathrooms). The nearby fitness centre has a pool and sauna. **www.hotelkangerlussuaq.gl**

NUUK Bed and Breakfast

Ilivinnguaq 1, P.O. Box 2291, 3900 Nuuk **Tel** *31 32 18* **Fax** *31 32 17* **Rooms** *3*

Not one location but many are available through Tupilak Travel, which organizes stays (and meals) with local families at very affordable prices. While comfort may vary, you are nearly always guaranteed a memorable time, since as everyone knows, the best way to get to know Greenland is from its people. **www.tupilaktravel.gl**

Key to Price Guide *see p244* **Key to Symbols** *see back cover flap*

NUUK Sømandshjemmet   🏠 🅿️   ⓚⓚⓚ
Marinevej 3, 3900 Nuuk **Tel** *32 10 29* **Fax** *32 21 04* **Rooms** *41*

Made up of several red wooden buildings at the foot of a mountain, the Sømandshjemmet (Seaman's Home) offers modern, bright, clean rooms, a TV lounge and meeting rooms with Wi-Fi. Be sure to ask for a room with a view, as they can be spectacular. The cafeteria-restaurant produces warming stews and desserts. **www.soemandshjem.gl**

NUUK Hotel Hans Egede   📶 🏠 🅿️   ⓚⓚⓚⓚ
Aqqusinersuaq 1–5, 3900 Nuuk **Tel** *32 42 22* **Fax** *32 44 87* **Rooms** *140*

This luxurious four-star establishment is right in the centre of Nuuk. The rooms are modern and somewhat soulless, but the service is superb. The hotel's gourmet restaurant and bar are on the top floor, and both offer unequalled views to the harbour and icebergs further out. Popular with large conference groups. **www.hhe.gl**

QAANAAQ Hotel Qaanaaq   🏠 🍽️   ⓚⓚ
Box 88, 3971 Qaanaaq **Tel** *97 12 34* **Fax** *97 10 64* **Rooms** *5*

A tiny, red wooden building with a handful of small rooms, the Qaanaaq is the only hotel in town. It does away with "unnecessary" facilities such as television, instead offering a cheery sitting room with local art on the walls, a washing machine (for a small fee) and a quaint restaurant. Internet access is available. **www.hotelqaanaaq.dk**

UUMMANNAQ Hotel Uummannaq   🏠 🅿️   ⓚⓚⓚ
Trollep Aqqutaa B, 3961 Uummannaq **Tel** *95 15 18* **Rooms** *40*

This modern hotel, attractively situated with panoramic views across the ice fjord, has comfortable rooms with all mod cons, including TV and phone. The hotel's restaurant looks out onto the world's only year-round ice golf course. There are also cheaper dormitory-style beds in the hostel annex. **www.icecaphotels.gl**

THE FAROE ISLANDS

EYSTUROY Gjáargarður   🏠   ⓚⓚ
Gjógv, 476 **Tel** *42 31 71* **Fax** *42 35 05* **Rooms** *33*

The only hotel on the Faroes to be granted the environmentally friendly Green Key certification, the grass-roofed Gjáargarður has dramatic views of Slættaratindur, Faroes' highest point. In addition to the ensuite double rooms, there are a number of cheaper box rooms and a self-catering annex. **www.gjaargardur.fo**

MYKINES Kristianshus   🏠 🍽️   ⓚⓚ
Mykines, 388 **Tel** *31 29 85* **Fax** *32 19 85* **Rooms** *12*

A colourful and quaint guesthouse run by a jovial local woman who also runs many nature expeditions out to the surrounding areas. The dozen rooms are furnished in a homely fashion, with basic amenities. There is also a small cafeteria: try the tasty fried puffin if it is available. **www.mykines.dk**

SUDUROY, TVØROYRI Gistingarhúsið undir Heygnum   ⓚ
Tvøroyri, 800 **Tel** *37 20 46* **Fax** *37 24 46* **Rooms** *9*

An excellent modern guesthouse set at the tip of the bay, with tables and chairs placed out front for taking in the sun (when it is shining). The rooms are clean and bright, and the comfortable common room has satellite TV and stereo. This hotel tends to get quite busy with groups of travellers, so book well in advance. **www.guest-house.dk**

TÓRSHAVN Bládýpi Guesthouse   ⓚ
Dr. Jakobsensgøta 14–16, 100 **Tel** *50 06 00* **Fax** *31 94 51* **Rooms** *19*

This guesthouse is close to the centre of town. The pristine rooms have views onto the street, and there are three dormitory-style rooms available for those travelling on a budget. There is a small kitchen available to guests, though breakfast is included in the price during the summer. Internet access is available. **www.bladypi.fo**

TÓRSHAVN Hotel Streym   🅿️   ⓚⓚ
Yviri við Strond 19, 100 **Tel** *35 55 00* **Fax** *35 55 01* **Rooms** *14*

This small place has bright rooms with comfortable beds, heated floors, satellite TV and Internet access; the double rooms also have views out to the sea. The lobby is decidedly modernist, with funky seating and polished matte wood floors. Friendly reception, complimentary breakfast and even a car rental service. **www.hotelstreym.com**

TÓRSHAVN Hotel Tórshavn   📶 🏠 🅿️   ⓚⓚⓚ
Tórsgøta 4, 100 **Tel** *35 00 00* **Fax** *35 00 01* **Rooms** *43*

Dating from 1923, this appealing establishment is one of the oldest in Faroes. Rooms (some with views) are decked out in warm colours, with flat-screen TVs and wireless Internet access. International fare is served in the hotel's brasserie restaurant. Good weekend rates. **www.hoteltorshavn.fo**

TÓRSHAVN Hotel Føroyar   🏠 🅿️   ⓚⓚⓚⓚ
Oyggjarvegur 45, 100 **Tel** *31 75 00* **Fax** *31 75 01* **Rooms** *108*

Set a bit above the town, the rooms and excellent restaurant in this four-star hotel have panoramic views over the colourful rooftops of Tórshavn. Great facilities and room service. The hotel also organises horse riding excursions in the countryside. Prices are slashed at weekends. **www.hotelforoyar.com**

WHERE TO EAT

Visitors to Denmark can be assured of a good meal wherever they go. The choice ranges from city restaurants serving New Nordic cuisine, featuring local produce and berries, to country inns catering for the lunchtime market with generous servings of *smørrebrød*. In small villages visitors can get a meal in a *kro* (inn), which often also provides overnight accommodation. Cafés are popular

Restaurant sign, Randers

in Denmark. As well as pastries and coffee, they often serve main meals and also beer and wine. Many cafés in Copenhagen open late into the night. At the bottom end of the spectrum are the street stalls selling *pølser*, a sausage or hot dog wrapped in a bun and served with onions and sauces. Spicier takeaway alternatives include Greek or Middle Eastern kebabs, which are in plentiful supply in larger towns.

The elegant interior of Era Ora in Copenhagen *(see p272)*

WHEN TO EAT

Danish breakfast tends to be a fairly modest affair. It is usually eaten at home, though there is no shortage of cafés serving delicious brunches. As an alternative, many bakeries sell bread, pastries and coffee and some provide a table at which to sit.

Frokost (lunch) is consumed between noon and 2pm. It can take various forms, from a light meal to a large banquet of open sandwiches and salads. At lunchtime many restaurants also serve hot main courses such as meatballs, but the helpings are smaller and prices lower than the same meal at dinnertime. *Aftensmad* (dinner) is from 6pm onwards and can be expensive. It is not unusual for prices to rise between lunch and dinner at the same establishment. At weekends many restaurants serve a

brunch between 11am and 3pm. Late night snacks are generally limited to hot dogs or kebabs from a stall.

OPENING HOURS

Bakeries open early; in some places it is enough to knock at the bakery door for the baker to open up and sell a loaf even before the shop is

open. Fast-food restaurants that serve breakfast open at around 8 or 9am. Restaurants that cater for the lunchtime trade generally open around 10 or 11am. Pubs remain closed until early afternoon, except for the village *kros* (inns), which open earlier, especially during the holiday season. Most restaurants finish serving by 10pm, and restaurants that are not licensed to remain open all night close at 1am. Cafés tend to stay open all day and often late into the night.

MENU

Many restaurants have menus written in English. In addition to the full menu, some offer a specially priced *dagens ret*, or "dish of the day", which is often written up on a board. Some restaurants serve good value fixed-price two-, three- or four-course lunches.

Glass-fronted counter displaying cakes at La Glace *(see p269)*

Visitors at tables in front of a herring smokehouse in Svaneke

CHILDREN

Most restaurants in Denmark offer high chairs and special "child-friendly" menus and activity packs. The best time to take children to a restaurant is late afternoon, when they are far less busy. This time of day is less stressful and generally means that no one need wait long to be served.

Café terraces lining one of Nykøbing F's little streets

PRICES AND TIPS

Prices in restaurants vary enormously. Many cheaper Danish establishments offer set-price all-you-can-eat buffets at lunchtime, as do some of the Thai and Indonesian restaurants. Some hostels also serve good value lunch and evening meals for about 60 Dkr. A three-course meal in a restaurant will cost about 200–400 Dkr not including alcohol, while

at an upmarket restaurant, diners should be prepared to pay in excess of 800 Dkr.

Soft drinks, beer and *akvavit* (a kind of schnapps) cost about the same in most places; however, prices for wines and liqueurs vary greatly and tend to be steep in some of the upmarket restaurants.

In Denmark, a service charge and tax are automatically included in the price. Leaving no tip is not considered bad manners; however, it is customary to round up the bill. Note that tipping is not practised in fast-food restaurants.

Most restaurants accept credit cards and display the appropriate signs at their entrance.

RESERVATIONS

Guests are generally required to book well in advance at the most popular restaurants. Even in quieter restaurants it is advisable to make a booking at the weekend, especially for Sunday brunch, which is often a busy time.

If it is too late to book, then the best option is to go somewhere where there are clusters of restaurants. For small groups, there will normally be at least one restaurant that will have a table available after a short wait.

DRESS CODE

The Danes are, for the most part, a relaxed people and do not attach too much importance to etiquette concerning their appearance. Nevertheless, it is customary

to smarten up when visiting a restaurant. Dress requirements become stricter as the prices on the menu increase; some upmarket restaurants expect diners to wear evening attire or at least a shirt and tie.

VEGETARIANS

The diet in Denmark is heavily based on meat and fish. However, most restaurants have at least a few vegetarian dishes on their menus, as well as a selection of salads. Restaurants that serve only vegetarian food are rare.

DISABLED GUESTS

As elsewhere in Europe, restaurants providing facilities for disabled people cannot be taken for granted. However, many restaurants in Denmark are accessible for patrons with special needs, but it is advisable to check when making a reservation.

A Danish-language database, researched by Danish wheelchair users, lists all the restaurants (as well as attractions and cultural institutions) that are accessible to wheelchair-bound people. Local tourist offices should be able to help with obtaining this information. Another useful source for tourists is the Accessibility Label Scheme website (www.godadgang. dk), which lists establishments that have signed-up to confirm they are accessible to those with special needs.

Aalborg's Mortens Kro *(see p283)*, with its floor-to-ceiling windows

The Flavours of Denmark

Denmark's cuisine, like that of other Scandinavian countries, has always been rich in meat and fish dishes. Specialities from the sea include smoked salmon, pickled herring, eel and haddock. Cod is served baked, steamed, fried or dried *(klipfisk)*. The *kolde bord*, a lunchtime buffet, is a good way to try out various local dishes, with a selection of *smørrebrød*, cold cuts and hearty pork dishes. Most Danes have a sweet tooth and *wienerbrød* (Danish pastries) are eaten at any time of day. Berries appear in many desserts, and Danish ice cream is among the best in the world.

Danish pastries

Punnets of ripe strawberries, freshly harvested on Samsø Island

SMØRREBRØD

The classic *smørrebrød* (open sandwich) is as popular as ever with the Danes. Preparation is easy enough: buttered slices of *rugbrød* (unleavened rye bread) are topped with any number of sliced meats, fish or cheeses, such as prawns, smoked eel, ham, lamb and beef. They are then garnished with dill,

cucumber, tomato or lemon, a remoulade (mayonnaise-based sauce), caviar, or even a raw egg yolk served in its shell. Among national favourites are *Sol over Gudhjem* and *Bornholmer*, both variations on smoked herring fillets topped with an egg yolk, raw onion, chives and radishes. *Marineredesild* (vinegar-cured herring with onions and capers) and *Stjerneskud* ("shooting star",

fried fish fillet with prawns, lemon and dill) are also popular. Meat varieties include *dyrlægens natmad*, a towering creation laden with liver pâté, salt beef, flavoured lard, onion rings and watercress; *roastbeefmad*, rare roast beef with fried onions and grated horseradish; and *rullepølsemad,* slices of pork belly seasoned with raw onions, herbs, horseradish and watercress.

Roastbeefmad   Dyrlægens natmad   Prawns, caviar and lemon

Bornholmer   Stjerneskud

Marineredesild

Akvavit

Selection of typical Danish *smørrebrød*

DANISH DISHES AND SPECIALITIES

To this day, Danish cuisine retains a flavour of pre-industrial times, when the diet centred around rye bread, salted pork and herring – basically whatever could be grown and harvested in a short summer or pulled from the sea and preserved. This type of cuisine is enjoying quite a resurgence. Typical are dishes such as *øllebrød* (barley porridge), *æbleflæsk* (slices of pork with apples fried in the fat) and *grønlangkål* (thick kale stew with sausages and mustard). Many dishes are served with new potatoes and root vegetables. Cucumber salad, pickled beetroot, and peas and carrots in white sauce also appear. Desserts include Apple Charlotte with whipped cream, breadcrumbs and almonds, and *rødgrød med fløde*, a jellied fruit juice served with thick cream.

Dill

Frikadeller *meatballs made of pork and veal are fried in Danish butter and served with boiled new potatoes.*

Herrings hanging in a Bornholm smokery

FISH & SEAFOOD

With its 406 islands, Denmark abounds with seafood. Herring is the most caught, cooked and consumed fish in the country. It is eaten fresh or preserved by salting, drying and smoking, and is served with sauces including curry, garlic, mustard and tomato. Salmon also features prominently, smoked, roasted, poached or cured in a salt-sugar-dill mixture, as do smoked eel, roe, mackerel and plaice. Fish fillets are often fried in butter and served with new potatoes and a buttery parsley sauce, washed down with lager or *akvavit* (Danish schnapps). Seafood is best enjoyed in the distinctive *røgeri* (smokehouses) found in harbours and pier restaurants all over the country.

MEAT

Pork is the most common meat; there are four times as many pigs as people in Denmark, and Danish bacon is famous throughout the world. Traditional prepara-

Snegl (literally "snail") pastries in a baker's window

tions include *stegt flæsk med persillesovs,* fried slices of pork with parsley sauce, served with potatoes; and *medisterpølse,* a thick and spicy pork sausage.

Sausages are popular, no more so than the ubiquitous *pølse,* a hotdog that is sold in kiosks everywhere and flavoured with any number of toppings. Though it is hardly *haute cuisine*, it is still a must for any visitor.

Beef, veal and lamb appear widely on menus, often in stews or minced to make rissoles and *frikadeller* (meatballs). In season, there are also game birds such as pheasant or duck, and venison and red deer.

DANISH PASTRIES

The "Danish" was introduced to Denmark in the 1870s, when striking breadmakers were replaced by Viennese immigrant bakers, with their repertoire of sweet breads, cakes and puff pastries. Pastries come in all shapes and sizes, and are filled with raisins, fruit compotes, custards and *remonce* (a very rich butter), then topped with nuts and sweet icing. Some of the best examples are marzipan horn, a crispy swirl of flaky pastry rolled up with *remonce, spandauer,* a flat twist of dough filled with vanilla custard, and the almond-filled *hanekam*. Moist and light, all are perfect with a coffee. Note that the same cakes and buns will have different names in different regions.

Flæskesteg *is a joint of roasted pork with crackling. It is usually served with cabbage and gravy.*

Rødbeder *is a side dish that consists of sliced pickled beetroot (beets). Horseradish sauce is also popular.*

Risalamande *is a Christmas rice pudding with almonds. It is served cold, topped with a rich, fruity cherry sauce.*

What to Drink in Denmark

As far as drinks are concerned the Danes have two passions – coffee and beer. People over 60 are also very attached to their liqueurs, which come in a variety of flavours and appear under the common name of *akvavit*. The beer market is dominated by a handful of companies, of which Carlsberg is the best known, but there are also many micro-breweries. Danish beer comes in a variety of strengths and colours, from fairly tame draught Pilsner through to stout with an alcohol content of about 10 per cent. Wine was not always so popular but is readily available in super-markets and restaurants. Non-alcoholic drinks include mineral water and numerous soft drinks.

Drinkers enjoying the sun outside one of Denmark's extremely popular bars

LAGER

Faxe Royal lager

Lager is the most popular Danish beverage. Most Danish beers are of the Pilsner type with an alcohol content of about 4.5 per cent. They include brands such as Carlsberg, Grøn Tuborg, Faxe and Star. Before Christmas and Easter the shops sell Julebryg and Påskebryg in standard and strong varieties. These beers are slightly sweet and make perfect additions to *akvavit*. Bars and restaurants serve both draught beer (*fadøl*) and bottled beers. Sometimes draught beer is ordered in a jug. Beer is most often sold in bottles rather than cans.

Beer is consumed throughout the day. It is not uncommon, and perfectly respectable, for Danes to drink beer in the park at lunchtime. Drunkenness is rare and drink-driving is not tolerated.

Logo of the Carlsberg brewery

Carlsberg Pilsner   **Tuborg lager**   **Faxe Classic**

BROWN ALE

There are over 400 varieties of beer produced in Denmark, including many fine brown ales. These generally have more flavour and are often stronger than Pilsner beers, with an alcoholic content of about 8 per cent or above. Some cafés and bars specialize in these beers, which tend to be slightly sweeter and less fizzy than lager. Among the popular brown ales are Carlsberg's Elephant and Sort Guld from the Tuborg brewery. The darkest beers are stouts and porters; these often have a higher percentage of alcohol. Organic micro-brews, such as Thy Bryghus, also have a slice of the market.

Carlsberg stout   **Carlsberg Elephant**

WINE

The Danish climate does not allow for the cultivation of grapes, although a few enthusiasts are trying to introduce the hardier varieties to southern Scandinavia. So far their efforts have not yielded any commercially viable vintages, and Danes, who are increasingly swapping a tankard of beer for a glass of wine, have to settle for imported wines. White wine is referred to as *hvidvin*, red wine is *rødvin* and sparkling wine is *mousserende-vin*. Hot mulled wine, or *gløgg*, is served with almonds and raisins in the run–up to Christmas.

Gløgg – mulled wine

HOT DRINKS

The Danes are coffee connoisseurs and coffee is the most popular drink in the country. Roasted beans are freshly ground on café premises and brewed in special jugs. Strong Italian espressos are also available, as are cappuccinos and increasingly popular lattes. Caffeine-free coffee is rarely found, but a delicious hot chocolate served with whipped cream is a fine alternative. Tea is not as popular in Denmark as coffee and consists of no more than a tea bag placed in a cup. Herbal teas are available in most cafés.

An aromatic herbal tea

A cup of black coffee

LIQUEURS

The traditional Christmas feast is often accompanied in Denmark by chilled *akvavit*. This schnapps-like beverage comes in a variety of herbal flavours and often bears the name *akvavit* on the label. It is usually drunk in a single shot and is followed by a glass of beer. As well as schnapps, the Danes drink other strong alcoholic herb infusions. The most popular of these is Gammel Dansk, which is traditionally drunk early in the morning. Danes used to regard a small glass of this bitter herbal preparation as a preventative medicine. Another local drink is Peter Heering, a sweet liqueur made from cherries, which is sipped after meals.

Herb-flavoured Gammel Dansk

Akvavit – **Danish schnapps**

SOFT DRINKS

When ordering a meal it is customary to ask for a bottle or jug of water. Danish tap water *(postevand)* is perfectly safe. Still bottled water is *minaralvand;* the sparkling variety bears the proud name of *danskvand* (Danish carbonated water). All restaurants, bars and pubs also serve low-alcohol beer, known as *let øl*. Soft drinks such as Coca-Cola go by the name of *sodavand*; bottled fruit juices are known as *saft*. Drinking chocolate – both hot *(varm chokolade)* and cold *(chokolademælk)* – is popular.

Sparkling mineral water

Fizzy soft drink

Bottle of chocolate milk

Choosing a Restaurant

The restaurants listed here have been selected across a wide price range for their fine food, good value and interesting location. They are listed alphabetically according to area, beginning with Copenhagen. For Copenhagen map references *see pp106–111*, for regional map references *see inside back cover*.

PRICE CATEGORIES:
The following price categories are for a two-course meal for one without alcohol or tip, but including tax:

Ⓚ Under 150 Dkr
ⓀⓀ 150–200 Dkr
ⓀⓀⓀ 200–300 Dkr
ⓀⓀⓀⓀ 300–350 Dkr
ⓀⓀⓀⓀⓀ Over 350 Dkr

COPENHAGEN

NORTH COPENHAGEN The Coffee Factory
Ⓚ

Gothersgade 21, 1123 **Tel** *33 14 15 82*   **Map** *1 A4*

A complete experience for coffee lovers, this has to be one the most outstanding places to drink coffee in Copenhagen. There are also brownies, croissants, and chocolate-chip cookies. And if you are not into coffee, there are smoothies or chai, served with milk and honey. Free wireless internet access too.

NORTH COPENHAGEN Café Petersborg
ⓀⓀ

Bredgade 76, 1260 **Tel** *33 12 50 16*   **Map** *2 D5*

Housed in what was once the Russian consulate, this charming old place dates back to the early 18th century. Among the Danish dishes served here are *biksemad* (a meat and potato hash), smoked salmon, and curried *sild* (herring). There is also a varied selection of *smørrebrød* dishes.

NORTH COPENHAGEN Eastern Corner
ⓀⓀ

Sølvgade 85A, 1307 **Tel** *33 11 58 35*   **Map** *1 B3*

You will get a very friendly reception at this large, much-loved Thai restaurant whose affordable prices make it a big hit with Danish families, though it would make a great spot for a date, too. Favourite dishes include chicken and coconut milk soup, grilled whole fish *á la thailandaise*, and pork filet with basil, chilli and garlic. Closed Sun.

NORTH COPENHAGEN Ida Davidsen
ⓀⓀ

Store Kongensgade 70, 1264 **Tel** *33 91 36 55*   **Map** *2 D3*

With nearly 250 *smørrebrød* sandwiches on offer, this lunchtime-only restaurant is a great place to try out this Nordic speciality. Best are the smoked duck, lobster, liver pâté, and the many variations on herring. The staff are well-informed about everything they serve and the walls are covered in photographs of famous Danes. Closed Sat, Sun; Jul.

NORTH COPENHAGEN O's American Breakfast & Barbeque
ⓀⓀ

Gothersgade 15, 1123 **Tel** *33 12 96 12*   **Map** *1 A4*

Here the "early morning brunch" begins at 3am, making this a good place for those leaving the city's clubs or bars. This American-style restaurant, with Cajun and Caribbean flavours, is best known for its filling pancakes, doused in maple syrup. There are also barbecued meats, including great burgers and inexpensive grilled chicken or ribs.

NORTH COPENHAGEN Sult
ⓀⓀ

Vognmagergade 8B, 1120 **Tel** *33 74 34 17*   **Map** *1 C5*

Somewhat confusingly named after Knut Hamsun's novel *Sult* (Hunger). The fusion menu here includes scrumptious dishes with influences from all over the world. Set inside the Danish Film Institute's cultural centre, Sult is ideal both for a quick snack or a longer, more filling meal. Its weekend brunch is especially popular. Closed Mon; Jul.

NORTH COPENHAGEN Biscaya Tapas Bar
ⓀⓀⓀ

Jernbanegade 4, 1608 **Tel** *33 32 44 77*   **Map** *3 A2*

One of Copenhagen's better tapas bars, this authentic Spanish restaurant (including Spanish pop music) is spread over two floors. Dozens of tapas dishes are on offer as well as other, more filling Iberian fare, as well as a good list of Spanish wines and *sangria*. Close to several cinemas so ideal as a pre- or post-film meeting place.

NORTH COPENHAGEN Restaurationen
ⓀⓀⓀⓀ

Møntergade 19, 1116 **Tel** *33 14 94 95*   **Map** *1 C5*

Placed a few blocks from Nørreport station at Gothersgade, this is a modern bistro where you can enjoy gourmet Danish cuisine in rooms lined with classical paintings. The dishes on the menu change according to what is fresh and in season. Closed Sun, Mon.

NORTH COPENHAGEN Umami
ⓀⓀⓀⓀⓀ

Store Kongensgade 59, 1264 **Tel** *33 38 75 00*   **Map** *2 D3*

Heralded as Copenhagen's best Japanese restaurant, but with a French twist, Umami's menu includes rabbit loin stuffed with shiitake mushrooms. The decor is decidedly minimalist, with brushed wood floors and massive portraits on the walls. On weekends the local hip crowd are attracted to the DJ sets of smooth low-key music.

Key to Symbols *see back cover flap*

CENTRAL COPENHAGEN La Galette

Larsbjørnsstræde 9, 1454 **Tel** *33 32 37 90*   **Map** *3 B1*

This Breton-style restaurant serves only *galettes* (savoury pancakes) topped or filled with any number of items including smoked salmon, ham, eggs, tomatoes, goat's cheese, or walnuts. There are also a number of sweet pancakes too. La Galette is small so you may want to book ahead.

CENTRAL COPENHAGEN La Glace

Skoubogade 3, 1158 **Tel** *33 14 46 46*   **Map** *3 B1*

Situated in a small maze of streets just south of the university, this is Copenhagen's oldest *konditori* (cake shop) and serves great cakes and pastries along with coffee and hot chocolate. Locals come here for a take-away or to enjoy a quick bite over the morning paper. An institution that should not be missed during your stay in the capital.

CENTRAL COPENHAGEN MakkeKafe

Nybrogade 18, 1203   **Map** *3 C2*

This friendly café located between the Nationalmuseet and Gammel Strand is run by two Italian women. It's simply furnished and offers healthy sandwiches, salads, home-made cakes and cookies, as well as great coffee. There are toys and drawing materials for small children and comfy sofas for their parents. Open until 6:30pm daily.

CENTRAL COPENHAGEN Atlas Bar

Larsbjørnsstr. 18, 1454 **Tel** *33 15 03 52*   **Map** *3 B1*

This cosy and unpretentious basement bar serves, in its own words, "food from the hot countries". Antique maps adorn the walls, alluding to the changing menu of dishes from all over the world; though the focus is on Asia and India. The Atlas is also known for its freshly pressed juices. Very busy, especially in the evenings. Excellent service.

CENTRAL COPENHAGEN Café Bjørg's

Vester Voldgade 19, 1552 **Tel** *33 14 53 20*   **Map** *3 A1*

A very social café-restaurant decorated in the style of an American diner. They serve good-sized brunches and lunches during the day and hot meals at night, including excellent club sandwiches accompanied by *jalapeños*, olives, and red pesto. There are also tasty curries, Mexican dishes, ample salads and wireless internet access.

CENTRAL COPENHAGEN Café Dan Turèll

Store Regnegade 3–5, 1110 **Tel** *33 14 10 47*   **Map** *1 C5*

This comfy place is named after renowned Danish author Dan Turéll and decorated with the covers from his many books. Locals come here for morning coffee and pastries, but there are also sandwiches, soups and burgers. In summer the outside terrace gets busy in the evenings and on weekends. Wireless internet access available.

CENTRAL COPENHAGEN Cafe Flottenheimer

Skindergade 20, 1159 **Tel** *35 38 32 12*   **Map** *3 C1*

Flottenheimer is located just a stone's throw away from popular Grabrødre Torv. Striking a balance between old and new Scandinavian design, it is a cosy little café with a well-assorted menu. In addition, it offers wireless internet access and a selection of papers and magazines. From Thursday to Saturday, it is also possible to enjoy cocktails.

CENTRAL COPENHAGEN Det Lille Apotek

Store Kannikestrade 15, 1169 **Tel** *33 12 56 06*   **Map** *3 B1*

The interior of Det Lille Apotek is decorated in deep, dark woods and gilded lamps. The menu features classic Danish dishes including roast pork, prawn cocktail with tournedos, and a wide variety of pickled *sild* (herring). Their speciality is *apotekergryde*, a tasty stew of pork tenderloin in a paprika cream sauce with mushrooms and pineapple.

CENTRAL COPENHAGEN Glyptoteket

Ny Carlsberg Glyptotek, Dantes Plads, 1556 **Tel** *33 41 81 28*   **Map** *3 B3*

This tranquil, atrium café-restaurant is set within the Glyptoteket Museum winter garden. It is a great place to stop for a fair-trade, organic coffee or quick snack. Here you will find some of the best cookies and cakes in Copenhagen. Beware, however, of the crowds on Sunday, when the museum opens its doors for free.

CENTRAL COPENHAGEN Himalaya

Herluf Trolles Gade 5 **Tel** *33 32 37 08*   **Map** *4 E1*

A rare opportunity to taste Tibetan (and Nepalese) food in Denmark, the Himalaya is presided over by the affable Tibetan chef/owner who knows his *thenthuk* from his *tukpa*. A house speciality is *momo*, a steamed dumpling filled with vegetables, chicken or beef, and served with a mouth-scalding chilli sauce.

CENTRAL COPENHAGEN Huset Med Det Grønne Træ

Gammeltorv 20, 1457 **Tel** *33 12 87 86*   **Map** *3 B1*

This well-liked lunch restaurant is popular with lawyers and businessmen. It is an excellent place to try typical Danish meals, such as *smørrebrød* sandwiches, local cheeses, *frikadeller* (Danish meatballs), as well as any of a dozen varieties of Danish schnapps. Well worth a stop if you are in the area. Also open in the evenings Wed–Sat.

CENTRAL COPENHAGEN Indian Taj

Jernbanegade 5, 1608 **Tel** *33 13 10 10*   **Map** *3 A2*

Copenhagen's first Indian restaurant is centrally located just a block away from the train station and serves unforgettable classic Indian cuisine. Here you will find a wide range of dishes, including a large number of vegetarian options, as well as favourites such as spicy jingha soup with king prawn and saffron.

CENTRAL COPENHAGEN Kanal Cafèen
Frederiksholms Kanal 18, 1220 **Tel** *33 11 57 70*   **Map** *4 F2*

This simple lunch restaurant opposite the Frederiksholms Kanal is best known for its wealth of *smørrebrød* dishes. The boiled, pickled herring is a well-regarded house speciality. The decor is maritime in theme, though it also sports signed photographs of its more famous diners.

CENTRAL COPENHAGEN Madklubben Bistro de Luxe
St Kongensgade 66, 1262 **Tel** *33 32 32 34*   **Map** *2 D5*

This Nordic bistro in the centre of Copenhagen serves traditional Scandinavian dishes with a modern touch. The relaxed and trendy surroundings, friendly service and simple, affordable menu attract a wide variety of diners. There is a selection of fixed-price menus offering one, two, three or four courses.

CENTRAL COPENHAGEN Magstræde 16, Spiseri & Enotek
Magstræde 16, 1204 **Tel** *33 16 12 92*   **Map** *3 B2*

This restaurant is housed in a building dating back to 1733 and features a rustic and relaxed interior. On the menu is Italian food with a Nordic twist, which translates into a selection of antipasti, snacks and some of the best pizzas in town, as well as three-course meals accompanied by a great range of Italian wines.

CENTRAL COPENHAGEN Slotskælderen hos Gittekik
Fortunstræde 4, 1065 **Tel** *33 11 15 37*   **Map** *3 C1*

Excellent, well-known lunch-only spot right by the Strøget that specializes is *smørrebrød*. Select what you want from behind the glass counters and they bring it to your table. Slotskælderen also serve good *frikadeller* (meatballs) and *sild* (herring). Popular with the parliamentarians who hold sessions nearby. Closed Sun, Mon; Jul.

CENTRAL COPENHAGEN The Living Room
Larsbjørnstræde 17, 1454 **Tel** *33 32 66 10*   **Map** *3 A1*

Come to The Living Room for a range of natural and organic foods and drinks, including soups, sandwiches, muffins, smoothies, milkshakes and juices. The place has a grungey, funky look, and diners can relax downstairs by the fireplace or head upstairs for views of the Latin Quarter.

CENTRAL COPENHAGEN Wagamama
Tietgensgade 20, 1704 **Tel** *33 75 06 58*   **Map** *3 A3*

This pan-Asian noodle bar ranks as one of the most popular casual dining spots in the city. With seating for 250, the Wagamama team offer inexpensive soups, dim sum, noodles, rice dishes and curries. Guests can also enter directly into the Tivoli park from the restaurant.

CENTRAL COPENHAGEN Café Sari
Nytorv 5, 1450 **Tel** *33 14 84 55*   **Map** *3 B1*

This café serves standard Danish fare as well as international café food, with a menu that includes *smørrebrød*, sandwiches, salads and light meals. However, its real draw is its outdoor seating on Nytorv square, one of the most central locations in Copenhagen. It can get busy at lunchtime.

CENTRAL COPENHAGEN Dubrovnik
Studiestræde 32, 1455 **Tel** *33 13 05 64*   **Map** *3 A1*

A convivial atmosphere is to be enjoyed here where the waiters walk around in Croatian costumes. The menu features a colourful and eclectic selection of Balkan cuisine, including rich grilled meat and fish dishes, such as thick soups, tripe and whitefish. All in all, a unique dining experience for downtown Copenhagen.

CENTRAL COPENHAGEN Firefly
Frederiksborggade 26, 1360 **Tel** *33 36 33 30*   **Map** *1 B5*

Located across the road from the Torvehallerne market, this biodynamic vegan restaurant serves Copenhagen's only vegan brunch. For dinner, choose from a raw food menu or a selection of international hot dishes. After closing the kitchen, Firefly becomes a nightclub serving organic cocktails and champagne. Open daily.

CENTRAL COPENHAGEN Maven
Nikolaj Plads 10, 1067 **Tel** *32 20 11 00*   **Map** *3 C1*

Boasting a lovely historic location in Nikolaj Plads, the square that was once the site for the city's butcher shops, Maven (Danish for "stomach") offers both lunch and dinner. The fairly upmarket cuisine is contemporary Danish. In summer, tables are placed outside and there's also live music. Closed Sun.

CENTRAL COPENHAGEN Nyhavns Færgekro
Nyhavn 5, 1051 **Tel** *33 15 15 88*   **Map** *4 D1*

A Danish restaurant in a building that once served as the last stop for immigrants on their way to the New World. The fetching interior features a spiral staircase from an old tram and marble floors from the old Dagmar theatre. The popular lunch buffet includes a host of herring dishes alongside Danish favourites including smoked salmon.

CENTRAL COPENHAGEN Peder Oxe
Gråbrødretorv 11, 1154 **Tel** *33 11 00 77*   **Map** *3 C1*

One of Copenhagen's most established restaurants, Peder Oxe serves good lunch dishes – the organic beefburgers are a big hit – but they are best known for their salad bar buffet, which includes such exotic vegetables as escarole endives and poupier. There is also a wine bar in the basement.

CENTRAL COPENHAGEN Restaurant Cap Horn

Nyhavn 21, 1051 **Tel** *33 12 85 04* **Map** *4 D1*

Weathered walls, original wood floors, and an open fireplace are the setting for the Cap Horn's classic Danish menu, which focuses on regularly changing seafood and organic dishes. The organic theme extends to the beer, wine, and coffee. Service is fast and courteous and they occasionally have live jazz sessions.

CENTRAL COPENHAGEN Krogs Fiskerestaurant

Gammel Strand 38, 1202 **Tel** *33 15 89 15* **Map** *3 C1*

This gourmet seafood restaurant with a focus on sustainable fishing has been a fixture on the Gammel Strand waterfront since 1910. Krogs is renowned as a fine dining destination and as the caterer to nearby Christiansborg. The set lunch and dinner menus offer a great, affordable deal.

CENTRAL COPENHAGEN Alberto K

Hammerischsgade 1, 1611 **Tel** *33 42 61 61* **Map** *3 A1*

Every detail (including the cutlery) of the Alberto K was designed by Arne Jacobsen. The Italian-inspired menu includes lumpfish roe, king crab *tortellini*, and thyme-spiced lamb. Outstanding Italian wine list. Located on the top floor of the Radisson Blu Royal Hotel, with superb views across the city. Booking essential. Closed mid-Jul–mid-Aug.

CENTRAL COPENHAGEN AOC & Co

Dronningens Tværgade 2, 1302 **Tel** *33 11 11 45* **Map** *4 D3*

Set under the vaulted ceilings of the Molktes Palæ, this adventurous restaurant is right in the centre of royal Frederiksstaden. Head chef Ronny Emborg's refined ten-course sensory menu is sheer decadence, especially when accompanied with a wine from the restaurant's award-winning selection. Reservations are essential.

CENTRAL COPENHAGEN Nimb Louise

Bernstorffsgade 5, 1577 **Tel** *88 70 00 00* **Map** *3 A3*

Nimb Louise features one of Denmark's best chefs, Allan Poulsen, at the helm. It's named after 19th-century restaurateur Louise Nimb and, unlike most of Tivoli, it is formal and upmarket. There's an extravagant set menu called Summer's Flora, as well as a range of *à la carte* dishes. Reservations essential. Closed Sat lunch, Sun.

SOUTH COPENHAGEN Lagkagehuset

Torvegade 45, 1400 **Tel** *32 57 36 07* **Map** *4 D2*

Out by the Christianshavn canal, this gem of a bakery is one of the best in the city. Locals in the know come here to stock up on muffins, breads, and, of course, Danish pastries. Light lunches of well-prepared sandwiches and salads are also served. Great coffee.

SOUTH COPENHAGEN Morgenstedet

Bådsmandsstræde 43, 1407 **Map** *4 F2*

Set in the alternative society of Christiania, this bright and unpretentious rustic community restaurant serves an exclusively organic and vegetarian menu, with items such as tofu, vegetable curries, hoummus, and great salads. The tables are laid out with small pots of fresh rosemary, pickled ginger, and chilli to use as a garnish. Closed Mon.

SOUTH COPENHAGEN Nemoland

Fabriksområde 52, 1440 **Tel** *32 95 89 31* **Map** *4 E2*

This is one of Christiania's best-known café-bistros and has an appropriately laid-back hippie atmosphere. The food is simple and hearty, and most people eat outside in the small courtyard when the weather is good. A great place to come to after a walk around this wonderful part of Copenhagen.

SOUTH COPENHAGEN Café Wilder

Wildersgade 56, 1408 **Tel** *32 54 71 83* **Map** *4 E3*

A relaxed, corner café on a quiet street in Christianshavn. The seasonal, French-inspired menu here changes quite often, but it always includes great meat and fish dishes. Wilders is a good choice for a late-night meal, and if you need to save your money then try the *dagens rett* ("selection of the day"). Vegetarian meals are booked in advance.

SOUTH COPENHAGEN La Novo

Torvegade 49–51, 1400 **Tel** *32 57 75 10* **Map** *4 D2*

Classic Italian fare served in an Italian setting. The interior of dark wood, terracotta, and wine bottles sets the ambiance, where you will find a wide range of tasty pizza and pasta dishes. Their *tiramisu* dessert is the best in the city. Tends to get lively later on, with lots of drinking and, occasionally, some dancing in the dining room.

SOUTH COPENHAGEN Oven Vande Café

Overgaden Oven Vandet 44, 1415 **Tel** *32 95 96 02* **Map** *4 D3*

An inviting café serving big brunches and good fish dishes at tables in front of large bay windows, perfect for watching the world (and well-dressed Danes) go by along the Christianshavn canal. The café fare is typically Danish, but with an added French touch. Open for breakfast, lunch and dinner.

SOUTH COPENHAGEN Ravelinen

Torvegade 79, 1400 **Tel** *32 96 20 45* **Map** *4 D2*

This garden restaurant on a tiny island, accessible via a small bridge, proudly serves traditional Danish cuisine, with a focus on *smørrebrød*. Their dishes include several types of herring, Danish potatoes, apple pie with whipped cream, and the much beloved *gammel ost* cheese, all of which should be accompanied by an *akvavit* (Danish schnapps).

SOUTH COPENHAGEN Spiseloppen

Bådsmandsstræde 43, 1407 **Tel** *32 57 95 58*

Map *4 E2*

This gourmet restaurant, with an international kitchen team, attracts a well-heeled but casually dressed crowd to its candle-lit tables in a large warehouse. A range of global, organic meals – including at least one veggie option – is on the menu, which changes weekly.

SOUTH COPENHAGEN Bastionen og Løven

Christianshavns Voldgade 50, 1424 **Tel** *32 95 09 40*

Map *4 D3*

One of the defining spots of Christianshavn, this one-time mill is a very popular place given its lush outdoor garden and views to the Vor Frelsers Kirke. The food is typically Danish, and includes filet of wild boar with red wine sauce, blue mussels steamed in white wine, and oven-baked flounder doused in saffron butter.

SOUTH COPENHAGEN Era Ora

Overgaden Neden Vandet 33B, 1414 **Tel** *32 54 06 93*

Map *4 E2*

Regularly nominated as the best Italian restaurant in Denmark, Era Ora has had its Michelin star for well over a decade for its sophisticated Tuscan-inspired menu. Diners here should expect a range of set menus rather than individual dishes, and an extensive wine cellar. Reservations essential.

SOUTH COPENHAGEN Kanalen

Wilders Plads 2, 1403 **Tel** *32 95 13 30*

Map *2 F4*

This quaint café serves great candlelit meals along one of Christianshavn's most idyllic canals. The food is seasonally-inspired Danish cuisine such as roasted gurnard fish and lamb with asparagus. French items such as oysters and an inventive goat's cheese *creme brulée* also show up. Choose from the modern dining room or the terrace umbrellas.

SOUTH COPENHAGEN Noma

Strandgade 93, 1401 **Tel** *32 96 32 97*

Map *4 D2*

Copenhagen's only two-star Michelin restaurant requires booking months in advance. Located in an old warehouse on Christianshavn's waterfront, Noma serves seasonal set menus using Scandinavian ingredients, many indigenous to a specific region. The place for an expensive, but definitely memorable, meal.

SOUTH COPENHAGEN Søren K

Søren Kierkegaards Plads 1, 1221 **Tel** *33 47 49 49*

Map *4 D2*

Businessmen and fashionistas alike come to this minimalist restaurant located in the "Black Diamond" *(see p88)*, for its fabulous views and great cuisine. There are lots of fish dishes and the six-course "tasting" menu is reasonably priced. If it is sunny out then take a table next to the water. Great wine list.

FURTHER AFIELD Café 22

Sortedam Dossering 21, 2200 **Tel** *35 37 38 27*

Right by one of Copenhagen's lakes, Café 22 is a great place for brunch, which is served seven days a week. The tasty Danish and continental meals served here are light and elegantly prepared, and the views from the tables overlooking the lake add to the appeal.

FURTHER AFIELD Castro

Nørrebrogade 209, 2200 **Tel** *35 85 35 85*

Pictures of Fidel Castro adorn the walls of this enormous Cuban-themed café-bistro. In addition to salads, burgers, and other hot dishes, they serve a range of fabulous coffees (Haitian, Colombian, and Kenyan brews) that are unrivalled in the city. Salsa and Afro-Cuban music accompanies everything.

FURTHER AFIELD Den Persiske Stue

Nørrebrogade 102, 2200 **Tel** *35 35 35 72*

Small, simple, and cosy ethnic restaurant offering affordable Persian and Turkish food. Beside the usual kebabs, yoghurt dips, and some tasty vegetarian main courses, the house speciality is the traditional Persian dish *koresht khemer*, delicately-prepared lamb with peas, potatoes, and saffron rice.

FURTHER AFIELD Golden Bamboo

Vesterbrogade 41, 1620 **Tel** *33 21 71 58*

The interior of Golden Bamboo, one of Copenhagen's oldest Chinese restaurants, can feel a bit dated at times, but do not let that keep you from ordering off their delicious pan-Asian menu. Recommendations include the king prawns with sweet and sour sauce, curry chicken with vegetables, and beef with mushrooms and bamboo shoots.

FURTHER AFIELD Kate's Joint

Blågårdsgade 12, 2200 **Tel** *35 37 44 96*

A simple, much-loved budget restaurant serving Asian and Caribbean fusion cuisine, much of which is geared towards vegetarians. The feel of the place is vaguely bohemian and there is always interesting world music being played. Be sure to try the mango lassi.

FURTHER AFIELD Sticks 'n' Sushi

Gammel Kongevej 120, 1850 **Tel** *33 29 00 10*

This chain of child-friendly sushi bars has a number of restaurants in Copenhagen. On the menu you will find sushi, sashimi, and all the trimmings, including lots of great spicy dipping sauces, as well as other traditional Japanese (non-raw) fish and meat dishes.

Key to Price Guide *see p268* **Key to Symbols** *see back cover flap*

FURTHER AFIELD Ankara

Vesterbrogade 35, 1620 **Tel** *33 31 92 33*

A large, dimly lit, buffet-style Turkish restaurant with reasonably priced Middle Eastern dishes – hoummous, falafel, mousakka – in addition to an inexpensive buffet of warm and cold items. Views from the top floor windows look out onto the lively Vesterbrogade. There is a sister branch on the same street at number 96.

FURTHER AFIELD Café Det Gule Hus

Istedgade 48, 1650 **Tel** *33 25 90 71*

This café serves *smørrebrød*-type lunches, with toppings that include local cheese, Danish ham, smoked bacon, fresh melon, garden tomato, spicy sausage, and marmelade. Some of their other popular menu items include pancakes and smoothies. Often remains packed throughout the day.

FURTHER AFIELD Den Franske Café

Sortedam Dossering 101, 2100 **Tel** *35 42 48 45*

Set right in the atmospheric Trianglen near a "lake" (really an old reservoir) at the heart of Østerbro, this typically Danish café has a relaxed feel and offers great views over the water. There are a number of well-priced lunch dishes and good coffee.

FURTHER AFIELD Floras Kaffebar

Blågårdsgade 27, 2200 **Tel** *35 39 00 18*

Fairly standard café fare, including soups, cakes, and coffees either in the sleek but casual interior or else outside when the sun is shining. During the evenings Floras turns into a popular place for drinks serving some of the cheapest beer in the neighbourhood.

FURTHER AFIELD Kaffesalonen

Peblinge Dossering 6, 2200 **Tel** *35 35 12 19*

This classic and colourful café with a maritime flavour has been around since 1933. It occupies an enviable location right on the small Peblinge lake and serves cakes, pastries, and drinks both inside and out. Opens early, so you can get your breakfast coffee and croissant from 8am. Wi-Fi is also available.

FURTHER AFIELD Pussy Galore's Flying Circus

Sankt Hans Torv 30, 2200 **Tel** *35 37 68 00*

Salads, burgers, and interesting renditions of Danish classics are served at this cosmopolitan but casual restaurant. They prepare brunch, lunch, and dinner as well as café-style snacks and well-priced drinks at a cocktail bar. When the weather's fine, be sure to get a spot out on the square.

FURTHER AFIELD Thai Esan 1

Lille Istedgade 7, 1700 **Tel** *33 24 98 54*

This Thai restaurant has large windows, atmospheric lighting, and spicy meals to enliven your day. Their Tom Yom shrimp soup is worth trying, and although the food is inexpensive the chefs do not skimp on quality ingredients. There are many other Thai restaurants in the vicinity, most run by the same family.

FURTHER AFIELD BioMio

Halmtorvet 19, 1700 **Tel** *33 31 20 00*

Located in the rejuvenated Kødbyen district of Vesterbro, in an old Bosch showroom the façade of which has been retained, this organic, eco-friendly "people's kitchen" serves vegetarian and meat dishes on long, communal tables. Everything – including the crockery – has been chosen with consideration for the environment.

FURTHER AFIELD Lê Lê Nhà Hàng

Vesterbrogade 40, 1620 **Tel** *33 22 71 35*

Outstanding Vietnamese food with a French touch is served here in the evenings. Instead of having a traditional single-plate meal, it is worth putting together a number of tasty noodles, soups, curries and spring rolls to sample all the great tastes that come out of the kitchen. Do not miss their great Thai milkshakes. Take-away available next door.

FURTHER AFIELD Radio

Julius Thomsens Gade 12, 1632 **Tel** *25 10 27 33*

Claus Meyer, co-owner of Noma, started Danish folk kitchen Radio on similar principles of seasonal, Nordic cuisine but without the gourmet exclusivity. Order the three-course menu (300 Dkr) or come at lunchtime, when you can order one course only. Located near Forum metro station. Closed Tue–Thu lunch; Sun, Mon; mid-Jul–early Aug.

FURTHER AFIELD Kadeau København

Vesterbrogade 135, 1620 **Tel** *33 25 22 23*

One of Bornholm's best-known summertime restaurants has brought its kitchen to the historic inn Den Sorte Hest, at the end of Vesterbrogade, near the hill that leads to the Carlsberg Brewery. The three-course seasonal set menu blends unusual ingredients, all imaginatively presented. Reservations advised. Closed lunch; Sun, Mon; Jul–early Aug.

FURTHER AFIELD Kødbyens Fiskebar

Flæsketorvet 100, 1711 **Tel** *32 15 56 56*

Inside one of the white and blue buildings of Vesterbro's old meat-packing district, the Fish Bar serves fresh fish and seafood in an informal setting. No ordinary fish and chip shop, the restaurant is Michelin-recommended and has a good wine list. The weekend lunchtime menu is considerably cheaper. Closed Tue–Fri lunch; Sat & Sun dinner; Mon.

FURTHER AFIELD Restaurant Relæ

Jægersborggade 41, 2200 **Tel** 36 96 66 09

In a gritty neighbourhood, Relæ appeals with its gourmet combination of Italian and New Nordic cuisines, which has earned it a Michelin star. There are two four-course seasonal menus on offer, one of them aimed at vegetarians. Reservations are essential. Closed lunchtime; Sun–Tue; Jul.

FURTHER AFIELD Formel B

Vesterbrogade 182, 1800 **Tel** 33 25 10 66

This Michelin-starred boutique restaurant serves delectable Danish-French dishes created by two talented young cooks. The divine dining room attracts its fair share of businessmen looking to impress and wealthy jetsetters. Reservation essential.

NORTHWESTERN ZEALAND

FREDENSBORG Restaurant Skipperhuset

Skipperallé 6, 3480 **Tel** 48 48 17 17   **Map** F4

The long Skipperallé leads past the castle down towards the sea, where this one-time boathouse serves great Danish meals in a charming ambiance right at the water's edge. Chicken and delicately-prepared fish dishes are some menu favourites, though it would be hard to go wrong with anything they serve here. Open lunch only (May–Sep).

FREDERIKSSUND Regnbuen

Ny Østergade 5C, 3600 **Tel** 47 38 58 10   **Map** F4

This cosy little restaurant offers a rather large menu of international dishes, including Danish, Italian, Turkish and Greek. There are nearly two dozen different pizzas, and as many types of steak, including *tournedos*, gorgonzola and T-bone. The lobster tail or French onion soup starters are both worth trying.

FREDERIKSSUND Toldboden

Færgevej 1, 3600 **Tel** 47 36 17 77   **Map** F4

Situated in an old tax collector's home, Toldboden offers meals with strong roots in traditional Danish cooking complemented with touches of modern European cuisine. The finely-prepared dishes are extremely tasty, as are the wines picked to go with them. Pricy, but the waterside location is idyllic.

GILLELEJE Røgeriet Bornholm

Havnen 4, 3250 **Tel** 48 39 22 31   **Map** F4

This smokehouse, with its location right on the harbour, is one of the most atmospheric of Gilleleje's eating spots. Ideal for those on a budget, Røgeriet Bornholm sells seasoned filets of mackerel, halibut, herring, eel and salmon from the counter which can then be eaten on the picnic tables out front.

GILLELEJE Gilleleje Havn

Havnevej 14, 3250 **Tel** 48 30 30 39   **Map** F4

Impeccably turned-out restaurant in an old merchants' inn on the harbour. Arrive early to get one of the booths at the front, each with individual French doors, that look out to the harbour. The lunch menu features many simple herring, salmon and other fish dishes; while for dinner the offerings are pricier and more sophisticated.

HELSINGØR Cafeteria San Remo

Stengade 53, 3000 **Tel** 49 21 00 55   **Map** F4

An inexpensive restaurant that features friendly service and no-frills Danish fare served from a counter. The dishes include fish and chips, scampi, *smørrebrød*, burgers and the *dagens ret* (day's selection). Moreover, the menu has photos of everything so you know exactly what you are getting. Ideal for a quick snack.

HELSINGØR Pakhus Pizza

Stengade 26, 3000 **Tel** 49 21 10 50   **Map** F4

This country-style *trattoria* serves excellent pastas and pizzas, drawing families from as far away as Copenhagen for its low-key atmosphere, friendly staff and central location. Situated on a pedestrianised street in downtown Helsingør, Pakhus Pizza offers an easy-going meal out.

HELSINGØR Rådmand Davids Hus

Strandgade 70, 3000 **Tel** 49 26 10 43   **Map** F4

One of the oldest addresses in town, this café-style restaurant has a few delectable dishes on the traditional Danish menu but the real attraction is the interior: meticulously restored stonework and evocative furnishings. There is even a view into the cellar, whose passageways reportedly run all the way up to Kronborg castle. Open for lunch only.

HELSINGØR Madame Sprunck

Stengade 48, 3000 **Tel** 49 26 48 49   **Map** F4

A café-restaurant in an atmospheric old building with a menu of Danish and international dishes. The five-course "tasting menu" gives a great sample of what the superb chef is capable of cooking. A large wine list, including some exceptional (and pricey) vintages, complements all the dishes served here. The café menu is cheaper and kid-friendly.

HILLERØD Spisestedet Leonora

🅰🚹 ⓀⓀ

Frederiksborg Slot, 3400 **Tel** *48 26 75 16*

Map F4

A lunch-only restaurant, with a large terrace garden, delightfully placed near the Frederiksborg Slot. The menu is extensive, but to order something typically Danish try *det store kolde bord* (a *smorgasbord*-like selection of fish, meat, vegetables and cheese dishes): a filling sampler of the best the country has to offer.

HILLERØD Castello Rufo Ruffo

🆅 ⓀⓀⓀ

Helsingørsgade 20, 3400 **Tel** *48 25 25 85*

Map F4

Named after a town in Sicily, this small Italian restaurant has aspirations well above your average pizzeria. The *à la carte* menu comprises classic antipasti, pasta, meat and fish dishes; alternatively, you can order the three-course set menu. Lengthy wine list. Open for dinner Mon–Sat.

HOLBÆK Bryghuset No.5

🅰🚹 ⓀⓀ

Nygade 5, 4300 **Tel** *45 34 55 55*

Map E4

This micro-brewery with café-restaurant attached has a good value *à la carte* menu. As well as snacks, it offers larger plates such as beef carpaccio, salmon roulade and beer-battered steamed mussels. There is also a large weekend brunch buffet and live music on Fridays and Saturdays.

HOLTE Søllerød Kro

🆅 ⓀⓀⓀⓀⓀ

Søllerødvej 35, 2840 **Tel** *45 80 25 05*

Map F4

One of Denmark's most prestigious restaurants, Michelin-starred Søllerød Kro is housed in an idyllic 17th-century inn at the edge of woodland, by the village church and pond. The French/Scandinavian lunch and dinner menus are fresh and inspired; it's also possible to order *à la carte*. Huge wine list. Reservations essential. Closed Mon, Tue; Jul.

HORNBÆK Restaurant Hansens Café

🍽🅰🚹 ⓀⓀⓀ

Havnevej 19, 3100 **Tel** *49 70 04 79*

Map F4

Just inside Hornbæk's oldest house, this inn-style restaurant has a changing menu that features a variety of typical Danish dishes. There are two terraces, for eating outdoors, and on Sundays the brunch menu attracts many locals to the place creating quite an atmosphere.

HORNBÆK Søstrene Olsen

🍽🅰 ⓀⓀⓀ

Øresundsvej 10, 3100 **Tel** *49 70 05 50*

Map F4

Set within a thatched, late-19th-century summer cottage next to the town beach, this traditional Danish restaurant looks towards France for flashes of inspiration. The menu changes every two weeks, but you can always find a selection of fine seafood dishes on offer. Closed Tue.

HUNDESTED Lynæs Kro

🚹▶ ⓀⓀⓀ

Frederiksværkvej 6, 3390 **Tel** *47 98 01 81*

Map E4

An old Danish inn serving a range of Danish favourites as well as a selection of international dishes including an especially tasty mulligatawny soup. The children's menu reverts to such standbys as fish and chips and nuggets. The interior is filled with antique furniture, adding to the bygone atmosphere of the place.

HØRSHOLM Mikkelgaard

🅰 ⓀⓀⓀⓀ

Rungsted Strandvej 302, 2970 **Tel** *45 76 63 13*

Map F4

The walls of this French restaurant are lined with wine bottles, adding to the homely feel of the bright interior. There are a few *à la carte* dishes, but most diners are confident enough in the skills of the chefs to choose one of the fixed-price meals.

KALUNDBORG Café Bogart

🅰🚹🆅 Ⓚ

Kordilgade 17, 4400 **Tel** *59 51 00 57*

Map E4

Café Bogart owes its popularity to its good food and its convenient location right on a pedestrian area in the centre of town. It serves baguettes, sandwiches, salads and baked potatoes topped with any assortment of fillings including bacon, shrimp, tuna and garlic butter. A great place for watching the world go by.

KORSØR Madam Bagger

🚹 ⓀⓀ

Havnegade 17, City Parkeringen, 4220 **Tel** *58 37 01 49*

Map E5

Named after an 18th-century innkeeper renowned for her culinary talent, this restaurant has retained its wooden beams. The varied, traditional menu includes plenty of herring on the lunch menu, and dinner specials like beef tenderloin and *Wienerschnitzel*. Centrally – though uninspiringly – located next to the town car park. Closed Sun.

NYKØBING SJ Madkunsten

ⓀⓀ

Algade 44, 4500 **Tel** *59 93 17 27*

Map F6

The food at this little hole in the wall will make your mouth water (its name means "The Art of Food"). For lunch they serve inventive dishes, often incorporating seafood, though there are good burgers, omelettes and snack-sized meals. Dinner is a bit more formal, accompanied by a surprisingly extensive wine list. Closed Mon.

ROSKILDE Snekken

🅰🚹🆅 ⓀⓀⓀ

Vindeboder 16, 4000 **Tel** *46 35 98 16*

Map F4

Located on the harbourfront, this bright restaurant has teamed up with the Vikingeskibsmuseet next door to create its own concept food, New Nordic Viking cuisine. Ancient Scandinavian ingredients are used to prepare imaginative dishes, including a children's menu. There's also outdoor seating and an extensive weekend buffet.

ROSKILDE Store Bors
Havnevej 43, 4000 **Tel** *46 32 50 45*

Map F4

Fresh and local sums up the approach of this upmarket restaurant, with views onto the harbour. The menu features fresh fish and shellfish straight out of the water in front, whilst many of the other ingredients are locally sourced or produced, including cheeses, smoked salmon, vegetables and beer. Closed Mon.

RØRVIG Rørvig Fisk og Røgeri
Toldbodvej 81, 4581 **Tel** *59 91 81 33*

Map E4

A simple, family-run smokehouse-cum-restaurant right at the ferry terminal, where boats leave to cross the fjord to Hundested. Do not expect anything more than fish and shellfish: herring, salmon, mackerel, pike, perch and shrimp, all caught from the fjord that morning. Fresher (and tastier) fish would be hard to find.

SORØ Hotel Postgården
Storgade 25, 4180 **Tel** *57 83 22 22*

Map E5

The warm and cosy atmosphere at this *à la carte*, candlelit restaurant make it a popular place. The menu is traditional Danish, with a few surprises from further afield. The interior features a fireplace and light music. Recommendations include the fish soup and the venison medallions.

SORØ Støvlet Katrines Hus
Slagelsevej 63, 4180 **Tel** *57 83 50 80*

Map E5

Located in a half-timbered country house, this inn has plenty of character. The interior is as traditional as the menu, which features plenty of herring, fillets of fish and a half-dozen steak dishes prepared according to century-old recipes. A short walk from the town centre, but by far the most atmospheric place to eat in Sorø. Closed early–mid-Jul.

TISVILDELEJE Tisvildeleje Caféen
Hovedgaden 55, 3220 **Tel** *48 70 88 86*

Map F4

This indoor/outdoor informal restaurant, with checkered tablecloths and a family atmosphere, could easily pass for a barbecue joint on Cape Cod. They put on a popular unlimited grilled buffet of steaks and fish, but there is also an inexpensive *à la carte* lunch menu. Perfect after a day at the beach.

SOUTHERN ZEALAND AND THE ISLANDS

BANDHOLM Bandholm Restaurant
Havnegade 37, 4941 **Tel** *54 75 54 76*

Map E6

Located in North Lolland, not far from Knuthenborg Safari Park, the restaurant of the historic Bandholm Hotel is open all day to non-guests and has a covered terrace with sea views. Drop in for brunch, a sandwich or something more substantial. The international fare includes steaks, burgers and lasagne.

KØGE Christians Minde
Brogade 7, 4600 **Tel** *56 63 68 56*

Map F5

Housed in a building from 1850, this Chinese-Danish restaurant is centrally located in Køge. European fare includes meat dishes like *Wienerschnitzel* and beef stroganoff, as well as fish dishes – or choose something from the extensive Cantonese selection. Danish lunch buffet and outside seating during the summer months.

KØGE Slagter Stig & Co Brasserie Bassin
Carlsensvej 8, 4600 **Tel** *56 65 48 09*

Map F5

With a host of burgers, fish filets, *charcuterie* and cheese plates, this brasserie-style restaurant is a good local option for picking up a quick tasty Danish meal. Unusually there is no menu: you just point at what you want from the counter and they prepare it before your eyes. Closed Mon.

MARIBO Panya Thai
Vesterbrogade 55, 4930 **Tel** *72 17 07 73*

Map E6

Should you find yourself craving Asian cuisine while in Lolland, this pleasant, friendly Thai restaurant has an extensive menu with varying degrees of spiciness and is reasonably priced. The children's menu offers dishes like chicken nuggets. A take-away service is also available. Open for dinner daily.

MARIELYST Larsens Plads
Marielyst Strandvej 57, 4873 **Tel** *54 13 21 70*

Map F6

This large indoor/outdoor establishment has room for 700 and has long been the most popular place to eat – and drink – in Marielyst. They have a number of themed rooms, all of which are usually teeming with Danish families. Their large all-you-can-eat buffet offers a dozen types of meat, a huge salad bar and any number of side dishes.

NAKSKOV Lido
Søndergade 8–10, 4900 **Tel** *54 92 23 13*

Map E6

The Danish menu at this long-standing cafeteria features a number of fairly priced dishes, such as fish fillet, *Wienerschnitzel*, many different burgers, and a number of tasty *smørrebrød* dishes. Many of the starters are also competitively priced, including the prawn cocktail, so it is worth giving them a try. Closed Sun.

NÆSTVED Café Oliver   ⊠ 🕭 🏃   ⓦⓦ
Jernbanegade 2, 4700 **Tel** 55 77 88 81   **Map** E5

A bright, airy brasserie-style restaurant right at the centre of Næstved. Their lunch offerings include sandwiches, bruschetta, burgers and nachos. With only three dishes, dinner is somewhat less varied. Ideal for a quick bite before heading out to explore the town.

NÆSTVED Rådhuskroen   ⊠ 🕭 🏃 ⓥ   ⓦⓦⓦ
Skomagerrækken 8, 4700 **Tel** 55 72 01 56   **Map** E5

The name means "Town Hall Inn", yet once inside it seems more like an English gentlemen's club with a decor of deep dark woods, tanned leather seats and shelves of antique tomes. The menu comprises a collection of Danish and French dishes such as pepper and garlic steaks and *Wienerschnitzel* with mashed potatoes, peas and gravy.

RINGSTED Café Aspendos   🕭 🏃 ⓥ   ⓦⓦ
Møllegade 11, 4100 **Tel** 57 67 05 08   **Map** E5

A relaxed corner café which is also a popular hangout for local teenagers. The menu is what you would expect from such a place – salads, burgers, sandwiches and the like, but it is also just a great place to come and have a coffee or a beer as you watch the world go by.

RINGSTED Rådhuskroen   🏃   ⓦⓦⓦ
Sct. Bendtsgade 8, 4100 **Tel** 57 61 68 97   **Map** E5

This local Danish inn is about as traditional as you are going to find in this part of Denmark, and it is very popular with the locals. It specialises in beef and steak dishes – English, French, garden, pepper and Bearnaise – though there are a few unexpected (but equally good) items such as blini and *escargot*.

STEGE Slagter Stig & Co. Støberiet   ⊠ 🕭 🏃 ⓥ   ⓦⓦ
Storegade 59, 4780 **Tel** 55 81 42 67   **Map** F6

This nationwide charcuterie chain combines an eclectically decorated, cosy brasserie with a well-stocked delicatessen shop. On the menu is Danish food with worldwide inspiration. Help yourself at the side-dish buffet and the draught beer bar, then choose your own cut of meat and leave it up to the expert staff to grill it and serve it to your liking.

STEGE David's   🏃 ⓥ   ⓦⓦⓦ
Storegade 11, 4780 **Tel** 33 13 80 57   **Map** F6

A pleasant Danish-French café-restaurant serving breakfast, brunch, tapas plates and lunch snacks, as well as special two- and three-course menus from 6pm onwards (Friday and Saturday only). Children's menus are also available. A charming courtyard in the back looks out over the old church tower. Open from 10am daily.

VORDINGBORG Babette   🍽 ▶   ⓦⓦⓦⓦⓦ
Kildemarksvej 5, 4760 **Tel** 55 34 30 30   **Map** E5

One of the best restaurants in Denmark. Named after the 1987 Danish film *Babette's Feast*, this gourmet establishment has a changing menu featuring Danish and French delicacies such as local asparagus with fjord prawns and Italian sardines *au gratin*. A worthwhile treat if you are in this part of the country. Closed Sun–Tue; mid-Jul–late Jul.

FUNEN

KERTEMINDE Rudolf Mathis   🕭 🏃 🍽   ⓦⓦⓦⓦⓦ
Dosseringen 13, 5300 **Tel** 65 32 32 33   **Map** D5

This well-regarded fish restaurant sits right on the waterfront in Kerteminde. Inside find cosy rooms elegantly decorated. Here the multiple-course set menus are excellent samplings of Danish gastronomy. The "daily catch" at lunchtime is a reliable option.

MIDDELFART Hindsgavl Slot   🕭 🍽   ⓦⓦⓦⓦⓦ
Hindsgavl Allé 7, 5500 **Tel** 64 41 88 00   **Map** C5

Set within a fetching old manor estate, this upmarket restaurant offers seasonal and locally sourced food served in a relaxed environment. Patrons can choose from a few fixed-priced menus, all of which are quite delicious. A wonderful place to splash out, eat well and relish the surrounding scenery.

MILLINGE Falsled Kro   🏃 ▶ ⓥ   ⓦⓦⓦⓦⓦ
Assensvet 513, 5642 **Tel** 62 68 11 11   **Map** D5

This charming old inn offers gourmet Danish cuisine created with local ingredients and home-grown produce. The set menus change according to the seasons and might include such delights as roe deer and crispy turbot. Falsled Kro is rated among the best restaurants in Denmark, and the prices reflect this. Advance booking is required.

MUNKEBO Restaurant Anden   ⓥ   ⓦⓦⓦⓦⓦ
Fjordvej 56, 5330 **Tel** 65 97 40 30   **Map** D5

A charming Danish inn, the Munkebo Kro has a nationwide reputation for its food, even hosting the Danish royal family on occasion. The menu is dominated by fish dishes, though the seasonal menus can bring surprises to your table. There is also an enormous wine list. Booking is advisable.

NYBORG Teglværksskoven
Strandalleen 92, 5800 **Tel** *65 31 41 40*
Map D5

An indoor/outdoor establishment that does a good trade in a range of herring dishes, though there are lots of other items on the menu including Funen *æggekage* (omelette), catch of the day, and shellfish salad. Be sure to get a table on the terrace, which has a wonderful view out to sea.

ODENSE Café Biografen
Brandts Passage 39–41, 5000 **Tel** *66 13 16 16*
Map D5

For a long time now Biografen has been one of the most popular places in Odense for lingering lazily over a tasty meal. The menu includes a good brunch or a dinner of *chile con carne*, burgers, or a selection of *tapas*. Afterwards, head further inside to catch one of the art house films at the restaurant's cinema.

ODENSE Bryggeriet Flakhaven
Flakhaven 2, 5000 **Tel** *66 12 02 99*
Map D5

A multi-level restaurant on the town square that doubles as a micro-brewery, with all the beer-making paraphernalia and plumbing running throughout the eating areas. The food includes spare ribs, steak and scampi, as well as a selection of *smørrebrød* offerings. Be sure to try their homemade brews.

ODENSE Café Cuckoo's Nest
Vestergade 73, 5000 **Tel** *65 91 57 87*
Map D5

Cosy intimate tables, deep sofas, and several different rooms for dining and hanging out make this chic café-style restaurant popular among students and young professionals. They serve lots of *tacos*, pastas, salads, *nachos* and steaks. The weekend brunches are especially enjoyable, when a jazz group usually plays outside.

ODENSE Djengis Khan
Overgade 24–26, 5000 **Tel** *66 12 88 38*
Map D5

Exotically decorated, Djengis Khan's speciality is Mongolian barbecue, a massive offering where you select from dozens of meat and vegetable ingredients to be topped with any number of exotic sauces. There is also a large salad bar, and the wine list includes French, Spanish and Californian vintages.

ODENSE Druen & Bønnen
Vestergade 15, 5000 **Tel** *66 11 18 13*
Map D5

This friendly, airy café and bistro serves a combination of simply prepared Danish and Mediterranean *tapas*-like dishes: think *charcuterie* platters and freshly made sandwiches with fresh olives and *tzatziki*. There are chess tables and board games in the back room, making it a great place to spend the day.

ODENSE Den Gamle Kro
Overgade 23, 5000 **Tel** *66 12 14 33*
Map D5

Set in a wonderful old building dating from 1683, this atmospheric restaurant is decorated with memorabilia from the past. Some of the Danish dishes on the menu include cured salmon, Kerteminde plaice, and vanilla parfait with summer berries from Funen. There are several dining rooms to choose from and a great wine cellar.

ODENSE Sortebro Kro
Sejerskovvej 20, 5260 **Tel** *66 13 28 26*
Map D5

Part of the open-air museum Den Fynske Landsby and located in luxuriant grounds, Sortebro Kro is a thatch-roofed historic inn with a cosy atmosphere. In the daytime, you can stop here just for coffee and cake, or enjoy a full meal prepared with produce grown in the museum's garden. The evening *à la carte* menu features Danish and French contemporary cuisine.

ODENSE Under Lindetræet
Ramsherred 2, 5000 **Tel** *66 12 92 86*
Map D5

Just minutes from the H.C. Andersen museum, this formal restaurant is housed in an original half-timbered building dating from 1771. The dishes tend to be pricey but come excellently prepared, often with local Funen produce. The best place in Odense for a romantic meal.

RUDKØBING Thummelumsen
Østergade 15, 5900 **Tel** *63 51 00 43*
Map D6

Located in an old townhouse, Thummelumsen is a cosy little restaurant that serves fresh fish (sourced from Bagenkop, on the southern tip of Langeland), home-made burgers (beef, chicken or vegetarian) and a range of traditional Danish dishes. Weather permitting, it is possible to eat alfresco.

SVENDBORG Jettes Diner
Kullinggade 1, 5700 **Tel** *62 22 17 48*
Map D5

Just next to the ferry terminal, this burger bar is popular among families on their way to visit the islands off Svendborg's coast. It serves up sandwiches, steaks, salads, snacks and, most famously, outstanding burgers – Danes come from all over Funen to have one. The weekend brunch is popular with locals.

SVENDBORG Pichardt's
Brogade 13, 5700 **Tel** *62 53 33 53*
Map D6

The friendly Pichardt's features gastronomic delights at reasonable prices. The menu includes such things as pâté of Danish lamb, cream of asparagus soup and hot smoked salmon served with Funen smoked cheese. The dessert menu is equally fine, and the chef/owner is happy to share his knowledge of the food.

SVENDBORG Restaurant 5

♟ ⓒⓒⓒⓒ

Brogade 1–3, 5700 **Tel** *72 18 55 55*   **Map** *D5*

Considered to be one of the best restaurants in Funen, Restaurant 5 is located in the 19th-century Hotel Ærø, on Svendborg's harbour. It specializes in both unusual and classic dishes from the New Nordic repertoire, with gourmet dinners and more down-to-earth lunches. Service is friendly and enthusiastic, children's dishes available.

ÆRØSKØBING Mumm

♿ ♟ V   ⓒⓒⓒ

Søndergade 12, 5970 **Tel** *62 52 12 12*   **Map** *D6*

Although the building dates back several centuries and the decor is mostly traditional, a few touches, such as umbrellas out back, add somewhat of a modern feel to Mumm. The menu includes both American and Scandinavian standards – steak, salads and seafood. Recommended are the snails, shrimp and sole.

SOUTHERN AND CENTRAL JUTLAND

EBELTOFT Molskroen

♟ ➔ V   ⓒⓒⓒⓒⓒ

Hovedgaden 16, 8400 **Tel** *86 36 22 00*   **Map** *D3*

The chef at Molskroen has a reputation for conjuring up a range of French fare with imaginative Danish twists, such as salted cod with peas and bacon, or turbot with lobster bisque. In the evening there are two menus to choose from (Short and Classic), plus a set Long Menu featuring nine courses. Wheelchair access is available in some areas.

ESBJERG Jensens Bøfhus

♿ ♟ ➔   ⓒⓒⓒ

Torvegade 10, 6700 **Tel** *75 18 18 70*   **Map** *B5*

Located in the centre of Esbjerg, this family restaurant (part of a nationwide chain) has its own courtyard, which is a pleasant place to enjoy the grilled meats in the summer. The menu consists mainly of meat dishes, served in generous portions, and there is a large salad bar to choose from too. To finish off, do not miss the ice cream bar.

ESBJERG Brasserie B

♿ ♟ ➔ V   ⓒⓒⓒ

Torvet v, Hotel Britannia, 6700 **Tel** *75 13 01 11*   **Map** *B5*

A popular pub-like restaurant, Brasserie B serves a selection of crowd-pleasing dishes created with local and seasonal ingredients. Highlights include beef Bearnaise and salmon sourced in the Wadden Sea. For dessert, choose pancakes with ice cream. There is live music five days a week.

FREDERICIA Yamamomo

V   ⓒⓒⓒ

Torvegade 2, 7000 **Tel** *75 91 49 11*   **Map** *C5*

Located in Axeltorv, in the centre of town, this Oriental restaurant serves sushi, noodle soups, uramaki rice rolls with a wide range of fillings (from snowcrab and smoked salmon to tuna and lobster) and Japanese grilled meat dishes. There is also a large selection of sake and Japanese beers.

GRENÅ Café & Restaurant Casablanca

♟ V   ⓒⓒⓒ

Skakkes Holm 8–12, 8500 **Tel** *86 32 35 39*   **Map** *D3*

Come to this Italian-inspired restaurant in Grenå's marina for delicious stone-baked pizzas, as well as pasta and meat dishes, not to mention classic desserts like ice cream and tiramisu. The popular all-you-can eat pizza buffet offers the best value. Children's and take-away menus are also available.

HADERSLEV LMNT Café and Lounge

♟ V   ⓒⓒ

Apotekergade 1, 6100 **Tel** *74 52 00 82*   **Map** *C5*

Frequented by locals, LMNT is a smart, family-friendly café. The tapas lunch selection is popular, if not authentically Spanish in flavour; choose a handful of options from a range of small dishes and enjoy the variety. A children's menu and vegetarian options are available. All-day cocktails are on offer, too. Closed Sun.

HERNING Herreford Beefstouw

♿ ♟   ⓒⓒⓒⓒⓒ

Lundvej 16, 7400 **Tel** *97 12 35 44*   **Map** *C4*

Now part of a leading chain of restaurants, this is the perfect place for all meat-lovers who dream of high quality, juicy steaks and spare ribs – and for vegetarians there is a salad bar. The paintings on the walls are by the former owner, Aage Damgaard. Wheelchair access needs to be arranged in advance. Closes at 9:30pm.

HORSENS Lille Hejmdal

♿ ♟ ➔   ⓒⓒⓒ

Rædersgade 8–10, 8700 **Tel** *75 61 02 00*   **Map** *C4*

A family restaurant that originally opened its doors as a café back in 1888. Lille Hejmdal is the town's oldest and largest restaurant, with a huge à la carte menu that includes Danish open sandwiches, organic chocolate fondue and a fantastic selection of other delicacies and organic dishes.

JELLING Jelling Kro

♟   ⓒⓒⓒ

Gormsgade 16, 7300 **Tel** *75 87 10 06*   **Map** *C4*

A historic inn dating from 1842, Jelling Kro is beautifully situated amid a verdant landscape. The house specialities include steak of Scottish Highland beef and smoked trout fillet with new potatoes and dill dressing. For dessert, try the *skyr*, a Viking-era yogurt served with mixed berries. You can dine alfresco when the weather is mild.

KOLDING Den Blå Café
     🔲 ⟩   Ⓚ Ⓚ Ⓚ
Slotsgade 4, 6000 **Tel** *75 50 65 12*   **Map** *C5*

Offering a cosy, intimate atmosphere, Den Blå is Kolding's oldest café. The menu includes wraps, sandwiches and salads. For a mouth-watering experience try the Monster Burger, with beef, scrambled eggs, tomatoes, bacon and cheese. Live music every Thursday from 11pm. Outdoor seating available in the summer.

KOLDING Den Gyldne Hane
     🔲 ⫙ Ⓥ   Ⓚ Ⓚ Ⓚ
Christian IV's Vej 23, 6000 **Tel** *75 52 97 20*   **Map** *C5*

Located only a few minutes from the centre of town in a timber-framed house, this restaurant provides excellent Danish and French cuisine in a lovely setting. The menu is constantly being tweaked, but at the same time "tried and tested" classics are always present. Outside tables are available.

KOLDING Herreford Beefstouw
     🔲 ⫙ ⟩   Ⓚ Ⓚ Ⓚ Ⓚ Ⓚ
Helligkorsgade 20, 6000 **Tel** *75 52 00 87*   **Map** *C5*

One of a reliable chain of meat restaurants known for stylish interiors serving juicy steaks and ribs in rich sauces. In Kolding, the building dates back to the 17th century and a massive olive mill stands in the middle of the restaurant. Gaining a good reputation for itself locally.

RIBE Sælhunden
     🖥 🔲 ⫙   Ⓚ Ⓚ Ⓚ
Skibbroen 13, 6760 **Tel** *75 42 09 46*   **Map** *B5*

As the name, which means "seal tavern", might suggest, this restaurant is know for its selection of reasonably priced fish dishes. Situated next to a river, the menu also includes non-fish dishes such as *Wienerschnitzel* served in a butter sauce. A terrace is open in the summer.

RIBE Kammerslusen
     🔲 ⫙   Ⓚ Ⓚ Ⓚ Ⓚ
Bjerrumvej 30, 6760 **Tel** *46 40 00 02*   **Map** *B5*

Located 15 km (9.5 miles) east of Ribe, right in the marshes, this popular hotel restaurant has several 19th-century dining rooms and space to seat 120 guests. The menu is Danish in flavour, and includes some good beef and fish dishes. The selection of local cheeses is another highlight.

RY Hotel Julsø
     🔲 ⫙ Ⓥ   Ⓚ Ⓚ Ⓚ
Julsøvej 14–16, 8680 **Tel** *86 89 80 40*   **Map** *C4*

Housed in a former hotel in the heart of the Danish lake district, Hotel Julsø is known for its experimental gourmet cuisine – their Adventure Menu changes every couple of months and might include dishes such as pigeon roulade with foie gras torrone. The fare is international, with an Italian twist. Highly recommended.

SILKEBORG Angus Steak House
     🔲 ⫙   Ⓚ Ⓚ Ⓚ
Christian d.8 Vej 7, 8600 **Tel** *86 82 28 54*   **Map** *C4*

Located in the heart of town, this family-friendly steakhouse serves a variety of grilled meat dishes, as well as fish. The decor is bright and cheery, and the desserts, such as pancakes with ice cream and fresh fruit, are definitely worth saving space for. There is also a good selection of wines.

SILKEBORG Piaf
     🔲 ⟩   Ⓚ Ⓚ Ⓚ Ⓚ Ⓚ
Nygade 31, 8600 **Tel** *86 81 12 55*   **Map** *C4*

Named because of the owner's resemblance to the French cabaret singer Edith Piaf, this popular restaurant strives to be a little different. Chef Marc Noël grew up in the south of France and brings a distinctive Mediterranean influence to his dishes. Fish and seafood are the highlights of the menu, which includes a six-course fish extravaganza.

TØNDER Torvets
     🔲 ⫙ Ⓥ   Ⓚ Ⓚ Ⓚ Ⓚ
Storegade 1, 6270 **Tel** *74 72 43 73*   **Map** *B6*

Situated in a former bank on the market square, this restaurant offers a wide selection of dishes in its restaurant and bistro. The restaurant is more upmarket and consequently more expensive, while the bistro offers a range of *smørrebrød*, pickled herring and pasta dishes. A large salad bar is available.

TØNDER Schackenborg Slotskro
     🔲   Ⓚ Ⓚ Ⓚ Ⓚ Ⓚ
Slotsgade 42, 6270 **Tel** *74 73 83 83*   **Map** *B6*

Prince Joachim, who lives in the nearby Schackenborg Slot, has designated this restaurant as his official royal inn. The hotel's gourmet restaurant is highly regarded and serves a mix of French and Danish cuisine. The local marsh lamb and shrimps are particularly good. Reservations are recommended.

VEJLE Merlot
     🔲 ⫙ Ⓥ   Ⓚ Ⓚ Ⓚ Ⓚ Ⓚ
Skyttehusgade 42, 7100 **Tel** *75 83 88 44*   **Map** *B4*

This small intimate restaurant, situated in a historic building, serves a selection of French food and wines. Particularly fine are the *foie gras* and the delicious desserts. For wine lovers, the Merlot also has its own wine shop. In summer, outdoor tables are available.

ÅBENRA Royal
     ⫙ ⟩   Ⓚ Ⓚ Ⓚ
Nørretorv 1, 6200 **Tel** *74 62 03 30*   **Map** *C6*

Located in the town's oldest hotel, the Royal serves sumptuous roast beef, grilled meats and hamburgers all at reasonable prices. It is renowned for its quick and efficient service. It is wise to book in advance, as it is popular with locals and tourists alike.

Key to Price Guide *see p268* **Key to Symbols** *see back cover flap*

ÅBENRÅ Knapp

Stennevej 79, Stollig, 6200 **Tel** *74 62 00 92*

Map *C6*

A smart hotel-restaurant situated in a former water mill that offers an extensive menu, formal but friendly atmosphere and excellent service, which makes you instantly feel expected. Its small size, only 35 places, adds an air of intimacy. Good for a romantic meal.

AARHUS Italia

Åboulevarden 9, 8000 **Tel** *86 19 80 22*

Map *D4*

The classic Italian cuisine on offer here includes pasta, grilled meat and fish. The pizzas, cooked in a wood-fired oven, are especially good. Not only that but there is an excellent Italian buffet, the prices are low, and the setting truly romantic. Italian all the way.

AARHUS Kähler Spisesalon

MP Bruuns Gade 33, 8000 **Tel** *86 12 20 53*

Map *D4*

A small Parisian-style brasserie decorated with mirrors, Kähler has redesigned the traditional Danish open sandwich. It serves these and other items with poetic names such as Wild Spring, Golden Delight and Midsummer by Constable. This is also a great place for the breakfast buffet and weekend brunch. Located a short walk from the train station.

AARHUS Olive

Kaløgade 2, 8000 **Tel** *86 12 95 61*

Map *D4*

Drawing inspiration from southern European cuisines, the menu in this cosy restaurant is small but varied. Reasonably priced and with the chance to bring your own bottle of wine, Olive is a popular place to eat and can get crowded and somewhat noisy at the weekends. The desserts are simply divine.

AARHUS Jacob's BarBQ

Vestergade 3, 8000 **Tel** *87 32 24 20*

Map *D4*

The restaurant is situated in an attractive 18th-century merchant's house. The menu consists mainly of grilled meats and a selection of fish dishes. Once you have finished your meal, you can move on to the bar where there is live piano music from Tuesday until Saturday, and dancing from 11pm at weekends.

AARHUS Navigator

Marselisborg Havnevej 46D, 8000 **Tel** *86 20 20 58*

Map *D4*

A lively restaurant in the Marselisborg marina, with splendid views of the sea, Navigator serves the catch of the day, as well as perfectly cooked Danish-French staples in tune with the seasons. When the weather permits, there is an outdoor grill and salad bar. It is necessary to book in advance.

AARHUS Dauphine

Frederiksgade 43, 8000 **Tel** *86 19 39 22*

Map *D4*

Rapidly gaining a reputation for its experimental cuisine using the finest ingredients, the Dauphine offers a constantly changing French-based menu in a pleasant, relaxed atmosphere. Foie gras and local cheeses are two of the highlights, and the food is accompanied by an extensive wine list.

AARHUS L'Estragon

Klostergade 6, 8000 **Tel** *86 12 40 66*

Map *D4*

Located in the heart of the city's Latin quarter, this intimate restaurant concentrates on producing high-quality French food using the best of local ingredients. The atmosphere is cosy, with only 22 guests, and on Sundays the menu extends to classic as well as experimental dishes.

NORTHERN JUTLAND

ERSLEV Øst Vildsund Gl. Færgekro

Sundbyvej 238, Sundby, 7950 **Tel** *97 74 60 67*

Map *B2*

Serving traditional Danish cuisine, this cosy little inn is located at a former ferry landing (now the Vildsund Bridge). The house speciality is fjord eels, which are sourced locally and served between May and November, but there is also a nice selection of *smørrebrod*, meat balls and fried and grilled fish dishes. Reservations recommended.

FREDERIKSHAVN Nikolines Cafeteria

Nordvej 4, 9900 **Tel** *98 47 90 16*

Map *D1*

Fast service and a wide selection of filling food are offered by this classic Danish café-restaurant. The menu is simple and unfussy, and there are many dishes that will appeal to children. Every Sunday they serve a traditional Danish meal of pork and red cabbage with potatoes and sauce.

FREDERIKSHAVN Møllehuset

Skovalléen 45, 9900 **Tel** *98 43 44 00*

Map *D1*

Ideal for coffee, lunch or an evening meal, the idyllic Møllehuset, housed in a former mill dating back to 1750, offers a mainly Danish *à la carte* menu with a good selection of dishes, all of which are made from fresh ingredients. Their Oriental Surf 'n' Turf (chicken breast and shrimps with pineapple curry sauce and fries) is recommended.

GRENEN De 2 Have
⊗⊗⊗⊗

Fyrvej 42, 9990 **Tel** *98 44 24 35*
Map *D1*

Located in Grenen, the northernmost tip of Jutland, this restaurant enjoys beautiful views of where the two seas meet (hence the name). The Cool Climate Menu relies heavily on fish and seafood caught in local waters and cooked with herbs and flowers. There is also a gastropub for a more affordable lunch menu. Reservations recommended.

HJØRRING Jensens Bøfhus
🔥 🏃 ⊗⊗⊗

Sankt Olai Plads 1, 9800 **Tel** *98 90 35 55*
Map *D1*

One of the Bøfhus chain, known for using only top-quality meat, this reliable, centrally located restaurant serves tasty grilled meat and stews as well as a variety of tempting desserts. The atmosphere is cosy and relaxed, the salad bar extensive, and there is a good children's menu.

RANDERS Niels Ebbesens Spisehus
🔥 🏃 V ⊗⊗⊗

Storegade 13, 8900 **Tel** *86 43 32 26*
Map *D3*

The ghost of Niels Ebbesen, a local hero who is thought to have lit the fuse against German occupation in 1340, is said to roam in this house. However, do not let that put you off the restaurant's delectable offerings, which include steaks and pancakes with home-made ice cream. Outdoor serving is available in the summer.

RANDERS Fru Larsen
🔥 ➦ V ⊗⊗⊗⊗⊗

Østergade 1, 8870 Langå **Tel** *86 46 83 88*
Map *D3*

This is a small, romantic hotel-restaurant where the guests are made to feel whole-heartedly welcome. Fru Larsen is known for its exceptional quality and attention to detail: from growing their own vegetables and herbs for the table to the exquisite Nordic cuisine that they serve. The service is friendly.

SALTUM Fårup Skovhus
🔥 🏃 ⊗⊗⊗

Saltum Strandvej 63, 9493 **Tel** *98 88 11 45*
Map *C1*

Charming and reasonably priced, this restaurant has gained a good reputation over the years for its traditional kitchen. Worth trying are their *frikadeller* with rye bread and red cabbage. The varied menu provides something for all tastes.

SKAGEN McCurdies
🔥 🏃 ⊗⊗

Sct Laurirtiivej 56, 9990 **Tel** *98 44 39 00*
Map *D1*

With the Stars and Stripes on the wall, McCurdies American-influenced menu includes hot wings, barbecue spare ribs, burgers and salads, along with an excellent Mexican buffet. The decor is bright and cosy, and children are welcome. Take-away available. Wi-Fi hotspot.

SKAGEN Jakobs Café & Bar
🍴 🔥 ➦ V ⊗⊗⊗⊗⊗

Havnevej 4, 9990 **Tel** *98 44 16 90*
Map *D1*

A popular Skagen café-bar, this lively establishment has good food and often hosts live music at the weekend. The varied menu is mainly Danish in character, featuring delicacies such as bisque of Norway lobster and fresh fish. There is also a decent wine selection. When the weather allows, it is possible to eat alfresco, on the terrace.

SKØRPING Røverstuen
⊗⊗⊗⊗

Rebildvej 17B, Rebild, 9520 **Tel** *98 39 27 11*
Map *C2*

The "Robbers' Den" is found in the village of Rebild, near the Rold Skov forest. On the menu is good, hearty Danish food prepared with fresh and, where possible, locally sourced ingredients. Try the roulade of chicken breast and Serrano ham with pesto cream, or one of the steaks, served with chips and a pepper, whiskey or Bearnaise sauce.

VIBORG Bones
🔥 🏃 ⊗⊗⊗

Preislers Plads 5, 8800 **Tel** *86 60 36 66*
Map *C3*

American-style salads and steaks are the main feature of the menu at this reasonably priced chain restaurant. You can design your own burger, with all the trimmings, and choose from the extensive salad bar, before a visit to the equally tempting ice cream bar. Children's menu and playroom are provided.

VIBORG Mønsted Kro
🔥 🏃 ⊗⊗⊗

Viborgvej 43, Mønsted, 8800 **Tel** *86 64 50 17*
Map *C3*

Serving traditional Danish food, Mønsted Kro is located in a historic building in a quiet setting. The lunch menu includes excellent soups and scrumptious desserts, including home-made ice cream. The restaurant can also cater for large groups and parties.

AALBORG Duus Vinkælder
🍴 🏃 ➦ ⊗⊗⊗

Østerågade 9, 9000 **Tel** *98 12 50 56*
Map *D2*

Located in the cellar of the famous Jens Bang's Stenhus, this is a convivial restaurant and bar which serves light lunches only. Duus Vinkælder is known for its delicious *frikadeller* and summer menu, which includes a wide variety of Danish *smørrebrød*. This place is full of character and makes a good stopping-off point while sightseeing.

AALBORG Vero Gusto
➦ V ⊗⊗⊗

Ved Stranden 14–16, 9000 **Tel** *98 12 39 99*
Map *D2*

Set in an 18th-century warehouse, this gourmet Italian restaurant has a traditional menu that includes a varied selection of pasta dishes, grilled meats and pizza. All the pasta is home-made and freshly rolled each day. The Casino Aalborg shares the same address and is located downstairs.

Key to Price Guide *see p268* **Key to Symbols** *see back cover flap*

AALBORG Provence   🅰 ⟩   ⓀⓀⓀⓀ
Ved Stranden 11, 9000 **Tel** *98 13 51 33*   **Map** *D2*

Inspired by French tradition, the interior design, music and gastronomy of Provence all reflects this. The bread is imported from the world famous bakery Poilâne in Paris, while the classic menu includes soufflés, fish and meats. Several times a year the restaurant stages exhibitions with works by Danish and international artists.

AALBORG Fusion   🅰 Ⓥ   ⓀⓀⓀⓀⓀ
Strandvejen 4, 9000 **Tel** *35 12 33 31*   **Map** *D2*

Reservations are recommended at this exciting restaurant that offers a heady combination of French and Asian flavours. The floor-to-ceiling windows allow diners to admire views of the Limfjord Bridge while they enjoy fine dishes, such as roasted monkfish on bok choi with oyster sauce.

AALBORG Mortens Kro   🅴 Ⓥ   ⓀⓀⓀⓀⓀ
Mølleå 4–6, 9000 **Tel** *98 12 48 60*   **Map** *D2*

Morten Nielsen, owner and head chef, is something of a celebrity cook in Denmark. The wide-ranging menu reflects his attention to detail: your meal might include filets of red snapper with an apricot-flavoured curry sauce. Every weekend the restaurant plays host to local and international DJs.

AALBORG Restaurant Brigaderen   🅰 🅴 ⟩   ⓀⓀⓀⓀⓀ
Vesterbro 77, 9000 **Tel** *98 12 00 11*   **Map** *D2*

Bright and spacious, with cream-coloured walls and gold furnishings, Brigaderen offers Danish and international dishes on an *à la carte* menu. It is located in the Helnan Phønix Hotel, Aalborg's oldest hotel, and is known for its cosy atmosphere, excellent service and outstanding wine list. Closed on Sundays.

BORNHOLM

ALLINGE Algarve   🅰 🅴   ⓀⓀⓀ
Havnegade 9, 3770 **Tel** *56 48 11 08*

A modest inn-style restaurant with a relaxed atmosphere and good selection of beautifully prepared Danish and French favourites. The restaurant is right on the harbour in Allinge, which means it can get quite busy at night, though reservations are not a necessity.

ALLINGE Cafe Sommer   🅴 Ⓥ   ⓀⓀⓀ
Havnegade 19, 3770 **Tel** *56 48 48 49*

With its chic modern interior, Cafe Sommer is particularly well known for its fish dishes. Though the portions are rather small, all the food is well cooked and served with a smile. Ask for the scrumptious *bruschetta* appetizer, with island mushrooms, berries, rosemary and parmesan. Food is served on a terrace during the summer.

CHRISTIANSØ Christiansø Gæstgiveri   ⓀⓀⓀ
Christiansø 10, 3760 **Tel** *56 46 20 15*

Lunches here are crowded with day trippers coming over to Christiansø for a few hours, but if you are staying the night then you will be treated to a wonderful evening meal. The dishes are traditional Danish prepared with an island flare. The baked cod and the salt-fried herring seasoned with island-grown sloe schnapps are especially tasty.

GUDHJEM Gudhjem Røgeri   🅰   Ⓚ
Ejner Mikkelsensvej 9, 3760 **Tel** *56 48 57 08*

The best place in Bornholm to try Sol Over Gudhjem, a *smørrebrød* sandwich with herring, onion and egg that is surprisingly tasty. If it is fish you are after, then there are nearly a dozen varieties, depending on the day's catch. The best option is to buy inside and then picnic on the harbourside. Live music in July.

GUDHJEM Pandekagehuset   🅴 ⟩ Ⓥ   Ⓚ
Brøddegade 15, 3760 **Tel** *56 48 55 17*

A great place for a quick bite, this roadside *crêperie* serves great savoury and sweet pancakes. The fillings include everything from mushrooms and local cheese to peaches, chocolate and almonds. There is diner-style seating inside, or you can sit outside at one the cast-iron tables and watch the world go by.

GUDHJEM Bokulhus   🅰 🅴 Ⓥ   ⓀⓀⓀ
Bokulvej 4, 3760 **Tel** *56 48 52 97*

Situated in a large estate on top of a hill, Bokulhus serves a great mix of traditional Danish cuisine and local island specialities. It is worth trying one of their sampler plates, which give a taste of local herring, shrimp and Bornholm cheeses; alternatively, there are tuna and cod main courses. The dining room looks out onto a beautiful garden.

HASLE Silderøgeriet   🅰   Ⓚ
Fælledvej 53, 3790 **Tel** *56 96 44 11*

Characterized by the island's traditional four-chimney design, this smokehouse is a characterful place where you can sample the catch of the day. Inexpensive fish, such as mackerel, herring and salmon, are served as pre-prepared fillets ready to eat inside or to take with you down to the harbour.

HASLE Le Port
Vang 81, 3790 **Tel** *56 96 92 01*

A traditional restaurant offering excellent food in a spectacular location overlooking the sea and Hammerhus Slot, perfect for a romantic sunset dinner. During the summer, diners can sit out on the terrace and choose one of several French dishes that are Le Port's speciality. The lunch menu, which is served until 3pm, is a cheaper option.

NEXØ Dueodde Badehotel
Sirenevej 2, 3730 **Tel** *56 48 86 49*

Set within one of the best beach hotels on the island, this café-restaurant offers a hearty salad buffet and light sandwich-based meals during the day. On summer evenings, fresh fish and meats are cooked on a mesquite-fired barbecue on the beach – well worth staying around for.

RØNNE Casa Mia
Antoniestræde 3, 3700 **Tel** *56 95 95 73*

Run by a born-and-bred Italian who has since settled on Bornholm, the rustic-style decor of Casa Mia recalls a Tuscan countryside inn, with lots of authentic decorations on the walls. The pizza and pasta dishes here are excellently prepared and well priced too. Closed Tue.

RØNNE Fyrtøjet
Store Torvegade 22, 3700 **Tel** *56 95 30 12*

Popular for its buffets, this restaurant serves international staples, such as *coq au vin*, as well as many local Bornholm specialities including grilled Baltic salmon. The atmosphere is very bright and airy, and there is an abundant salad bar. Good weekend brunch. Closed Sun, Mon.

RØNNE Di 5 Stâuerna
Strandvejen 116, 3700 **Tel** *56 90 44 44*

Spread across five separate rooms inside the Radisson Blu hotel, this popular restaurant is known for its award-winning chefs and superb Danish-French cuisine. All the dishes on the menu are top-notch and there is also a very impressive wine cellar.

SVANEKE Pakhuset
Brænderigænget 3, 3740 **Tel** *56 49 65 85*

Just off Svaneke's market square, Pakhuset is known for its steaks, which they serve with many different sauces, including Bearnaise, chilli, onion and blue cheese. There are also fish and vegetarian options. Especially popular with families just back from the beach.

SVANEKE Bryghuset
Torvet 5, Havnebryggen 12, 3740 **Tel** *56 49 73 21*

Right on the central square in Svaneke, where there is always lots of lively goings-on, the Bryghuset's typically Danish menu includes braised lamb, breast of chicken with a creamy pepper sauce, and marinated and grilled spare ribs, which can be washed down with beer from the restaurant's own brewery.

ÅKIRKEBY Restaurant Kadeau
Baunevej 18, Vestre Sømark, Pedersker, 3720 **Tel** *56 97 82 50*

Open only from early May until mid-September, this restaurant offers Nordic-inspired food prepared with local produce. Kadeau is located right on the coast, and diners can enjoy splendid ocean views while sampling dishes such as seasonal fish with hollandaise sauce and dill, or Piggy-Wiggy (pork loin and brisket). Book ahead.

GREENLAND

ILULISSAT Ulo
Hotel Arctic, Postcode 1501, 3952 **Tel** *94 41 53*

The restaurant attached to the Hotel Arctic has superb views of icebergs afloat in the bay. The menu includes international dishes as well as Greenlandic shrimps and other good fish platters. In the summer, weekend parties are held out on the deck.

ILULISSAT Mamartut
Sermermiut Aqqutaat 4, P.O. Box 487, 3952 **Tel** *94 51 00*

Probably the best place to eat in Ilulissat, Mamartut offers friendly service and fresh local produce – try, for example, the musk ox burger or the local ammassat, a herring-like fish. A huge Greenlandic buffet is offered mid-week during the summer, when it's also possible to sit outside on the terrace. Open 6–10pm Mon–Sat.

KANGERLUSSUAQ Roklubben
3910 **Tel** *84 19 96 or 52 45 26*

Just south of Kangerlussuaq on the shores of the idyllic Lake Tasersuatsiaq (Lake Ferguson), the "Rowing Club" serves local dishes, including fried reindeer fillet and marinated musk ox. After a meal, you can walk or cycle around the lake to see reindeer and musk oxen grazing. A great spot to catch the Northern Lights. Hourly buses from town.

Key to Price Guide *see p268* **Key to Symbols** *see back cover flap*

NUUK Isikkivik

Narsaviaq 2G 1sal, 3905 **Tel** 34 85 06

Set in Nuussuaq, just outside of central Nuuk by the marina, this canteen-style restaurant has simple, well-cooked meals that include burgers and pizzas, though you can also get a decent fixed-price meal. The tables have pleasant views across the harbour.

NUUK Charoen Porn

Aqqusinersuaq 5, 3900 **Tel** 32 57 59

Alongside some excellent Thai dishes and several types of sushi, expect to find a few unique dishes here, including whale meat and crocodile satay. Their renowned "Greenlandic coffee" consists of coffee, sugar and three different spirits topped with whipped cream. The decor is "pan-Asian" which makes a nice change from Danish-Greenlandic.

NUUK Nipisa

Hans Egedesvej 29, 1. sal, 3900 **Tel** 32 12 10

Nuuk's premiere dining spot manages at the same time to feel wonderfully low-key. The menu features lamb, reindeer, musk ox and fish. All the dishes are elegantly prepared and served, and some even border on works of art. The traditional lunch dishes are more affordable. Reservations a must.

UUMMANNAQ Hotel Uummannaq

Trollep Aqqutaa B, 3961 **Tel** 95 15 18

A hotel restaurant with some spectacular views of the sea. This is really the only place in town to have a decent, sit down meal. On the menu are tasty Arctic char, caribou and lamb dishes, as well as a few standard international dishes including pasta and burgers.

THE FAROE ISLANDS

EYSTUROY Gjáargarður

Gjógv, 476 **Tel** 42 31 71

In the summer months (May–Sep), this eco-friendly hotel in the northernmost village on Eysturoy opens its restaurant to outside visitors, as well as guests, between 6 and 8pm. It is also open for Sunday lunch, breakfast or just a late afternoon coffee and cake break while hiking through the mountains. Closed dinner Oct–Apr; Jan, Dec.

KLAKSVIK Hereford

Klaksvíksvegur 45, 700 **Tel** 45 64 34

An atmospheric old steakhouse with lots of rustic charm. The menu is full of scrumptious steak dishes and burgers, but there are also a couple of surprises such as *escargot*. The restaurant is in the same building as a popular café, great for morning coffees or a glass of island beer during the day. Closed Mon.

SUDUROY Hotel Øravik

Øravik 827 **Tel** 37 13 02

Situated in a remote, creek-side town along Suduroy's eastern coast, the Øravik occupies a rickety old building near to the town's harbour. This hotel-restaurant serves good pizzas and salads, but hold out if you can for a unique Faroese speciality: a tasty mélange of dried lamb, dried fish and whale blubber.

TÓRSHAVN Glitnir Irish Pub

Grim Kambansgøta 13, 110 **Tel** 31 90 91

Simple, reasonably priced pub food – like fish and chips or a good piece of beef or lamb – is served at Tórshavn's Irish pub, which also has a wide selection of Faroese beers in addition to the obvious Irish ones. The pub also does a weekend brunch between 10am and 2pm.

TÓRSHAVN Áarstova

Gongin 1, 100 **Tel** 21 75 10

Located in one of Tórshavn's oldest properties, the childhood home of the literary Áarstovu brothers, this charming restaurant offers one of the best gourmet experiences in the Faroes. Choose the adventurous five-course tasting menu or a local meat or fish dish from the à la carte menu. Open for dinner daily.

TÓRSHAVN Marco Polo

Sverrisgøta 12, P.O. Box 1140, 110 **Tel** 47 15 05

This casual diner in the centre of town is the ideal place for an evening with friends. The menu includes dishes such as grilled fillet of salmon with a green herb sauce, and fillet of venison served with Waldorf salad and fig confit. Marco Polo is also renowned for its griddled steaks. Reservations recommended.

TÓRSHAVN Koks

Oyggjarvegur 45, 100 **Tel** 33 39 99

Under Faroese chef Leif Sørensen, a staunch supporter of New Nordic cuisine, the restaurant of Hotel Føroyar has blossomed into a world-class eatery serving contemporary Faroese food. Memorable and expensive, the four-, six- and eight-course set menus are served with one of the best views in town. Open for dinner only; closed Sun.

SHOPPING IN DENMARK

Most major towns in Denmark have large, shopping centres and department stores such as the country-wide chain Magasin du Nord. Prices can be high, however, especially in the more exclusive shops such as those found along Strøget in Copenhagen. Many bargains on clothes can be found, especially during the post-seasonal sales. Flea markets are widespread in

Denmark. Much of what is on sale is tat, but persistence and a keen eye can sometimes uncover real treasures. The many independently run shops selling beautiful household goods satisfy the Danes' love of good design. Jewellery made from Danish amber is also popular and relatively cheap. Danish herb-flavoured *akvavit* (a kind of schnapps) comes in a variety of flavours and colours and makes a good present.

Bearded Viking toy

Busy Saturday market in Svaneke, popular with Danes and visitors

OPENING HOURS

In Denmark shopping days and opening hours are regulated due to union demands for reasonable working hours. The regulated hours are, for the most part, rigorously adhered to, although during the Christmas season and around busy tourist resorts longer openings are usual. Most shops open at 9 or 9:30am and remain open until 5:30pm Monday to Thursday. On Fridays many shops are open until 7 or 8pm. On Saturdays most shops close at about 2pm; some larger shops and department stores remain open until 4pm. Most shops are closed on Sundays, but some open on the first and last Sundays of the month.

Some smaller, independent shops keep longer opening hours. Stores attached to

petrol stations and kiosks found in town centres remain open 24 hours but offer a limited choice of goods.

In the run-up to Christmas and other festivals many shops and department stores in the capital and in larger towns extend their opening hours and often trade on Sundays.

MARKETS

Produce markets are very popular in Denmark, often held twice weekly in most towns; one of the best is the upscale Torvehallerne market in Copenhagen (*see p100*). The Danes also relish their flea markets, which are held periodically in many towns. Genuine antiques are mixed up with piles of bric à brac.

Sign in Ærøskøbing

A morning spent at a flea market offers a trip down memory lane for many Danes and also provides a good opportunity to munch on a hot sausage from one of the many snack bars. Pre-Christmas fairs are also common. Seasonal fairs sell a variety of festive decorations including handmade wooden or knitted items, candles and colourful elves and gnomes fashioned from balls of bright wool.

VAT

The rate of VAT (known as MOMS) is 25 per cent in Denmark; this is always already included in the selling price quoted. Some goods, such as alcohol, tobacco and petrochemical products, carry an additional excise. Visitors from outside

12th-century cellars being used for wine storage

Hvide Hus – a handicraft shop in Gudhjem on Bornholm

the EU can claim a tax refund of between 13 and 19 per cent of the total price of an item on purchases over 300 Dkr. Shops operating this scheme carry a Tax Free logo. When making a purchase ask for a Global Refund certificate. The shopkeeper may ask to see a passport. On leaving the country the certificate must be stamped by a customs officer, who will need to see that the product is intact in its original packaging. The stamped certificate may be used when reclaiming VAT in allocated banks or border agencies. For more information, visit *www.taxfreeworldwide.com*.

SEASONAL REDUCTIONS

Reductions on many items can be obtained by shopping during the sales, which are known locally as "Udsalg". In Denmark, the traditional months for sales are January and June/July, although many stores shift their dates by one or two weeks either way. Sales are also held to mark the anniversary of a shop's opening or even the founding of a chain. As with most promotions, it pays to be cautious, however, as reductions can often be quite insignificant or apply only to a limited number of goods.

METHODS OF PAYMENT

Cash is the easiest form of payment but for larger sums it is safer to use credit cards, which are widely accepted throughout the country. Cards can be used in many shops, restaurants, hotels and museums. This method of payment carries a small surcharge.

CONTEMPORARY DESIGN

Denmark is famous for its cutting edge design of ceramics, contemporary furniture and home accessories. Copenhagen has a wealth of independent outlets, but many brands are available throughout the country. The price of such merchandise can be high, especially for items by major designers, but smaller, more affordable items are available such as glasses by Bodum, silver Christmas tree decorations by Georg Jensen, cheese cutters or small porcelain items.

FOOD PRODUCTS

Many types of cheese are produced in Denmark so there is no excuse for sticking to a simple Danish blue. Those who like sharp-tasting cheeses should go for "Gamle Ole". This strongly flavoured cheese goes particularly well with Danish rye bread, a dense and healthy loaf made with seeds and grains.

For those with a sweet tooth, chocolates and sweets are also well worth seeking out. Often these are handmade,

beautifully presented and far superior to the mass-produced variety. Hand-made boiled sweets are also good quality.

One of the Danes' favourite foodstuffs is pickled herring, which is served on its own and often on bread as *smørrebrød*. Many different recipes are used when marinating the fish to produce a wide range of tastes. Smoked fish, especially from Bornholm, is also popular.

The southern region of Jutland is famous for its meat products, which include salamis of various flavours and seasonings, all of which are delicious.

Assorted coffee-related gadgets such as grinders and percolators are often on sale in coffee shops, which sell a bewildering range of roasted beans from around the world.

ALCOHOLIC DRINKS

While in Denmark it is worth sampling *akvavit* (a form of schnapps). Many regions, and even individual restaurants, have their own special recipes for these flavoursome drinks, which are then sold as *husets snaps*. Visitors can, for instance, savour an Aalborg Porse flavoured with Jutland herbs. As well as *akvavit*, Denmark produces some excellent beers (*see p266*). Some of the lesser known brands and dark beers are worth trying, and make a welcome alternative to the ubiquitous light Pilsners.

An antique shop in Copenhagen

ENTERTAINMENT IN DENMARK

Denmark is a vibrant country with a wide range of culture and entertainment on offer. Clubs and bars promote all kinds of music from mainstream pop and jazz to the latest in alternative sounds, while venues such as Det Kongelige Teater (The Royal Theatre) put on world-class theatre and ballet. Summer time is the season for a number of high-profile festivals such as Roskilde's rock festival in

Viking Festival

early July. Local festivals include re-creations of Denmark's Viking past. Cinemas can be found in most towns and often screen English language films with Danish subtitles. Sport, too, is popular, and Danish soccer clubs are among the best in Europe. Children are sure to enjoy a visit to one of the country's amusement parks, including LEGOLAND®. For entertainment in Copenhagen see pages 102–105.

Pierrot, Harlequin and Columbine at Tivoli

THEATRE, MUSIC AND DANCE

A visit to the theatre is one of the most popular pastimes in Denmark. Cultural life blossoms throughout the country, and university towns, such as Aarhus, Aalborg and Odense, have much to offer.

Aarhus is the biggest cultural centre after Copenhagen and has the **Musikhuset Aarhus**, a modern concert hall with four venues that stages musical and dance performances. It is home to Den Jyske Opera (The Jutland Opera) and the Jutland Symphony. Aalborg, in northern Jutland, has the cultural centre Nordkraft and a resident symphony orchestra, which often gives concerts in the **Aalborg Kongres og Kulturcenter**.

In Odense, the **Odense Koncerthus** has a regular programme of classical music, which includes performances of music by Carl Nielsen

(1865–1931), a native of the city.

Most large towns have a hall putting on concerts, theatre, ballet and modern dance performances. During the summer, Denmark hosts a number of open-air concerts, often in the grounds of manor houses. People bring along picnics for an evening of opera or classical music. There are also several rock, pop and folk music festivals. Visit *http://live-music.dk* for more details of live music in Denmark.

AMUSEMENT PARKS

Denmark's amusement parks provide entertainment for children and adults alike. The parks are open mainly

in summer, although some of them start their season earlier. One of the most famous is **LEGOLAND®** in central Jutland *(see pp192–3)*, which includes LEGO® sculptures along with high-octane rides. As with many of Denmark's amusement parks, the admission price to LEGOLAND® includes free use of all the attractions. Less high-profile amusement parks are dotted throughout the country and include fairgrounds, water parks and science centres. **BonBon-Land** in southern Zealand *(see p157)*, for instance, is packed with rides and amusements as is **Fårup Sommerland** in northern Jutland *(see p204)*.

In addition to its traditional zoos, Denmark has numerous safari parks and aquariums where visitors can see wild animals and aquatic creatures. Two of the best known are **Knuthenborg Safari Park**

Miniature buildings in LEGOLAND®

Royal Theatre performance in Copenhagen *(see p69)*

(see pp160–61) and Esbjerg's **Fiskeri-og Søfartsmuseet** aquarium *(see p194).*

NIGHTLIFE

The best clubs, apart from Copenhagen, are in university towns, such as Aarhus, Aalborg and Odense, where they cater for the exacting demands of the student population. Among the most popular places in Aarhus are **Train**, **VoxHall** and **Musikcaféen**, which play a mixture of rock and techno depending on the night. In Aalborg **Skråen** and **The Irish House** have a lively feel. Two of the best clubs in Odense are **Posten** and **Jazzhus Dexter**. The latter has live jazz at the weekend.

Performances in Danish music venues range from local bands to major acts from abroad. Many concerts are free although prices can be fairly steep for the biggest international names. Nightclubs are also popular and can be found even in some of the smaller towns. Clubwise, nothing really gets going until about 11pm in Denmark. Pubs and clubs usually stay open until 1am on weekdays. At weekends many of them don't close their doors until dawn.

SPECTATOR SPORTS

Football (soccer) is a passion in Denmark and the Danish national side is one of the top teams in Europe.

Watching football is a popular pastime and many games are attended by entire families. Three of the best-known clubs are **FC Midtjylland**, **FC København** and **Aalborg BK**. International matches are played at Parken, Denmark's national stadium and home ground of FC København.

Handball has quite a high profile following the gold-medal success of the women's team at the 2000 Olympics. Other common sports include ice hockey, badminton, dirt-bike racing and cycling. Gymnastics clubs are also popular, and shows and competitions are frequently advertised in smaller towns.

Feeding the seals at the Fiskeri-og Søfartsmuseet, southern Jutland

DIRECTORY

THEATRE, MUSIC AND DANCE

Granhøj Dans
Klosterport 6, 8000
Aarhus C. **Tel** 86 19 26
22. **www**.granhoj.dk

Musikhuset Aarhus
Thomas Jensens Allé,
8000 Aarhus C.
Tel 89 40 40 40.
www.musikhuset
aarhus.dk

Odense Koncerthus
Claus Bergs Gade 9,
Odense C.
Tel 62 12 13 14.

Odense Teater
Jernbanegade 21,
5100 Odense C.
Tel 62 12 00 52.
www.odenseteater.dk

Aalborg Kongres og Kulturcenter
Europaplads 4, 9000
Aalborg. **Tel** 99 35 55 66.

Aarhus Teater
Teatergaden,
8000 Aarhus C.
Tel 70 21 30 21.
www.aahusteater.dk

NIGHTLIFE

The Irish House
Østerågade 25,
9000 Aalborg.

Jazzhus Dexter
Vindegade 65,
5000 Odense C.

Musikcaféen
Mejlgade 53,
8000 Aarhus C.

Posten
Ostre Stationsvej 35,
5000 Odense C.

Skråen
Nordkraft, Kjellerup Torv 5,
9000 Aalborg.

Train
Toldbodgade 6,
8000 Aarhus C.

VoxHall
Vester Allé 15,
8000 Aarhus C.

SPECTATOR SPORTS

FC København
Parken, Øster Allé 50,
2110 Copenhagen.
Tel 35 43 74 00.
www.fck.dk

FC Midtjylland
Kaj Zartowsvej 5,
7400 Herning.
Tel 96 27 10 40.
www.fcm.dk

Aalborg BK
Hornevej 2,
9220 Aalborg Øst.
Tel 96 35 59 00.
www.aabsport.dk

OUTDOOR ACTIVITIES

The Danes are keen on sport and fitness, and many adults and most children participate in one sport or another. The country's gentle terrain and the many miles of well maintained cycle routes have helped to make cycling an integral part of Danish culture – it is not unusual for entire Danish families to embark on cycling holidays. Golfers are also well catered for and Denmark has over 100 courses, many of which can be found close to hotels and camp sites. With its many fjords, protected waters and tiny islands to explore, Denmark is a good place for sailors. The country is also ideal for water sports such as windsurfing and canoeing. The same sheltered fjords are perfect for novice windsurfers, and there are many companies near Danish holiday resorts that can arrange lessons. Horse riding and fishing are other popular activities.

A successful catch

HORSE RIDING

Equestrian pursuits are popular in Denmark and the country has a large number of riding stables. Some Danes have their own horses and keep them in community-style stables. Those who are unable to keep their own horses make use of the numerous riding clubs that offer riding lessons and provide horses for individual unsupervised rides. A small number of clubs will accept riders paying an hourly rate. Rides are also on offer in beach resorts such as Rømø, Thy and Løkken.

A good way for beginners to learn about riding and looking after horses is to sign up for a farm holiday (*see p243*), some of which include riding lessons and accompanied treks through the countryside. Riding holidays on Icelandic

Horse riding – a popular pastime in Denmark

horses (the traditional Viking horse) are available in Mols National Park.

For something a little different, it is possible to travel the country by wagon. Four to six people can usually be carried in the wagons, which are hired complete with horses from companies such as **Prærievognsferie Og Hesteud-lejning** on Funen. Training is provided and the wagon is equipped with everything that travellers might need while on the road. A map is supplied marking the route to the camp site, where there is pasture for horses and often a welcoming bonfire. Prairie wagon holidays can be great fun, particularly for children. Contact **Dansk Ride Forbund** (The Danish Equestrian Federation) for details of activities in the area you are visiting.

For those who prefer to spectate, horse races are held in several towns, including Klampenborg, Aarhus, Fyn, Aalborg and Bornholm.

Horse and driver on a carriage racetrack

WATER SPORTS

The many Danish lakes and some 7,300 km (4,536 miles) of coastline make Denmark a perfect location for water sports enthusiasts. Equipment for windsurfing, water skiing and sea kayaking can be hired in waterside resorts, as can jet skis and other gear. In Silkeborg it is possible to book canoeing holidays.

Visitors intending to take up some form of water sport should check in advance whether the region they plan to visit allows for such pursuits – for example, water skiing is prohibited in some ecologically sensitive areas.

FISHING

Denmark is an ideal destination for anglers. Its many streams and lakes are well maintained and have healthy stocks of fish including plentiful supplies of pike and trout both for coarse and fly-

Windsurfers making the most of Denmark's coastal waters

fishing. The long coastline is also good for saltwater fishing and anglers can hope to catch sea trout, plaice, mackerel and cod. Anglers between the age of 18 and 67 must carry an appropriate licence. These are sold at post offices, tourist information offices and shops that sell angling equipment; they are also available at *www.fisketegn.dk*. Licences are issued for one day, one week or annually and cost 40, 130 and 185 Dkr respectively. Fishing in lakes and streams requires the permission of the owner, which often is the local angling club. Tourist offices will have details of angling holidays and some camp sites are especially geared for anglers with rooms set aside for gutting and cleaning fish.

Anyone fishing in Denmark will be expected to know the regulations concerning the size and types of species that may be caught. Some clubs may impose restrictions concerning the number or the total weight of the catch.

Those keen on deep-sea fishing can join the crew of a fishing vessel and head out to offshore fishing grounds, such as Gule Rev, in the North Sea off Hanstholm. The cutter **T-248 Skagerak** sails to this reef daily (weather permitting).

Anyone interested in a fishing holiday in Denmark should contact the local tourist office. The website *www.fiskekort.dk* provides maps of good fishing areas.

MOTORCYCLE TOURS

Touring around Denmark by motorcycle is a pleasant way to get to know the country. Traffic is reasonably light and many Danes are themselves keen motorcyclists.

Motorcycle rallies, known as *motorcykeltrief*, are organized countrywide. The size of events varies from small weekly meetings to large rallies that feature live music and competitions for the most impressive bikes. Major events can last days and attract locals as well as foreign enthusiasts.

Denmark has a network of scenic roads known as the Marguerite Route, which takes in some of the most beautiful parts of the country. The route consists mostly of secondary and minor roads and is marked on road signs by a white daisy on a brown background *(see p308)*. Maps mark the route with green dots or a green line.

Anyone travelling in Denmark on a motorcycle should take into account the wind, which at times can be very strong and make riding difficult and sometimes even hazardous. When crossing bridges, particularly over some of the long straits, the wind can be especially strong and take the form of sudden and unexpected gusts. When strong winds prevail, motorcyclists may be banned from using these bridges.

Motorcyclists in Denmark must adhere to the highway code. Riders and passengers are required by law to wear helmets and carry the necessary documentation.

Cyclists on one of the country's many cycling routes

CYCLING

Riding a bike is a hugely popular activity in Denmark and the lowland areas especially are excellent regions for a cycling holiday, as is the island of Bornholm *(see p227)*. The whole country is criss-crossed with an extensive network of cycling routes. It is easy to plan a journey and routes take in most of the big towns and cities as well as more rural parts of the country.

Organized cycle races are common in Denmark. Many cover short distances and are open to amateurs. Races for elite riders include the Grand Prix Aalborg and the prestigious CSC Classic, where teams compete to earn points for use on the world ranking list. Races such as the CSC Classic are for serious competitors only.

Bikers and bikes at an annual motorcycle rally

Playing the green at a golf club near Gilleleje, northwestern Zealand

CYCLING TOURS

Cycling is an excellent way to tour Denmark, and enthusiasts are very well catered for. Specialist bicycle shops are found throughout the country. Alongside traditional touring bikes, they sell the very latest in cycling equipment. Dedicated cycling maps make planning a cycling tour fairly straightforward. Maps are widely available and cover virtually every part of the country. The maps include not only cycle routes but all the major sights along the way such as museums and castles. In addition, they indicate which roads have cycle paths and on which roads it is forbidden or too dangerous to ride. Cycling maps are useful in a number of other ways. They often include details of camp sites and hostels, for instance, as well as grocery stores. Maps can be ordered from **Dansk**

Cyklist Forbund (The Danish Cycling Federation) as well as from bookshops and tourist offices.

The Dansk Cyklist Forbund can also provide details of packaged cycling tours. Tours can be expensive but they have the advantage of providing suitable cycles and organizing the accommodation along the route. Tour operators often arrange for luggage to be carried, so that riders need not be weighed down by tents and other items.

There are several places in Denmark where visitors can hire a bicycle; the local tourist office will be able to help. Larger towns usually have free city bikes available for short rides. Finding someone to fix a bike is easy. Most cycling maps include details of cycle workshops where minor repairs such as mending a punctured tyre or fixing a spoke can be carried out quickly and cheaply.

Tandem bicycle, popular in Denmark

GOLF

Denmark has more than 100 golf courses. Most of them will honour the membership card of your own club, and most clubs admit novices as well as experienced players. Green fees vary but are fairly reasonable, averaging around 300 Dkr per day (370 Dkr at weekends). Buying a package golfing holiday that also includes accommodation can work out cheaper. Golf clubs generally hire and sell golfing equipment and also run improvement courses for all levels. The **Dansk Golf Union** can provide information about the country's golf courses.

SAILING

The waters around Denmark are dotted with islands, many of which have harbours in which to moor a boat. The coastline is highly diversified and there is plenty of scope for sailing at all levels of ability. Storms and gales are uncommon in bodies of water such as the sea between Zealand and Lolland as well as many of the fjords and these calm, forgiving conditions are perfect for less experienced sailors and novices.

If you wish to hire a sailing boat in Denmark, local tourist offices will be able to point you in the direction of a reputable company.

All craft intended for charter must carry a seaworthiness certificate issued by the State Inspectorate of Shipping. When chartering a boat, it is important to ask to see this certificate before sailing.

Sailing boats, a common sight on Danish waters

Coastal dunes, an ideal area for walks

BOAT CRUISES

Boat cruises are popular in Denmark and depart regularly from Nyhavn in Copenhagen, bound for the islands situated in the Øresund (Sound). It is even possible to book a cruise on a reconstructed Viking ship. Stationed in Roskilde harbour are several small ships that are faithful copies of 10th-century wooden Viking boats and these embark on regular cruises. Cruises of the lakes and rivers are another option. One popular jaunt is to jump aboard one of the small ships that depart from Ry harbour on a cruise along the Gudena river. Another alternative is to take a trip back in time on the *Hjejlen*, a paddle steamer that travels daily from Silkeborg to Himmelbjerget. A trip on one of the many ferries that link the various islands can be considered a pleasant cruise too.

WALKING

Walking trails in Denmark are clearly signposted, with information boards giving the names of the destination points and the length of the route. In Denmark the public have conditional access to the coast even if the land is privately owned. Many signed walks follow the shoreline and are especially beautiful. The country's forests are also good for walking. Some marked trails lead across private land. When this is the case it is important to stick to the trail, otherwise walkers risk being arrested (although this is highly unlikely). Many routes are through nature reserves and may be marked with the sign of a daisy. Tourist offices and libraries often have brochures listing some of Denmark's best walks. The town of Viborg has a walking festival along old drove and army roads.

Denmark's hostels and inns are used to catering for the needs of walkers, as are the country's camp sites. **Dansk Vandrelaug** (The Danish Ramblers Association) provides maps (in Danish) for visitors.

SWIMMING

Denmark has many beautiful beaches. Most are ideal for swimming although the temperature can be on the chilly side. Even in summer, the water temperature rarely rises above 17° C (63° F). As an alternative, virtually all cities and major towns have swimming baths, which are well maintained.

Children may enjoy a visit to one of the many water parks, such as **Fårup Sommerland** (*see p204*) and **Joboland** (*see p226*), which have splash pools and waterslides.

DIRECTORY

VisitDenmark
www.visitdenmark.com

SPORTING ORGANIZATIONS

Dansk Idræt Forbund
Idrættens Hus, Brøndby Stadion 20, 2605 Brøndby.
Tel 43 26 26 26.
www.dif.dk

HORSE RIDING

Dansk Ride Forbund
Idrættens Hus, Brøndby Stadion 20, 2605 Brøndby.
Tel 43 26 28 28.
www.rideforbund.dk

Prærievognsferie Og Hesteudlejning
Holmdrup Huse 3, 5881 Skårup, Funen.
Tel 62 23 18 25.

FISHING

Danmarks Sportsfiskerforbund
Skyltevej 4, Vingsted, 7082 Bredsten.
Tel 75 82 06 99.
www.sportsfiskeren.dk

T-248 Skagerak
Vorupør Strand, 7700 Thisted.
Tel 97 93 85 77.
www.skagerak-t248.dk

CYCLING TOURS

Bornholm Velcomstcenter (Visitors Centre)
Nordre Kystvej 3, 3700 Rønne.
Tel 56 95 95 00.
www.bornholminfo.dk

Dansk Cyklist Forbund
Rømersgade 5, 1362 Copenhagen K.
Tel 33 32 31 21.
www.dcf.dk

GOLF

Dansk Golf Union
Idrættens Hus, Brøndby Stadion 20, 2605 Brøndby.
Tel 43 26 27 00.
www.danskgolfunion.dk
www.golf.dk

WALKING

Dansk Vandrelaug
Kultorvet 7, DK-1175 Copenhagen K.
Tel 33 12 11 65.
www.dvl.dk

SURVIVAL
GUIDE

PRACTICAL INFORMATION 296–303

TRAVEL INFORMATION 304–313

PRACTICAL INFORMATION

Large numbers of holiday-makers travel to Denmark each year, drawn by the wide range of attractions and accommodation on offer. The peak season is relatively short, however, since the winter months are cold and daylight hours few. The country has a good tourism infrastructure, with a network of efficient tourist offices. Information is easy to obtain, especially on the Internet, and planning a trip should be a straightforward undertaking, since most hotels and attractions have excellent English websites. Denmark's hotels and inns are welcoming and clean, as are the many good-value camp sites and hostels. The major museums and galleries display world-class collections, accompanied by English-language displays, guidebooks and even digital guides and apps to help visitors get the most from the exhibits.

Bicycling tourists

WHEN TO GO

The best time to visit Denmark is during the milder months (mid-April–mid-October) or in December, when most of the country's towns and villages sparkle with festive Christmas decorations. The ideal time for cycling holidays is between mid-June and late August.

Most Danes go on holiday between late June and mid-August, to coincide with school vacations. During this time the camp sites, beaches and resorts tend to be full. A good time to visit, then, is in mid-August, after the schools have reopened – the beaches and attractions are less busy, but the days are still warm.

VISAS AND PASSPORTS

EU citizens do not need a visa to enter Denmark; visitors from other parts of the world should check if their country has reciprocal agreements on waiving visa requirements. Visitors not obliged to have a visa are allowed to stay in Denmark for up to 90 days.

Contact your embassy in an emergency, such as the loss of your passport or a motoring accident. However, note that embassies expect you to have your own travel insurance *(see p299)*, and they are not likely to help if you have been jailed or fined for committing a crime. Most embassies are in Copenhagen, but there are some in other cities too – visit the **Ministry of Foreign Affairs** website for a list.

CUSTOMS INFORMATION

The customs allowance for EU visitors travelling to Denmark is 800 cigarettes and 10 litres of spirits; for people travelling from non-EU countries, it is 200 cigarettes and 1 litre of spirits. All food articles must be vacuum-packed by the manufacturer. Commercial quantities and presents of a value exceeding 1,350 Dkr are subject to customs duty.

There is no limit – within reason – on how much alcohol or tobacco EU citizens can take out of the country. US citizens are allowed to take home $400 worth of goods before duty must be paid.

TOURIST INFORMATION

Most Danish towns have tourist information centres with multilingual staff. They can supply maps and information on local sights, festivals and events; they will also hand out free pamphlets containing information on hotels, cycling routes, walking trails and disabled access to various attractions. In smaller towns with no tourist centres, visitors can usually get information from their hotel. The official website of the Danish Tourist Board, **VisitDenmark**, is also very useful.

Aarhus, Denmark's second-largest city, relies heavily on QR tags and the Internet to deliver information to tourists.

Sign for a historical site

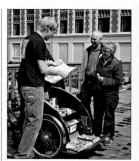

Tourist information at the Shopping Street in Aarhus

ADMISSION PRICES AND OPENING HOURS

Some museums and historic attractions, especially those in Copenhagen, waive admission charges once a week (usually on Wednesday). In larger cities, visitors can purchase passes that combine reduced entry fees to museums and other attractions with unlimited use of public transport *(see p310)*.

Many museums and galleries are closed on Monday, while some art museums, such as Louisiana and Aarhus' AroS, stay open late on selected days.

Shops are usually open 9am–5:30pm; on Friday they close at 7 or 8pm, and on Saturday any time between noon and 4pm. Most shops are closed on Sunday, though some larger stores open on the first and last Sundays of the month. In tourist resorts, shops are generally open seven days a week during July and August.

Danish churches are open only on certain days and between certain hours, so it is wise to check in advance. Note that churches are closed to sightseers during services.

Tourist attractions often make seasonal changes to their opening hours. Some attractions and seaside restaurants close completely in January and February, while many restaurants and cafés in Copenhagen close in July.

TRAVELLERS WITH SPECIAL NEEDS

With a little forward planning, travellers with special needs should find a holiday in Denmark straightforward and enjoyable. Modern holiday centres, hotels, museums and other attractions generally provide wheelchair-accessible ramps and lifts, as well as facilities for the visually and hearing-impaired. However, hotels, museums and restaurants located in older buildings may not have such resources, and so you could find you have to negotiate stairs at street level and face space restrictions. It pays to check well in advance, either online or by phone.

TRAVELLING WITH CHILDREN

Hotels, holiday centres and cottage letting agencies in Denmark will often provide travel cots, high chairs, and garden toys such as swings. Taking children to a restaurant is perfectly acceptable, though it's best to go before 8pm.

Restaurants generally have children's menus, high chairs and changing facilities.

Most buses and stations on the public transport network are equipped with lifts that allow easy access for buggies.

TRAVELLING ON A BUDGET

Farm holidays and B&Bs offer fairly cheap accommodation, as do camp sites and hostels. YHA hostels have private rooms as well as dorms, and camp sites often offer accommodation in wooden chalets, a cheaper alternative to summer houses. Note that there is a charge at all Danish official camp sites; a free solution is to pitch a tent at a "nature camp" with only basic amenities (running water and a public toilet). See the VisitDenmark website for more information. **CouchSurfing** is free of charge, and is also a fun way to meet local people.

Savings can be made on train travel by booking tickets well in advance at "orange" saver rates *(see p306)*. Alternatively, you can travel around the country by sharing a private car ride. Visit the **GoMore** website for a list of destinations and quotes.

RESPONSIBLE TOURISM

Denmark has always been progressive when it comes to environmental issues. Any bottles marked with the recycling logo can be placed in the machines *(flaskeautomat)* found in supermarket foyers. Press the green button for your receipt,

which can then be redeemed inside the shop for cash or goods. Other glass can be placed in the green recycling containers outside.

Many hotels and holiday centres are **Green Key**-certified, meaning they have adopted a number of eco-friendly initiatives. Organic, or *økologisk*, food is widely available, and there are also some organic restaurants. "Klima+" restaurants combine organic food with a policy of reducing carbon emissions.

DIRECTORY

VISAS AND PASSPORTS

Ministry of Foreign Affairs
http://um.dk

TOURIST INFORMATION

Aalborg Tourist Office
Kjellerup Torv 5,
Niveau 13, 9000 Aalborg.
Tel 99 31 75 00.
www.visitaalborg.com

Bornholms Visitor Centre
Ndr Kystvej 3, 3770 Rønne.
Tel 56 95 95 00.
www.bornholm.info

Copenhagen Visitor Centre
Vesterbrogade 4A,
1620 Copenhagen V.
Tel 70 22 24 42.
www.visitcopenhagen.com

Odense Tourist Office
Rådhuset, 5000 Odense C.
Tel 63 75 75 39.
www.visitodense.com

VisitDenmark
Islands Brygge 43,
2300 Copenhagen S.
Tel 32 88 99 00.
www.visitdenmark.com

TRAVELLING ON A BUDGET

CouchSurfing
www.couchsurfing.org

GoMore
http://gomore.dk

RESPONSIBLE TOURISM

Green Key
www.green-key.org

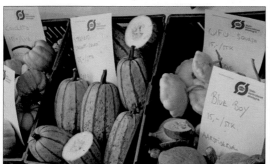
Certified organic vegetables for sale at a market stall

Personal Security and Health

Denmark is a safe country with low levels of crime. Even in the larger cities there is little likelihood of visitors encountering problems. The chances of falling victim to crime can be further minimized by not carrying excessive amounts of cash and by keeping credit cards, mobile phones and other valuables hidden away. In the event of a crime or accident, the Danish police and emergency services work very efficiently. It is also worth asking passers-by or witnesses to the event for their help. As a rule, Danes will not refuse such a request.

Ambulance with its lights on, attending to an emergency

White police patrol car parked in front of a shopping centre in Odense

POLICE

During the summer season the Danish **police** are dressed in blue shirts and black trousers; in winter they also wear black jackets. Road police generally wear all-in-one leather suits and ride large white motorcycles. Ordinary police patrol cars are white with the word "POLITI" in blue lettering, while the cars driven by the criminal division are dark blue. Criminal division police usually wear civilian clothes and will show their ID cards when required.

The majority of Danish policemen and policewomen will have at least a working knowledge of the English language. In most cases they will be able to provide some assistance, such as giving you directions or helping you contact a break-down service.

Although they are not part of the police force, traffic wardens, are entitled to check if someone has a valid parking ticket and can impose a fine for illegal parking *(see pp309 and 311)*. Traffic wardens in Copenhagen wear dark green jackets.

WHAT TO BE AWARE OF

The summer months and the run-up to Christmas are the times when thieves are most likely to be operating, especially in busy places. Visitors are advised to be on their guard, particularly in the main train stations, such as Copenhagen's Central Station, as well as in the prime shopping areas. Valuables should be deposited at the hotel reception or kept in the safe in your room; money and documents should be carried under clothing rather than in handbags or trouser pockets. Make sure all valuable items are out of sight if left in a car.

IN AN EMERGENCY

In the event of a road accident, life-threatening situation, fire, attack or any other predicament that requires immediate intervention by the **emergency services**, visitors should call 112. This toll-free line is staffed by qualified operators who are able to speak several foreign languages, including English; they will determine which service should be sent to the scene of the incident.

Emergency telephones installed along the hard shoulders of motorways can be used to report a breakdown or accident. Special telephones found in S-tog railway stations and on metro lines enable passengers to contact railway duty officers when needed.

An accident or mugging should be reported to the police. The victim and any witnesses to the incident are entitled to give evidence in their native language.

Consulates and embassies *(see p297)* can help to contact a visitor's family in the event of an incident, and they may also be able to provide financial help or advance the money for a ticket home.

LOST AND STOLEN PROPERTY

Any theft of money, travel documents, credit cards or other valuables, as well as any theft from a car or hotel room, should be reported immediately at the local police station, where an officer will issue a note confirming that the crime has been reported. This note may well be required when filling out an insurance claim or visiting an embassy or consulate to obtain a temporary passport.

If you have lost any personal belongings, enquire at the **lost property office** *(hittegods)* closest to the area where they went missing. There are *hittegods* at all local police stations. Any items left behind on a train, S-tog or metro should be reported to the duty personnel at the station; if lost on a bus, report it to the passenger service office of the appropriate bus company. Lost or stolen credit cards should be reported to the card issuer as soon as possible.

The entrance to a hospital in Copenhagen

HOSPITALS AND PHARMACIES

Addresses of doctors and hospitals can be obtained from hotel receptionists and camp site managers, or found in a telephone directory. Most Danish doctors speak English.

Note that not all hospitals in Denmark have an emergency department, and that the old word for emergency room, *skadestue*, is being replaced by *akutklinik*.

Pharmacies *(apotek)* are usually open from 9am to 5:30pm on weekdays and until 1pm on Saturdays. In larger towns there is always one pharmacy that is open 24 hours a day; the address will be displayed on the doors or windows of any pharmacy. You will usually have to call or buzz at a side entrance outside of normal opening hours (after 8pm Monday to Friday, after 4pm on Saturday and all day Sunday). A small surcharge is generally added to the cost of non-prescription medicines purchased during these times.

If you require constant medication, be sure to take an adequate supply with you – medicines can be expensive in Denmark. Controlled drugs require a doctor's prescription.

MINOR HAZARDS

Travellers to Denmark do not require any special vaccinations. Mosquitoes can be a problem near large lakes in the summer; spray-on repellents can be bought in any pharmacy. Those on hiking or camping holidays should check regularly for blood-sucking ticks, especially on children; ticks must be removed completely and any subsequent redness treated promptly with antibiotics. Note that antiseptic lotions, such as Savlon, are not available in Denmark, so it is advisable to bring some with you.

It is safe to drink tap water in Denmark, and stomach upsets are uncommon.

TRAVEL AND HEALTH INSURANCE

Anyone with a medical emergency is entitled to free treatment in hospitals and doctor's surgeries in Denmark, provided that the person has not arrived in the country specifically for that treatment and is unfit to return home. EU visitors in possession of a European Health Insurance Card (EHIC) are covered by Danish national health insurance. Greenland and the Faroe Islands are not part of the EHIC scheme. Non-EU citizens must have health insurance.

Travel insurance is advisable for all visitors, as it can make it easier to get treatment and should cover the cost of an ambulance (which the patient is responsible for) or an emergency flight home.

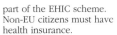

DIRECTORY

IN AN EMERGENCY

Emergency services
Tel 112 (toll free).

Police
Tel 114 (toll free).

LOST AND STOLEN PROPERTY

Lost Property Office, (Copenhagen)
Copenhagen police station, Slotsherrensvej 113, 2720 Vanløse.
Tel 38 74 88 22.

HOSPITALS

Aarhus Universitets Hospital
Nørrebrogade 44, 8000 Aarhus C.
Tel 87 31 50 50.

Amager Hospital (Copenhagen)
Italiensvej 1, 2300 Copenhagen S.
Tel 32 34 32 34.

Odense Universitets Hospital
Sønder Blvd 29, 5000 Odense C.
Tel 65 41 22 71.

24-HOUR PHARMACIES

Aalborg Budolfi Apotek
Algade 60, 9000 Aalborg.
Tel 98 12 06 77.

Aarhus Løve Apotek
Store Torv 5, 8000 Aarhus C.
Tel 86 12 00 22.

Copenhagen Steno Apotek
Vesterbrogade 6C, 1620
Copenhagen V. *Tel 33 14 82 66.*

Copenhagen Sønderbro Apotek
Amagerbrogade 158, 2300
Copenhagen S. *Tel 32 58 01 40.*

Odense Apoteket Ørnen
Vestergade 80, 5000 Odense C.
Tel 66 12 29 70.

A pharmacy in Copenhagen

Banks and Currency

Visitors arriving in Denmark from outside the EU are obliged to have adequate means to support themselves for the duration of their stay. Immigration authorities are usually satisfied with a verbal assurance regarding a visitor's credit card limit. While credit cards can be used almost anywhere, it's worth having some Danish kroner to hand for buying small treats like ice creams, or to use on public transport and when travelling to the more remote islands.

A branch of Jyske Bank in Copenhagen

BANKS AND BUREAUX DE CHANGE

Banks in Denmark are open from 10am until 4pm Monday to Friday, with extended opening hours on Thursday (until 6pm). Banks are closed on Saturday, Sunday and public holidays.

Be aware that banks in Denmark's smaller towns generally do not carry cash and will be able to provide money only from the ATM (Automated Teller Machine).

Foreign currency can be exchanged at many places throughout the country. Exchange booths at Copenhagen Airport are open most of the day. Hotels can also exchange money, though they offer the least favourable rates. Banks and special automatic money-exchange machines offer slightly better rates, but they also charge a commission. The best deals can generally be obtained at branches of **Forex**, since they do not charge a commission. In addition, their opening hours are usually more flexible than those of the banks. Exchange rates are usually displayed by the door.

Anyone who wishes to bring more than 40,000 Dkr into the country or make a deposit of a similar sum must have a certificate confirming the legality of the money's source.

ATMS

All Danish banks have cash machines from which kroner can be withdrawn with a credit or debit card. ATMs are widespread in the towns and cities, and they all provide directions in English, as well as a number of other European languages.

ATMs are not so readily available in more remote parts of Denmark, including some of its smaller islands, camp sites and summer house areas; those visiting these parts should have enough Danish kroner to last until they return to a larger town.

CREDIT AND DEBIT CARDS

Visitors to Denmark should have no problem using credit cards such as MasterCard, VISA or Eurocard, though some restaurants may charge a small fee for non-Danish cards. American Express and

DIRECTORY

BANKS

Danske Bank
Højbro Plads 5, 1200
Copenhagen K. **Map** 3 C1.
Tel 45 12 45 50.
www.danskebank.dk

Jyske Bank
Vesterbrogade 9, 1780
Copenhagen V. **Map** 3 A2.
Tel 89 89 00 10.
www.jyskebank.dk

Nordea
Kongens Nytorv 28, 1050
Copenhagen K. **Map** 4 D1.
Tel 33 12 11 11.
www.nordea.dk

Sydbank A/S
Kongens Nytorv 30, 1050
Copenhagen K. **Map** 4 D1.
Tel 74 37 78 00.
www.sydbank.dk

BUREAUX DE CHANGE

Forex Aalborg
Ved Stranden 22.
Tel 98 18 97 00.

Forex Aarhus
Banegårdspladsen 20.
Tel 86 80 03 40.

Forex Copenhagen
Nørre Voldgade 90.
Map 1 B5.
Tel 33 32 81 03.
Hovedbanegården.
Map 3 A3.
Tel 33 11 22 25.

Forex Odense
Banegardscentret,
Østre Stationsvej 27.
Tel 66 11 66 18.

Diners Club are less readily accepted. Be aware that some shops may refuse to take credit cards as payment for low-cost items, while others accept only a Danish debit card called Dankort.

In many restaurants and shops, staff will use a reader to enter a card's data and ask the customer to sign a receipt or key in the card's PIN code.

In order to ensure your card works overseas, contact your bank or credit card provider before travelling.

If your credit or debit card is lost or stolen, report it to your card issuer immediately.

CURRENCY

Denmark is one of the few EU countries to reject joining the European monetary union, keeping the krone (plural: kroner) instead. In large towns and tourist resorts, however, prices are often quoted in both kroner and euros. The Danish krone (or crown) is divided into 100 øre. Coins come in denominations of 50 øre, and 1, 2, 5, 10 and 20 kroner. Notes come in denominations of 50, 100, 200, 500 and 1,000 kroner. The Danish krone is written as DKK in most international money markets, but as Dkr in northern Europe and simply as kr in Denmark.

The Faroe Islands have their own version of the Danish krone, known as the Faroese krona, which has exactly the same value as its Danish counterpart. Danish currency is accepted on the Faroe Islands, but the Faroese krona is not accepted in Denmark, so exchange any Faroese krona notes at a bureau de change.

The Danish krone is the official currency in Greenland. Be aware that while all Scandinavian currencies are called krone or krona, they are not interchangeable. Swedish kronar and Norwegian kroner, for example, are not valid currencies in Denmark.

Bank notes
Danish bank notes differ from each other in terms of size and colour. The lowest denomination bank note in circulation is the violet-blue 50-Dkr note. The largest denomination is the red-and-green 1,000-Dkr note.

50 kroner

100 kroner

200 kroner

500 kroner

Coins
The 10- and most of the 20-Dkr coins are golden in colour, with the queen's image on the reverse. The 1-, 2- and 5-Dkr coins are nickel with a hole in the centre. The 50-øre coin is copper-coloured.

50 øre

1 krone

20 kroner

10 kroner

5 kroner

2 kroner

Communications and Media

Telia

Logo for mobile
phone network Telia

Danish postal services are very efficient. Letters and postcards take one to two days to reach their destinations within the country, and about two to four days within Europe. Telephoning abroad is straightforward, although public telephones are becoming increasingly rare due to the popularity of mobile phones. Nevertheless, visitors should be able to find a public telephone at a post office, railway station, camp site reception or hotel lobby. Making calls from your hotel room usually incurs a steep fee, so check in advance.

A public telephone that accepts both coins and phone cards

DIALLING CODES

- To make an international call, dial 00, the country code, the area code and the number.
- Calling Denmark from abroad: 0045
- Country codes: UK 44; US/Canada 1.
- Directory enquiries: 118 (inland), 80 60 40 55 (overseas).

INTERNATIONAL AND LOCAL TELEPHONE CALLS

Denmark has no area codes, and all numbers consist of eight digits, generally written and read out by Danes in blocks of two. Numbers starting with 20 through to 31 are mobile numbers, while those starting with 32 through to 39 are Copenhagen landline numbers. Numbers starting with 80 are toll-free, while premium rate lines start with 90. Danes refer to land lines as *fastnet*.

Prepaid phone cards for calling overseas are available in many kiosks in the larger cities, and they offer better value for money than a **TDC** (Denmark's main telecommunications company) phone card. Always state where you're calling for the best rates to that country. Prepaid phone cards can also be used with mobile phones.

Calling from a payphone is more expensive than using a private phone, but cheaper than phoning from a hotel room. The minimum charge for a call from a public phone is 5 Dkr, and denominations of 1, 2, 5 and 10 Dkr are accepted; many payphones also take euros. All calls, including local calls, are charged by the minute. Clear instructions on how to make a call are displayed in English, and a list of dialling codes for other countries is usually available.

Skype is a free alternative to costly international phone calls. Anyone with a computer or phone with Internet access can use Skype, as long as they have registered for an account.

MOBILE PHONES

Most mobile phone networks provide the facilities for making international calls. Before departure, make sure that your phone will work in Denmark. If not, it is sometimes possible to get an upgrade for the duration of your

holiday. When using a prepaid mobile phone in Denmark, you should check whether your package covers international roaming. Danish mobile phone providers include TDC, **Telia** and **Oister**.

Making calls from Denmark is more expensive than calling from home; incoming calls will also be charged at a higher rate. Receiving texts from abroad is free, but sending them is usually subject to a substantial fee.

PUBLIC TELEPHONES

The increase of mobile phones in Denmark means that public telephone boxes are not as common as they used to be. However, those that do remain – usually outside train stations – are well maintained. There are two types of phone booths: those that accept both coins and cards, and those that take cards only. Card phones also accept credit cards. Phone cards are available in about 1,500 outlets, including post offices and many shops.

INTERNET

Denmark moved swiftly into the broadband era, and free Wi-Fi connections are commonplace – not only in most hotel rooms (even the cheaper ones), but also in cafés and on some public transport, including the high-speed ICE train from Copenhagen to Aarhus, the regional S-tog in Copenhagen

A Danish man using a mobile phone while riding a bicycle

and some buses. Wi-Fi is also available throughout Copenhagen Airport for a small charge. If you plan on using your own laptop, be sure to bring an adaptor suitable for Denmark's plug sockets.

Most hotels in Danish holiday resorts can provide Internet access at reception. Many youth hostels and camp sites also have computers with Internet access.

Danish postal services' logo

The number of Internet cafés has declined, due to Wi-Fi becoming more widespread, but, these can still be found in towns and cities. Free Wi-Fi hotspots are available throughout Denmark. You can search for locations using **openwifi**.

POSTAL AND COURIER SERVICES

Danish post offices are indicated by the word "POST" in white letters on a red background. Most post offices are open 10am–5pm Monday to Friday (until 6pm on Thursday) and 10am–noon on Saturday. You can post parcels, send registered letters and collect *poste restante* mail from all of Denmark's post offices.

Stamps can be purchased at post offices, in many souvenir shops and from vending machines. A letter sent to a European country requires a "Europa" tariff postage stamp.

Danish post boxes are painted red. They feature the crown and trumpet insignia

Bright-red Danish letterbox, showing collection times

of the national postal service and display the time of the next collection. International mail sent from Copenhagen should leave the country within 24 hours.

When posting something to a Danish address, you should include the name of the recipient, street, house number, town and a four-digit post code. It is very important to include the post code, since many Danish towns, as well as many streets in Copenhagen, have the same name. For details of post codes, visit the website of **Post Danmark**, the national postal service provider. The address for an apartment may sometimes include the floor and staircase, as well as the number of the flat within a building. For example, the address may be written as "Bjergvej 20, 3.tv", where "3" stands for 3rd floor and "tv" stands for *til venstre*, meaning "to the left".

Express courier services such as **DHL** and **UPS** usually provide a telephone booking service in English.

NEWSPAPERS AND MAGAZINES

Most of the major foreign papers, including US and UK dailies such as *The Times*, *The Guardian* and the *Wall Street Journal*, can be found at train station kiosks and in some of the main newsagents in Copenhagen, and other large towns. Magazines such as *Time* and *The Economist* are also readily available. Libraries often provide free access to international newspapers.

Denmark's own press consists of about 50 regional and national daily newspapers. Of these, *Politiken* and *Jyllandsposten* have the largest circulation. The weekly *Copenhagen Post* has national news and a pull-out listings section in English; it can be found at kiosks and newsagents in Copenhagen, as well as in many cafés, public libraries and tourist offices.

DIRECTORY

INTERNATIONAL AND LOCAL TELEPHONE CALLS

Skype
www.skype.com

TDC
Tel 80 80 80 20.

MOBILE PHONES

Oister
Tel 70 31 30 70.
www.oister.dk

Telia
Tel 80 40 40 40.
http://telia.dk

INTERNET

openwifi
www.openwifi.dk

POSTAL AND COURIER SERVICES

DHL
Tel 70 34 53 45.
www.dhl.dk

Post Danmark
Tel 80 20 70 30.
www.postdanmark.dk

UPS
Tel 86 28 66 30 (Aarhus).
Tel 35 25 80 80 (Zealand).
www.ups.com

TELEVISION AND RADIO

All television in Denmark is broadcast digitally. There are two public-service channels, DR1 and DR2, screening news and current affairs along with light entertainment. Other channels are more commercial in character, showing a large amount of soap operas and comedies. Many US and British programmes are shown with Danish subtitles. English-language news is often available on cable and satellite TV.

Many summer houses have satellite dishes that receive German, Norwegian and Swedish channels. German channels are largely available in Southern Jutland, while viewers in Northern Jutland should be able to pick up Swedish and Norwegian TV.

TRAVEL INFORMATION

Flights to Denmark from most parts of northern Europe are frequent. Planes from over 100 cities worldwide land at Copenhagen, and the airport receives more than 20 million passengers a year. Fewer people arrive by train and ferry, although ferries are popular with visitors from elsewhere in Scandinavia. Ease of travel has increased with the construction of the Store Bælt (Great Belt) Bridge, linking Zealand and Funen, and the fixed-link Øresund Bridge between Zealand and Sweden, but many of the smaller Danish islands can be reached only by ferry. Travelling on the mainland and around the major islands is easy, thanks to a network of well-maintained motorways and railways, and an efficient coach service.

SAS aircraft

ARRIVING BY AIR

Most visitors to Denmark arrive at Copenhagen Airport, located 12 km (7 miles) southeast of the city centre. **SAS** connects Copenhagen to most European capitals, and it also has non-stop flights from New York and Chicago. From Australasia the best connections to Denmark are via Bangkok. Other airlines serving Copenhagen include **British Airways**, **Norwegian**, **bmi** (from Edinburgh and Glasgow) and **easyJet** (from London Gatwick, London Stansted and Manchester, as well as other airports in Europe). **Ryanair** has daily flights from London Stansted to Aarhus and Billund, and also to Malmö, in Sweden, with a special connecting coach to Copenhagen.

Jutland can be reached via the international airports of Aarhus, Aalborg and Billund. **Aarhus Airport**, which is 40 km (25 miles) northeast of the city, receives flights from London Stansted and Barcelona among others. Buses link the airport to the city, dropping passengers off at Aarhus's railway station. The journey time is about 45 minutes.

Billund Airport (for LEGOLAND®) is the largest international airport in West Denmark, and it receives flights from many European cities, including London (Stansted and City), Frankfurt and Amsterdam. Bus routes operate from here to Vejle, Horsens, Aarhus, Kolding and Esbjerg.

Aalborg Airport offers easy access to the very north of the country and receives flights from such places as London Gatwick, Berlin and Oslo. An express bus links the airport with the city centre.

COPENHAGEN AIRPORT

The country's main airport is **Copenhagen Airport** (formerly known as Kastrup), situated on Amager Island, a short way from the city centre. It has four terminals: three for international flights

Bilingual information board at Copenhagen Airport

and one for domestic flights. Terminal 4, which is known as CphGo, is used exclusively by easyJet and other low-cost airlines.

Copenhagen Airport has helpful staff and excellent information services. Facilities include shops and restaurants, cash machines and lockers. Cars can be hired at terminals 1 and 3.

The CPH Advantage programme is available to all passengers and allows free Wi-Fi access through all of Copenhagen Airport. Passengers flying business class can also enjoy the CPH Apartment, located within the transit hall, for free Wi-Fi, printing and recharging facilities, and light meals and drinks at a nominal fee.

Special assistance for passengers with disabilities is provided by **Falck**. However, note that this service should be booked in advance either via the airport website or by calling Falck directly.

A fast and economical train service runs every 10 minutes from the airport's Terminal 3 to Central Station in Copenhagen (a journey of about

Sleek, streamlined interior of Copenhagen Airport

SAS aircraft on the tarmac at Aalborg Airport

12 minutes). Trains run throughout the day, as well as during the night, albeit less frequently. Many trains are listed as running to Helsingør because they continue up the coast after stopping at Copenhagen's Central Station. Be aware that trains from Copenhagen Airport also run in the other direction, to Sweden, so it's important to check the correct platform.

The metro also runs from the airport to the city centre, taking about 15 minutes and stopping at Kongens Nytorv and Nørreport stations. It's also possible to take the bus, which drops passengers off at Rådhuspladsen. The price of a bus ticket is the same as the train (36 Dkr), however, and the journey time is nearly three times as long.

Visitors with a lot of heavy luggage will find a taxi rank by the exit of Terminal 3. Rates to the city centre start around 250 Dkr and fares can be paid by credit card.

TICKETS AND FARES

Intense competition, rising airport taxes and CO2 tariffs mean that airlines vary their prices continuously and it is difficult to be precise about fares. Booking in advance is recommended, as travellers who book at short notice invariably pay higher prices. It is always worth shopping around, and often the best deals can be found online.

It is possible to purchase a one-way, non-refundable ticket on a low-cost airline for as little as €35–45 (including taxes) from London, Berlin and other European capitals.

Direct return flights with SAS from New York or Chicago to Copenhagen cost around US$700, with no refunds or flexibility.

Most airlines connecting Denmark to other European destinations charge for light snacks. SAS still allows one piece of 23-kg (50-lb) luggage free of charge, as well as offering discounts to people over 65 and to children and students. Low-cost airlines offer good deals to people who bring only an item of hand luggage.

INTERNAL FLIGHTS

Air travel within Denmark is fairly inexpensive, as long as you book your tickets a couple of weeks in advance of your departure date. The major domestic carrier is SAS.

A route particularly worth recommending is the one from Copenhagen to Aalborg (a 5-hour journey by car). Connections are frequent, especially on weekdays. Another important domestic hub is **Karup Airport**, located in the flatlands around Herning, in Jutland.

ON ARRIVAL

All visitors from EU countries must have their passport or ID card ready for exiting the arrivals area; this is usually a fairly quick process. Citizens of many non-EU countries, such as the USA and Australia, do not need a visa to enter Denmark, but they may need to show a return ticket and evidence of sufficient funds to cover their stay.

Logo of SAS (Scandinavian Airlines)

DIRECTORY

ARRIVING BY AIR

Aalborg Airport
Ny Lufthavnsvej 100,
9400 Nørresundby.
Tel 98 17 11 44.
www.aal.dk

Aarhus Airport
Ny Lufthavnsvej 24,
8560 Kolind.
Tel 87 75 70 00.
www.aar.dk

Billund Airport
Passagerterminalen 10,
7190 Billund.
Tel 76 50 50 50.
www.bll.dk

bmi (British Midland)
Tel 0844 848 4888 (UK).
www.flybmi.com

British Airways
Tel 0844 493 0787 (UK).
www.britishairways.com

easyJet
Tel 0843 104 5000 (UK).
www.easyjet.com

Norwegian
Tel 020 8099 7254 (UK).
www.norwegian.com

Ryanair
Tel 0871 246 0000 (UK).
www.ryanair.com

SAS
Denmark *Tel* 70 10 20 00.
Ireland *Tel* 01 844 5440.
UK *Tel* 0871 226 7760.
USA/Canada
Tel 1800 221 2350 (toll free).
www.flysas.com

COPENHAGEN AIRPORT

Copenhagen Airport
Lufthavnsboulevarden 6,
2770 Kastrup.
Tel 32 31 32 31.
www.cph.dk

Falck
Tel 32 31 41 20.

INTERNAL FLIGHTS

Karup Airport
N.O. Hansens Vej 4,
7470 Karup J.
Tel 97 10 06 10.
www.krp.dk

Travelling Around by Train, Coach and Ferry

Color Line ferry logo

Danish trains are mostly run by the Danish State Railway (DSB) and Arriva; they are reliable and fast, making it possible to travel between Copenhagen and Aarhus in under 3 hours. Coaches run between the large cities and to other destinations in Europe; they take longer than the train, but they are cheaper. A network of ferry links provides a convenient way to travel to some of Denmark's many islands, including the Faroe Islands, as well as between Denmark and countries such as England, Germany, Sweden, Norway and Iceland.

ARRIVING BY TRAIN

The most common railway routes into Denmark are from Germany to Jutland or via the Puttgarden-Rødby ferry from Hamburg to Lolland and up to Zealand. Many people also travel to Zealand by train from Sweden across the Øresund Bridge. Travel from the UK is generally via the Netherlands and through Germany.

Trans-European trains are fast and efficient, particularly the high-speed ICE services between Copenhagen and Gothenburg and Stockholm, in Sweden; and between Copenhagen and Hamburg and Berlin, in Germany.

Copenhagen's Central Station, in the heart of the city, is the main point of arrival for international rail services.

MAIN STATIONS

Danish railway stations are clean and well maintained. Facilities often include heated waiting rooms and snack bars. Copenhagen's Central Station has shops, ATMs, cafés, a supermarket, a post office and a police station. Aarhus's Central Station is set in the middle of a shopping mall.

DOMESTIC TRAINS

DSB's extensive network covers both local and long-distance lines. Long-distance trains, such as those that run between Copenhagen and Aarhus, are modern, safe and stylish. Seats are arranged in

pairs facing each other. Above each seat is a reading light and, often, individual music jacks for headphones and power supply sockets for laptop computers. Many trains have Wi-Fi connections for an additional charge (29 Dkr); trains with Internet access are marked with a white logo on a dark background and the word "Internet". Intercity trains also offer payphones, baby-changing facilities and even children's play areas. Information displayed above each seat indicates whether a seat has been reserved and to which station. In some parts of the train, known as *stille zoner*, silence must be maintained, and the use of mobile phones is prohibited. On many routes, DSB also operates "business class" carriages, which supply passengers with Wi-Fi, free drinks, snacks and papers.

Local trains, many of which have double-decker carriages, tend to be slower and have fewer facilities.

On some routes, such as from Copenhagen to Aarhus, Bornholm and Odden, it's possible to buy a combined train-and-ferry ticket.

Details of the network and main schedules are available from all DSB stations.

TRAIN TICKETS AND FARES

Tickets can be bought at train stations or by calling the DSB reservation line or logging on to their website. The

Rejseplanen website offers useful information on train and coach travel.

Train passes such as Inter-Rail (available to European travellers) and Eurail (for visitors from outside Europe) give the holders substantial discounts on travel in Europe and a flexible range of options. There are many other rail concessions within Denmark, so it pays to ask about discounts for off-peak travel, family tickets and return fares. Often the best prices can be obtained by booking early and online. Those travelling between Copenhagen and Jutland and Funen can get the best savings by booking an "orange" ticket well in advance via the DSB website.

Children aged between 10 and 15 travel for half price; adults with valid tickets can take up to two children under 12 for free. Further information can be obtained from DSB ticket offices.

A coach is often the cheapest way to travel around Denmark

TRAVELLING BY COACH

Abildskou travels to Aarhus from Berlin via Hamburg Airport. It also operates daily services from Copenhagen to Aarhus and Aalborg. Tickets can be bought on board, but it is wise to reserve a seat in advance. Between Monday and Thursday, discounts are available for students and the over-65s. The bus leaves from outside **Valby Station**, arriving in Jutland via Odden or the Mols-Linien ferry *(see opposite)*.

Eurolines operates coach journeys from the larger Danish cities to various European destinations. In Copenhagen, they depart from Ingerslevsgade, below the Central Station.

A domestic ferry sailing between Denmark's islands

ARRIVING BY FERRY

The major international ferry companies are **DFDS Seaways**, **Stena Line**, **Color Line**, **Fjord Line** and **Scandlines**.

The opening of the bridges spanning the Øresund (Sound) and the Store Bælt has greatly reduced the demand for ferries between Zealand and Sweden, and between Zealand and Funen. However, ferry travel remains a popular option with many visitors.

MAIN TERMINALS

Most ferry travellers from the UK will arrive at the port of Esbjerg. Other main terminals are located in Copenhagen, just north of the city centre, and Frederikshavn and Hirtshals, in northern Jutland.

There is usually a bus link between the port and the town's train station, as well as a taxi rank and long- and short-stay car parking.

Ferry passengers will often be asked to check in at least 1 hour before departure.

DOMESTIC FERRIES

Ferry services, such as those provided by **Færgen**, play a vital role in Denmark's transport infrastructure, linking a number of islands. Some routes are very short, taking a matter of minutes, while the longest route (Køge–Bornholm) takes nearly 7 hours.

Ferries also link different parts of mainland Denmark. The **Mols-Linien**, from Odden in West Zealand to Ebeltoft or Aarhus in Jutland, is a popular alternative to the Store Bælt Bridge, as it saves paying the bridge toll charge; the same is true of the **Kattegatruten** (Kalundborg–Aarhus). In the summer, **Smyril Line** runs two weekly ferries from Hirtshals to the Faroe Islands (journey time: a day and a half).

Most ferries take both foot passengers and cars, but there are some small islands where passenger-only ferries operate.

FERRY TICKETS AND FARES

Tickets for ferry services can usually be reserved online. Fares vary widely, depending on the season and the time of day. Substantial discounts are often available for students and young people with an international rail pass.

There is no need to book in advance on short routes, but it is compulsory to do so for longer journeys. Reservations should also be made when travelling at busy times (like Christmas) or with a vehicle.

DIRECTORY

DOMESTIC TRAINS

DSB
Tel 70 13 14 15.
www.dsb.dk

Rejseplanen
www.rejseplanen.dk

TRAVELLING BY COACH

Abildskou
Tel 70 21 08 88.
www.abildskou.dk

Eurolines
Tel 33 88 70 00.
www.eurolines-travel.com

Valby Station
Lyshøjgårdsvej, Copenhagen V.

ARRIVING BY FERRY

Color Line
Tel 99 56 19 00.
www.colorline.com

DFDS Seaways
Tel 0871 522 9955 (UK).
www.dfdsseaways.co.uk

Fjord Line
Tel 97 96 30 00.
www.fjordline.com

Scandlines
Tel 33 15 15 15.
www.scandlines.eu

Stena Line
Tel 96 20 02 00.
www.stenaline.dk

DOMESTIC FERRIES

Aerøfærgenrne
Tel 62 52 40 00.
www.aeroe-ferry.com

Færgen
Tel 70 23 15 15
www.faergen.com

Kattegatruten
Tel 38 11 12 22
www.kattegat-ruten.dk

Mols-Linien
Tel 70 10 14 18.
www.mols-linien.dk

Smyril Line
Tel (+298) 34 59 00.
www.smyril-line.com

International ferry connecting Denmark with Germany and Sweden

Travelling by Car

Sign indicating scenic route

Although Denmark's public transport network is excellent, a car can still be a convenient way of travelling, especially when visiting out-of-the-way places. For groups of three or four people, a car can also reduce travel costs significantly. Danish motorways are toll-free, but the Store Bælt and Øresund bridges are not. The major roads are well signposted and of a good standard, and travelling over one of the bridges, such as the Store Bælt Bridge between Zealand and Funen, can be a truly breathtaking experience.

ARRIVING BY CAR

Most people driving to Denmark arrive from Germany, the country's only land border, or from Sweden via the Øresund Bridge. Immigration checkpoints between EU countries have been abolished; however, there are still customs checkpoints at sea and land borders with Germany.

The main routes into the country are the E45, running from the German border all the way through Jutland up to Frederikshavn; the E47, which connects Lübeck and Hamburg with Lolland via the car ferry from Puttgarden to Rødby; and the E20, which travels over the Øresund Bridge from Malmø in Sweden. From 2020, the Puttgarden–Rødby ferry will be replaced by the Fehmarn Belt Fixed Link, which will connect the German island of Fehmarn, north of Lübeck, with Lolland.

WHAT YOU NEED

Anyone driving in Denmark must have all the relevant documents, including insurance and an international driver's licence. Check that you have breakdown cover with a company that has reciprocal arrangements with Denmark. **FDM**, the Danish motoring organization, can provide further information.

While it is not compulsory to carry a first-aid kit, it is a good idea to have one in the car, in addition to a car fire extinguisher, a torch and a tow rope. A warning triangle must be kept in the car in case of a breakdown.

Motorway road signs

ROADS AND TOLLS

Motorway signs in Denmark are colour-coded and easy to understand. The blue signs indicate exits, while the green ones indicate the cities that can be reached along the motorway.

Denmark has five trans-European motorways. The E20 runs west–east from Esbjerg through Kolding and Odense, across the Store Bælt and on to Køge and Copenhagen; the E29 links Hirtshals to Nørresundby; the E45 crosses the German border and links Kolding, Aarhus, Aalborg and Frederikshavn; the E47 links Helsingør, Copenhagen, Køge, Maribo and Rødby harbour; and the E55 runs between Helsingør, Copenhagen, Køge, Nykøbing F and Gedser.

Part of the E20 consists of bridges over the Store Bælt and Øresund (Sound). The toll charged to cross is collected at entry or exit points. The toll stations are equipped with card machines or manned by staff at busier

Danish motorway sign

times. The yellow *Manuel* lanes are for payment by credit card or cash.

The toll charge on the **Store Bælt Bridge** is 275–370 Dkr, depending on the size and height of your vehicle. Similar toll charges apply for the **Øresund Bridge**. A BroBizz pass – a small transponder that you affix on the windscreen behind the rear-view mirror – can be used on both bridges and offers considerable discounts if you're making regular trips. Visit www.storebaelt.dk for more information.

Other major bridges in Denmark include the Farø Bridges that connect Zealand and Falster; the Lille Bælt Bridge, between Jutland and Funen; the Sallingsund Bridge, between Mors and Salling; and the bridge from Fyn to the island of Langeland. These bridges are toll-free.

A proposal that is likely to become reality within the next decade is the Kattegat Bridge, a bridge and tunnel connecting Kalundborg in Zealand with Aarhus via the island of Samsø.

RULES OF THE ROAD

As in all continental European countries, the Danes drive on the right. Both cars and motorcycles must have dipped headlights on during the day (cars from the UK will need to have their headlights adjusted). Seat belts must be worn at all times, and children under three must be in a child seat. When turning right, drivers must give way to cyclists on the inside.

The speed limit is usually 50 km/h (30 mph) in towns, 80 km/h (50 mph) on most roads and up to 130 km/h (80 mph) on motorways. A hefty on-the-spot fine may be charged for breaking the speed limit and for other motoring offences, such as not wearing a seat belt or talking on a mobile phone while driving. Being

A pretty country road alongside a rape field

caught driving under the influence of alcohol will incur even stiffer penalties and possibly imprisonment.

PARKING

Tickets for parking are obtained from kerbside machines (*billet-automat*), which accept most coins. In many smaller towns, parking is free and regulated by a parking disk, available from all garages, that has an hour hand. Different zones are marked with a blue sign with the letter "P". Also on the sign is the time limit for parking; signs marked as *1 time* mean you can stay for an hour; *2 timer* is two hours and so on. When parking within these time zones, set the hour hand on your parking disk to indicate the time when you arrived and leave it on the dashboard, so that the wardens can check whether the limit has been exceeded. In larger towns, parking is

often free 6pm–8am on weekdays, after 2pm on Saturday and all day Sunday. The Danish for "no parking" is *parkering forbudt*. For more details about parking in towns see p311.

PETROL

There is no shortage of petrol stations in Denmark, and most international brands are represented. Pumps are generally self-service, with daily opening hours from 6 or 7am to midnight. At 24-hour petrol stations, payment facilities are automated using Dkr notes, though you are unlikely to find instructions in English. Petrol is expensive, with prices slightly higher than in Britain or Germany. Autogas (LPG) is not widely used and is available only at a few selected petrol stations.

BREAKDOWN SERVICES

In the event of a breakdown, telephone the emergency number supplied by your car hire company or breakdown organization. Phones on motorways are placed at 2-km (1-mile) intervals. For other emergencies, dial 112 and ask for the relevant service. The main breakdown companies in Denmark are **Falck Autohjælp** and **Dansk Autohjælp**.

CAR HIRE

Representatives of most major car hire firms can be found at airports, upmarket hotels and in city centres.

Car hire tends to be expensive in Denmark; booking beforehand through an international firm can work out much cheaper. Three of the major firms in Denmark are **Avis**, **Europcar** and **Hertz**.

GREAT DRIVES

The Marguerite or Daisy Route (*Margueritruten* in Danish) is a scenic motoring route signposted by a daisy on a brown background. It was started in 1991 and named after Queen Margrethe II and Denmark's national flower. The route passes through more than 100 major attractions, including the castles of Egeskov and Kronborg, providing a pleasant alternative to the main highways.

One of the roads on the scenic Marguerite Route

Getting Around Danish Towns

Bicycle route sign

Most Danish towns and cities can be easily explored on foot or by bicycle. Cycling is popular, and motorists treat cyclists as they would any other legitimate road users. Public transport in most cities is efficient, safe and reasonably priced. Taxis are another good way to get around, and they are especially convenient for anyone who is carrying heavy luggage or large amounts of shopping.

City bus – tickets can be bought on board or in advance

GREEN TRAVEL

It is possible to travel around Denmark without leaving a massive carbon footprint thanks to the country's great train network and many ferry connections. Electric buses and cars are not as common as in neighbouring Sweden, but they are becoming more popular. The country's first electric taxis operate in Odense, and at least one taxi firm in Copenhagen is working towards making the move by 2020. In Copenhagen, some bus routes, including the sightseeing bus CityCirkel, use electric vehicles.

Cycling is widespread and it has been estimated that Danes cycle, on average, more than 600 km (373 miles) a year. Danish cities make many allowances for cyclists, including cycle paths and favourable laws regarding right of way.

Some small islands are virtually car-free, while some others offer the possibility of hiring a horse-drawn gypsy wagon for an especially green vacation.

PUBLIC TRANSPORT

Most cities in Denmark have well-run, modern public transport networks, so there is little need for a car. There are also well-maintained bus routes on all Danish islands, even the small ones. Here, bus timetables usually run in conjunction with ferry schedules, and a bus is likely to be waiting at the port as you disembark the ferry.

Central bus stations in towns and cities are usually situated next to the main train station or by the ferry terminal. Maps and timetables that list the major bus and rail routes, as well as the most important sights, are available from tourist offices.

More information on public transport in Copenhagen can be found on pages 312–13.

TICKETS

Multi-ticket clip cards (*klippekort*), valid on buses and local trains, are readily available in the major cities, such as Copenhagen, Aarhus and Odense. Travel passes bought in Copenhagen are also valid in other towns in the Greater Copenhagen (HT) region, including Roskilde, Helsingør and Hillerød. The Aarhus Pass and Odense City Pass allow unlimited travel on public transport and include discounted or free admission to some city attractions. Reduced-fare travel cards for children up to the age of 16 are also available.

In smaller towns, it is also possible to buy single tickets directly from the driver upon boarding. This is the best option if you are unlikely to be making multiple journeys. On the island of Mors, in the Limfjord, local buses are free.

WALKING

All of Denmark's towns and cities are compact, and most have pedestrianized areas. In addition, many sights tend to be closely grouped together, making getting around on foot a pleasant experience.

Nevertheless, pedestrians should observe the traffic regulations. Take care when crossing the road, although Danish drivers are very attentive towards pedestrians and would never enter a crossing when there are people on it. However, pedestrians who step on to the cycle lanes that run along beside the pavements are strongly frowned upon, especially during rush hour.

Walking tours provide a fun, alternative way to explore the major towns and cities in Denmark. Local tourist offices (*see pp296–7*) will be able to provide details of tours that are available in the area, as well as maps for those who wish to explore the city on foot without a guide

Pedestrianized street in Aalborg

Visitors enjoying a walking tour

DIRECTORY

TAXIS

Aarhus Taxa
Aarhus. *Tel* 89 48 48 48.

Dantaxi
Nationwide. *Tel* 70 25 25 25.

Taxa Fyn
Funen (incl. Odense).
Tel 66 15 44 15.

CYCLING

Baisikeli Bike Rental
Copenhagen.
www.cph-bike-rental.dk

Bikes4rent.dk
Aarhus. *Tel* 20 26 10 20.
www.bikes4rent.dk

CSV Cykeludlejning
Odense.
Tel 63 75 39 64 (May–Sep);
66 12 12 58 (Oct–Apr).
www.odensecykler.dk
www.cityhotelodense.dk

TAXIS

Taxis in Danish cities are plentiful, but they can be rather expensive. Taxi ranks can be found in front of all railway stations, airports and ferry terminals, as well as in town centres and major shopping centres. Cabs with a lit sign saying *fri* can be flagged down in the street. Taxis can also be booked on the phone. Fares start around 40–50 Dkr and then increase by the kilometre. A higher rate is levied at night and when booked by phone. Most taxis in Denmark accept credit cards, and there is no need to tip the driver.

Sign for a taxi rank

DRIVING

Avoid driving in the larger towns if at all possible. As per its environmental policy, the Danish government does its best to discourage people from using their car. Most cities have designated car-free centres, and parking and fuel are very expensive, as is the cost of hiring a car. Cyclists and pedestrians take precedence on city roads, and when turning right, car drivers are obliged to give way to cyclists coming up on the inside and, even if there is a green light, to pedestrians crossing the road.

PARKING

A fee is charged for on-street parking in Denmark's city centres between 8am and 6pm Monday to Friday and between 8am and 2pm on Saturday. It can be difficult to find a parking space at any time of day, especially in the centre of towns and cities. It can also be expensive to park a car. Some Danish cities have parking zones, with zones closest to the centre costing the most. High fines are charged for failing to pay parking fees or exceeding the time limit. See page 309 for more on parking in Denmark.

CYCLING

Cycling is another popular and practical way to get around: bikes can be hired from hotels or special bike hire places. In Copenhagen and Aarhus, you can use free bikes supplied by the city and available at designated areas in the city centre *(see p313)*. Bicycle lanes exist all over the country, in rural areas as well as in big towns, and you can obtain a map of scenic routes from tourist offices. Many Danes spend their holidays touring an island like Samsø or Bornholm by bike.

Bikes and accessories such as helmets, child seats and even attachable trailers for transporting kids and heavy bags can be hired in many towns and cities from companies such as **Baisikeli**, **Bikes4rent.dk** and **CSV Cykeludlejning**.

Cycling is a fun way to get around, but a number of factors should be taken into account. Never leave a bike unlocked; expensive bikes, in particular, are highly desirable to thieves. In larger towns, attach the bicycle to a cycle rack. When using cycle lanes, cyclists must observe general traffic regulations, such as not jumping red lights. Buses often stop in areas allocated for bikers, so beware of people getting off. Bicycles must be equipped with lights after dark and have reflectors fitted at the back and front. Cyclists stopped under the influence of alcohol may not only incur a hefty fine but also lose their driver's licence. Everybody, especially children, should wear safety helmets.

Outside of peak hours, bicycles can be taken on to trains (excluding ICE trains) upon purchase of a special bicycle ticket. This is required on all trains, excluding Copenhagen's S-tog, but the cost is minimal.

Cycling is a popular form of transport in Danish towns

Getting Around Copenhagen

Logo of the S-tog train

Copenhagen has an excellent round-the-clock public transport system, and you can use the same *klippekort* (clip cards) and travel passes on the buses, metro, S-tog and regional trains. Walking and cycling are also pleasant options. Copenhagen is one of the safest cities in Europe, and there should be no problem travelling alone, even at night.

The platform of a metro station in Copenhagen

BUSES

Copenhagen's efficient bus network, run by **Movia**, shares its fare structure with the city's various train networks. Bus stops are marked by a yellow sign with the word "BUS" and display the relevant bus's timetable.

Insert your clip card into the yellow time clock next to the driver. If you don't have a clip card, you can pay the driver with cash; change is given, but be aware that large notes will not be appreciated. The next stop is displayed on a digital screen towards the front of the bus, and disembarking is via the central or back doors.

Buses, like trains, start running at about 5am (6am on Sunday). Less frequent night buses (marked by the prefix "N") operate on special routes.

METRO

Copenhagen's modern underground rail network, the **Metro**, has two lines, one of which links the airport to the city centre. The metro system, which complements the S-tog rail network, stops at Frederiksberg, Forum, Nørreport, Kongens Nytorv and Christianshavn in the city centre. A circle line (due by

2018) will stop at Nørrebro, Østerbro, Vesterbro and the Central Station. Metro stations are marked with the red letter "M" and can be spotted by the 5-m- (16-ft-) high illuminated information posts outside.

Metro trains are fully automated and consist of single driverless carriages that are sleek, bright and rarely feel crowded. The doors open automatically in line with the platform doors, making it impossible for anyone to fall on to the track. Call points by each of the carriage doors can be used in an emergency or by people with mobility issues. Travel cards must be punched into the yellow time clocks on the platform before boarding.

S-TOG

Copenhagen's rail system is known as **S-tog** and is run by the DSB state railway. This fast and convenient service consists of 10 lines that all pass through Central Station and run to the outskirts of the city. The DSB website *(see p307)* has a journey planner that allows you to find the best route around Copenhagen.

All S-tog trains have bright carriages with plenty of

space for passengers with bicycles, prams and wheelchairs (outside of peak times). Screens in the carriages show traffic information and news in Danish, and there is also free broadband connectivity.

Tickets can be bought at the station. Travel cards must be punched into one of the yellow time clocks on the platform by inserting it with the magnetic strip facing downwards.

All trains are marked with a red hexagon bearing a white letter "S". Those marked with an "X" are express trains with limited stops. Most of the system has been adapted for disabled passengers, and there are lifts from street level to the platforms.

Trains operate from about 5am until around 1am during the week and on Sundays, and throughout the night on Fridays and Saturdays.

Cyclists boarding a train at Copenhagen's Central Station

REGIONAL TRAINS

The Greater Copenhagen (HT) transport region stretches as far north as Helsingør and Hornbæk and as far east as Roskilde and Lejre. Many outlying attractions – including the Louisiana art galleries in Humlebæk – can be visited on a day trip using regional trains and a Copenhagen area *klippekort*.

TICKETS

Public transport tickets in Copenhagen are valid on trains, buses and the metro, and it is possible to transfer from one mode of transport to another on the same ticket. Tickets are available from ticket offices, vending machines at stations and bus drivers.

The metropolitan area is split into seven zones. The cheapest ticket *(billet)* allows you to travel within two zones. A *klippekort* is valid for 10 trips within two zones; for travel between three or more zones, you will need to buy the correct ticket or clip the appropriate number of *klippekort* tickets. Clipping stamps your travel card with the date, time and the zone from which you are departing. Cards stamped for journeys within the same zone or between two or three zones are valid for 1 hour. Four-, five- and six-zone tickets are valid for 90 minutes, and tickets and stamped 10-trip cards for all zones are valid for 2 hours. Fares on night buses are the same. Travelling without a valid ticket carries a high penalty.

Special tickets that allow for unlimited travel over a 24-hour period are available. Tourist passes like the Copenhagen Card (for dealers, visit the Copenhagen Visitor Centre website, *see p297*) allow unrestricted travel on public transport, as well as reduced entry to many attractions.

Two children up to the age of 12 travel free when accompanied by an adult with the correct ticket. Four children up to the age of 12 can travel on one ticket, or one clip of an adult *klippekort*. Children under 16 pay a child's fare when travelling alone.

DRIVING

Much of Copenhagen's city centre is car-free, and parking spaces are in high demand and expensive. Driving in central Copenhagen is therefore not recommended.

TAXIS

Taxis operate all over the city at all times. To hail a cab in the street, simply wave to any that displays a lit *fri* sign. There are taxi ranks outside the Central Station, Nørreport Station and Kongens Nytorv.

WALKING

Copenhagen is the perfect city for walking around. Green spaces and parks provide plenty of places to take a break. The tourist office *(see p297)* runs themed walking tours on subjects such as history, food and design. The energetic can join a **Running Copenhagen** tour.

CYCLING

Copenhagen is one of the most cycle-friendly cities in the world, with cycle lanes over much of it, and cycle- and footbridges crossing the canals. Nørrebrogade is open to bicycles, pedestrians and buses only.

The summer scheme Bycykler provides over 2,000 bikes for anyone who wishes to use one free of charge. The bicycles have solid wheels and punctureless tyres; to deter theft, they are unsuitable for travelling long distances. They are available from 125 stands throughout the city, located close to main attractions and at some of the larger S-tog stations. A 20 Dkr coin must be deposited in the stand to release a bike. This deposit is returned once the bike is placed back in a stand.

Cycling is a great way to see the city, and bikes can be taken free of charge on the S-tog. Guided tours, like **Bike Copenhagen With Mike**, are also available.

Take care when cycling in the city and obey the rules of the road at all times. Cycle lanes can be quite aggressive, especially at peak times.

DIRECTORY

BUSES

Movia
Tel 36 13 14 00.
www.moviatrafik.dk

METRO AND S-TOG

Metro
Tel 70 15 16 15. www.m.dk

S-tog / Regional Trains
Tel 70 13 14 15. www.dsb.dk

WALKING

Running Copenhagen
Tel 20 58 58 77.
www.running-copenhagen.dk

CYCLING

Bike Copenhagen With Mike
Tel 26 39 56 88.
www.bikecopenhagenwith
mike.dk

WATERBUSES

DFDS Canal Tours
Tel 32 96 30 00.
www.canaltours.dk

WATERBUSES

A trip on a waterbus is a good way to see Copenhagen, as the city's canals lead past many of the major sights. The trips run by **DFDS Canal Tours** are accompanied by a guide and are particularly appealing to people with children. The yellow harbour buses 991, 992 and 993, operated by Movia and subject to the same fare system as buses and trains, are a cheaper alternative.

Departure point for a waterbus on a canal in Copenhagen

General Index

Page numbers in **bold** type refer to main entries. The Danish letters å (aa), æ and ø fall at the end of the alphabet *(see p325)*.

A

Abildgaard, Nicolai 26
Abildskou 307
Absalon, Bishop 22, 36, 81, 86, 170
  Asserbo 130
  Christiansborg Slot 87
  Fanefjord Kirke 168
  monument 70
  Roskilde Domkirke 142
  Selsø Slot 138
  statue of 74
  tomb of 144
  Vordingborg 153
Absolutism **38–9**
A.C. Perch's Thehandel (Copenhagen) 101
Academy of Knights 38
Accessories, shopping **99**, 101
Adeler, Christian 150
Admission prices 296–7
Aerøfærgerne 307
Afstøbningssamling (Copenhagen) 53
Agersø 156
Agriculture 18
Air travel **304–5**
Akademiet (Sorø) 145
Akvavit 267, 287
Alexander III, Tsar 52
Alexander Newsky Kirke (Copenhagen) 52
Alexandra, Princess 55
Allinge 18, **220**
  hotels 258
  restaurants 283
Althings 236
Amager and Ørestad **96–7**
Amager Hospital (Copenhagen) 299
Amagertorv (Copenhagen) 70
Amaliehaven (Copenhagen) 53
Amalienborg Slot (Copenhagen) 39, **56–7**
  Street-by-Street map 52–3
Amber Museum (Copenhagen) 68
The Amber Specialist (Copenhagen) 101
Ambulances 299
Ammassalik (Tasiilaq) **233**
Amusement parks 288
  Bakken **120**
  BonBon-Land **157**
  Fårup Sommerland 204
  Joboland **226**
  Labyrinthia Park 187
  Legoland 183, **192–3**
  Sjælland Sommerland 151
  Småland (Knuthenborg Safari Park) 161
  Tivoli (Copenhagen) **76–7**
Ancher, Anna and Michael 26, 59, 62, 205, 206
Andelslandsbyen Nyvang (Holbæk) 139
Andersen, Eric 70
Andersen, Hans Christian 15, 42, 43, 71
  bicentenary 45
  BonBon-Land 157
  Brøndums Hotel (Skagen) 205
  Gisselfeld Kloster (Haslev) 156

Andersen, Hans Christian (cont.)
  H.C. Andersens Barndomshjem (Odense) 178
  H.C. Andersens Hus (Odense) 173, 179
  Karmeliterklosteret Sankt Mariæ Kirke (Helsingør) 124
  Lerchenborg Slot 147
  The Little Mermaid (Copenhagen) **54**
  Nyhavn (Copenhagen) 67
  plays (Odense) 29
  statues of 58, 74, 75
  tomb of 94
Anisse Nord 131
Anker, Poul 222
Ansgar 195
Antiques shops **100**, 101
Apostelhuset (Næstved) 158
Aquaparks
  Fårup Sommerland 204
  Joboland 226
  Lalandia 162
Aquariums
  Danmarks Akvarium (Copenhagen) **95**
  Fiskeri-og-Søfartsmuseet (Esbjerg) 194–5
  Fiskeriets Hus (Hvide Sande) 190
  Fjord&Bælt (Kerteminde) 176
  Nordsøen Oceanarium (Hirtshals) 204
  Øresundakvariet (Helsingør) 125
Arbejdernes Kampdag 28
Archaeological sites
  Grønjægers Høj (Møn) 168
  Grønnese Skov 134
  Jelling 191
  Klekkendehøj (Møn) 168
  Knudshoved Odde 155, 159
  Kong Asgers Høj (Møn) **168**
  Lejre Forsøgscentre 117, **138–9**
  Lindholm Høje **206–7**
  Madsebakke Helleristninger (Allinge) 220
  see also Vikings
Architecture 19, **22–3**, 35, 39
Arken Museum For Moderne Kunst (Copenhagen) **97**
ARoS Kunstmuseum (Aarhus) 188
Around Limfjorden Race 30
Arp, Jean 122
Arresø 117, **130–31**
Arsenal, Tøjhusmuseet (Copenhagen) 82, **88**
Art **26–7**
  "Golden Age" **42–3**, 62, 78
  shopping **100**, 101
Asnæs peninsula 147
Assens **176**
  hotels 251
Asserbo tour 130
Assistens Kirkegård (Copenhagen) **94**
Assurnasirpal II, King of Assyria 78
Astronomy
  Rundetårn (Copenhagen) **71**
  Tycho Brahe Planetarium (Copenhagen) 19, **92**
ATMs 300
Autumn in Denmark 30
Avis 309
Axeltorv (Helsingør) 124

B

Bache, Otto 41
Baggsen, Ida 158
Baisikeli Bike Rental 311
Bakken **120**
Baldaccini, Cesar 122
Ballet **288**, 289
  in Copenhagen **102–3**, 105
Bandholm 276
Bang, Jens 208
Bang & Olufsen 19, 24, 101
Bangsbo-Museet 206
Banknotes 301
Banks **300**
Baroque architecture 23
Baruël, Jean-Jacques 209
Beaches 18, 293
  Amager Strand 96–7
  Bornholm 217
  in Copenhagen **103**, 105
  Funen 173
  Hornbæk 128
  Langeland 180
  Limfjorden 210
  Marielyst 167
  Northern Jutland 201
  Odsherred 151
  Southern Zealand 153
Bed & breakfast **242**, 243
Beer 266, 287
  Carlsberg Brewery (Copenhagen) **92**
Bella and Hanna Nathansson (Eckersberg) 42
Belleforest, François de 126
Bellevue Strand (Copenhagen) 105
Bendz 59
Berg, Claus 27, 145, 178, 189
Bering, Vitus Jonassen 186
Bering Flowers (Copenhagen) 101
Big Thumb (Baldaccini) 122
Bike Copenhagen with Mike 313
Bikes4rent.dk 311
Billetnet 105
Billetnet 105
Billund 253
Billund Airport 305
Bindesbøll, Gottlieb 42
Birdwatching
  Bøto Nor bird sanctuary 167
  Faroe Islands 229, 236, 237
  Limfjorden 201, 211
  Nyord 170
  Selsø lake 138
  Tipperne Nature Reserve 190
Birkerød 247
Bjernede 145
Bjørck, Oskar 205
"Black Diamond" (Kongelige Bibliotek Copenhagen) 15, 23, 83, 88
Blixen, Karen 120, **121**
Blunck, Dietlev 43
bmi (British Midland) 305
Boats
  canal tours 313
  cruises **293**
  ferries **307**
  Fregatten Jylland (Ebeltoft) 186
  hiring 292
  Korsør By-og Overfartsmuseum 145
  Ladbyskibet 176
  Museet for Søfart (Helsingør) 125
  Søfartsmuseum (Marstal) 181

Boats (cont.)
  Viking 34–5, 293
  Vikingeskibsmuseet (Roskilde)
    19, 141
Bodum, Peter 24
Bohr, Niels Henrik 77
  statue of 74
  tomb of 94
Bolia (Copenhagen) 99
BonBon-Land **157**
Bornholm 11, 115, **217–27**
  cycling **227**, 291
  hotels 258–60
  landscape and flora 20
  map 13, 218–19
  restaurants 283–4
  round churches 22, 217, 218, **221**
Bornholm Velcomstcenter (Rønne)
    293
Bornholms Visitor Centre 297
Bornhøved, Battle of (1227) 36
Botanisk Have (Copenhagen) **59**
Bothwell, Lord James von 150
Brahe, Tycho 92
Brandenburger, Ernst 93
Brandes, Peter 141
Brandts (Odense) 178
Breakdowns 309
Bregentved Slot (Haslev) 156
Bresterson, Sigmund 237
Bridges 309
  Storebælt **146**, 309
  Øresund 91, **96**, 97, 309
Britain, wars with 40–41
British Airways 305
Brodersen, Anne Marie 179
Brokman, Hans 142
Bronze Age 33
Brown ale 266
Bruegel, Pieter 62, 63
Bruno, Francesco 60
Brunsvick, Queen Juliane Marie of
    86
Bruun Rasmussent (Copenhagen)
    101
Bruuns Bazaar (Copenhagen) 101
Brøndums Hotel (Skagen) 205
Budolfi Domkirke (Aalborg) 209
Buffalo 159
Bungaard, Anders 55
Bureaux de change 300
Buses, Copenhagen 312
By Malene Birger
    (Copenhagen) 101
Byron, Lord 85
Bysøparken (Holbæk) 139
Børsen (Copenhagen) 39, 83, **85**
Bøto Nor bird sanctuary (near
    Marielyst) 167
Bøtger family 150

C

Café Intime (Copenhagen) 105
Camp sites **241**, 243
Campingrådet 243
Canals
  Christianshavn (Copenhagen) 88
  Nyhavn (Copenhagen) 67, **68**
  tours (Copenhagen) 313
Canoeing and kayaking 30
  Glumsø 157
  Suså 156
Canute I (The Great), King 33
Canute II, King 178
Car hire 309
Canute III, King 22

Caritas Springvandet (Copenhagen)
    73
Carl XVI, King of Sweden 96
Carlsberg Brewery (Copenhagen)
    92
Carmen & Fantasio 101
Cars **308–9**
  driving in towns 311
  Gjern vintage car museum 187
  Sports Car Museum (Væggerløse)
    167
  see also Tours by car
Casa Shop (Copenhagen) 101
Castles and fortifications
  Asserbo 130
  Bregentved Slot (Haslev) 156
  Dragsholm Slot **150**
  Egeskov Slot (Funen) 11, 173, **177**
  Fredericia 197
  Frykat Viking fortress 35, 201,
    215
  Gisselfeld Kloster (Haslev) 156
  Hammershus Slot **220**
  Jægerspris Slot **135**
  Kalundborg 147
  Kastellet (Copenhagen) **54**
  Koldinghus 185, 197
  Korsør Fæstning 145
  Kronberg Slot (Helsingør) 23,
    115, **126–7**
  Krudttårnet (Frederikshavn) 206
  Lerchenborg Slot 147
  Nyborg Slot **177**
  Rosenholm Slot 215
  Selsø Slot **138**
  Skansin Fort (Tórshavn) 236
  Spøttrup Borg 210
  Tranekær Slot 181
  Trelleborg 115, **147**
  Valdemars Slot (Tåsinge) 180
  Vallø Slot **171**
  Voergård Slot 201, **206**
  Vordingborg 158–9
  Aalborghus Slot (Aalborg) 208
  Ålholm Slot 163
  see also Palaces
Cathedrals
  Budolfi Domkirke (Aalborg) 209
  Domkirke (Aarhus) 188
  Haderslev Domkirke 197
  Maribo 162
  Ribe Domkirke 22, 195
  Roskilde Domkirke 22, 27, 118,
    142–3
  Sankt Knuds Domkirke (Odense)
    22, 27, 178
  Sankt Olai Kirke (Helsingør) 125
  Viborg Domkirke 214
  Vor Frue Kirke (Copenhagen)
    72–3
  see also Churches
Catherine II, Tsarina 71, 93
Cemeteries
  Assistens Kirkegård
    (Copenhagen) **94**
  Lindholm Høje 201, **206–7**
  Russian cemetery (Allinge) 220
Central Copenhagen **65–79**
  area map 65
  hotels 244–5
  Kongens Nytorv:
    Street-by-Street map 66–7
  restaurants 268–70
Centralhjørnet (Copenhagen) 105
Changing of the guard
  (Amalienborg Slot) 57, 58

Chaplin, Charlie 71
Charlemagne, Emperor 33
Charlotte Amalie, Princess 95
Charlotte Amalie, Queen 69
Charlottenborg Slot (Copenhagen)
    23, 67, **68**
Charlottenlund Slot (Copenhagen)
    95
Children
  entertainment in Copenhagen
    104, 105
  Experimentarium (Copenhagen)
    94–5
  in hotels 242
  in restaurants 263
Christ as the Suffering Redeemer
  (Mantegna) 63
Christian I, King 72
Christian II, King 37, 124
  Sønderborg 196
  tomb of 144
  Ålholm Slot 163
Christian III, King 17
  tomb of 27
  Aalborghus Slot (Aalborg) 208
Christian IV, King 23, 26, 37
  Akademiet (Sorø) 145
  Caritas Springvandet
    (Copenhagen) 73
  Christiansborg Slot (Copenhagen)
    86
  Christianshavn (Copenhagen) 88
  Kongens Have (Copenhagen) 58
  Kronberg Slot (Helsingør) 126
  Rosenberg Slot (Copenhagen) 60,
    61
  Rundetårn (Copenhagen) 71
  tomb of 142
  Tøjhusmuseet (Copenhagen) 88
  Valdemars Slot (Tåsinge) 180
Christian V, King 38
  Frederiksborg Slot (Hillerød) 132
  statue of 67, 68–9
  Vor Frelsers Kirke (Copenhagen)
    81
Christian VI, King 86, 120
Christian VII
  abolishes serfdom 40
  Amalienborg Slot 39
  Frederiksberg Slot (Copenhagen)
    93
  Royal Copenhagen Porcelain 93
Christian IX, King 55
Christian X, King 44
Christian, Jacob 92
Christiania (Copenhagen) 18, **89**
Christianity 33
Christiansborg Slot (Copenhagen)
    23, **86–7**, 170
  Street-by-Street map 82–3
Christiansen, Ole Kirk 19, 24, 183,
    192
Christianshavn (Copenhagen) 81,
    88
Christiansø
  hotels 259
  restaurants 283
Christmas 30–31
Christoffer I 195
Christoffer III 124
Churches
  Alexander Newsky Kirke
    (Copenhagen) 52
  Bornholm round churches 22,
    217, 218, **221**
  Fanefjord Kirke **168**

Churches (cont.)
Grundtvigs Kirke (Copenhagen) **94**
Helligåndskirken (Copenhagen) **70**
Marmorkirken (Copenhagen) 48, 52, **58**, 115
Nyker round church **222**
Sankt Albans Kirke (Copenhagen) **54–5**
Sankt Ansgars Kirke (Copenhagen) 53, 55
Sankt Petri Kirke (Copenhagen) **72**
Tveje Merløse Kirke **144**
Vor Frelsers Kirke (Copenhagen) 23, 39, 81, **88–9**
Vor Frue Kirke (Copenhagen) 43
Østerlars Rundkirke (Sankt Laurentius) 221, **226**
see also Cathedrals; Monasteries *and individual towns and villages*
Churchillparken (Copenhagen) 55
Cinema **288**, 289
in Copenhagen **103**, 105
film festivals 28–30
Cinemateket (Copenhagen) 105
Cinemaxx (Copenhagen) 105
Cisternerne (Copenhagen) **93**
City Hall, Rådhus (Copenhagen) **74–5**
Cleopatra 71
Climate 28–31
Clothes
in restaurants 263
shopping **99**, 101
Clown festival (Klampenborg) 29
Club Christopher (Copenhagen) 105
Coach travel 306
CoBrA 27
Coffee 267, 287
Coins 301
Cold Museum (Ilulissat) 233
Color Line 307
Communications **302–3**
Concert Hall (Tivoli, Copenhagen) 77
Copencabana (Copenhagen) 105
Copenhagen 10, **47–111**, 115
airport 304–5
Amalienborg Slot: Street-by-Street map 52–3
boat trips 67
bureau de change 300
Central Copenhagen **65–79**
Christiansborg Slot: Street-by-Street map 82–3
entertainment **102–5**
events 28–31
Further Afield **91–7**
Golden Age in 43
hotels 244–7
Kongens Nytorv: Street-by-Street map 66–7
maps 48–9, 91
North Copenhagen **51–63**
public transport **312–13**
restaurants 268–74
shopping **98–101**
South Copenhagen **81–9**
Street Finder 106–11
Copenhagen Blues Festival 105
Copenhagen Cooking 29
Copenhagen Gay Life 105

Copenhagen Jazz Festival 105
Copenhagen Jazz House 105
Copenhagen Opera Festival 105
Copenhagen Right Now
Information and Booking Service 243
Copenhagen Steno Apotek 299
Copenhagen Sønderbro Apotek 299
Copenhagen Visitor Centre 297
Coppy, Maria 68
Cottages 242–3
CouchSurfing 297
Courier services 303
CPH:DOX (Copenhagen) 30
CPH:PIX (Copenhagen) 28
Credit cards 300
lost or stolen 298
in restaurants 263
in shops 99, 287
Crime 16, 298
Crocodiles
Krokodille Zoo (Eskilstrup) 167
Crown jewels 61
Cruises **293**
CSV Cykeludlejning 311
Cubism 27
Cultural Harvest 29
Culture Box (Copenhagen) 105
Currency **300–301**
Customs information 296
Cycling **291**, 293
bike hire 311
Bornholm 218, **227**, 291
in Copenhagen 313
Dansk Cykel & Knallert Museum (Glumsø) 157
Funen 173
Langeland 180
tours 292
in towns 311
Czarens Hus (Nykøbing F) 166

D

Dagmar (Copenhagen) 105
Dagmar, Queen 156, 195
Dajon, Nicolai 27
Dance **288**, 289
in Copenhagen **102–3**, 105
Danevirke 33
Danhostel Danmarks Vandrehjem 243
Danish Design Centre (Copenhagen) 24, 101
Danish Freedom Council 44–5
Danish pastries 265
Danland & DanCenter 243
Danmarks Akvarium (Copenhagen) **95**
Danmarks Borgcenter (Vordingborg) 159
Danmarks Saltcenter (Mariager) 215
Danmarks Sportsfiskerforbund 293
Danner, Countess 135
Dansecenen (Copenhagen) 105
Dansk B&B 243
Dansk Camping Union 243
Dansk Cykel & Knallert Museum (Glumsø) 157
Dansk Cyklist Forbund 293
Dansk Danseteater (Copenhagen) 105
Dansk Folkeferie 243
Dansk Golf Union 293
Dansk Idræt Forbund 293
Dansk Landbrugs-museum (Gammel Estrup) 215

Dansk Møbelkunst (Copenhagen) 101
Dansk Polarcenter (Copenhagen) 233
Dansk Ride Forbund 293
Dansk Slotte & Herregaarde 242
Dansk Vandrelaug 293
Danske Bank 300
Danske Kroer & Hoteller 243
Dansommer 243
Dantaxi 311
David, Christian Ludvig 58
David, Jacques Louis 26
Davids Samling (Copenhagen) **58**
Day Birger et Mikkelsen (Copenhagen) 101
De Vries, Adrian 23
Dead Drunk Danes (Jørn) 26
Degas, Edgar 78, 79
Le Déjeuner sur l'Herbe (Picasso) 122
Department stores **99**, 101
Design 19, **24–5**
shopping **99**, 101, 287
Designer Zoo (Copenhagen) 99
Designers Remix (Copenhagen) 101
DesignMuseum Danmark (Copenhagen) 24, 53, **55**
DFDS Canal Tours (Copenhagen) 313
DFDS Seaways 307
DHL 303
Dialling codes 302
Dinesen, Isak 120
Disabled travellers
in hotels 242
in restaurants 263
Disko Bay 233
DK-CAMP 2002 243
Doctors 299
Dog-sled trips, Greenland 229, 233
Dokøen (Copenhagen) 81
Domhuset (Copenhagen) 73
Domkirke *see* Cathedrals
Donaldson, Mary 45
Donatello 63
DR Koncerthuset (Copenhagen) 105
Drachmann, Holger 204, 205
Dragon's Leap Fountain (Copenhagen) 75
Dragsholm **150**
Dragør 91, 96, **97**
Drink *see* Food and drink
Driving **308–9**
in Copenhagen 313
in towns 311
Driving tours *see* Tours by car
Dronning Louises Bro (Copenhagen) 91
Dronningens Pakhus (Nakskov) 162
Dronninglund 256
Dråby Kirke 138
DSB (Danish railway services) 307
Dueodde 259
Dukkehuset (Ærøskøbing) 181
Dunkel (Copenhagen) 105
Dúvugarðar Museum (Saksun) 236
Dybbøl (Sønderborg) 196
Dyveke 124

E

E-mail 303
easyJet 305
Ebbesøn, Sune 145
Ebeltoft **186**
hotels 253–4
restaurants 279

Eckersberg, Christoffer Wilhelm 26, 40, 41
Bella and Hanna Nathansson 42
Hirschsprungske Samling (Copenhagen) 59
Statens Museum for Kunst (Copenhagen) 62
tomb of 94
Ecolarium (Vejle) 194
Ecological tax 240–41
Edward VII, King of England 55
Ege, Ole 71
Egede, Hans 232
Egeskov Slot (Funen) 11, 173, **177**
Eigtved, Nicolai 23
Amalienborg Slot (Copenhagen) 39, 56–7
Kunstindustrimuseet (Copenhagen) 55
Ledreborg Slot 139
Marmorkirken (Copenhagen) 58
Eigtved, Niels 129
Eliasson, Olafur 97
Elmelunde **169**
Elmelunde Master 168, 169
Elmuseet (Tange Sø) 187
Embassies 297
Emergencies 298
Emergency services 299
Empire Bio (Copenhagen) 105
Empiregården (Stege) 169
Entertainment **288–9**
ballet and contemporary dance **102–3**, 105
beaches **104**, 105
booking tickets **102**, 105
children's entertainment **104**, 105
cinema **103**, 105
gay and lesbian **104**, 105
in Copenhagen **102–5**
jazz clubs and live music **103**, 105
nightlife venues **103**, 105
opera and classical music **102**, 105
theatre **103**, 105
Environment 18
Erik IV, King 156
Erik V, King 36
Erik Klipping, King 176
Erik of Pomerania 37, 124, 140, 162
Erik the Red 229
Eriksen, Edvard 54
Erlandsen, Eric 56
Ermitagen hunting lodge 117, 120
Ernst, Frederik 176
Erslev 281
Esbjerg **194–5**
hotels 253
restaurants 279
Eskebjerg 247
Eskilstrup **166–7**
Esrum 128, 131
Esrum Møllegard 128
Esrum Sø **130–31**
Eurolines 307
Europcar 309
European Medieval Festival (Horsens) 29
European Union 18, 45
Events 28–31
Experimentarium (Copenhagen) **94–5**
Expressionism 27
Eysturoy **237**
hotels 261
restaurants 285

F
Faergen 307
Fakse **170**
Falck 305
Falster 153, 166–8
Falsters Minde (Nykøbing F) 166
Famjin 237
Fane, Queen 168
Fanefjord Kirke **168**
Fanø 29, 253
Farm holidays 243
Faroe Islands 11, 15, 229, **234–7**
hotels 261
map 12, 234–5
restaurants 285
Farsø 256
Fashion fair (Copenhagen) 31
Fastelavn 31
Fauna *see* Wildlife
FC København 289
FC Midtjylland 289
FDM 309
FDM Camping 243
Ferries **307**
Festivals 19, **28–31**
Fiddlers Museum (Rebild Bakker) 214
Fields (Copenhagen) 101
Figaros Bryllup (Copenhagen) 101
Film *see* Cinema
Fishing 18, **290–91**, 293
Fiskeri-og-Søfartsmuseet (Esbjerg) 194–5
Fiskeriets Hus (Hvide Sande) 190
Fisketorvet (Copenhagen) 101
Fjerritslev 211
Fjord&Bælt (Kerteminde) 176
Fjord Line 307
Flag 11
Flakhaven (Odense) 178
Flaske-Peters Samling (Ærøskøbing) 181
Flora **20–21**
Flora Danica porcelain 25, 55, **93**
Floris, Cornelius 27
Fluxus 70
Folketinget (Copenhagen) 16–17, 83, **85**
La Fontaine (Copenhagen) 105
Food and drink
Carlsberg Brewery (Copenhagen) **92**
The Flavours of Denmark **264–5**
shopping 287
what to drink **266–7**
see also Restaurants
Football 289
Forex 300
Forsorgsmuseet (Svendborg) 180
Forsvarsmuseet (Rønne) 223
Fotomuseum (Herning) 187
Fragonard, Jean Honoré 206
Fredensborg 131
restaurants 274
Fredensborg Slot 23, **129**, 131
Fredericia 185, **197**
hotels 253
restaurants 279
Frederik, Crown Prince 45
Frederik II, King 23
Frederiksborg Slot (Hillerød) 132
Kronborg Slot (Helsingør) 126–7
Marienlyst Slot (Helsingør) 125
Nationalmuseet (Copenhagen) 82

Frederik III, King 27, 37, 38, 39
Amalienborg Slot (Copenhagen) 57
Fredericia 197
Frederiksborg Slot (Hillerød) 133
Frederikssund 135
Kastellet (Copenhagen) 54
Frederik IV, King
Fredensborg Slot 129
Frederiksberg Slot (Copenhagen) 93
Rosenberg Slot (Copenhagen) 60, 61
Frederik V, King
Amalienborg Slot (Copenhagen) 52, 56
Charlottenborg Slot (Copenhagen) 69
Kongenshus Mindepark 207
Marmorkirken (Copenhagen) 58
Rådhuset (Aalborg) 208
statue of 57
Frederik VI, King 40, 43, 171
Frederik VII, King 39
Frederikshøj hunting pavilion 135
Jægerspris Slot 135
statue of 178
Frederik VIII, King 44, 95
Frederik IX, King 45, 71
Frederiksberg Slot and Have (Copenhagen) **93**
Frederiksborg Slot (Hillerød) 22, 119, **132–3**, 136–7
Neptune's Fountain 116
Slotskirken 38
Frederikshavn **206**
hotels 256–7
restaurants 281
Frederikshavn–Læsø 307
Frederikshøj (Nordskoven) 135
Frederikskirken *see* Marmorkirken (Copenhagen)
Frederikssund 35, **135**
hotels 248
restaurants 274
Frederikstad district (Copenhagen) 23
Frederiksværk 130
Fregatten Jylland (Ebeltoft) 186
Freuchen, Peter 134
Frihedsmuseet (Copenhagen) **55**
Frilandsmuseet (Maribo) 162
Frilandsmuseet (near Copenhagen) **120**
Fuglsang Kunstmuseum (Toreby) **163**
Funen 10–11, 114, **173–81**
hotels 251–3
landscape and flora 21
map 174–5
restaurants 277–9
Fyn *see* Funen
Fyns Kunstmuseum (Odense) 178–9
Fyrkat 35, 201, 202, **215**
Faaborg 174, **177**
hotels 251
Fårup **204**
hotels 256
Fårup Sommerland 204
Føroya Fornminnissavn (Tórshavn) 236
Føroyar *see* Faroe Islands

G
Det Gamle Apotek (Langeland) 181
Det Gamle Apotek (Tønder) 196
Den Gamle By (Aarhus) 189

Den Gamle Gaard (Faaborg) 174, 177
Det Gamle Rådhus (Ribe) 195
Den Gamle Smedie (Nakskov) 162
Gammel Estrup 17, **215**
Gammeltorv (Copenhagen) 73
Gardens *see* Parks and gardens
Gauguin, Paul 79
Gavnø **158**
Gay and lesbian travellers
  in Copenhagen **104**, 105
Gefion Springvandet (Copenhagen)
  48, **55**
Geocenter Møns Klint 168–9
Geologisk Museum (Copenhagen)
  59
Geologiske Museum (Fakse) 170
Giacometti, Alberto 122, 207
Gilbjergstien 129
Gilleleje **128–9**
  hotels 248
  restaurants 274
Gisselfeld Kloster (Haslev) 156
Givskud Zoo (Loveparken) **190–91**
Gjern 187
Gjorslev 170
Gjøgv 237
Glam Vintage (Copenhagen) 101
Glass
  Glasmuseet (Ebeltoft) 186
  Holmegård Glassworks 157
  Pernille Bulow (Svaneke) 223
  shopping for 101
Gloria (Copenhagen) 105
Glumsø **157**
Gniben 151
Godfred, King of Jutland 33
Godthåb *see* Nuuk
Golden Age 26, 41, **42–3**, 62, 78
Golden Days (Copenhagen) 30
Goldgubber (gold tablets) 222
Golf **292**, 293
GoMore 297
Gorm the Old 33, 191
Gothic architecture 22
Government 16–17
Goya y Lucientes, Francisco José de
  206
Grand Teatret (Copenhagen) 105
Granhøj Dans (Aarhus) 289
Graubelle Man 186
Green Key 297
Green Square (Copenhagen) 101
Green travel 310
Greenland 15, **229–33**
  hotels 260–61
  map 12, 230–31
  restaurants 284–5
Grenen 201, **204**
  restaurants 282
Grenå
  hotels 254
  restaurants 279
Gribskov 130, 131
*Group of Danish Artists Visiting
  Rome* (Hansen) 42–3
Grund, J.G. 129
Grundtvig, Nicolai Frederik Severin
  94
Grundtvigs Kirke (Copenhagen) **94**
Gråbrødre Kirkegård (Roskilde) 141
Gråbrødretorv (Copenhagen) **72**
Græsted 129
Grøn Jæger, King 168
Grønjægers Høj (Møn) 168
Grønnesse Skov **134**
Gudenå 187

Gudhjem 11, **226**, 227
  hotels 259
  restaurants 283
Guinness World Records Museum
  (Copenhagen) 66, **69**
Gunderslev Kirke (Skelby) 157
Gunhilde, Queen 194
Gustav Vasa, King of Sweden 37
Gåsetårnet (Vordingborg) 159

H

Haag, Carl 34
Haakon, King of Norway 36
Haderslev **197**
  restaurants 279
Halsnæsstien 134
Hamlet (Shakespeare) 115, 124,
  126
Hamlet Summer (Helsingør) 29
Hammershaimb, Venceslaus Ulricus
  236
Hammershus Slot **220**
Handball 289
Hans Christian's Wonderful World
  (Copenhagen) 105
Hanseatic League 36, 159
Hansen, Christian Frederik
  43, 72, 73
Hansen, Constantin 42, 59
  *Group of Danish Artists Visiting
  Rome* 42–3
  Universitet (Copenhagen) 72
Hansen, Jacob 190
Hansen, Peter 177
Hansen, Svend Wiig 195, 198–9
Hanstholm 256
Harald I (Bluetooth) 17, 33
  Jelling 191
  Roskilde 140, 142
  Trelleborg 147
Harboøre 210
Hardcanute 36
Harsdorf, Caspar Frederik 129
Hasle **222**
  restaurants 283–4
Haslev 156
Haven, Lambert van 39, 89
Havnebadet (Copenhagen) 105
Havneby 196
Havnebyen 151
Hay Cph (Copenhagen) 101
Health **299**
Heart Made (Copenhagen) 101
Helgoland swimming pool complex
  (Amager) 97
Helgsen, Paul 138
Hellebæk 25
Helligåndhuset (Næstved) 158
Helligåndskirken (Copenhagen) **70**
Helligåndsklosteret (Aalborg) 209
Helsingør **124–7**
  events 29
  hotels 248
  map 125
  restaurants 274
Helsingør Bymuseum 124
Helvig, Queen 128
Henningsen, Poul 25
Herning **187**
  hotels 254
  restaurants 279
Herrings
  pickled 287
  smoked 217, 222, 226
Hertz 309
Hestetorvet (Roskilde) 141

Hillerød 275
Himmelbjerget 21, 187
Hindsholm **176**
Hirschsprung, Heinrich 59
Hirschsprungske Samling
  (Copenhagen) **59**
Hirtshals **204**
  hotels 256
Historic house hotels **241**, 243
Historiecenter Dybbøl Banke
  (Sønderborg) 196–7
Historiske Museum (Aalborg) 209
History **33–45**
Hitler, Adolf 44, 71
Hjerl Hedes Frilandsmuseum **207**,
  210
Hjertetjeldet mountain 233
Hjørring 282
Hobro 282
Hog, Count Henrik 158
Holberg, Ludvig 69, 145
Holbæk **139**
  hotels 248
  restaurants 275
Holger Danske 126
Holiday centres 242–3
Holidays, public 31
Holly Golightly (Copenhagen) 101
Holmegård glassworks 19, 24
Holmegaard Park 157
Holmen (Copenhagen) 81, 88
Holmens Kirke (Copenhagen) 27,
  38
Holstein, Count Johan Ludvig 139
Holsterbro **207**
  hotels 256
  restaurants 279
Holte 275
Home exchanges 243
Honthorst, Gerrit van 26, 126
Hornbæk **128**
  hotels 248
  restaurants 275
Horns Rev Lightship (Esbjerg) 195
Hornslet 215
Horse riding **290**, 293
Horsens **186**
  events 29
  hotels 254
  restaurants 279
Hospitals 299
Hostels **242**, 243
Hot springs
  Uunartoq 232
  Varmakelda 237
Hotel d'Angleterre (Copenhagen)
  66, **68**
Hotels **240–61**
  booking 240
  Bornholm 258–60
  chain hotels 241
  children in 242
  choosing 240
  Copenhagen 244–7
  disabled guests 242
  Faroe Islands 261
  Funen 251–3
  Greenland 260–61
  historic house **241**, 243
  Northern Jutland 256–8
  Northwestern Zealand 247–9
  prices 240
  Southern and Central Jutland
  253–5
  Southern Zealand and the Islands
  249–51

House of Amber (Copenhagen) 101
Hundested 117, **134**
    hotels 248
    restaurants 275
Hunting and Fishing Museum
    (Ilulissat) 233
Husmoderstrand 204
Hvalba 237
Hvalsey 232
Hvide Sande 190
Højbro Plads (Copenhagen) **70**
Højby 151
Højby Sø 151
Højerup 170
Hørsholm 275
Hørve 248
Høst, Oluf 226

I

Icebergs 233
Illum (Copenhagen) 101
Illums Bolighus (Copenhagen) 101
Ilulissat (Jakobshavn) **233**
    hotels 260
    restaurants 284
IMAX cinema (Copenhagen) 92
Immigration 17
Imperial (Copenhagen) 105
Indrio, Anna Maria 62
Inns **241**, 243
Interior decoration, shopping
    99, 101
Interior of a House (Marstrand) 42
Internet 302–3
Inuit 230
    Nationalmuseet (Copenhagen) 84
    Qilaqitsoq 233
Irish festival (Copenhagen) 30
The Irish House (Aalborg) 289
Iron Age 33
Isefjord 134
Isenstein, Harald 145

J

Jacobsen, Arne 19, 24, **25**, 123, 188
Jacobsen, Carl 54, 78, 132
Jacobsen, Hans Sandgren 25
Jacobsen, Peter 181
Jacobsen Brewhouse (Copenhagen)
    92
Jacobson, Robert 178
Jailhouse (Copenhagen) 105
Jakobshavn *see* Ilulissat
Jardin, Nicolas-Henri 56, 125
Jazz **103**, 105
    festivals 19, 29, 31
Jazzhus Dexter (Odense) 289
Jazzhus Montmartre (Copenhagen)
    105
Jelling **191**
    restaurants 279
Jens Bangs Stenhus (Aalborg) 23,
    208
Jensen, Christian Albrecht 26
Jensen, Georg 19, 24
    showroom (Copenhagen) 70, 101
Jerichau, Jens Adolph 78
Jesperhus Park (Limfjorden) 210
Jewellery shops **100**, 101
Joboland **226**
Jorn, Asger 26, 27, 97, 122, 187
Juel, Jens 26
Juel, Admiral Niels 153, 171, 180
Juliane Marie, Queen 86, 125
Julianehåb (Qaqortoq) **232**
Julie Sandlau (Copenhagen) 101

Jutes 183
Jutland *see* Northern Jutland;
    Southern and Central Jutland
Jutland Code 36, 73, 158–9
Juvre 196
Jylland *see* Northern Jutland;
    Southern and Central Jutland
Jyske Bank 300
Jægersborg Dyrehave **120**
Jægerspris Slot **135**

K

Kalmar Union 36–7, 124
Kalsoy **237**
Kalundborg **147**
    restaurants 275
Kalvehave Labyrintpark 159
Kangerlussuaq (Søndre Strømfjord)
    232–3
    hotels 260
    restaurants 284
Kap Kallur 237
Karen Blixen's house
    (Rungstedlund) 120, 121
Karlsstenen (Grønnese Skov) 134
Karmeliterklosteret Sankt Mariæ
    Kirke (Helsingør) 124
Karup Airport 305
Kastellet (Copenhagen) **54**
Kattegatruten 307
KB3 (Copenhagen) 105
Keldby 169
Kellerøddysen 145
Kerteminde **176**
    hotels 251
    restaurants 277
Kettinge 163
Kiel, Treaty of (1814) 40–41, 229
Kierkegaard, Søren 42, 43, 55
    statue of 88
    tomb of 94
Kikhavn 134
Kil Kafeen (Copenhagen) 105
Kirkeby 196
Kirkeby, Per 88, 97
Kirkjubøur 236
Kirkjuvatn 237
Kirsten Pils Kilde 120
The Kiss (Rodin) 78
Kite festival (Fanø) 29
Kjaer & Sommerfeldt (Copenhagen)
    101
Klaksvik 235
    restaurants 285
Klassik (Copenhagen) 101
Klekkendehøj (Møn) 168
Klint, Kaare 24
Klint, P.V. Jensen 94
Klintholm Havn 169
Klosterkirke (Sorø) 144–5
Knieper, Hans 126
Knud Rasmussens Hus (Hundested)
    134
Knudshoved 177
Knudshoved Odde 155, **159**
Knuth, Eggert Christoffer 160
Knuthenborg Safari Park **160–61**
Kolding 185, **197**
    hotels 254
    restaurants 280
Koltur 234
Komandørgaard (Toftum) 196
Kong Asgers Høj (Møn) **168**
Kongeegen (Nordskoven) 134, 135
Det Kongelige Bibliotek
    (Copenhagen) 15, 23, 83, **88**

Det Kongelige Kunstakademi
    (Copenhagen) 67
Det Kongelige Teater
    (Copenhagen) 67, 68, **69**, 105
Kongens Have (Copenhagen) **58**
Kongens Nytorv (Copenhagen) 65,
    68–9
    Street-by-Street map 66–7
Kongenshus Mindepark **207**
Kongernes Jelling 191
Konpagnihuset (Næstved) 158
Korsør **145**
    hotels 248
    restaurants 275
Korsør By-og Overfartsmuseet 145
Krageland family 204
Krieger, Johann Cornelius 23
Kristkirken (Tønder) 196
Krock, Henrik 129
Krogh, Christian 205
Krokodille Zoo (Eskilstrup) 167
Kronberg Slot (Helsingør) 23, 115,
    126–7
Krudttårnet (Frederikshavn) 206
Krøyer, Peder S. 26, 59, 205
Küchler, Albert 43
Kunsten Museum of Modern Art
    Aalborg 209, 211
Kunstforeningen GL Strand
    (Copenhagen) **71**
Kunsthallen Brandts (Odense) 178
Kunstmuseet Trapholt (Kolding) 197
Kvindemuseet (Aarhus) 189
Købelevhaven 162
Københavns Musikteater 105
Købke, Christen 26, 59
    tomb of 94
Køfod, Jens 222
Køge 153, **171**
    hotels 249
    restaurants 276
Køge Bay 153

L

Ladbyskibet 176
Lager 266
Lakes
    Arresø 117, **130–31**
    Esrum Sø **130–31**
    Højby Sø 151
    Mossø 187
    Silkeborg Lake District 187
Lalandia **162–3**
Landscape **20–21**
Landscape from Saint-Rémy
    (Van Gogh) 79
Landsforeningen for Landboturisme
    243
Landsoldaten monument
    (Fredericia) 197
Landsting 156
Langeland 173, **180–81**
Langeland, Rasmus 145
Larsen, Henning 89
Larsen, Johannes 59, 176, 177
Larssøn, Peter Jakob 206
The Last Supper (Nolde) 62
Laurvig, Count Conrad Danneskiold
    68
Laward, Knud 156
Le Clerk 39
Le Corbusier 25
Ledreborg Slot 23, **139**
Lego 19, 24
LEGOLAND® 183, **192–3**
Lejre **138–9**

Lente, Margarete von 150
Leonora Christina, Princess 220
Lerche, Christian 147
Lerchenborg Slot 147
Libraries
  Christiansborg Slot (Copenhagen) 87
  Det Kongelige Bibliotek (Copenhagen) 15, 23, 83, **88**
Lichtenberg Palace (Horsens) 186
Lighthouses
  Horns Rev Lightship (Esbjerg) 195
  Kap Kallur 237
  Nakkehoved Østre Fyr 128
  Nøre Lyngvig 190
  Oddesund Nord 212–13
  Rønne 222, 227
  Røsnæs 147
Lille Bælt 173, 197
Limfjorden 201, **210–11**
Lindholm Høje 34, 201, **206–7**
Liqueurs 267
Liselund Slot **169**
The Little Dancer (Degas) 79
Little Mermaid (Copenhagen) **54**
Livgarden 49
Livgardens Historiske Samling (Copenhagen) **58–9**
Locher, Carl 205
Lolland 153, 159–66
Lolland-Falster Stiftsmuseet (Maribo) 162
London Toast (Copenhagen) 105
Loppen (Copenhagen) 105
Lorentzen, C.A. 40
Lost property 298, 299
Louis Poulsen (Copenhagen) 101
Louise, Princess 44, 95
Louisiana Museum **122–3**
Lovns Bredning 211
Ludwig XV, King 56
Lumsås Mølle 151
Lund, Søren Robert 23, 97
Lundstrom, Vilhelm 27
Lungholm (Tågerup) 163
Lutheranism 17, 37
Lynæs 134
Lysberg (Copenhagen) 101
Løgstør 30
Løveapoteket (Næstved) 158

M

Madsebakke Helleristininger (Allinge) 220
Magasin du Nord (Copenhagen) 66, 101
Magazines 303
Malmö 91, 96
Man Meets the Sea (Hansen) 195, 198–9
Manet, Edouard 122
Mantegna, Andrea 63
Maps
  Bornholm 218–19
  Copenhagen 48–9
  Copenhagen: around Amalienborg Slot 52–3
  Copenhagen: around Christiansborg Slot 82–3
  Copenhagen: around Kongens Nytorv 66–7
  Copenhagen: Central Copenhagen 65
  Copenhagen: North Copenhagen 51

Maps (cont.)
  Copenhagen: outside city centre 91
  Copenhagen: South Copenhagen 81
  Copenhagen: Street Finder 106–11
  cycling on Bornholm 227
  Denmark 12–13, 114–15
  Faroe Islands 234–5
  Funen 174–5
  Greenland 230–31
  Helsingør 125
  Legoland 192–3
  Limfjorden 210–11
  Northern Jutland 202–3
  Northwestern Zealand 118–19
  Odense 179
  Odsherred tour 151
  Roskilde 141
  Southern and Central Jutland 184–5
  Southern Zealand and the islands 154–5
  Aalborg 209
  Aarhus 189
Marathon, Copenhagen 28
Marchal, Jean 68
Margrete I, Queen 36–7, 124
  Gavnø 158
  Roskilde 141
  tomb of 143, 144
Margrethe II, Queen 16, 45
  Amalienborg Slot (Copenhagen) 52
  birthday 28
  Christiansborg Slot (Copenhagen) 83, 86
  Folketing (Copenhagen) 85
  Royal Copenhagen Porcelain 93
  Vor Frue Kirke (Copenhagen) 73
  Øresund Bridge 96
Marguerite Route 291
Marhøj knoll (Hindsholm) 176
Mariager **214–15**
Maribo 17, **162**
  hotels 250
  restaurants 276
Marielyst **167**
  hotels 250
  restaurants 276
Marilyn Monroe (Warhol) 123
Marionet Teatret (Copenhagen) 105
Markets **100**, 101, **286**
Marmorkirken (Copenhagen) 48, 52, **58**, 115
Marsk Stig 176
Marstal **181**
  hotels 251
Marstrand, Wilhelm 42
Marx, Karl 71
Mary Queen of Scots 150
Masken Bar (Copenhagen) 105
Matisse, Henri 62, 207
Media 303
Medical care 299
Medicinsk-Historisk Museum (Copenhagen) 52
Mediemuseum (Odense) 178
Mens Bar (Copenhagen) 105
Menus 262
Merian, Maria 60
Meteorites 59
Metro, Copenhagen 312, 313
Meyers Bakery (Copenhagen) 101
Middelaldercenter (Østerlars Kirke) 226

Middelaldercentret (Lolland) **166**
Middelfart
  hotels 251–2
  restaurants 277
Midsummer Eve 29
Midvagur 236
Millinge 277
Milner, Edward 160
Mines, Mønsted **214**
Mix Copenhagen 30, 104
Mobile phones 302
Model railways
  Svinninge Modeljernbane 150
Moesgård **186**
Mojo Blues Bar (Copenhagen) 105
Mols Linien 307
Moltke, Count 56
Monasteries
  Cistercian monastery, Esrum 128
  convent (Gavnø) 158
  Esrum 131
  Helligåndsklosteret (Aalborg) 209
  Karmeliterklosteret Sankt Mariæ Kirke (Helsingør) 124
  Roskilde Kloster 140
  Æbelhof Kloster 130
Monet, Claude 79
Money **300–301**
Monroe, Marilyn 71, 123
Montre (Copenhagen) 101
Moore, Henry 122, 123
Mores, Jakob 132
Mors 210
Morstrand, Wilhelm 43
Moseløkken quarry (Allinge) 220
Motorcycle tours 291
Motorways 308
A Mountain Climber (J.F. Willumsen) 62
Movia 313
Mummies
  Graubelle Man 186
  Qilaqitsoq 233
  Queen Gungilde (Vejle) 194
  Tollund Man 187
Munk, Knud 92
Munkastovan (Tórshavn) 236
Munkebakken Park (Næstved) 158
Munkebo
  restaurants 277
Munthe plus Simonsen (Copenhagen) 101
Museums and galleries
  opening hours 296
  Afstøbningssamling (Copenhagen) 53
  Amber Museum (Copenhagen) 68
  Andelslandsbyen Nyvang (Holbaek) 139
  Arken Museum For Moderne Kunst **97**
  ARoS Kunstmuseum (Aarhus) 188
  art collection (Gavnø) 158
  Bangsbo-Museet 206
  Bishop's Palace (Roskilde) 140
  Bornholms Museum (Rønne) 222, 223
  Brandts (Odense) 178
  Carl Nielsen Museet (Odense) 179
  Cisternerne (Copenhagen) **93**
  Cold Museum (Ilulissat) 233
  Culture Museum (Silkeborg) 187
  Danish Design Centre (Copenhagen) 24
  Danmarks Fotomuseum (Herning) 187

Museums and galleries (cont.)
Danmarks Saltcenter (Mariager) 215
Dansk Cykel & Knallert Museum (Glumsø) 157
Dansk Landbrugs-museum (Gammel Estrup) 215
Davids Samling (Copenhagen) **58**
Denmark's Sugar Museum (Nakskov) 162
DesignMuseum Danmark (Copenhagen) 24, 53, **55**
Doll Museum (Skuldelev) 138
Dragør Museum 97
Dúvugarðar Museum (Saksun) 236
Ecolarium (Vejle) 194
Elmuseet (Tange Sø) 187
Empiregården (Stege) 169
Esbjerg Museum 194, 195
Experimentarium (Copenhagen) **94–5**
Fakse Geologiske Museum 170
Falsters Minder (Nykøbing F) 166
Fiddlers Museum (Rebild Bakker) 214
Fiskeri-og-Søfartsmuseet (Esbjerg) 194–5
Fiskeriets Hus (Hvide Sande) 190
Flaske-Peters Samling (Ærøskøbing) 181
Forsorgsmuseet (Svendborg) 180
Forsvarsmuseet (Rønne) 223
Fredericia Museum 197
Fregatten Jylland (Ebeltoft) 186
Frihedsmuseet (Copenhagen) **55**
Frilandsmuseet (Maribo) 162
Frilandsmuseet (near Copenhagen) **120**
Fuglsang Kunstmuseum (Toreby) **163**
Fyns Kunstmuseum (Odense) 178–9
Faaborg Museum 177
Føroya Fornminnissavn (Tórshavn) 236
Den Gamle By (Aarhus) 189
Det Gamle Hus (Gilleleje) 128, 129
Geologisk Museum (Copenhagen) **59**
Gilleleje Museum 128, 129
Gjern vintage car museum 187
Glasmuseet (Ebeltoft) 186
Gudhjem Museum 226
Guinness World Records Museum (Copenhagen) 66, **69**
Haderslev Museum 197
H.C. Andersens Barndomshjem (Odense) 178
H.C. Andersens Hus (Odense) 179
Heart (Herning) 187
Helsingør Bymuseum 124
Herning Kunstmuseum 187
Herning Museum 187
Hirschsprungske Samling (Copenhagen) **59**
Historiecenter Dybbøl Banke (Sønderborg) 196–7
Historiske Museum (Aalborg) 209
Hjerl Hedes Frilandsmuseum **207**, 210
Holbæk Museum 139
Holstebro Kunstmuseum 207
Horsens Kunstmuseum 186
Horsens Museum 186
Hunting and Fishing Museum (Ilulissat) 233

Museums and galleries (cont.)
J.F. Willumsens Museum (Frederikssund) 135
Johannes Larsen Museum (Kerteminde) 176
Kalundborg 147
Kangerlussuaq military museum 232
Karen Blixen's house (Rungstedlund) 120, 121
Kikhavn open-air museum 134
Klosterkirke museum (Sorø) 144–5
Knud Rasmussen house (Ilulissat) 233
Knud Rasmussens Hus (Hundested) 134
Koldkrigsmuseum (Langeland) 181
Komandørgaard (Toftum) 196
Kongernes Jelling 191
Korsør By-og Overfartsmuseet 145
Krudttårnet (Frederikshavn) 206
Kunsten Museum of Modern Art Aalborg 209, 211
Kunstforeningen GL Strand (Copenhagen) **71**
Kunsthallen Brandts (Odense) 178
Kunstmuseet Trapholt (Kolding) 197
Kvindemuseet (Aarhus) 189
Køge Museum 171
Lejre Museum **139**
Livgardens Historiske Samling (Copenhagen) **58–9**
Lolland-Falster Stiftsmuseet (Maribo) 162
Louisiana Museum **122–3**
Mariager Museum 215
Medicinsk-Historisk Museum (Copenhagen) 52
Mediemuseet (Odense) 178
Middelaldercenter (Østerlars Kirke) 226
Middelaldercentret (Lolland) **166**
Moesgård **186**
Museet for Fotokunst (Odense) 178
Museet for Søfart (Helsingør) 125
Museet på Koldinghus (Kolding) 197
Museet for Moderne Kunst (Arken) 23
Museum Jorn (Silkeborg) 187
Museum of Southern Jutland (Sønderborg) 196
National History Museum (Frederiksborg Slot) **132–3**
National Museum (Nuuk) 232
Nationalmuseet (Copenhagen) 19, 82, **84–5**
NaturBornholm (Aakirkeby) 217, 223
Nikolaj, Copenhagen Contemporary Art Centre 66, **70**
Ny Carlsberg Glyptotek (Copenhagen) 19, **78–9**
Næstved museum 158
Oluf Høst Museet (Gudhjem) 226
Orlogsmuseet (Copenhagen) **89**
Post & Tele Museum (Copenhagen) **69**
Ribe Kunstmuseum 195
Ribes Vikinger 195
Ringkøbing Museum 190
Ripley's Believe It Or Not! (Copenhagen) **73**

Museums and galleries (cont.)
Roskilde Museum 140
SAK Kunstbygningen (Svendborg) 180
Silderogerierne Museum (Hasle) 222
Silkeborg Bad 187
Skagens Museum 205
Skovgaard Museet (Viborg) 214
Sports Car Museum (Væggerløse) 167
Statens Museum for Kunst (Copenhagen) 49, **62–3**
Stevns Museum 170
Strandingsmuseet St George (Thorsminde) 207
Sydsjællands Museum (Vordingborg) 159
Sydvestsjællands Museum (Sorø) 144
Sæby Museum 206
Søfartmuseum (Marstal) 181
Søfartsmuseet (Troense) 180
Thorvaldsens Museum (Copenhagen) 27, 43, 82, **85**
Traktormuseum (Eskilstrup) 166–7
Tåsinge Museum 180
Tøjhusmuseet (Copenhagen) 82, **88**
Tønder Museum 196
Uummannaq 233
Vejle Museum 194
Viborg Museum 214
Viking centre (Frykat) 202, 215
Vikingecenter (Ribe) 195
Vikingemuseet (Aarhus) 188
Vikingeskibsmuseet (Roskilde) 19, 117, 141
Willemoesgården (Assens) 176
Ærø Museum (Ærøskøbing) 181
Music **288**, 289
Concert Hall (Tivoli, Copenhagen) 77
in Copenhagen **102**, **103**, 105
festivals 28–9, 31
Musikcaféen (Aarhus) 289
Musikhuset (Aarhus) 188, 289
Musikhuset (Esbjerg) 194
Mykines 11, **237**
hotels 261
Møller, Erik 188
Møn 153, 168–9
hotels 250
Møns Klint 10, 152, **168–9**
Mønsted **214**

N
Nakkehoved Østre Fyr 128
Nakskov **162**
hotels 250
restaurants 276
Napoleon I, Emperor 206
Napoleonic Wars 40–41
National Museum (Nuuk) 232
National parks
North and East Greenland 233
Rebild Bakker 15, 201, **214**
Nationalmuseet (Copenhagen) 19, 82, **84–5**
NATO 45
NaturBornholm (Aakirkeby) 217, 223
Nature reserves
Kongenshus Mindepark **207**

Nazis 44–5
Nelson, Horatio 176
Never Mind (Copenhagen) 105
New Year 31
Newspapers 303
Nexø
  hotels 259
  restaurants 284
Nibe 211
Nielsen, Carl 19
  Carl Nielsen Museet (Odense)
  179
Nielsen, Jais 27
Nielsen, Kai 79, 177, 180
Nielsen, Ole Martin 144
Night of Culture
  (Copenhagen) 30
Nightlife 289
  in Copenhagen **103**, 105
Nikolaj, Copenhagen Contemporary
  Art Centre 66, **70**
Nimb Building (Tivoli,
  Copenhagen) 65, 77
Nolde, Emil 62
Nordbrandt, Henrik 141
Nordea 300
Nordic Wars 129
Nordskoven **134–5**
Nordsøen Oceanarium (Hirtshals)
  204
Normann Copenhagen 101
North Copenhagen **51–63**
  Amalienborg Slot:
    Street-by-Street map 52–3
  area map 51
  hotels 245–6
  restaurants 272–3
Northern Jutland 11, 114, **201–15**
  hotels 256–8
  landscape and flora 21
  map 202–3
  restaurants 281–3
Northwestern Zealand 10, 115,
  116–51
  hotels 247–9
  landscape and flora 20
  map 118–19
  restaurants 274–6
Norwegian 305
Notke, Bernt 188, 189
Novasol 243
Nuuk (Godthåb) **232**
  hotels 260–61
  restaurants 285
Ny Carlsberg Glyptotek
  (Copenhagen) 19, **78–9**
Nyborg **177**
  hotels 252
  restaurants 278
Nyhavn (Copenhagen) 67, **68**
Nyker 221, **222**
Nykøbing F **166**, 275
Nykøbing M 257
Nykøbing S 249
Nykøbing SJ 275
Nylars 22, **223**
Nyord **170**
Nyrop, Martin 74
Nysted **163**
Nytorv (Copenhagen) **73**
Næstved 154, **158**
  hotels 250
  restaurants 277
Nødebo 131
Nørgaard, Bjørn 86
Nørre Jernlose Mølle **144**

O

Oak trees, Nordskoven 134, 135
Oddesund Nord lighthouse 212–13
Odense 173, **178–9**
  bureau de change 300
  events 29
  hotels 252
  map 179
  restaurants 278
Odense Apotek Ørnen 299
Odense Koncerthus 289
Odense Teater 289
Odense Tourist Office 297
Odense Universitets Hospital 299
Odsherred **151**
Oehlenschläger, Adam 42, 69
Oister 303
Olaf, St 220
Olsen, Jens 74, 181
Olsen, Peder 222
Olsker **220**
Oluf III, King 144
Oluf Høst Museet (Gudhjem) 226
Opening hours 296–7
  banks 300
  museums and historic sights 296
  restaurants 262
  shops 98, 286
Opera
  Aalborg opera festival 28
  in Copenhagen **102**, 105
  Operaen (Copenhagen) 69, **89**,
  105
Orlogsmuseet (Copenhagen) **89**
Oscar Bar & Café (Copenhagen) 105
Otto, Statius 73
Outdoor activities **290–93**
Oynadarfjordur 237

P

Pagoda (Tivoli, Copenhagen) 77
Painting **26–7**
Palaces
  Amalienborg Slot (Copenhagen)
  39, 52, **56–7**
  Bishop's Palace (Roskilde) 140
  Charlottenborg Slot
  (Copenhagen) 23, 67, **69**
  Charlottenlund Slot
  (Copenhagen) **95**
  Christiansborg Slot (Copenhagen)
  23, 82–3, **86–7**
  Fredensborg Slot 23, **129**, 131
  Frederiksberg Slot (Copenhagen)
  93
  Frederiksborg Slot (Hillerød) 22,
  119, **132–3**, 136–7
  Gråsten (Sønderborg) 197
  Jægerspris Slot **135**
  Ledreborg Slot 23, **139**
  Lichtenberg Palace (Horsens) 186
  Liselund Slot **169**
  Rosenborg Slot (Copenhagen) 26,
  60–61
  see also Castles
Pantomime Theatre (Tivoli,
  Copenhagen) 76
Parking 309, 311
  at hotels 240
Parks and gardens
  Amaliehaven (Copenhagen) 53
  Botanisk Have (Copenhagen) **59**
  Bysøparken (Holbæk) 139
  Charlottenlund (Copenhagen) 95
  Churchillparken (Copenhagen) 55

Parks and gardens (cont.)
  Dragsholm Slot 150
  Fredensborg Slot 129
  Frederiksberg Slot (Copenhagen)
  93
  Frederiksborg Slot (Hillerød) 133
  Gavnø 158
  Gråbrødre Kirkegård (Roskilde)
  141
  Jesperhus Park (Limfjorden) 210
  Jægersborg Dyrehave **120**
  Jægerspris Slot 135
  Kongens Have (Copenhagen) **58**
  Købelevhaven 162
  Labyrinthia Park 187
  Ledreborg Slot 139
  Lungholm (Tågerup) 163
  Munkebakken Park (Næstved) 158
  Tivoli (Copenhagen) **76–7**
  Vallø Slot 171
  Winter Garden (Ny Carlsberg
  Glyptotek) 79
  Østre Anlæg (Holbæk) 139
Parliament (Copenhagen)
  17, 83, **85**
Paustian (Copenhagen) 101
Pedersen, Carl-Henning
  187, 195
Penelope (Jerichau) 78
Pernille Bulow (Svaneke) 223
Peter the Great, Tsar 71, 93, 166
Peter Hertz (Copenhagen) 101
Petersen, Knud 70
Petersen, Carl 177
Petrol 309
Pharmacies 299
Phone cards 302
Photography
  Danmarks Fotomuseum
  (Herning) 187
  Museet for Fotokunst (Odense)
  178
Picasso, Pablo 19, 62
  Le Déjeuner sur l'Herbe 122
  Holstebro Kunstmuseum 207
Pilo, Carl Gustaf 26
Pinsedag 28
Planetarium, Tycho Brahe
  (Copenhagen) 19, **92**
Polakkasernen (Tågerup) 163
Police 298
Polish immigrants 159, 162, 163
Politics 16–17
Pollack, Sydney 121
Porcelain 25
  Royal Copenhagen 70, **93**
Portrait of Madame Matisse
  (Matisse) 62
Post Danmark 303
Post & Tele Museum (Copenhagen)
  69
Postal services **303**
Postbåden (Nakskov) 162
Posten (Odense) 289
Poulsen, Louis & Co 25
Prærievognsferie Og Hesteudlejning
  293
Præstø 250
Public holidays 31
Public telephones 302
Public transport 310
  in Copenhagen **312–13**
Puppets
  Dukketeaterfestival (Silkeborg) 30
  Marionet Teatret (Copenhagen)
  105

Q

Qaanaaq (Thule) **233**
hotels 261
Qaqortoq (Julianehåb) 229, **232**
Qilaqitsoq 233
Quellinus, Thomas 27

R

Radio 303
Rail travel **306**
in Copenhagen 312
Svinninge Modeljernbane
(model railway) 150
Rainfall 30
Ramløse 130
Ramses II, Pharaoh 78
Randers **215**
hotels 257
restaurants 282
Raphael 206
Rasmussen, Anders Fogh 45
Rasmussen, Knud **134**, 233
Rasmussen, Niels Peter 144
Ravmuseet (Copenhagen) **68**
Rebild Bakker 15, 201, **214**
Red Army 220
Reformation 27, 128
Rejseplanen 307
Religion 17
Rembrandt 26, 62
Renaissance architecture 23
Renoir, Pierre Auguste 78
Resistance movement 44–5
Frihedsmuseet (Copenhagen) **55**
Responsible tourism 297
Restaurants **262–85**
Bornholm 283–4
children in 263
Copenhagen 268–74
disabled guests 263
dress code 263
Faroe Islands 285
The Flavours of Denmark **264–5**
Funen 277–8
Greenland 284–5
menus 262
Northern Jutland 281–3
Northwestern Zealand 274–6
opening hours 262
prices 263
reservations 263
Southern and Central Jutland
278–81
Southern Zealand and the Islands
276
vegetarian food 263
what to drink **266–7**
Ribe **195**
events 28
hotels 254
restaurants 280
Richter, Johan 188
Ringkøbing 190
hotels 254
Ringkøbing Fjord **190**
Ringridning 29
Ringsted 153, **156**
hotels 250
restaurants 277
Ripley's Believe It Or Not!
(Copenhagen) **73**
River Boat Jazz Festival (Silkeborg)
29
Road travel **308–9**
Rock paintings 220
Rodin, Auguste 78

Rold Skov 201, 214
Romanesque architecture 22
Rosenberg Slot (Copenhagen) 26,
50, **60–61**
Rosenfeldt Estate 159
Rosenholm Slot 215
Rosenkrantz, Mette and Birgitte 171
Roskilde **140–43**
Domkirke 118, **142–3**
events 19, 29
hotels 249
map 141
restaurants 275–6
Roskilde, Treaty of (1658) 37
Roskilde Fjord 134–5
Roskilde Palace 140
Rousseau, Jean-Jacques 71
Royal Copenhagen 101
Royal shopping **100**, 101
Royal Theatre (Copenhagen) 105
Rubens, Peter Paul 62, 206
Rudkøbing 180–81
hotels 253
restaurants 278
Rules of the road 308–9
Runavik 285
Rundetårn (Copenhagen) **71**
Rungstedlund **120**
Runic stones 191, 222, 226
Running Copenhagen 313
Russells Glacier 233
Rust (Copenhagen) 105
Ry 280
Ryanair 305
Rådhus (Aarhus) 188
Rådhus (Copenhagen) **74–5**
Rådhuset (Aalborg) 208
Rådhuspladsen (Copenhagen) 49, **75**
Røddinge 168
Rødvig Stevns 170
hotels 251
Rømø **196**
hotels 254
Rønne 16, 219, **222–5**, 227
hotels 259–60
restaurants 284
Rønnede 156
Rørbye, Martinus 42
Rørvig 276
Røsnæs **147**

S

S-tog 312, 313
Sabro 254
Safari Park (Knuthenborg) **160–61**
Sagnlandet Lejre 117, **138–9**
Sahl church 27
Sailing 29, 30, **292**
St George's Frigate III (Tivoli,
Copenhagen) 76
SAK Kunstbygningen (Svendborg)
180
Sakskøbing **159**
hotels 251
Saksun 236
Sales 287
Saltcenter (Mariager) 215
Saltum 282
Saly, Jacques 57
Sand dunes 201, 204
Sand sculpture festival 29
Sandavagur 236
Sandvig 220
hotels 260
Sankt Hans Eve 29
Santa Claus 232

SAS 305
Saxo Grammaticus 126
Scandlines 307
Schleswig-Holstein 41, 44, 183
Schrøder, Abel 37
Schubertiade (Roskilde) 29
Sculpture **27**
Security and Health **298–9**
Selsø Slot **138**
Shakespeare, William
Hamlet 115, 124, **126**
Ships *see* Boats
Shopping **286–7**
art and antiques **100**, 101
clothes and accessories **99**, 101
in Copenhagen **98–101**
department stores **99**, 101
design and interior decoration
99, 101
how to pay 98–9, 287
jewellery **100**, 101
markets **100**, 101
opening hours 98, 286
royal shopping **100**, 101
sales 287
specialist shops **100**, 101
VAT 286–7
where to shop 98
Shrovetide 31
Silderogerierne Museum (Hasle)
222
Silkeborg 183, **187**
events 29, 30
hotels 254–5
restaurants 280
Silkeborg Lake District **187**
SIN CITY (Copenhagen) 105
Sjælland *see* Northwestern Zealand;
Southern Zealand
Sjælland Sommerland 151
Skagen 201, **205**
hotels 257
restaurants 282
Skagen Odde Naturcenter 204
Skagen School 26, 62, 201, 205
Skanderborg 255
Skelby 157
Skibby **138**
hotels 249
Skibby Chronicle 138
Skive 257
Skovgaard, Joakim 87, 144, 214
Skråen (Aalborg) 289
Skuespilhuset (Copenhagen) 71
Skuldelev 134
Skype 303
Skørping 257
restaurants 282
Slotskirken (Frederiksborg Slot)
132
Smyril Line 307
Småland (Knuthenborg Safari Park)
161
Smørrebrød 264
Snare, Esbern 118, 147
Soft drinks 267
Sol & Strand 243
Solar power 18
Sonne, Jørgen 43, 85
Sophie, Queen 133, 166
Sophie Amalie, Queen 57
Sophie Hedevig, Princess 61
Sophie Magdalene, Queen 171
Sorø **144–5**
hotels 249
restaurants 276

South Copenhagen **81–9**
area map 81
Christiansborg Slot: Street-by-Street map 82–3
hotels 246
restaurants 273–4
Southern and Central Jutland 11, 114, **183–99**
hotels 253–5
landscape and flora 21
map 184–5
restaurants 279–81
Southern Zealand and the islands 10, 115, **153–71**
hotels 249–51
landscape and flora 20
map 154–5
restaurants 276–7
Sport 289, **290–93**
Sports Car Museum (Væggerløse) 167
Spring in Denmark 28
Sprogø 146
Spøttrup Borg 210
Stadil church 27
Statens Museum for Kunst (Copenhagen) 49, **62–3**
Steam trains 129
Steenwinckel, Hans van 85, 180
Steenwinckel, Lorentz 85
Stege **169**
restaurants 277
Stena Line 307
Stengade (Helsingør) 125
Stevns Klint **170**
Stevns Museum 170
Stock Exchange see Børsen
Stockholm Bloodbath (1520) 37
Stone and Man programme (Greenland) 232
Store Bælt (strait) 145, 173
Store Bededag 28
Storebælt Bridge **146**, 309
Storkespringvandet (Copenhagen) 70
Storre Heddinge 171
Streymoy **236**
The Strife of Lent Against Carnival (Bruegel) 63
Strøget (Copenhagen) 68, **70**
Stændertorvet (Roskilde) 140
Submarine U-359 (Nakskov) 162
Supuroy **237**
hotels 261
restaurants 285
Sugar Museum (Nakskov) 162
Sugarloaf Mountain 233
Summer in Denmark 29
Sunesen, Jakob 169
Sunshine 29
Suså **156**, 157
Svane Lys (Nysted) 163
Svaneke 217, **223**
hotels 260
restaurants 284
Svendborg 174, **180**
hotels 253
restaurants 278–9
Svinninge **150**
Svinninge Modeljernbane 150
Sweyn I, King 33
Sweyn II, King 36
Swimming **293**
Sydbank A/S 300
Sydvestsjællands Museum (Sorø) 144

Sylt 196
Sæby 203, **206**
hotels 257
Sæbygård 206
Søfartmuseum (Marstal) 181
Søfartsmuseet (Troense) 180
Søhøjlandet 187
Sømods Bolcher (Copenhagen) 101
Sønderborg **196–7**
hotels 255
restaurants 280
Søndre Strømfjord see Kangerlussuaq

T
T-248 Skagerak 293
Tasiilaq (Ammassalik) **233**
Taxa Fyn 311
Taxes
hotel 240–41
VAT 286–7
Taxis 311
in Copenhagen 313
TDC 303
Telephone services **302**
Television 303
Telia 303
Temperatures 31
Tessin, Nicodemus 89
Theatres **288**, 289
Concert Hall (Tivoli, Copenhagen) 77
in Copenhagen **103**, 105
Det Kongelige Teater (Copenhagen) 67, **69**, 105
DR Koncerthuset (Copenhagen) 105
Musikhuset (Aarhus) 188
Musikhuset (Esbjerg) 194
Operaen (Copenhagen) 69, **89**
Pantomime (Tivoli, Copenhagen) 76
Rønne Theatre 222
Skuespilhuset (Copenhagen) 71
Theft 298
Thirty Years War (1616–48) 37
Thorvaldsen, Bertel 19, 26, 27, 42
Christiansborg Slot (Copenhagen) 87
Roskilde Domkirke 142
Sankt Albans Kirke (Copenhagen) 55
self-portrait 27
statue of 74
Thorvaldsens Museum (Copenhagen) 27, 43, 82, **85**
Vor Frue Kirke (Copenhagen) 72–3
Thorvaldsens Plads Antique Market (Copenhagen) 101
Thule see Qaanaaq
Thurah, Lauritz de 39, 89, 129, 140
Thyborøn 210
Tickets
for entertainment 102
for transport 306, 307, 310, 312–13
Tiger Reserve (Knuthenborg Safari Park) 160
Timm, Reinchold 26
Tipperne Nature Reserve 190
Tipping, in restaurants 263
Tisvildeleje
hotels 249
restaurants 276
Tivoli (Copenhagen) 10, 30, **76–7**
Tivoli Boys Guard **77**

Tivoli Festival (Copenhagen) 105
Tivoli Koncertsal (Copenhagen) 105
Toll charges 308
Tollund Man 187
Torftum 196
Tórshavn 235, **236**
hotels 261
restaurants 285
Torvehallerne København 101
Toulouse-Lautrec, Henri de 71, 79
Tourde Gudenå 30
Tourist information 296
Tours by car
Esrum Sø and Arresø **130–31**
Odsherred **151**
Toy Museum (Skuldelev) 138
Traditions 16
Traffic wardens 298
Train (Aarhus) 289
Trains see Rail travel
Traktormuseum (Eskilstrup) 166–7
Tranekær 181
Travel **304–13**
air **304–5**
Bornholm 219
car **308–9**
coach 306
in Copenhagen **312–13**
Faroe Islands 235
ferries **307**
Funen 175
Greenland 231
Northern Jutland 203
Northwestern Zealand 118
rail **306**
Southern and Central Jutland 184
Southern Zealand and the islands 154
Travellers with special needs 297
Travelling on a budget 297
Travelling with children 297
Trelleborg 115, **147**
Trianon Bakery (Copenhagen) 101
Troense 180
Troldbjerg (Hvide Sande) 190
Tuxen, Lauritz 205
Tveje Merløse Kirke **144**
Tvøroyri 237
Two Piece Reclining Figure No. 5 (Moore) 123
Tycho Brahe Planetarium (Copenhagen) 19, **92**
Tystrup-Bavelse (near Sorø) 145
Tågerup **163**
Tårnborg **145**
Tåsinge 173, **180**
Tøjhusmuseet (Copenhagen) 82, **88**
Tønder **196**
events 30
hotels 255
restaurants 280

U
Ulfeldt, Corfitz 39
Ulstrup 147
UNESCO World Heritage Sites
Jelling Kirke 191
Kronberg Slot (Helsingør) 126
Roskilde Domkirke **142–3**
Universitet (Copenhagen) **72**
UPS 303
Urban Factory (Copenhagen) 101
Utzon, Jørn 19, 25
Musikhuset (Esbjerg) 194
Skagen Odde Naturcenter 204
Utzon Center (Aalborg) 208

Uummannaq **233**
  hotels 261
  restaurants 285

V

Vadehauscentret (Vester Vedsted)
  195
Vágar **236**
Valby Station 307
Valdemar I (The Great), King 22, 36
  Nyborg Slot 177
  Sønderborg 196
  Vordingborg 158
Valdemar II, King 33, 36
  Jutland Code 158–9
  Ribe 195
Valdemar IV, King 36, 128
  Sankt Peder Kirke (Næstved) 158
  tomb of 144
  Vordingborg 159
Valdemar the Victorious 147
Valdemar dynasty 153
Valdemars Slot (Tåsinge) 180
"Valley of the Flowers" (Greenland)
  233
Vallø Slot **171**
Van Gogh, Vincent 79
Vandtårnet (Esbjerg) 194, 195
Varmakelda hot springs 237
VAT 286–7
VEGA (Copenhagen) 105
Vegetarian food 263
Vejle **194**
  hotels 255
  restaurants 280
Vejle Fjord 183
Veng 187
Vénus de Meudon (Arp) 122
Versailles, Treaty of (1919) 44
Vest, Nils 89
Vester Vov Vov (Copenhagen) 105
Viborg 202, **214**
  hotels 257
  restaurants 282
Viby 176
*View from the Loft of the Grain
  Store at the Bakery in the Citadel*
  (Købke) 26
Vikings
  architecture 35
  history 33, **34–5**
  Jelling 191
  Ladbyskibet 176
  Lindholm Høje 201, **206–7**
  Moesgård 186
  Ribes Vikinge 195
  ships 34–5, 191, 293
  Trelleborg 117, **147**
  Viking centre (Frykat) 201, 202,
    215
  Viking Market (Ribe) 28
  Viking Village (Frederikssund)
    135
  Vikingecenter (Ribe) 195
  Vikingemuseet (Aarhus) 188
  Vikingeskibsmuseet (Roskilde)
    19, 117, 141
Visas 296
VisitDenmark 293, 297
Voergård Slot 201, **206**
Vogt, Adelgund 135
Vor Frue Plads (Copenhagen) 72
Vordingborg 153, **158–9**
  hotels 251
  restaurants 277
VoxHall (Aarhus) 289
Væggerløse **167**

W

Wagons, horse-drawn 290
Wahl, Johan Salomon 26
Walking **293**, 310–11
  in Copenhagen 313
Wallmans Saloner (Copenhagen)
  105
Warhol, Andy 122, 123
Water, drinking 267, 299
Water Mother (Nielsen) 79
Water parks *see* Aquaparks
Water sports **290**, 293
Waterbuses, Copenhagen 313
Weather 28–31
Wegener, Alfred 233
Wellington, Duke of 40
Whale watching, Greenland 232,
  233
Whaling, Rømø 196
When to visit 296
Whitsun Carnival
  (Copenhagen) 28
Wi-Fi 302, 303
Wiedewelt, Johanes 27
Wildlife **20–21**
  Danmarks Akvarium
    (Copenhagen) **95**
  Fjord&Bælt (Kerteminde) 176
  Jesperhus Park (Limfjorden) 210
  Knuthenborg Safari Park **160–61**
  Nordsøen Oceanarium (Hirtshals)
    204
  Randers Regnskov 215
  Tystrup-Bavelse (near Sorø) 145
  Øresundakvariet (Helsingør) 125
  see also Aquariums;
    Birdwatching; Zoos
Willemoes, Peter 176
Willumsen, J.F. 135
  A Mountain Climber 62
Wind turbines 18, 96, 97, 218
Windmills
  Agersø Mølle 156
  Dybbøl Mølle (Sønderborg) 196
  Kettinge 163
  Langeland 180
  Nørre Jernlose Mølle 144
  Ramløse 130
  Ulstrup 147
  Vejle Vindmølle 194
  Viby 176
  Væggerløse 167
  Årsdale Mølle (Svaneke) 223
Wine 267
Winter in Denmark 31
Winter Garden (Ny Carlsberg
  Glyptotek) 79
Women 17
  Kvindemuseet (Aarhus) 189
  Vallø Slot 171
Wondercool (Copenhagen) 31
World Clock (Rådhus, Copenhagen)
  74
World War I 44
World War II 44–5
  anchor memorial (Copenhagen)
    67, 68
  Frihedsmuseet (Copenhagen) **55**
Wounded Philoctetes (Abildgaard)
  26

Y

Yding Skovhøj 21
Yellow Pages 303
Youth hostels **242**, 243

Z

Zealand *see* Northwestern Zealand;
  Southern Zealand
Zebu (Copenhagen) 105
Zoo Bar (Copenhagen) 105
Zoos
  Givskud Zoo (Loveparken)
    190–91
  Guldborgsund Zoo (Nykøbing F)
    166
  Joboland 226
  Krokodille Zoo (Eskilstrup) 167
  Randers Regnskov 215
  Zoologisk Have (Copenhagen)
    92–3
  see also Wildlife

A (AA)

Aalborg 201, **208–9**, 211
  airport 305
  bureau de change 300
  entertainment 28
  hotels 258
  map 209
  restaurants 282–3
Aalborg BK 289
Aalborg Budolfi Apotek 299
Aalborg Kongres og Kulturcenter
  289
Aalborg Tourist Office 297
Aalborghus Slot (Aalborg) 208
Aalto, Alvar 209
Aarsdale Mølle (Svaneke) 223
Åbenrå 280–81
Åkirkeby 217, **223**, 227
  hotels 260
  restaurants 284
Aarhus 183, **188–9**
  airport 305
  bureau de change 300
  events 29
  hotels 255
  map 189
  restaurants 281
Aarhus Løve Apotek 299
Aarhus Taxa 311
Aarhus Teater 289
Aarhus Universitets Hospital 299

Æ

Æbelhof Kloster 130
Ærø 18, 173, 181
Ærøskøbing **181**
  hotels 253
  restaurants 279

Ø

Ølfestival (Copenhagen) 28
Øresund 37, 40
Øresund Bridge 91, **96**, 97, 309
Øresundakvariet (Helsingør) 125
Øro island 139
Ørsted, Hans Christian 180–81
Østbro 146
Østerlars Kirke 221, **226**
Østre Anlæg (Holbæk) 139

Acknowledgments

Hachette Livre Polska would like to thank the following people whose contribution and assistance have made the preparation of the book possible:

Additional Text
Sue Dobson, Roger Norum, Marek Pernal, Jakub Sito, Barbara Sudnik-Wójcikowska, Jennifer Wattam Klit.

Additional Illustrations
Dorota Jarymowicz, Paweł Pasternak.

Additional Photographs
Oldrich Karasek, Ian O'Leary, Laura Pilgaard Rasmussen, Jakub Sito, Jon Spaul, Barbara Sudnik-Wójcikowska, Monika Witkowska, Andrzej Zygmuntowicz and Ireneusz Winnicki, Juliusz Żebrowski.

Dorling Kindersley would like to thank the following people whose contribution and assistance have made the preparation of the book possible:

Publisher
Douglas Amrine.

Publishing Managers
Anna Streiffert, Vicki Ingle.

Managing Art Director
Kate Poole.

Senior Editor
Kathryn Lane.

Editorial Assistance
Sam Fletcher, Anna Freiberger.

Additional Picture Research
Rachel Barber, Ellen Root.

Cartography
Vinod Harish, Vincent Kurien, Azeem Siddiqui, Casper Morris.

DTP Designers
Uma Bhattacharya, Mohammad Hassan, Jasneet Kaur, Alistair Richardson.

Factcheckers
Britt Lightbody, Katrine Anker Møller.

Proofreader
Stewart J. Wild.

Indexer
Helen Peters.

Jacket Design
Tessa Bindloss.

Revisions Team
Marta Bescos, Lokesh Bisht, Imogen Corke, Mariana Evmolpidou, Elisabeth Fogh, Jane Graham, Claire Jones, Laura Jones, Sumita Khatwani, Priya Kukadia, Delphine Lawrance, Carly Madden, Alison McGill, Vikki Nousiainen, Catherine Palmi, Laura Pilgaard Rasmussen, Pollyanna Poulter, Lucy Richards, Ellen Root, Simon Ryder, Sands Publishing Solutions, Susana Smith, Dora Whitaker, Conrad van Dyk.

Special Assistance and Permissions
The Publishers also wish to thank all persons and institutions for their permission to reproduce photographs of their property, for allowing us to photograph inside the buildings and to use photographs from their archives:

Amager Youth Hostel; Amalienborg, Copenhagen (S. Haslund-Christensen, Lord Chamberlain and Colonel Jens Greve, Palace Steward); Amber Museum, Copenhagen; Aquarium, Charlottenlund; Arbejdermuseet, Copenhagen (Peter Ludvigsen); Bornholm Tourist Information Centre (Pernille Larsen); Carlsberg Brewery; Ceramics Museum, Rønne; Christiansborg, Copenhagen; Copenhagen Airports A/S (Bente Schmidt – Event- and visitor department); Copenhagen Town Hall (Allan Johansen); Corbis (Łukasz Wyrzykowski); Danish Tourist Board Photo Database (Christian Moritz – Area Sales Manager); Dansk Moebelkunst (Dorte Slot) (Bredgade 32, Copenhagen K) www.dmk.dk; Davids Samling, Copenhagen; Danish Chamber of Tourism & SAS Group PR (Agnieszka Blandzi, Director); Egeskov Castle; Experimentarium, Copenhagen; H. Ch. Andersen Museum, Odense; Holmegaard Glass Factory; Jagna Noren – a guide to Bornholm; Jesper T. Møller and other employees of the National Museum in Copenhagen; Karen Blixen Museum; Knud Rasmussens Haus; Kronborg castle; Legoland, Billund; Lene Henrichsen – assistant to the director of the Louisiana museum; Louisiana – Museum for Modern Kunst (Susanne Hartz); The Museum of Holbæk and Environs, Holbæk; Det Nationalhistoriske Museum på Frederiksborg, Hillerød; Nationalmuseet, Copenhagen (Heidi Lykke Petersen); The Nobel Foundation (Annika Ekdahl); Ny Carlsberg Glyptotek in Copenhagen (Jan Stubbe Østergaard); Palaces and Properties Agency, Denmark (Peder Lind Pedersen); Pritzker Prize (Keith Walker) for making available the photographs of the interiors of Jørn Utzon's house; Ribe VikingeCenter (Bjarne Clement – manager); Rosenborg Castle – The Royal Danish Collection (Peter Kristiansen – curator); Roskilde Cathedral; The Royal Library, Copenhagen (Karsten Bundgaard – photographer); Royal Porcelain Factory, Copenhagen; Skagens Museum (Mette Bøgh Jensen – curator); Scandinavian Airlines SAS (Wanda Brociek i Małgorzata Grążka); Statens Historiska Museum, Stockholm; Statens Museum for Kunst (Eva Maria Gertung & Marianne Saederup); Stine Møller Jensen (Press coordinator, Copenhagen Metro); Bo Streiffert; Tivoli, Copenhagen – Stine Lolk; Tobaksmuseet, Copenhagen (W.Ø. Larsens); Tycho Brahe Planetarium, Copenhagen; Tønder Tourist Office (Lis Langelund-Larsen – tourist officer); Voergård Slot; Aalborg Symfoniorkester (Jan Bo Rasmussen); Østerlars Kirke, Bornholm (Ernst A Grunwald).

Picture Credits
Key: a-above; b-below/bottom; c-centre; f-far; l-left; r-right; t-top.

Wilhelm Eckersberg 42tr; Thorvaldsens Museum, Copenhagen *Shepherd Boy* (1817) Bertel Thorvaldsen 42bl.

CINEMAXX DANMARK: 103br. CISTERNERNE: 93crb. COLOUR LINE GMBH: 306tl. COPENHAGEN AIRPORTS: Arne V. Petersen 304bl. CORBIS: © ARCHIVO ICONOGRAFICO, S. A. 38–39c, 41br; © Bettmann 37bl, 38tc, 43 bl, 44cr, 121 crb; Francis Dean 299bl, 302tr; © Werner Forman 34b, 36bl; © Hulton–Deutsch Collection 45t; © Robbie Jack 122b; © Wolfgang Kaehler 236t, 236b; © Douglas Kirkland 121bl; © Bob Krist 135b, 182, 200, 205tl, 205cr; © Stefan Lindblom 28tclb, 45br; © Massimo Listri 27b, 50; © Wally McNamee 45c; © Adam Woolfitt 54br, 172.

DANISHEVPHOTOS: Rasmus 298cl. DANSK MOEBELKUNST; 24clb, 25cla. NIELS JAKOB DARGER; 89b. DAVIDS SAMLING: 58cra. DREAMSTIME.COM: Laser143 126tr; Tupungato 300cl.

FREDENSBORG; 129tr, 131ca. FREDERIKSBORG: Hans Petersen 39t, 40c, 41t, 41crb; Larsen, Lennart 38cla, 40t; Ole Haupt 36t. FÆRGEN: 307tl.

GETTY IMAGES. AFP/Stringer 298clb; Chris Jackson 299tl.

DAVE HANLON: 193tr. HEMISPHERES IMAGES: Jean du Boisberranger 11br. HORSENS KOMMUNE: Hartmann-Schmidt Fotografi 29br.

JAKUB SITO: 22t, 23tc, 23ca, 27tr, 27cl.

OLDRICH KARASEK: 48t, 48b, 49b, 57b, 228, 230tl, 233t, 290t. KNUTHENBORG SAFARIPARK: 160cla, 160clb, 160br, 161cra, 161crb, 161bc.

LALANDIA A/S: 162br. ©2012 THE LEGO GROUP: LEGO, the LEGO logo, the Brick and Knob configurations, the Minifigure and LEGOLAND are trademarks of the LEGO Group. 192cla, 193bl, 193tl, 193ca, 193crb. LOUISIANA – MUSEUM FOR MODERNE KUNST: 123tc; *Dead Drunk Danes* (1960) Asger Jorn © DACS, London 2011 26b; *Big Thumb* (1968) Cesar Baldaccini © ADAGP, Paris and DACS, London 2011 122tr; Poul Buchard/Brøndum & Co 122bl, Poul Buchard/Strüwing 123bl; *Breakfast on the Grass* (1961) Pablo Picasso © Succession Picasso/DACS, London 2011 122cra; *Venus de Meudon* (1956) Jean Arp © DACS, London 2011 122clb; *Marilyn Monroe* (1967) Andy Warhol © Licensed by the Andy Warhol Foundation for the Visual Arts, Inc/ARS, New York and DACS, London 2011 123cra; Henry Moore, *Two Piece Reclining Figure No.5* (1963–4) © by kind permission of the Henry Moore Foundation 123clb.

METRO KUNDESERVICE: 312cl. MEPL: 9c, 34clb, 36cr, 37t, 37bra, 38bl, 42bl, 43t, 44t, 44bla, 44brb, 47c, 113c, 239c, 295c. MUNTHE PLUS SIMONSEN: 99tr.

NATIONALMUSEET: 33bl, 84t, 84cra, 84clb, 84b, 85cla. NATUREPL.COM: Michael Hutchinson 19tr. NIMB HOTEL AND RESTAURANT: 64, 77bl.

B. V. PETERSEN; 20cl, 20clb, 20cra, 20c, 21cla, 21clb, 21cra, 21ca, 21crb. POLFOTO: Hansen Claus 167br.

RESTAURANT ERA ORA: 262cl; RIBE VIKINGE CENTER: 28b; ROSENBORG CASTLE: 60b, 61ca, 61b. ROYAL LIBRARY: (Karsten Bundgaard) 121br

SAFARI PARK: (Finn Brasen) 160t, 160b, 161cra, 161crb. SCANDLINES: 307bl. SHUTTERSTOCK: 311br. SKAGENS MUSEUM P. S. Krøyer, Michael Ancher (1886) phot. Esben Thorning 205br. SKUESPILHUSET - ROYAL DANISH PLAYHOUSE: JensMarkus Lindhe 71bl; ANNA AND JANUSZ STAROŚCIK: 5t. STATENS MUSEUM FOR KUNST (COPENHAGEN): SMK Foto 26tra, 26tlb, 32, 42cl, 42br, 42–43c, 62cla, 62clb, 63cra, 63cr; *Seated Woman* (1934) Henri Laurens © ADAGP, Paris and DACS, London 2011 63bc; *Portrait of Mrs Matisse* (1905) Henry Matisse © Succession H Matisse/DACS, London 2011 63crb; *Last supper* (1909) Emil Nolde 63tl. BARBARA SUDNIK-WÓJCIKOWSKA; 20bla, 21cl.

TELIASONERA: 302tl. TIVOLI: Henrik Stenberg 76cla, 77t. TØNDER TOURIST OFFICE: 30t.

JØRN UTZON: 24–25c.

VISITDENMARK: 59b, 83c; Aalborg Tourist- og Kongressbureau 211ca; Bent Næsly 29c, 117, 205cl; Bob Krist 288c; Cees van Roeden 2–3, 34cra, 100t, 174b, 183b, 210bla, 291cr; Danmarks Turistråd 125cl, 216; DigiEye Z A/S 296tc; Ditte Isager 296cr; Dorte Krogh 287b, 308tr; Henrik Steberg 164–165; Ireneusz Cyranek 90; Jan Kofoed Winther 96b; Jette Jørs 102cr; John Sommmer 38cl, 58clb, 201d, 292c, 309tc; Jørgen Schytte 266t, 309tl; Juliusz Żebrowski 229b, 234t, 234b, 235t; Kim Wyon 297bl; Klaus Bentzen 136–137, 278–279; Lars-Kristian Crone 310tl, 312cr; Peter Søllner 33t; Strüwing 25br; Ted Fahn 46–47, 112–113; Thomas Nykrog 238–239, 309bl; ; ukendt 1, 289t; VisitAalborg 263br; VisitAalborg/Michael Damsgaard 305t, 310br, 311tl; Wedigo Ferchland 212–213; WoCo 6b.

MONIKA WITKOWSKA: 230b, 231t, 231b, 232t, 232b. WONDERFUL COPENHAGEN: 297bl.

JACKET
Front - 4CORNERS: Huber/Reinhard Schmid; Back - ALAMY IMAGES: Alex Hare clb, Frantisek Staud bl; DORLING KINDERSLEY: Rough Guides/Roger Norum cla; SUPERSTOCK: Steve Vidler tl; Spine - 4CORNERS: Huber/Reinhard Schmid t.

All other images Dorling Kindersley.
For further information see www.dkimages.com

SPECIAL EDITIONS OF DK TRAVEL GUIDES

DK Travel Guides can be purchased in bulk quantities at discounted prices for use in promotions or as premiums. We are also able to offer special editions and personalized jackets, corporate imprints, and excerpts from all of our books, tailored specifically to meet your own needs.

To find out more, please contact:
(in the United States) **SpecialSales@dk.com**
(in the UK) **TravelSpecialSales@uk.dk.com**
(in Canada) DK Special Sales at **general@tourmaline.ca**
(in Australia) **business.development@pearson.com.au**

Phrasebook

In an Emergency

Can you call an ambulance?	Kan du tilkalde en ambulance?	kann do till-kalleh ehn ahm-boo-lang-seh?
Can you call the police?	Kan du tilkalde politiet?	kann do till-kalleh po-ly-tee'd?
Can you call the fire brigade?	Kan du tilkalde brand-væsenet?	kann do till-kalleh brahn-vaiys-ned?
Is there a telephone here?	Er der en telefon i nærheden?	e-ah dah ehn tele--fohn ee neya-hethen?
Where is the nearest hospital?	Hvor er det nærmeste hospital?	voa e-ah deh neh-meste hoh-spee-tahl

Useful Phrases

Sorry	Undskyld	ons-gull
Goodnight	Godnat	goh-nad
Goodbye	Farvel	fah-vell
Good evening	Godaften	goh-ahf-tehn
Good morning	Godmorgen	goh-moh'n
Good morning (after about 9am)	Goddag	goh-dah
Yes	Ja	yah
No	Nej	nye
Please	Værsgo/ Velbekomme	vehs-goh/ vell-beh-commeh
Thank you	Tak	tahgg
How are you?	Hvordan har du det?/ Hvordan går det?	voh-dann hah do deh?/voh-dan go deh?
Pleased to have met you	Det var rart at møde dig	deh vah rahd add meutheh die
See you!	Vi ses!	vee sehs!
I understand	Jeg forstår	yay fuh-stoah
I don't understand	Jeg forstår ikke	yay fuh-stoah egge
Does anyone speak English?	Er der nogen, der kan tale engelsk?	e-ah dah noh-enn dah kann tah-leh eng-ellsgg?
on the left	til venstre	till vehn-streh
on the right	til højre	till hoy-reh
open	åben	oh-ben
closed	lukket	luh-geth
warm	varm	vahm
cold	kold	koll
big	stor	stoah
little	lille	lee-leh

Making a Telephone Call

I would like to call...	Jeg vil gerne ringe til...	yay vill geh-neh ring-eh till...
I will telephone again	Jeg ringer en gang til	yay ring-ah ehn gahng till

In a Hotel

Do you have double rooms?	Findes her dobbelt-værelser?	feh-ness he-ah dob-belld vah-hel-sah?
With bathroom	Med bade-værelse	meth bah-the-vah-hel-sah
With washbasin	Med hånd-vask	meth hohn-vasgg
key	nøgle	noy-leh
I have a reservation	Jeg har en reservation	yay hah ehn res-sah-vah-shohn

Sightseeing

cathedral	domkirke	dom-kia-keh
church	kirke	kia-keh
museum	museum	muh-seh-uhm
railway station	banegård	bah-neh-goh
airport	lufthavn	luhft-havn
train	tog	toh
ferry terminal	færgehavn	fah-veh-havn
a public toilet	et offentligt toilet	ehd off-end-ligd toa-led

Shopping

I wish to buy...	Jeg vil gerne købe...	yay vill geh-neh kyh-beh...
Do you have...?	Findes der...?	feh-ness de-ah...?
How much does it cost?	Hvad koster det?	vath koh-stah deh
expensive	dyr	dyh-ah
cheap	billig	billy
size	størrelse	stoh-ell-seh
general store	købmand	keuhb-mann
greengrocer	grønthandler	grund-handla
supermarket	supermarked	suh-pah-mah-keth
market	marked	mah-keth

Eating Out

Do you have a table for... people?	Har I et bord til... personer?	hah ee ed boah till... peh-soh-nah?
I wish to order...	Jeg vil gerne bestille...	yay vill geh-neh beh-stilleh...
I'm a vegetarian	Jeg er vegetar	yay eh-ah veh-gehta
children's menu	børnemenu	byeh-neh-meh-nye
starter	forret	foh-red
main course	hovedret	hoh-veth-red
dessert	dessert	deh-seh'd
wine list	vinkort	veen-cod
May I have the bill?	Må jeg bede om regningen?	moh yay beh-theh uhm rahy-ning-ehn

Menu Decoder

Danish	English	Pronunciation
brød	bread	bruth
danskvand	mineral water	dansg vann
fisk	fish	fesgg
fløde	cream	flu-theh
grøntsager	vegetables	grunn-saha
is	ice cream	ees
kaffe	coffee	kah-feh
kartofler	potatoes	kah-toff-lah
kød	meat	kuth
kylling	chicken	killing
laks	salmon	lahggs
lam	lamb	lahm
leverpostej	liver paté	leh-vah-poh-stie
mælk	milk	mailgg
oksekød	beef	ogg-seh-kuth
ost	cheese	ossd
pølse	sausage	pill-seh
rejer	shrimps	rah-yah
røget fisk	smoked fish	roy-heth fesgg
saftevand	squash	sah-fteh-vann
salat	salad	sah-lad
salt	salt	sald
sild	herring	sil
skaldyr	shellfish	sgall-dya
skinke	ham	sgeng-geh
smør	butter	smuah
sodavand	fizzy drink	sodah-vann
svinekød	pork	svee-neh-kuth
te	tea	teh
torsk	cod	tohsgg
vand	water	vann
wienerbrød	Danish pastry	vee-nah-bryd
æg	egg	egg
øl	beer	uhl

Numbers

	Danish	Pronunciation
0	nul	noll
1	en	ehn
2	to	toh
3	tre	tray
4	fire	fee-ah
5	fem	femm
6	seks	seggs
7	syv	siu
8	otte	oh-deh
9	ni	nee
10	ti	tee
20	tyve	tyh-veh
30	tredive	traith-veh
40	fyrre	fyr-reh
50	halvtreds	hahl-traiths
60	tres	traiths
70	halvfjerds	hahl-fyads
80	firs	fee-ahs
90	halvfems	hahl-femms
100	hundrede	hoon-dreh-the
200	tohundrede	toh-hoon-dreh-the
1,000	tusind	tooh-sin-deh
2,000	totusinde	toh-tooh-sin-deh